Robert Altman's America

MIST

I don't believe the sleepers in this house
Know where they are.

SMOKE

They've been here long enough
To push the woods back from around the house
And part them in the middle with a path.

MIST

And still I doubt if they know where they are.
And I begin to fear they never will.
All they maintain the path for is the comfort
Of visiting with the equally bewildered.
Nearer in plight their neighbors are than distance.

From "A Cabin in the Clearing,"
by Robert Frost

ROBERT
ALTMAN'S
AMERICA

Helene Keyssar

New York   Oxford
OXFORD UNIVERSITY PRESS
1991

Oxford University Press

Oxford   New York   Toronto
Delhi   Bombay   Calcutta   Madras   Karachi
Petaling Jaya   Singapore   Hong Kong   Tokyo
Nairobi   Dar es Salaam   Cape Town
Melbourne   Auckland

and associated companies in
Berlin   Ibadan

Copyright © 1991 by Helene Keyssar

Published by Oxford University Press, Inc.,
200 Madison Avenue, New York, New York 10016

Oxford is a registered trademark of Oxford University Press

Library of Congress Cataloging-in-Publication Data
Keyssar, Helene.
Robert Altman's America / Helene Keyssar.
p. cm.   Includes bibliographical references and index.
ISBN 0-19-504869-5
ISBN 0-19-504870-9 (pbk.)
1. Altman, Robert, 1925–   —Criticism and interpretation.
I. Title.
PN1998.3.A48K49   1991
791.43′0233′092—dc20   90-23733

Excerpt from "A Cabin in the Clearing" from *The Poetry of Robert Frost,* edited by Edward Connery Lathem. Copyright 1951, © 1962 by Robert Frost. Copyright © 1969 by Holt, Rinehart and Winston. Reprinted by permission of Henry Holt and Company, Inc.; and of the Estate of Robert Frost, the source and Jonathan Cape as publishers.

9 8 7 6 5 4 3 2 1

Printed in the United States of America
on acid-free paper

For Tracy

PREFACE

I began writing this book more than ten years ago, in 1976 to be exact, and my relationship to it has been peculiar. Some, including friends, family, and several voices inside my own head, might describe this relationship as one of compulsive attachment combined with separation anxiety, and that would not be inaccurate, although it would be incomplete. One cannot reside in academia for very long without knowing someone (at times meaning oneself) who has slipped into middle age without yet finishing those revisions and additions that will make a doctoral dissertation, finally, into the important book it must necessarily be. In my experience, the most unfortunate aspect of this syndrome (and here, out of due modesty, I exclude myself from the pattern) is that the authors of such works are often more brilliant and eloquent writers than most of us who publish with some regularity, and in many instances, the works of these men and women are not trivial but substantial manuscripts, the publication of which would benefit many, even if they fall short of the ever-increasing goals of their creators.

I managed to participate in this syndrome while simultaneously protecting myself from its worst pitfalls. My doctoral thesis, which was on black American drama and not on Robert Altman's films, was duly revised and published, as were subsequent articles and books. In the meantime, however, I began writing, what was clear from the beginning would be a long work, on Altman's films, and over the years as the manuscript was repeatedly shelved and unshelved, my vision of what it would be grew, as did the number of pages it contained and the number of films it needed to address.

The more important perversity in my relationship to this book goes back to its origins. My interest in Altman's films coincided with the beginning of my serious interest in movies as a medium and as sets of texts. From the beginning, I was ridden with guilt and sadness over both these interests. My academic training was in theater and in American literature; in the fall of 1975, I was happily established in a position teaching and directing drama at Amherst College, and there was little reason for anyone, including myself, to think that the teaching and writing I was doing on film signified anything but a casual, subordinate interest that happened also to serve the curricular needs of the institution that employed me.

This, however, was not the truth of the situation at all. I had always been a moviegoer, which is to say no more or less than that, like many people my age, my childhood weekends were structured and lightened by double-feature Saturday matinees, and in my memories of childhood, my first viewings of *Dumbo* and *The Greatest Show on Earth* are at least as vivid as my memories of Peter Pan flying across the stage and Julie Andrews singing "I Could Have Danced All Night." (Among those who should be the first acknowledged as contributing to this book are my aunts and parents who made certain that all these wonderful worlds were part of my education and who somehow never managed to make any hierarchical discriminations between stage drama and screen drama.)

The second period of my relationship to movies was no less ordinary. During the sixties (meaning until roughly 1973) I went to the movies at least twice a week, sometimes as many as three or four times, and my recollections of those bright and shadowed years are still ordered, and to a great degree made available, by the movies that accompanied the relentless turmoil of the period. Black and white images of mourners passing the bier of John Kennedy mingle in my mind with snapshots of *Bonnie and Clyde; Johnny Got His Gun* was inseparable for me from the March on the Pentagon, and I remember *Easy Rider* as the movie I saw just before a long-haired friend and I were threatened with physical violence at a Mississippi truck stop.

In the late sixties and early seventies, while I continued to go to the movies, my relationship to film took a somewhat different turn. I had had a child and had been divorced in the typically rapid succession of the era, and I was teaching full-time at Newark College of Engineering while trying, futilely, to continue full-time graduate studies out on "the island," more than a hundred miles away. With little money and less "free" time and bombarded by daily rumors of rapes and murders in the elevators of my inner-city apartment building, I was not much tempted to venture outside when I returned home from one classroom or another. (I heard recently of a study in progress of the relationship between inner-city residence, violence, and television, in which the hypothesis is that inner-cities are not prone to violence because the dwellers in these areas watch so much television but rather that inner-city dwellers watch more television because they are afraid of the violence outside. My own experience confirms this view.) The only safe temptation available to me, a temptation to which I yielded repeatedly for two years, was late-night television. And as everyone who has lived in or near New York City knows, the best thing about late-night television in the metropolitan area is the movies.

For that time, the movies were not a problem but salvation. Several years later, however, my relationship to movies had changed and not in entirely pleasing ways. Just at the moment when I found myself free—personally, parentally, financially—to go out at night, a moment when I no longer had to settle for a movie but could and should for professional reasons see every live theater performance around, I found myself horridly bored with theater. Like a well-behaved child, I sat through one live show after another, dutifully recording my critical responses; then, like the bad child I knew myself increasingly to be, I would sneak off to the movies.

It was in this context and spirit that I became determined to teach a course about film: if the only way to overcome temptation was to yield to it, I would immerse myself in the movies, and much as I had once overcome my infatuation with historical romances and found much deeper pleasure in "good" literature, I would be able to return with renewed respect and pleasure to the authentic art and politics of the theater.

In retrospect, it seems transparently clear that my attraction early on to the films of Robert Altman was inseparable from my conflicted loyalties to theater and film. At the time, however, I had no notion that this was the case. All I knew was that although I had seen all of the "foreign" movies that one was supposed to see as a matter of course when living in and around academic institutions, what I liked best were American movies, and of all the American movies I had seen in theaters and on television, the ones that I returned to repeatedly were made by four directors: Frank Capra, Charlie Chaplin, Stanley Kubrick, and Robert Altman. All of the films of these directors attracted my attention, but for reasons that were then as obscure and threatening as my suspicion that I preferred film to theater because I was lazy. The movie that seemed to hold the key to my interest was Altman's *Brewster McCloud* (1970), and I found myself only slightly less intrigued by my passionate attachment to three other Altman films—*The Long Goodbye, Thieves Like Us,* and *California Split.*

With the release in 1975 of *Nashville,* I leapt to a new stage of involvement with Altman's work and with movies in general. I became both an addict and a missionary, as a generation of students and colleagues from Massachusetts to California will attest. To all of these students, from Amherst College in the seventies and from the University of California, San Diego, in the eighties, I and this book owe more than I can recall specifically but not more than I can remember.

My entrancement with movies and with Altman's work in particular has also been key to most of the friendships that have given and continue to give my life meaning. I would not have the privilege of knowing and acknowledging Richard Pini, Karen Hendricksen, Stanley Cavell, George Kateb, Barry O'Connell, Catherine Portuges, Carol Axel, Mark Jaster, Jan Stuart, Patricia Stockhausen, Richard Ledes, Marguerite Waller, Michael Schudsen, Rachel Klein, Robert Westman, Mary Walshok, Marco Walshok, Laura Nathanson, Chuck Nathanson, and Michael Cole were it not for what I have come to think of as the mediation of the movies. Movies, I like to say, are our modern medium for gossip. In a culture inhospitable to intimacy, movies provide us with a context for conversation, conversation that is authentically if indirectly about ourselves, our values, and our practices.

During the period that I have been writing this book, the most important change in the world of film—both on the screen and in reflections about what is screened—has undoubtedly been the intervention of contemporary feminism. Blatant sexism and patriarchical values continue to dominate the screen—*Tootsie* and *Fatal Attraction* as well as hundreds of movies that do not merit naming can stand as examples—but thanks to a substantial group of feminist film critics and an emergent body of feminist films, viewers now have ways to see films differently, to see many of them as powerful instances of the objectification and repression of women. Teresa De Lauretis, Kaja Silverman, Catherine Portuges, Laura Mulvey, Tania Modleski, Virginia Wright Wexman, Molly Haskell, Joan Mellon, Claire Johnston, Julia Lesage, E. Ann Kaplan, Mary Ann Doane, Bill Nichols, Robert Stam, and the unacknowledged first feminist of film criticism, Pauline Kael, have changed the shape of the field of film criticism and have deeply informed my own thinking about movies. If my notes fail sufficiently to acknowledge their contributions to my work, it is because, more often than not, my debt is to the instigation of a conversation rather than the naming of a specific point.

Within the domain of drama criticism, where much of my published work is situated, my debt and commitment to a wide range of feminist theorizings are clear. I am aware, nonetheless, that even given the above acknowledgment of my debt to feminist film critics, my position in relation to feminist endeavors may well seem odd or ambiguous to many readers of this book. Most feminist film criticism has focused on the unveiling of the gendered relations of power and pleasure in the work of male directors; more recently, as in the Indiana University Press series International Women Filmmakers, feminist film critics have begun to generate a body of writing concerned with women filmmakers. This book does not fit neatly within either of these projects. I come not to bury Robert Altman's films but to reflect upon and with them, and yes, at times, to praise them. It is my hope that the following pages will reveal me not as traitor but as contributor to feminist thinking.

Over the years and through my many revisions of this book, Jillaine Smith and Elizabeth Vaughn, have given me help cleaning up and producing this manuscript—far beyond the call of duty— and offered important encouragement and support. In recent years, Lisa Cecere has also been wonderfully helpful in assisting me to find and use film and tape resources. During the last six months, while I have had to put some of my energy into a battle with cancer, Jennifer Troutner has been an extraordinary source of support, both with this book and with my life. I thank these four with much gratitude.

For the first ten years or so of this book's development, I steadfastly refused to show it to any publisher, for fear, I suppose, that someone might offer me a contract that would require that I actually finish the manuscript. Then at just the right moment, or at least at a moment when my resistances to completing this work were low, along came Sheldon Meyer, an editor whom I had respected from a distance for many years. It was not only Sheldon Meyer's interest but also his clear understanding of what I was attempting that led me to contract with Oxford University Press. I take full responsibility for what lies between the covers of this book, but only now can I say how much I owe to Sheldon for the fact that these pages do exist between covers. That this book is being published by Oxford University Press has also given me the opportunity to work, gratefully, for a second time with Scott Lenz, whose editorial wisdom is only transcended by his deep decency.

To Veronica Welch I owe many thanks for support and for leading me to the understanding that I could finish this book and not lose myself in the process. My sister, Redwing, has also been a source of strength.

Two people are missing from the group of friends named above. One of these is Jack Cameron, my colleague at Amherst College, who began to articulate his passion for movies at about the same time that I did. In the first chapter of this book, I attempt to describe the collaborative nature of Altman's authorship, of his relation to actors, editors, cinematographers, and writers, as one like that of the Soviet critic M. M. Bakhtin with his circle of collegial friends. It is not only because Jack Cameron taught me the necessity of confronting the problem of *auteurship*/authorship in examining Altman's films, but also because so many of the sentences in this book occur in and out of conversations (written and oral) with Jack Cameron that I hesitate to use my name alone as author of these pages.

The second friend omitted from the group above is my husband, Tracy Burr Strong, to whom this book is dedicated. The beginnings of *Robert Altman's America* were coincident with my marriage to Tracy Strong. That this book nears its completion at a time when we have joined together in a remarriage of affection and interest may not be coincidental.

Those who are acknowledged—and thanked—here will understand that the ghost of Elizabeth Bruss haunts the pages I have written from beginning to end.

La Jolla, Calif.   H. K.
November 1990

CONTENTS

Robert Altman's America

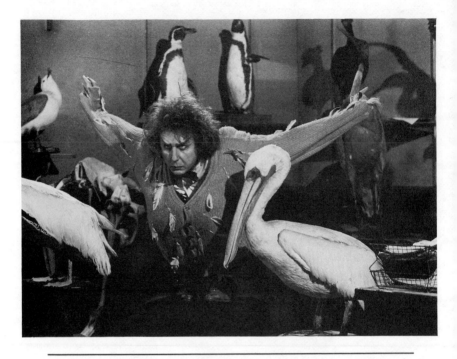

The lecturer demonstrates the relationship between birds and humans in *Brewster McCloud.* He hopes we will draw no conclusions, "elsewhere the subject will cease to fascinate us and another dream would be lost." (*The Museum of Modern Art/Film Stills Archive, New York City*)

CHAPTER 1

THE ALTMAN SIGNATURE:
A WORLD IN MOTION

It is late December 1970. In the darkness of the theater, the first light projected on the screen reveals, familiarly, the MGM lion. But this lion does not roar; instead, it confesses that it has forgotten its line. The movie cuts to a classroom setting with a stuffed bird perched screen-right on a teacher's desk. A beady-eyed, wild-haired professor appears in the left of the frame, crosses in front of the desk, pats the stuffed bird as he moves around and behind the desk, opens a book, and announces, "Enough of that Hobbes." A toy bird flutters toward the desk from the unseen and vaguely heard class, which, like the audience, is situated behind the camera, in front of the projected scene. The professor (René Auberjonois) quietly begins his lecture: "Flight of Birds, flight of man, man's similarity to birds, birds similarity to man. These are the subjects at hand. We will deal with them for about an hour or so and hope we will draw no conclusions, elsewise the subject will cease to fascinate us and another dream would be lost. There are far too few."

A reflection of/on the opening of
Brewster McCloud (1970), directed by Robert Altman

More than any other contemporary American film director, Robert Altman recognizes that we enjoy our despair in who we are. Altman's twenty-four[1] films of America since the sixties describe a culture and its inhabitants, stuck like a top in mud and prevented from sinking only by the force of its self-perpetuated spinning. As

3

spectators, we are often disoriented by Altman's defiance of ordinary filmic syntax, yet our seeing and hearing of our present society can be meaningfully reorientated by the movies that bear Altman's name. We may be able to reduce a viewing of *M*A*S*H* or *McCabe and Mrs. Miller* or *Nashville* to the clichéd question, "How could this happen in America?" but this would be a foolish response, not because we should know the answer, but because the instances *do* occur. We learn from the work of Robert Altman that we can only rightly ask how individual Americans include in their consciousness of self the knowledge of racism, of the corruption of the American Dream, of extraordinary violence, and yet remain Americans.

Most movies are easy to forget. Either the relationship they establish between the world projected and the viewer is static and predictable or they provide no sufficient grounds to inform or to transform the relationship between the world projected, the viewers, and their culture. The movies that stay on our minds, or that resist forgetting (sometimes disconcertingly), do so because they have either loosened some previous bond to the world or provided a new tie, a new thread of connection.

Serious writing about film, like serious thinking in the making of movies, has always been concerned with the relationship of the medium to the world it represents and the audience it captures. Sergei Eisenstein's investigations of film form, André Bazin's discussions of the ambiguity of moving images, Robert Warshow's explorations of movie genres, Laura Mulvey's analyses of visual pleasures, and Stanley Cavell's investigations of the ontology of film, all begin from the common assumption of this triangulation of the moving picture, the off-screen world, and the audience. In both the movies and the writings about movies that we remember, what matters is not knowledge of film *as* film but understanding of what we can know—and not know—of the world as mediated through film. This has remained the case despite numerous attempts to loft film to the realm of high art. The medium is remarkably resistant to separation from ordinary life.

Robert Altman's films are not easy to forget, precisely because they renegotiate both our detachments from and attachments to American culture. The Altman signature distinguishes itself from other filmic signatures by its attention both to the politics of representation[2] and to the representation of culture and politics. This is not simply or only an illustration of Marshall McLuhan's aphorism, "the medium is the message"; it is more like the basic phenomenon of vision: two eyes each perceive or contact the world separately, then conjoin the images they capture to make meaning.

Equally important, Altman is not concerned with culture, politics, or representation as general concepts; the Altman signature is emphatically and specifically American, both in the territories it explores and in its styles of exploration. Stanley Kubrick's *Paths of Glory, Dr. Strangelove,* and *Full-Metal Jacket* are films about war and its elemental threats to humanity; Altman's *M*A*S*H* is not about "war" but about peculiarly American ways of practicing war. Like the Doonesberry comic strips of his 1988 partner, Garry Trudeau, Altman's work for film and television is a blatantly seductive invitation to all Americans to engage in a conversation about the past, present, and future of the promised land.

The necessary qualities of that conversation are its insistence on diversity and its resistance to resolution. The diversity of points of view, the variety and types of genres exploited, the range of settings and landscapes, the tension between individual stars and the community, the attention to the distinctive voices of women and blacks in the articulation of culture, and the association of fraternity with political power in Altman's films assure what one might call the "democratization" of the movies. Altman knows and shows that there are multiple stories in every moment of American history, not one promised land but many. In his movies, film's capacity for multiple points of view, so often suppressed in filmmaking practice, is embraced and brought to the fore. That this may appear to situate film in a post-modernist sensibility is less important than that it is represented as profoundly American. The power in Altman's films is not in melting diversity in the pot of American culture but in the interanimation of authentically conflicting voices. Ironically, this celebration of a multiplicity of voices and styles has meant that many viewers will not identify such apparently different works as *M*A*S*H*, *McCabe and Mrs. Miller*, *Nashville*, *Popeye*, and *Vincent and Theo* as all Altman films.

That we sometimes remember movies under the name of or as the work of a particular director—the films of Charlie Chaplin, Alfred Hitchcock, and Ingmar Bergman stand as obvious examples—is not a simple matter. Chaplin, Hitchcock, and Bergman each have vivid directorial signatures, and so does Robert Altman. Contexts of production and distribution, the American propensity, especially with American movies, to identify a movie with its star or stars, an almost equally strong tendency to recall American movies in terms of genre, all contribute to the ways in which we remember or forget particular movies.

Even if most people did remember most of Robert Altman's films *as* Altman films, I could still not write unreflexively about "the films of Robert Altman." For those who are aware that Altman has, at two different points in his career, directed and produced works for television and live theater as well as for film, there is, at the least, an immediate ambiguity in what I mean when I say "the films of Robert Altman." I can clarify part of this issue by stating that I am here concerned primarily with movies initially intended for theatrical distribution that bear Altman's name as director and with the work he has produced in his recent return to television. I can further specify my interest by noting that the movies to which I refer in this study as "Altman's productions" refer to works directed by Robert Altman between 1968 and 1988. But while the quantity of work and the evidence of interrelated elements among the twenty-four movies and twelve television programs[3] are more pronounced than is true in many instances of "authors" of dramatic works (including conventional television dramas and theater as well as film), Altman's particular position in relation to these films and in relation to others who have worked with him in making them is so eloquently ambiguous that it makes the question of his position as an author paradoxically central to the rationale for approaching him and his work in these terms.

*   *   *   *

In the late eighties, to organize a study of movies under the rubric of the work of one film director implies an acceptance of the post-World War II *auteur* school of film criticism or a willingness to defend the particular director's position as an "author" in the post-modern, Foucaultian sense of the term. This is to say no more or less than that at least two critical positions converge and command attention in any contemporary discussion of the work of one film director.[4] The first of these positions, initiated in the 1950s by French filmmakers and critics associated with the film journal *Cahiers du Cinéma,* emphasized the aesthetic, intellectual, and ideological coherence of sets of movies made by selected directors. Articulated at first as a somewhat perversely French appreciation of the works of classical American studio film directors (including such diverse directors as Chaplin, Ford, Hawks, Hitchcock, and Welles), the *auteurists* claimed the authority of the *auteur*-director over the discourse of the film; the filmmaker had to be the scenarist or had to have taken control of the book or script of the film. What mattered in the original identification of American *auteurs* was the success of the individual director in transcending the economic, social, and political constraints of the Hollywood studio system such that he did take control of the film's discourse.

By calling attention to groups of films as the work of a single director, *auteur* theorists asserted the stylistic and social intentionality of movies as always potentially and sometimes in fact transcendent over the commercial interests and transient entertainment values of the medium. This enabled movies to be interpreted or "read" as works of art and was especially important in legitimizing serious readings and positive evaluations of such popular movies as American "screwball" comedies and Westerns (many of which were not seen in Europe until after World War II). That directors became *auteurs* within this critical school was not just a quirk of the French language or intellectual mode; the term (especially in its original phrasing as *la politique des auteurs*) implied both a general vagueness about what a director of film actually did as well as a confidence that movie audiences did know and value what literary authors did. *Auteur* theory thus urged that movie directors merited the same kind of serious attention as literary authors: both could be creators of stories and unique visions of the world.

From the start, in the early fifties, despite the (perhaps deliberate) absence of a coherent theoretical description,[5] the *auteur* theory met strong resistance from film critics and film artists in Europe and the United States. The controversies that this approach instigated focused on three concerns. First, there was the problem of criteria. On what grounds would one determine which film artists were *auteurs* and which were not? Did the directorial authorship of two films with common, recognizable characteristics suffice? Did directors' signatures necessarily become more vivid and interesting in relation to the number of movies they made?

Aside from issues of quantity, what were the components of an authorial signature? Andrew Sarris argued in 1962 that technical competence, the recognizable presence of a directorial personality, and "interior meaning" (or the "tension between a director's personality and his material") were the three "concentric circles" of an authorial signature. Pauline Kael's celebrated retort to Sarris argues that the circles of Sarris's *auteur* theory delineate a female moviegoer's vision of hell: a mystified region in which motion picture trash is misrepresented by narcissistic adult males as meaningful art.[6]

While Kael's critique of Sarris and his *auteurist* cohorts is scathing and worthy of celebration as a ground-breaking assault on the dominance of male fantasies in film, common sense can function between these two poles. Enough of us recognize repeated patterns of themes, coloration, character types, styles of camera movement, articulations of points of view, acting styles, and modes of editing as indicators of a particular filmic signature to allow for the meaningful identification of a group of films as those of Hitchcock or Renoir. We also know, from our experiences as viewers, that unity and repetition of themes and stylistic devices do not suffice to locate a film director in a pantheon of his or her peers. To the contrary, the works of a director that tend to call forth film festivals, critical studies, and college courses are almost always those that exhibit a coherent but nonredundant ideology and semiology. The persistent sentimentality, wit, and American parochialisms of Frank Capra's movies are key to his signature, but these elements would not confirm his position as an *auteur* were there not significant differences between *It Happened One Night* (1934) and *Meet John Doe* (1941).

A second, and related problem of *auteur* theory has been that of possibly misfocused evaluation.[7] Critics (including Kael) have repeatedly contended that the *auteurist* approach inflates the value of trivial films that would rightly be ignored were they not associated with the name of a director who may have, in fact, made only one or two good movies. Supporters of *auteur* theory contend that one of the great values of this approach was that, in requiring careful scrutiny of all of a director's work, the method revealed hidden treasures that might otherwise be lost because of such factors as poor distribution, the absence or presence of stars, or shifts in political and cultural climates. The third problem that arose was the inverse of the second: by emphasizing the body of work of a selected director, the *auteurist* approach is vulnerable to erroneous dismissal of first efforts or of singular masterpieces.

More than thirty years after the advent of the *politique des auteurs,* debate over the criteria for *auteur* status and over the validity of the approach continues. The debate is invigorated, on the one hand, by the prevalence in the practices of teaching, publication, television programming, and film festivals of the organization of movie materials in terms of directors. Denaturalizing these practices, on the other hand, is a collection of recent forms of interpretation (deconstruction, semiotics, discourse analysis, feminism, new historical analysis, Lacanian psychoanalysis) that, from diverse perspectives, call into question the very idea of authorship.[8] In 1962, Sarris could, in rebuttal to André Bazin's attack on *auteur* theory, unselfconsciously reaffirm Truffaut's citation of Giraudoux's claim that "there are no works; there are only authors." By the 1980s, a theory identified as focused on authorship would more likely reverse Giraudoux's epigram; under the influence of Jacques Derrida and deconstruction, "there are no authors, there are only works [or, more precisely, texts]." As some would put it, punning on the name Derrida, "'dere ain't no reada / 'dere ain't no wrider / Eider."[9]

Given these ongoing debates, as Robert Self[10] and others have reminded us, to write about "Altman's films" without confronting the concept of authorship would be to write on the false premise of a critical vacuum in regard to this topic. Since, instead, we have a critical cornucopia, what can we say about Altman and the idea of authorship beyond acknowledging the disappearance of the author as inherent to post-modernism and then, either recklessly or paradoxically asserting (and subsequently demonstrating) the obvious— that is, that Robert Altman's name appears as the director of twenty-seven films (three made before 1968) and dozens of television programs, that he has served as writer or co-writer and as producer of many of these same productions, and that there is a recognizable Altman signature evident in each of these works?

What I believe we can say is what I intend the sentences that follow to say: there are meanings and visions in a set of filmic representations of American society associated with the name Robert Altman, which, when addressed, make an unusual and provocative sense of the world of American culture (a sense that cannot be reduced, despite critical compulsions to do so, to a single or basic "theme"). The name of an author, as Michel Foucault suggests, " . . . can group together a number of texts and thus differentiate them from others. A name also establishes different forms of relationships among texts." And as Foucault concludes, the author's name serves a specific function: it "characterizes a particular manner of discourse."[11]

I now arrive at the wonderful irony that the first thing to say in an attempt to specify the particular manner of discourse meant by this particular author's name—Robert Altman—is that this name subverts several conventional notions of authorship in film. In the first place, the "particular manner of discourse" of Altman's films is one that undermines the singular authority of the director both by its insistence on ambiguity, on diverse ways of reading the world viewed, and by its explicit embrace of alternative voices in the making and the projection of the filmic text. This is, in part, simply a reminder of the well-known information that Altman's films are collaboratively constructed. More than any American filmmaker, Altman has not only depended on others—actors, writers, editors,

Robert Altman directs a scene from *A Wedding* with Mia Farrow as Buffy Brenner (the maid of honor) and Vittorio Gassman as Luigi Corelli (the father of the groom). (*The Museum of Modern Art/Film Stills Archive, New York City*)

cinematographers—as resources but has made the presence of these other voices central to his texts. This is not so simple, however, if we understand that Altman's films are always what Soviet critic M. M. Bakhtin calls "dialogic"; that is, they are always representations of interacting points of view, of the constantly shifting and interactive nature of culture and of human activities.[12] We might represent this relationship of Altman to others in a variation of the typographical convention that Tzvetan Todorov invents to signify Bakhtin's own relationships to other possible co-authors; in this case, we would follow the name Altman with a slash and the name(s) of others with whom the particular text at hand was created, preserving, as Todorov suggests, the ambiguity of whether the relations are those of collaborators, substitutes or communicants. Thus we would have Altman/Shepard; Altman/Duvall/Tewkesbury/ Tomlin/Baskin . . . ; Altman/Trudeau/. . . .

Even this convention would not suffice, however, to convey the complexity of Altman's authorship, because this function is further complicated by the plasticity of his own relationship to specific historical moments, to contexts of production, to each filmic text, and to its makers. The constant in Altman's function as director is not only the presence of his own point of view but also the interaction of that perspective with others' points of view. Some directors of theater and film conceive of their task as that of using the media of actors, sets, costumes, scripts, and lights to express or represent a "concept" or unified authorial interpretation. Altman, in contrast, appears to see his role as coordinator of many readings of several texts that become one film. Beyond this, there is flux. In his films of the seventies, the director's dialogue with actors is prominent; in many Altman films of the eighties, the director's dialogue is additionally with the playwright or writer. At the same time, and varying in form and extent from movie to movie, Altman's ways of seeing and the stories he selects to tell intersect with historical conditions, genre conventions, and the grammars of both classical and post-classical Hollywood cinema.

Robert Altman as film director could be a character in a deconstructionist's dream. If so, however, the dream would have to deal with the usually mystified role of the director of any form of drama and might in fact be called a deconstructionist's nightmare because it deals with the displacement of the father-author by the *reader* of culture and cultural forms who simultaneously cannot escape the perimeters of the language in which s/he reads. A director interprets texts, including lived situations, photographs, and stories as texts.[13] Robert Altman makes situations and episodes into texts, thereby creating discourse and reinventing the author or the reader as author—the ultimate fulfillment of the deconstructionists' wish and fear. We might say that Robert Altman reads American culture from the particular point of view of someone who is always conscious of the ostensible role of the media in which this culture makes its meanings.

*   *   *   *

Film, more than any other art, is a student of its masters. Better than any other American director, Robert Altman understands that this is film's strength, not its weakness. Like many other contemporary filmmakers, Altman's style is eclectic. Traditional oppositions between film as a reflection of life and film as a projection of an artist's vision of life, between film as a recorder and film as creator, dissolve in the movies of Stanley Kubrick and Francis Ford Coppola; in Altman's movies, such historically antithetical positions become recognizably conjoined. While it is usual to think of theater as either the more virtuous foe or subordinated elder sibling of film, Altman's films embrace both overt theatricality and specific theatrical conventions. Altman's films have been both praised and faulted for their structural and stylistic innovations, but while no single film or director anticipates Altman's work, or allows us to anticipate our relation to his films, his movies acknowledge their indebtedness to film history by their exploitation and extension of every element of the medium. Sound, in Altman's films, complicates the world projected rather than simplifying it; color is codified, selected with a painter's sense of deliberateness. The cinemascope screen becomes a means not only to cover more terrain but also to multiply the possibilities of meaning within one shot.

Altman's films at once ignore and affirm the leap to modernism that occurred in movies in the sixties.[14] The self-referential, self-questioning gestures that we associate with directors like Ingmar Bergman, Alain Renais, Jean-Luc Godard and François Truffaut, and with a few Americans, such as John Cassavetes and Woody Allen, are an arrest in film history; they pause to ask what film *is*, and they make us pause to confront the experience of watching movies. These are the films of the metaphysicians in the dark, twanging their instruments to provide the dissonance that will remind us that these are someone else's dreams we behold. Unlike these directors, Altman's acknowledgment that film has a history is neither confrontational nor nostalgic. In the instances where an Altman film directly alludes to an earlier movie, it is deeply consistent with the events of modernism in other art forms; that is, such instances recollect the mythology from which our present experience is drawn. But the implication in Altman films is that we should recognize such mythology or its filmic contexts not as dead but as embedded in our consciousness such that we must use this knowledge to move on. The whimsical allusions to the *Wizard of Oz* at the beginning of *Brewster McCloud* are too perverse in their presentation to engage us for long in sentimental journeying; what these allusions do is to name the place from which our experience of this film takes off.

Altman's films are thus poised in dialectical stance toward the works that precede them. This is most obvious and most publicly understood in the relationship each of his films has to recognizable film genres. If there is a cliché of Altman criticism, it is that he has taken on, one by one, each of the notable genres: *M*A*S*H* is a war film, *McCabe and Mrs. Miller* is a Western, *The Long Goodbye* combines the detective and gangster thrillers, *Quintet* is science fiction, and *Popeye* is a musical comedy. The attributes of each of these films that suggest these categories are obvious on viewing the films, yet in each instance I hesitate, not because the examples betray the models but because each film extenuates the characteristics of its genre such that the mold no longer looks like itself. (Stanley Cavell makes a convincing case that this is exactly what members of a genre do and should do; they do not share the same features but participate in a common practice and "inheritance," each attempting that practice in somewhat distinctive ways.)[15] Sergio Leone's *Once Upon a Time in the West* so successfully exaggerates and unveils the underside of the Western romance that it is subsequently difficult to view any conventional Western without boredom or disgust; yet finally, we revel in our superiority and repeat the ordinary experience of applauding the conquering hero. In contrast, *McCabe and Mrs. Miller* remains so close to the scheme of the traditional Western that where its codes do alter and its world sours, we are humbled by our loss of the romantic vision. Both are part of the Western genre in Cavell's terms.

Robert Kolker's essay on Altman in *A Cinema of Loneliness* provides one key to the seemingly relentless pursuit in Altman's films of established genres. Kolker concludes that Altman's films "take as their subject our cultural propensity toward passivity, our willingness to be oppressed by manufactured images that we accept as historical realities."[16] What seems to me to be key is that Altman does not simply remark or label this subject; instead, his films attempt to exploit those very images and work us back through our experience of them. Kolker is only half right when he continues, "But the images manufactured by Altman to inscribe these subjects refuse to dominate us."[17] The miracle, always at least present in potential in Altman's films, is that he arranges the very images that have dominated us in such a way as to reestablish our control over them.

Robert Altman not only establishes "democratic vistas"; he knows what he is doing. It is no simple coincidence that in *McCabe and Mrs. Miller,* Altman's revision of the classic American Western, the lawyer who encourages the "hero" McCabe to strike out on his own is called Clement Samuels. If this lawyer is a humorless inverse of the keenest American voice of the nineteenth century, it is because Altman reincarnates Mark Twain so aptly in his own parables of American life. The logo of Hal Phillip Walker, *Nashville*'s candidate for president, reads, "New Roots for the Nation." This logo and the platform of Walker's Replacement party are seductive for audiences both within the world of the film and outside that world. But while *Nashville* exposes the decay of the old roots, it also makes transparent the error in conceiving of roots as of the order of things that can be replaced or dismissed through analysis.

When Altman tells his interviewers that the response he ideally envisions is one in which viewers exit the movie theater unable to articulate what the film "meant,"[18] he is not, I think, denigrating meaning itself; nor is he facilely separating emotions and thoughts. Instead, his films mediate among the stories we, as Americans, tell ourselves about who we are, and those stories include those projected by the viewer as well as those imprinted on film. Altman's films represent a mythology that informs our lives but usually remains remote from ordinary living. Like all key stories in a culture, those screened in these movies can best be described in terms of points of tension and conflicts of values: community and individualism, woman and man, mediation and realism, reproduction and production are the primary oppositions in the stories Altman tells. Notably, however, these are rarely binary oppositions because in almost all instances, several of these points of tension interanimate each other: tensions between ideas of community and of individuality interact with gendered conflicts, and these, in one turn or another, modify ideas of production, reproduction, mediation, and realism.

The signs that provoke such an experience are many, varied, and intricately interrelated; they are aural and visual and often complexly aural *and* visual. Most important, such signs are rarely symbols, even when they might in isolation appear to be so. Because they cannot be simply equated with another fact, object, or assertion, they sometimes seem to limit our response to one of remarking moments isolated from a sense of narrative.

The quick response to Altman's films is that they do not make sense. Yet, their richness is located in the evidence that exactly what these movies *do* do is to make sense—not of themselves, but of the world, especially the world of modern America, in which they determinedly exist. Like modern journalism, movies might be thought of as a prelude to history. Movies read or interpret the cultures in which they exist, just a beat behind the present tense of events.

Although Altman's films are usually more rigorously and tightly structured than we at first perceived, they rarely leave us with a conceptual conclusion or with the satisfaction that the world projected is complete and distinct from the world in which we live. Either the attention of the film is dispersed, shared among many characters and locations, as most obviously occurs in *M*A*S*H, Nashville, A Wedding,* and *Health;* or motivations for characters' behavior remain emphatically unknown and unknowable, as in *That Cold Day in the Park, California Split, McCabe and Mrs. Miller, The Long Goodbye,* and *Quintet;* or our conventional engagement with the plot of the film carries the ambiance of a joke, and we sense that the center of the film exists elsewhere than in the obvious narrative, as in *Brewster McCloud, Thieves Like Us, Buf-*

falo Bill and the Indians, A Perfect Couple, and *Popeye.* In many instances, these various sources of our unease occur in the same movie.

It is not, then, that Altman's films capture vignettes or tell us *about* life in contemporary America, as in the case in more commercially successful films, such as *The Deer Hunter* or *Kramer vs. Kramer.* Rather, they embody the fusion of myths of American life and the knowable facts of American social history. Altman's films are profoundly historical, but that is less a matter of their competence in capturing particular times and places in American history than it is of their focus on the kinds of decisions that shape an American identity. Altman is an astute observer of daily life in modern America, but his films are not simply accurate recordings, they are complex attempts to transform the world projected as it is viewed.

This is accomplished most specifically by presenting us with characters whom we have difficulty judging and who force us to reassessments of human worth. While many of Altman's characters are discomforting, and very few are wholly admirable, even those who appear briefly on screen often surprise us. The inability to "anticipate what's coming," which Pauline Kael stresses in her reviews of Altman films,[19] is in part a matter of the persistent use of achronological editing and of the fecund filmic wit characteristic of Altman films. It is also a result of Altman's exploitation of our assumptions about our fellow Americans. The commonplace criticism of Altman's work, that it condescends to its characters, is slightly, but significantly, mistaken. Altman characters often initially present themselves to us as stereotypes, and the facile use of the stereotype is certainly an apt cue to a director's condescension to characters, but few characters in Altman's films remain as stereotypes. Even in *Popeye,* a context in which the possibilities of the stereotype might provide delight, the exactitude with which the cartoon figure is performed disguises the particularity of the character: this Popeye does *not* eat his spinach. The problem is not that Altman reduces individuals or "the American" to predictable images and behaviors but rather that we as audience are so ready to assume our knowledge of these people that we resist discrepancy and interpret eccentricity as condescension.

Vincent Canby's astute titling of his July 4, 1976, *New York Times* piece on Altman's work creates the right kind of space for critical entrance to Altman's films. Canby's notion that Altman presents a "Gallery of American Portraits" points in the right direction because Altman rarely allows us to examine or become immersed in one character as isolate and distinct from either the other characters who inhabit that same world or from those who surround us in our daily lives. Altman's directorial signature may appear most obviously to occur in what Kolker calls the "radical surface"[20] of Altman's films, but the interest in these movies is resolutely on the characters they present. Our more usual experience of characters on the screen is that they remain remote from us and from those who surround them on the screen because they so perfectly fulfill a stereotype; or they so fill the screen with their very wholeness and specificity that once they are gone, once the screen is dark, they are dead, and the best we can do is grieve at our loss. But Altman's gallery of portraits is permanent and resonant. He understands film's success in projecting types of characters as well as stereotypes, and he uses this understanding to extend the function of the filmic type. Whereas the stereotype is simply a social role, one that remains static no matter who (or which actor) fills it, as Stanley Cavell asserts, ". . . what makes someone a type is not his similarity with other members of that type but his striking separateness from other people."[21] Our pleasure (but also ultimately a restriction inherent in the traditional filmic type) is in the very distinctness of, say, the Bogart "type" or the Garbo goddess when she is not a stereotype; that I respond to some instances of these types with awe confirms my sense that this is a matter of separateness as well as distinctness. The astonishing, unremitting grace of the types created by Cary Grant[22] and Katherine Hepburn, or the transcendent wizardry of Chaplin's tramp, may satisfy our yearnings to imagine human beings who are radically better than we, but our aspirations to these models are as fleeting and vague as are our aspirations to paradise.

In reshaping the filmic type, Altman pursues the character who remains accessible to us. Altman characters fulfill social roles in particular ways, but the kinds of particular ways diverge sharply from the conventions of American film. With Altman's male characters especially, we recognize the type, and in the instant of recognition, the characters behave in a manner that defies tradition. Only Altman's Philip Marlow, his "detective" type, would have a cat in the first place; and certainly no previous film detective would try to feed his cat by disguising the brand of cat food. As will occur in many of Altman's disruptions of the traditions of American film, his conceptions of character adhere to the pattern that Cavell illuminates, but Altman refuses to accept its last step:

> They [the stars] realized the myth of singularity—that we can still be found, behind our disguises of bravado and cowardice, by someone, perhaps a god, capable of defeating our self-defeats. This was always more important than their distinction by beauty. Their singularity made them more like us—anyway, made their difference from us less a matter of metaphysics, to which we must accede, than a matter of responsibility, to which we must bend. But then that made them even more glamorous.[23]

And the more brilliantly the stars shone, the more powerfully they affected us, the more glamorous they appeared. That Cavell's description is an accurate rendering of even our more recent stars—of Dustin Hoffman or Jane Fonda—makes clear why it is important to specify just where and how Altman's types diverge from what appears to be an inevitable and irresistible pattern. To deny his stars and us their glamor, which is unabashedly what Altman does, is to alter not only our relationship to the stars but to ourselves.

Yet it is in part the very absence of glamor that raises the suspicion in many spectators that Altman condescends to his characters. It is precisely the tension between the glamorous and the pedestrian that causes pain for most of Altman's characters and that identifies them as undeniably American. The whole history of Shelley Duvall's screen life in Altman's films is circumscribed by this tension. As the tour guide in *Brewster McCloud*, she is briefly tempted by the glamor that she anticipates will accompany the public presentation of the wings Brewster is inventing, yet she manages to accomplish one of the least glamorous gestures ever projected on screen when she passionately kisses her boyfriend a moment after vomiting over a railing in the Astrodome. As the sweet and ordinary love of one of the "Thieves Like Us," Duvall is placed in the role of the woman anxiously awaiting the return of her not-so-innocent lover; she is not only remote from the adventures of the thieves, but is an emphatically unglamorous contrast to her prototype, Bonnie—Faye Dunaway of *Bonnie and Clyde*. In *McCabe and Mrs. Miller,* Duvall's character loses what distinction she may have in the context of the film's grundgy mining town when she is forced by sudden widowhood to join the community of whores. In *3 Women,* Duvall's awesome ordinariness and desperately futile attempts to become the perfect plastic glamor girl emit the central energy of the film. Duvall's portrayal of Olive in *Popeye* becomes the most natural gesture of casting accomplished in film since Fred Astaire played Daddy Long-Legs.

That Shelley Duvall—and Milly, Olive, L.A. Joan, et al.—is much a recurrent and tenacious presence in Altman's films is no simple matter of a director's ease with a particular actress; nor is this the case of a filmic style that rightfully belongs to the actor, not the director. We are neither in the world of an Alfred Hitchcock–Cary Grant relationship nor in the situation of a Humphrey Bogart or Marilyn Monroe. If there is a proximate analogue, it is perhaps Ingmar Bergman and Liv Ullman, an aesthetic and ontological relationship in which the director's projection of the world is perfectly satisfied by the precise ambiance and individual radiance of the actor. Like Bergman, Altman's interest is in the human beings, and voices, that wake us before we drown. And again like Bergman, Altman often demonstrates an uncanny ability to reflect the ineluctable qualities of his characters through the landscapes and interiors they inhabit. But the analogy is finally limiting, for at the end and in the beginning and in the middle of his films, Altman is always more like Renoir than Bergman in his unwillingness to dwell on solitary individuals. People and their behaviors, not souls, attract Robert Altman, and such portrayal, in turn, attracts us to his films. When Altman errs, when he embarrasses us as spectators, it is most often when he mistakes an attraction to a person for an interest in a soul.

What distinguishes a soul from a person, or what I might more straightforwardly here call a "citizen," is that for the soul the significant relationships are metaphysical, whereas for the citizen they are obviously but importantly social and political. And when Altman's camera seems to be desperately groping for the metaphysical, as in the hallucinations of *Images* or the water figures of *3 Women,* it inevitably either loses focus or, with somewhat bemused acquiescence, discovers not the godly and ephemeral but a pile of discarded tires. Nor are these tires symbols. Like Altman's characters, the objects the camera lands upon rarely represent a quality or concept; rather they are some*thing.*

The success of Altman's camera, of the vehicle of his vision, is in its insistence on finding and revealing people in relationship to one another. This is not to claim that Altman finds romance or community wherever he turns or places his camera; indeed, often the poignancy of the image is in the reminder of the missed moment of true contact or lasting community. It is to say that while Altman's interest is in people, and more specifically in people who are undeniably identifiable as Americans, what we learn from an Altman movie is not *why* a particular character behaves in a particular fashion but how people behave, what they *do* do (or avoid doing) such that they and we are led to acknowledge responsibility for the lives of others.

The perspective of Altman's films, then, is not psychological but social. This is true even in the films that apparently focus on a single central character or the films in which the extraordinary behavior of the characters elicits anxiety in their worlds and ours about their ability to function sensibly. We may conclude that Frances Austen (Sandy Dennis) is clinically crazy when, in *That Cold Day in the Park,* she kills the prostitute whom she has solicited for her foundling "boy," but neither the motivations nor the details of her psychosis are finally of interest to us or the camera. Like the Western cowboy who is the archetype for many of Altman's characters, Frances does what she does because she has to. We are meant to accept that and pay attention to what she does in the present in our presence; we will be frustrated if we search the film for clues in Frances's past as to why she lives in such enforced solitude or why she then brings the boy from the park in from the cold. Interest in such questions is really a desire for another film.[24] And part of what Altman's films teach us is to confront the world before us—if only because there is so much to see and hear there—and not make another film in our own image of the world.

The world projected in *That Cold Day in the Park* is not that of Frances's psyche or anguished soul but of a society that manages to contain but not connect the frivolous, impetuous communal interactions of the boy, his sister, and his friends with the formal, calculating isolation of the bourgeois spinster. The most Altman allows us is some tentative notion that the contrasting class backgrounds of Frances and the boy may contribute to the basic structures of behavior of each character. The individual motivations of each character are anchored in the performances of these characters; they are not explained by any form of directorial injection. Why the boy has chosen to play a manipulative game of silence (a game he has played repeatedly since childhood) and why Frances finds it necessary to speak incessantly are questions the film refuses to answer.

In later films, Altman will make such refusal more deliberate and assaultive on our sensibilities. A common experience during a first viewing of *Nashville* is to work hard at figuring out just what is happening and who is related to whom in what ways. The complementary experience at a second viewing is to search out the clues as to just why the seemingly innocuous young man who is barely identified as Kenny and whose visual image strays across the screen at apparently random moments should, in the end, kill the star singer, Barbara Jean. But no viewing of *Nashville* will provide this information, and the more intently we try to discover such knowledge in the film, the more clearly "clues" appear to be red herrings or obvious and clichéd explanations of experience. We may associate Barbara Jean's song about her mommy and daddy and their Idaho home with Kenny's strained conversation with his mother earlier in the film, but that is a story we tell ourselves, not one the movie tells us.

Similarly, and even more potently, when, in *3 Women*, Pinky's parents arrive at the hospital after their daughter's attempted suicide, we and Pinky's roommate, Millie, may gain some social, historical knowledge of Pinky, but the presence of the parents provides not a glimmer of insight into the particular sources of their daughter's behavior; not every young woman from a poor, rural family plunges into a pool from a dangerous height after confronting her roommate's paltry affair. And when Pinky awakens from her long coma, her adamant refusal to acknowledge her parents *as* her parents is presented not as a revelation of character but as a resolute signal that these parents are irrelevant to Pinky's relationship to the world and our relationship to her.

*   *   *   *

The absence in Altman's films of conventional gestures that provide or appear to provide insights into character motivation disorients and reorients us as spectators. It is not so strange that the philosopher Ludwig Wittgenstein, among whose concerns was how meaning is achieved through grammatical relationships, should have been personally obsessed with movies. Oddly enough, Altman shares with Wittgenstein a conception of knowing that argues that meaning is achieved by lateral, diachronic juxtaposition, not by layers that can be penetrated. For Wittgenstein (as it did at about the same time for J. L. Austin) this suggested that no amount of staring at a term would unveil it; one must examine what it does in a context and what is available to it to do. For Altman, this means approaching images and sounds—people, flags, cars on a highway—as actions in space and time. It also means approaching the juxtaposition and combinations of sounds and images as a central activity of film. Editing in Altman's films is thus not the hidden glue that binds one shot to another in order to create the illusion of continuity; Altman's editing truly merits the appellation montage, in the sense that Eisenstein proposed both in his films and writings. Images and sounds collide in Altman's films at least as frequently as they cohere, and in many instances it is the interpretation of shots that establishes narrative and makes the film mean.

Underlying the structures of most films is the assumption—called into question by Eisenstein—that the events of a film are most accessible when presented in chronological syntagmas: continuous autonomous segments that contain elements of consecutiveness within the temporality of the world of the film.[25] The frequent and sometimes predominant use of achronological syntagmas in Altman's films would then suggest that Altman is deliberately constructing barriers against our penetration of the world of the film. While movies like *Brewster McCloud, Nashville, Buffalo Bill and the Indians,* and *A Wedding* do assault or undermine our groundings in consecutiveness (and thus limit our reliance on plot, on superficial relationships of cause and effect), they are also transparently eager to tell us stories and to make us care about the worlds they project. The inserts in *Brewster McCloud* of the lecturer regaling his students on bird life interrupt the plot of the film; that is, the sequence of events that lead to Brewster's failed attempts to fly. But the shots of the lecturer and the recordings of his words at the same time clarify and enhance the narrative; the lecturer's diatribes on man's fascination with birds and the challenging, unyielding differences between the two species elevate Brewster's obsession with wings from a foolish adolescent project to a mythical enactment of an essential human yearning. Rather than distracting us from Brewster, the intercut shots of the lecturer lead us to care about Brewster's rise and fall and to dismiss the mundanity of his pimply adolescent countenance.

To achieve these ordinarily contradictory effects, Altman relies heavily on blatant but unconventional pairings of filmic signs when he cuts from one sequence to another. Within the usual conventions of film, continuity, whether in chronological or achronological sequences,[26] is most frequently established by information connected by the semantic content of verbal dialogue, by the repetition of some aspect of the visual image, or by some combination of these elements in which the linkage is clearly narratively based. In Hitchcock's *Psycho,* a cut within the first few minutes of the film from a cheap hotel room to an orderly office, does not perplex us at all because Marion (Janet Leigh) is visually present in both episodes. Later in that same film, when Hitchcock cuts from the symbolic sinking of Marion's car to the interior of an unfamiliar hardware store, we are quickly oriented both by the visual familiarity of her boyfriend and by the dialogue that concerns Marion. Even in less obviously causal linkages, such as the cut early in *Rules of the Game* from Jurieu's arrival at the airport to Christine's dressing room, we correctly assume the obvious narrative connection: that this unknown woman is she who has been proclaimed by Jurieu as the absent beloved.

Such conventional linkages do occur in Altman's films, but his films are more powerfully propelled by a mode of montage in which the key connecting elements present themselves initially in metaphoric rather than syntactical relationship to each other. In the striking final shots of *McCabe and Mrs. Miller,* the film cuts from the cold still image of the dead and frozen McCabe to a warm, intense close-up of Mrs. Miller's eye and a swirling jar she holds. The images provide sharp visual contrasts yet suggest the complementary isolations of each character. Similarly, in *Nashville,* Altman remarks the consanguinity of grief and delight by juxtaposing the sob of one character with the laughter of two others. We can speak about such cuts as blatant examples of Eisensteinian montage, but Altman has at the least extended Eisenstein's vision of the collision of images precisely because the collision is so frequently not simply of images but of images and sounds, and even more precisely, of phonic sound and musical sound, or phonic sound and graphic tracings. Perhaps more important still, Altman's montage is rarely didactic because its components often include depth-of-focus photography and depth of focus in sound. Even when the montage is momentarily pedantic, specific pairs of signs are almost always absorbed into more extensive codes of meaning and in these larger contexts become resonant. Each editorial gesture in *Nashville* and *McCabe and Mrs. Miller* adds a detail to at least one of the stories being told, and these films finally tell their most vivid stories not by any single series of incidents but by the accumulation of pairings of signs that become codes and then evolve into meaningful patterns.

*   *   *   *

For Altman, the assertion of meaning through tension and collision necessitates a minimal and very particular use of one of the most standard conventions of the Hollywood film, the close-up of the human face. In contrast to the illusion projected by most filmmakers that the close-up is one of film's most penetrating and characteristic acts, Altman often pointedly dismisses this gesture, moving restlessly or sitting fixedly at mid- or full distance from his characters. When he does use the close-up, it demonstrates the opposite of its traditional implication; in most instances we see the opacity not the transparency of the human face. The camera conveys delight in its observation of the processional that begins *A Wedding*, but when it is placed in the inevitable tight shot of the bride's face at the altar, it seems unable to hold its stance; we are removed abruptly back to the house where the wedding reception is being prepared and grandmother is dying. Our glimpse of the bride's face has told us nothing of her pleasure or dismay at this ritual union. (This leads me to recall that it was not the close-ups of their faces, but the distance shots of their dashing bodies that informed me of what was really on Claudette Colbert's—in *It Happened One Night*—and, thirty years later, on Katherine Ross's—in *The Graduate*—minds when they were at their respective wedding altars.)

A certain consanguinity between Altman's filmmaking and theater should be evident here. When the close-up came into persistent use in the twenties, it was embraced in part as a vivid sign of the separation of film and theater; indeed, it was part of the severance of the two media for many actors and directors. It allowed filmmakers to distinguish their work from theater not only in scale and projection of movement but also in terms of the signification of the image and its strategy. Most specifically, it argued a different degree and quality of intimacy with characters. "The close-up," Bela Belazs asserts in *Theory of Film*, "has not only widened our vision of life, it has also deepened it."[27] Drawing both from recollections of silent films and judgments about all "good" films, he elaborates:

> The close-up may sometimes give the impression of a mere naturalist preoccupation with detail. But good close-ups radiate a tender human attitude in the contemplation of hidden things, a delicate solicitude, a gentle bending over the intimacies of life-in-the-miniature, a warm sensibility. Good close-ups are lyrical; it is the heart, not the eye, that has perceived them. Close-ups are often dramatic revelations of what is really happening under the surface of appearances.[28]

According to such claims, film transcends theater. It captures the details and "hidden" elements veiled in the human face, accessible at best to those in the front rows of a "live" theater, and it focuses our attention on that face. The close-up is one key way that film uncovers what Cavell calls the "inner agenda of a culture."

The close-up implies a necessary equivalence of knowledge and intimacy on the one hand with specificity and focus on the image on the other. Belazs goes so far as to argue that the close-up renders objective the human face, "this most subjective and individual of human manifestations."[29] If I am standing next to someone such that all I in effect can see is that person's face, it is sensible to assume at least a momentary intimacy. It is not out of order to imagine that such proximity may yield greater knowledge of the other: I can feel her breath; I can touch her with little effort; we can whisper and hear each other and not be overheard; we can focus on each other's eyes and force a moment of connection or rejection. It is appropriate to assume that we are each more vulnerable to the other than we would be at a distance of twenty feet.

Because the close-up presents the visual portion of such proximity to an other, we tend to equate our experience of the close-up with our experience of physical intimacy in ordinary life. But the equation is false. The face on the screen remains doubly distant from us; it is as far away as is our seat from the screen (just exactly as far away as we are from a distance shot of the same person, or of that person among many), and it is removed by time and space as well. The eyes, the nose, the mouth do not necessarily yield any more or less information about the character than do the smiling lips and a fisted hand that together reveal character in a frame. In the theater, when actors move fully downstage, they at least are approaching us, and while we are no more or less vulnerable than we were when they were upstage, they are less protected, more withdrawn from the boundaries of their world, less able to escape quickly to the wings; we not only see their faces more clearly, but they are genuinely closer to us.

Rather than specifying, the close-up most often abstracts. Roland Barthes argues in his "The Face of Garbo," that:

> The most successful close-up of the most effective face is a mask, . . .
> Something even sharper than a mask is looming: A mask is but a sum

of lines; a face, on the contrary, is above all their thematic harmony. Garbo's face represents this fragile moment when the cinema is about to draw an existential from an essential beauty, when the archetype leans towards the fascination of mortal faces, when the clarity of the flesh as essence yields its place to lyricism of Woman.[30]

When Altman does employ a close-up of the human face, it is just such a tension between the mortal and the archtypical, between physical features and persona, that he depicts. The frozen face of McCabe at the end of *McCabe and Mrs. Miller,* the lyrically passive face of Lily Tomlin that the camera captures in the rear of a club in *Nashville,* the imperturbable harmony of Swee' Pea's visage in *Popeye,* are image-concepts that lead us not to investigation but to love. As with the rare close-up of Charlie Chaplin's face at the end of *City Lights,* when a face does fill the screen in an Altman film, it is a moment of paralysis for both viewed and viewer. Cause is irrelevant to effect; motion ceases.

The close-up, then, is, in essence, a still photograph; so, of course, is every frame of film. But it is the most natural act of film to endeavor to distract us from this knowledge, whereas the close-up reminds us of it. It is therefore not surprising that Altman abjures the close-up much as good writers hesitate thrice before inserting a mark of exclamation in their prose. The close-up arrests the activity of narrative, and while Altman's films subvert the conventional modes of filmic narrative, they do determinedly tell us stories. What Altman's films do resist is the notion that the close-up image of a character's face will tell us a better or truer story than any other image or sound. Belazs may be correct that the function of the close-up is similar to that of the soliloquy in classical drama; however, he fails to grasp that the contemporary playwright may spurn the soliloquy not because it is "unnatural" but because it is arrogant and deceptive. Both the soliloquy on stage and the close-up on film claim to speak truths that dispel other lies told on stage or on camera. But as Samuel Beckett and Harold Pinter repeatedly teach us, there is an impenetrable conspiracy between the dramatic character and the words he speaks; there is an at least equal conspiracy between the camera and the actor's face.

By denying us the illusion of access to the "interior" of characters, Altman's limited use of the close-up importantly draws our attention *away* from concern with those characters' past histories. It is a cliché of the post-Freudian sensibility that we will find ourselves in uncovering our pasts; with zealous facility, we have carried this notion to our knowledge of the fictive characters of stage, screen, and novel. As with most new tools, for a time the pursuit of the flashback seemed sufficient to achieve all important understanding. The continuing potency of a *Citizen Kane* or a *Death of a Salesman* notwithstanding, in music, in theater, in Southern California, and in Altman's films doubts are being raised. In much the same way that Beckett and Pinter reject the assumed dramatic activities of unraveling and deconstructing human actions, Altman takes us into space in which present actions *do* matter, even if isolated from individual and social history. In Beckett and Pinter, as in Altman, this offers us the pleasure of unpredictability. Clov, in Beckett's *Endgame*, repeatedly threatens to leave and repeatedly remains in the "shelter" with his surrogate father, Hamm; when, at the end of the play, Clov does appear before us and Hamm in hat and coat, with suitcase in hand, we must be surprised, because something new has happened. Whether Clov actually leaves is irrelevant; what is important is that without explanation, the seemingly predictable pattern has been broken. This kind of disruption is central to Altman's filmic strategies. The great irony of Altman's *California Split* is that while the pattern of Bill's (George Segal) final streak of gambling luck is never broken by a turn of the wheel, our patterns of expectation are jarred by Bill's sudden despondency at his triumph.

This tendency to renegotiate our expectations of movie characters ironically places Altman's movies in the avant-garde of the performance arts and at the same time in a fluid continuum with the traditions of American film. It is, after all, the cowboy and the gangster who have been and to some extent remain the most vivid and dominant types of American film. Our interest in these figures is surely in their style, in how they do what they do, and rarely in the sources of their behavior of their lives before we encounter them. When, at the end of Leone's *Once Upon a Time in the West*, we finally see an in-focus shot of the moment in Charles Bronson's family history that initiated Bronson's vendetta, the film separates itself fully from the genre that it has exploited; having challenged the myths of the Western in a variety of ways, in the end, it revokes that mythology by allowing us to explain the behavior of its hero such that he is no longer magical, no longer in fact a hero in the context of the kind of world in which he has dwelt. If Shane carries with him a haunted vision of a determining past, we do not wish to know it; we weep at the end of *Shane* not only because we know he cannot come back but because we know the boy's voice will haunt us more than it will haunt Shane.

Our willingness to accept these impenetrable filmic heroes and our complementary difficulty in accepting the limits of our knowledge of Altman's characters—or Beckett's or Pinter's—would be curious were it not for the obvious power of a genre to establish its own terms and its own mythology. The big cities and prairie towns of our gangster films and Westerns may be vaguely like the real cities and towns that contained the real gangs of our past and present, but that does not truly concern us; what matters is that these places establish their mythic authenticity and that these films cohere with a mythic structure. Within such a context, we understand and respect that a man's history—or occasionally, a woman's—is a burden, not an asset. Nowhere is this made clearer than in Altman's most overtly genre-specific film, *McCabe and Mrs. Miller.* Unlike *Once Upon a Time in the West, McCabe and Mrs. Miller* tenaciously holds to the conventions of the Western genre, not to parody or explode the form but to transform it by imposing the structure of the myth on a world that is persuasively ordinary, historical, and continuous with our present.

In this world, the imposition on the "hero," McCabe, of a personal past history is one cause of his undoing. Seeking to explain to themselves McCabe's sudden appearance in the tiny mining town of Presbyterian Church, the townsmen readily accept saloon-keeper Sheehan's story that McCabe was a gunslinger with a "big rep" and a particularly awesome killing behind him. The problem for McCabe, as the real gunslinger attests, is that, despite the fact that that man "Never killed nobody," McCabe must now behave as a solitary gunman. His "history" demands this of him, and the community is obedient to this history. In Altman's films, released from the remoteness of the confines of the perfectly mythical worlds of the conventional genres, personal history becomes an encumbrance both to the character and to the audience.

As the example of *McCabe and Mrs. Miller* suggests, while Altman's characters are freed from personal past history, they remain limited and affected by social context and social history. Altman's worlds partake of both historical and mythical understandings. The worlds of Beckett's *Endgame* and *Waiting for Godot,* like many of the worlds of great theater, finally exist outside of history; the worlds of *M*A*S*H,* of *Nashville,* of *McCabe and Mrs. Miller,* of *3 Women,* and of *Tanner '88* focus their attention on those points at which American mythology and American history intersect. The important paradox embodied in and repeatedly examined in Altman's films is that the history of Americans is the history of a people attempting to escape their history. That Altman leads us to regard characters whose personal histories are unimportant to our knowledge of them is then both an aesthetic and a political gesture. It is not so much, I would venture, that Altman embraces the American ideology of escape from one's "roots," but that he recognizes that to appropriately illuminate something like the "American character," one must confront the defining terms. It is no coincidence that not one of Altman's films is located in New England, that whether the place is called Houston or Nashville or Miami, it is in California that these movies exist most comfortably. And it may not be only a pragmatic choice that *Popeye* was filmed in Malta and that Sweethaven is where Americans go when they cannot escape their pasts in California.

I return then, to the claim that Altman's characters are decidedly *American* men and women. These characters fuse typical images of men and women in American film with pedestrian modes of behavior and appearance. Altman's characters strike us as out of place because they appear to us within the structures established by the myths of American film, yet their behaviors are contiguous with the actual society of American life.

The necessary accompaniment to the projection of characters who attract us without revealing their souls or psyches, who are types without the conventional glamor of the filmic type, is that almost all of our interest is focused on how these people's lives affect and are affected by those with whom we see them. While I would like to think that this is a truism, it is not of the order of understandings that has in fact controlled either American self-consciousness or American film. What distinguishes Altman's characters is that they are and remain part of the crowd. In every Altman film, including those that are most diffuse and "democratic" (such as *Nashville* and *A Wedding*), some characters do receive more attention than others, are picked out of the crowd by the telephoto lens or a blatant zoom. But those who are thus selected are inevitably also returned to the group or crowd from which they came by an equally deliberate reverse zoom or editorial gesture. Bill (George Segal) and Charlie (Elliot Gould) are discovered among the gamblers in the first casino scene of *California Split*, and while they isolate themselves and are isolated by the camera at many moments in the film, they are repeatedly returned to the gambling crowds in which they first appeared. McCabe rides into Presbyterian Church alone, but is quickly absorbed into a dusky, disorderly, and cacophonous saloon. The languorous shooting of this scene augments the diffusion of our attention; we must work hard at keeping McCabe in focus.

Even when the context or plot would seem to demand the separation of individuals from the crowd, Altman arranges his camera angles and environment such that the group is credibly present. Haven Hamilton's intimate clique is so literally and figuratively "onstage" when Haven sings at the Grand Ole Opry in *Nashville* that Haven never really accomplishes a solo performance. And whenever Barbara Jean performs in this same film, the camera (or the cutting) insists on interspersing glimpses of the audience and repeatedly catches the back-up group on whom Barbara Jean is dependent in a variety of ways. The deemphasis of the solitary individual is in part accomplished by and connected to what Robert Kolker calls Altman's imposition of "the peripheral action onto the central focus of the sequence, not merely indicating its presence but playing that presence over and against the main figure and her concerns."[31] This is different, as Kolker also notes, from the general tendency in American films of the sixties and seventies to take

"cognizance of peripheral acitivity. The periphery recognized usually encompases the onlooker, and the sense is that of giving the
extras a bit more work to do."[32] Kolker is just slightly off the mark
here in suggesting that the main figure (or figures) is played *against*
the crowd. The figure of interest in an Altman shot may be visually
and socially barred from membership in a proximate group but
remains one of that group in dependence upon them and likeness to
them. This is in sharp contrast to the gestures toward the peripheral
of recent American filmmakers and to classical American films in
which groups or crowds are significant forces. The presence and
potency of the crowd is one of the distinguishing attributes of Frank
Capra's films, but the Capra hero is never genuinely part of the
crowd, even if, as in *Mr. Deeds Goes to Town,* he might long to be
so. Chaplin, too, finds the crowd or associated group of people
necessary and hypnotically vital to the world he projects. Yet while
his tramp hero might be any one of the crowd, he is always isolated
from it. He is a gold digger among gold diggers but not of them; he
is a factor worker but "chosen" as a sample; he is a worker who
disrupts the assembly line by the distinctness of his habits.

Such relationships have serious implications. In Frank Capra's
films, the relationship between the central figure and the larger
group suggests that there are always in America communities that
are potentially available and good—if led well. In Chaplin's films,
the very fact of the tramp's isolation implies that there is not community, or that if there is community the actor/individual and the
chorus/community are separate forces, wholly other, one apart
from the other. Altman's more-elaborated characters are not only
visually drawn from and returned to the crowd but are neither
consistently leaders nor necessarily misfits; there is thus the temptation to feel pressed to a conclusion that his groups either firmly
deny or romantically assert the existence of community. Kolker
resists this temptation, suggesting instead that in the context of
McCabe and Mrs. Miller, we can tentatively infer some hope that "a
community might cohere on terms other than self-interest and a
brutality that arises out of greed."[33] But Kolker urges that we reach
this possibility through the absence of such alternatives, whereas
what seems to me more specifically to occur is that in Altman's

America there are groups or associations of people whose appearances as a community distort and even distract us from what really makes them a community. The lack of despair that I find in Altman's films for any remnants of community in America is founded neither in stoicism nor in the kind of oppositional optimism that we have been taught was the strategy of T. S. Eliot's *Wasteland*. As I shall pursue in subsequent chapters, although groups and crowds are most often only groups and crowds in these films, the possibility of community is revealed through presences and actions and not implied simply by absences. We are shown what we might do to achieve community, not just what we ought not to do.

*   *   *   *

To return to the theological language I initiated earlier, the issue here is revelation. The post-modern sensibility is so accustomed to the restriction of revelation to apocalyptic visions that it has difficulty perceiving and admitting any revelation that suggests a positive transformation of the world. Knowledge of this difficulty repeatedly informs Altman's work and the strategies of his filmmaking. His films are able to lead us to recognition of virtue and mutual responsibility; in the process, we must also acknowledge our denial of such gestures. *Nashville*'s Haven Hamilton is such a pompous and narcissistic character throughout most of the film that we may miss or dismiss his admirable concern for others when he as well as Barbara Jean are shot at the end of the movie; this is not a problem of focus in the film, but in us. The classical scene of revelation and recognition in *3 Women,* in which Millie rushes to aid Willie in the latter's maternal labor, is even more complex in its strategy: to dwell on the death of the baby or on Pinky's infuriating paralysis may be to miss the inspiration of Millie's acutely responsible attempt to assist Willie. When Altman does arrive at a full-scale projection of the apocalypse in *Quintet,* the physical qualities of the world extend our most terrifying poetic nightmares, but the relationships of persons remains unpredictable even within the framework of a game with rules.

Part of the difficulty posed by Altman's films is that they at once confront our social and our aesthetic assumptions, and they assume the inseparability of each. We expect epiphanies, and none are forth-coming. We defend against revelations; they imply the director's arrogance and our helplessness. Yet what we get in an oddly tradi-tional, Calvinist fashion is both revelation and freedom. The emer-gence of one character or another from the crowds that fill Altman's screens is as arbitrary and ultimately uncertain as the appearances of the elect in a Puritan community. No previous behavior—as actor or character—is sufficient evidence that someone who ap-pears in an Altman film will be among its select any more than good or bad behavior could *cause* election among the Calvinists. Nor does the shooting or editing pursue characters and continuity of time and space within the usual rhetorical structures of film. From *M*A*S*H* to *Tanner '88*, the camera in Altman's films is deter-minedly restless, unwilling to commit its focus to any single relation-ship to a character, or to yield its attention to an obvious visual or aural attraction. Perhaps our most proximate experience is in watch-ing the films of Jean Renoir, that other intimidating penetrator of a culture. Robin Wood's comments about Renoir's style seem pro-phetically appropriate to Altman as well:

> The camera style emphasizes the structure-patterns of the scenario by never allowing us more than transitory identification with one char-acter at the expense of others. The constant reframings in which the camera excludes some to include others, the continual entrances into and exits from the frame, the division of our attention between fore-ground and background—the style might be aptly described as per-petual visual promiscuity, quite breaking down the traditional one-to-one relationship of spectator to protagonist to which the cinema has habituated us.[34]

In Altman, as in Renoir, visual promiscuity is not just an aesthetic device to increase the activity of the spectator but is also, relentlessly, a reflection of the relationships projected. Promiscuity is a refusal of commitment to any one person or image; it makes intimacy difficult but not impossible. We encounter such difficulty in every one of Altman's films, both in our relationships to the characters on screen and in their relationships to each other. In some instances (such as with L.A. Joan in *Nashville*), this promiscuity is blatant and ordinary: each time we see L.A. Joan, she is in pursuit of still another male escort, and almost each time her physical appearance has changed such that we must relate to a new image. In other instances, the refusal of commitment of one character may prevent a possible commitment from another, or, as in *The Long Goodbye*, one personal commitment may ironically necessitate behavior that has the ambiance of promiscuity even if the accompanying detachment from others in appropriate. In none of these instances, however, is the visual promiscuity of the camera or the social or sexual promiscuity of characters automatically condemned—or damnable. We may crave more attachment to the characters on screen, and some of them clearly desire greater attachment to each other, but in neither instance is the kind of choice available that would allow for moral judgment. I am urging something stronger here than the claim that these films are what they are, that we cannot alter them. I am saying that while we have the choice to conclude that the worlds projected in these films have no connection to the world we know in our daily lives, there is an integrity between the visual promiscuity of the camera and the social promiscuity of the characters.

This suggests, but does not necessitate, our exclusion from the worlds of these films. If we are present to Altman's films, their own activity will catch us up in their ways of seeing.[35] Each of Altman's films has its own strategic traps to ensnare us; the elements that comprise these traps are rarely single or simple. When we do get caught up, it is because Altman's "way of seeing" is as richly aural as it is visual. Forty years ago, Orson Welles and Jean Renoir captured our visual attention with the use of depth-of-focus photography; the deliberate use of depth-of-focus photography, as André Bazin made lucid, not only allows the projected world to retain its inherent ambiguity but also radically increases our activity as spectators. Even with depth-of-focus photography, our activity as spectators has remained partial since it was only our eyes that were put to work; with brief moments of exception (most notably in the "screwball" comedies of the thirties), film has delivered to our ears little that necessitated more than simple recording.

For Robert Altman, this clearly does not suffice. In *Nashville*, especially, but even in Altman's earliest films, we find ourselves in the presence of depth of focus in *sound* as well as in visual images. Altman's use of sound has its precedents in earlier films—in the overlapping dialogue of Welles's *The Magnificent Ambersons* and Hitchcock's *Shadow of a Doubt*—but these are rare instances, employed more to establish an ambiance within the world of the film than to change our relationship to the film itself. For Altman, sounds (and silence) have as much depth, texture, and color as visual images; the world we hear is as complex as the world we see, and sound must thus be delivered to us both with all its inherent complexity and with sufficient structure to satisfy our efforts to listen. This means that if, as in the mess hall in *M*A*S*H* or in the recording-studio sequence early in *Nashville,* more than one person is speaking (or singing) at a given moment, we will hear more than one person. This is a deliberate choice, not only to seduce us to the authenticity of a space in which realistically no single voice would be isolated, but also to force us to decide how we will focus our listening.

To augment our difficulty—and our pleasure—much of the aural sorting out that Altman imposes upon us occurs because verbal sound shares its time and space with musical sound and recorded noise. French film semiotician Christian Metz asserts that the strictly cinematic signifiers fall into five physical types—the image, recorded phonic sound, recorded musical sound, recorded noise, and graphic tracing of written matter. Yet even within the innovative context of Metz's own methodology, the image elicits the bulk of attention.[36] Altman defies the assumption of the dominance of the image and implicitly suggests that this list is not a hierarchy. In *Nashville,* a sob is made poignant as much by the laughter posed as by the imaged of a bereaved face in the same frame; in *Brewster McCloud,* the rhythmic creakings of rocking chairs superimposed on the chirpings of crickets evoke the awkward romance of Keechie and Bowie at least as poignantly as do their words and facial expressions.

*   *   *   *

In a sense we are, of course, excluded from the worlds of Altman's films as we are from the world of any film. The characters and their relationships are separate and other; as with analogous devices in Brechtian theater, Altman's nonsynchronic editing and the very stress on visual and aural promiscuity, while arguably more like the multiplicity of ordinary life, persistently remind us that we are watching a movie. More than in many films, however, Altman's characters persistently reevaluate their relationships to each other and make us work at our relationships to them. Our attachment or detachment to a given character is rarely automatic or static in these films. In many films, the feelings portrayed and spoken by characters are our essential source of relationship to them; in Altman's films, there is instead an expressionistic tendency to elicit our response through sounds and images associated with but not performed by the actors-as-characters.[37] The signs and codes of meaning in Altman's films often appear in unanticipated time and space, but once recognized they attach us to the film because they engage us in dialogue with it. These films request a dialogic relationship with the audience; they do so in part by disrupting or elongating the connections between signifiers and signification and in part by relocating signs so as to interfer with the anticipated process of meaning.

Such a relationship challenges our passivity in much the same way that Soviet critic M. M. Bakhtin argues is the case in the assortment of works he gathers within the rubric of the "novel." The undermining of genre, the celebration of polyphony—multivoicedness—and openness of discourse that for Bakhtin distinguish novels from all other cultural actions, are as explicit in Altman's films as these gestures are "pure" in Bahktin's Dostoyevski. If this implies that Altman's films are to be taken seriously as oppositional representations it should also mean that we can laugh at their successes and learn from their failures. When Altman's films embarrass us or fail to accomplish the desired interactions among characters and with the audience, it is often because one voice shrieks or polyphony becomes cacophony; the pitfalls of expressionism gape in front of us, and we are confronted with either trite symbols or impenetrable ciphers. Sometimes, too, these films yield to the temptation of overabundance; there are shots in at least half of Altman's films that waste time and space with all the fecundity and disarray of a garbage heap. But, at the least, the abundance of signs we are offered makes it our responsibility to sort out and judge the rubbish from the treasures.

To read signs meaningfully we must assume some shared values among the readers; we must assume, in other words, some modicum of community in the audience. And this is where Altman's American vision, not unlike Walt Whitman's, assertively contains contradictions. Every one of Altman's characters is dependent on others, in some instances for sheer survival, at the least for release from vivid burdens of emotional and economic solitude. In most of Altman's films, such dependence is a matter of choice or social circumstance; that is, the interdependence of characters is not in these films a matter of family or imposed relationship, such as among prisoners or patients in a hospital, but is a matter of friendship, partnerships, an exchange of services, colleagueship, or romantic and sexual relationships including (infrequently) marriage.

We recall these films in terms of a pair or group of characters: Hawkeye Pierce, Trapper John, and Duke of *M*A*S*H;* McCabe and Mrs. Miller, as well as Mrs. Miller and the group of prostitutes; Bowie, Chicamaw and T-Dub, the three "thieves" of *Thieves Like Us* (and, here, the other alliance of Bowie and Keechie); Bill and Charlie, Barbara and Susan, of *California Split;* the Star, the Producer, the Relative, the Sure Shot—in other words, the "company"—of *Buffalo Bill;* and the candidates for the presidency of *Health. Nashville* not only presents the broadest projection of filmic characters as linked members of a group but also, within its cast of twenty-four-plus characters, includes almost every variation on the modes of dependence of two or more people; indeed it is the web of relationships that binds the fragments of the film together and binds us to it.

There is also a web of relationships among the people working on Altman's films. More noticeably than any other contemporary American director, Altman works with a company of actors and production people; the relationship of these people to the films on which they work might recall the old studio system, but lacking legal and economic ties, they in fact bear a closer resemblance to a theater company than to any conventional organization of film actors and crew. As in many contemporary American theater companies, while no two Altman films have been produced, photographed, edited, and acted by exactly the same group of people, the number of people who have worked on two or more of them is significant. These people are not exclusively bound to Altman or Lion's Gate, his production company; that Shelley Duvall, who has appeared in seven Altman films, has also starred in Stanley Kubrick's *The Shining* is a natural event, not a heresy or rejection of one director for another. And as in some theater companies, the status and function of the role played in any one film does not delimit or determine what will occur in the next: Henry Gibson is at the center of the frame and the events of *Nashville,* yet plays less-manifest roles in *Health* and *A Perfect Couple;* Maysie Hoy has acted in two of Altman's films and has served as an editor and production assistant for others.[38]

For the public that has craved information about the external relationships of those who make movies, recognition of the "Altman company" makes good news. And when an actor like Michael Murphy, who has performed in six Altman films, protests the notion of a "stock company" saying, "we're just good friends,"[39] the good public relations is extended, not defeated. Just as gossip about the romantic liaisons of the classical stars of Hollywood brought one kind of audience to the movie theaters, so gossip about the community of Altman people will bring to the theaters screening these films audiences with positive expectations drawn from a belief in communal, nonegocentric art. (The hostile gossip of Patrick McGilligan's biography, *Robert Altman: Jumping Off the Cliff,* intended, I presume, to deflate this image of community, may undermine this attraction, but I doubt it will have much effect.)

But does any of this mean anything when we actually watch and hear an Atlman film? No and yes. If the spectator's experience is confined to externally acquired knowledge of the "Altman company" and the viewing of only one Altman film, then the relationship of this knowledge to the experience of the film allows for superficial if not fallacious judgments; we are then in the muddy territory of Wimsatt and Beardsley's affective fallacy. If, however, we come to this sense of the company from the experience of watching Elliot Gould in *M*A*S*H* and then in *The Long Goodbye* and then in *California Split,* when we see him appear in *Nashville* as

Elliot Gould, our sense of an Altman company will not only be affirmed but complicated. We increase the pleasure gained from watching an actor transform into a variety of characters, a pleasure augmented by the capability it gives us to perceive nuances in character and characterization. We also learn from the distinctions in textures and tensions among one group of actors-as-characters[40] and another. We may never get enough of Spencer Tracy and Katherine Hepburn playing with and against each other, but there may be an even sharper enjoyment in juxtaposing Hepburn and Tracy to Hepburn and Bogart, to Hepburn and Grant. Not so simply, Altman takes this source of pleasure and multiplies it in seemingly infinite combinations: Shelley Duvall, Keith Carradine, Julie Christie, René Auberjonois, Michael Murphy, and Gwen Welles all appear in both *McCabe and Mrs. Miller* and *Nashville,* but the addition and absence of other actors to and from each film illuminate and shade our response to each individual and the various groupings in which they are arranged on screen. There is, also, a kind of evolutionary principle at work in the films; we never quite know who will appear next, in what kind of role, and with whom. We are at least as disconcerted by the appearance of Julie Christie and Elliot Gould as themselves in *Nashville* as are those on screen, not only because they appear undisguised but because we had accepted their absence from the film. Yet, if we have seen the other Altman films in which Christie and Gould appeared separately, we are also likely to be delighted by their containment within a single frame. We thus can turn to the next Altman film not just with simple empathy for the company ambiance but with secure expectations that we will meet both the familiar and the new. The web of relationships describes characters to characters, actors to actors, them to us, and one Altman film to another.

To create such a web is a burden and a responsibility; it is therefore important that all of the relationships referred to are those of adults. We and they are just in aspiring to mutual responsibility and in being disappointed if such responsibility is not fulfilled. A number of these relationships resemble family structures, but when such resemblances occur, we are markedly meant to note the semblance—and the differences. The parent-child relationship is often imaged in

Altman's films: Mrs. Miller cuddles McCabe and instructs the new whore Ida as she might a daughter; the fairy-godmother Louise obviously mothers Brewster in *Brewster McCloud;* Barbara rocking Susan in an archetypical madonna pose in *California Split* suggests a pseudofamilial relationship between the two. We never, however, mistake these relationships for families; rather, we infer that the mutual reliances of these people occur instead of reliances on families. Relatively few of Altman's characters have any literal family members actually in view or memory. In *3 Women,* which overtly exemplifies the imposition of family structure on an adult association, it is only after the parents of one member (Pinky) and the husband of another (Willie) have been forcefully rejected and eliminated that the relationship of the three women achieves stability.

One could reasonably argue that the distinctive pattern of relationships I am depicting here is accurate to most of Altman's earlier films but altered or transformed in his more recent works. *A Wedding* does appear to focus emphatically on families; Essex (Paul Newman) is initially in search of his brother in *Quintet;* the structural tension of *A Perfect Couple* is established through the parallel opposition of the families of each "mate"; Popeye is in search of his father and the Oyls are a stereotypical family; and Vincent and Theo are brothers. Some shift in the nature of given circumstances is apparent here. It is possible to argue that *3 Women* marks Altman's transition to a new attention to the traditional family. Such a claim falls apart quickly, however, the moment one considers anything but the obviously greater presence of families in these later films. *A Wedding* and *A Perfect Couple* present the most troublesome examples. By the end of *A Wedding* the lives of its forty-odd characters have become so absurdly intertwined and disrupted that we either must declare all three families to be one family or annihilate any notion of family with which we may have approached the film. And if *Popeye* appears to be the conventional family film, we must only remember that Swee' Pea makes no conventional arrival in this world, that Popeye chooses to become the child's parent with a freedom given few mothers or fathers, that Popeye and Olive share no conjugal space, and that Popeye's image of his father is an empty frame.

The consistency of attention to nonfamilial relationships, to various combinations of person, in Altman's films persistently suggests the possibilities of companionship, and even of community, but is rarely a sentimental or facile gesture. When a character does appear alone in a frame, both the physical posture of the actor and the effect of the surrounding space often connote desolation. Even more frequently, the space between and among characters projected in the same frame is a barrier not a gateway, a path of tension not of connection. Sueleen Gay, the would-be star who is manipulated into a public striptease in *Nashville*, appears distressingly alone as she dresses for her "performance," naively stuffing her bra with tissue paper; we could wish for her that she at least had a reassuring roommate. But her isolation is even more painfully reflected when she does appear in a frame with others; this is most obvious in the shots of her strip at the political dinner, shots that repeatedly include the hooting men as well as Sueleen. It is most unbearable near the end of the film when Sueleen is framed on the stage at the Parthenon among but utterly absent from the stars with whom she has longed to be.

Were these the only alternative images with which Altman presented us, it would be tempting and perhaps appropriate to conclude that all that these films offered us was still another vision of alienation: we are lonely when we are alone and even lonelier when we are together. This is the kind of conclusion that Robert Kolker nearly reaches in *A Cinema of Loneliness*:

> Isolation and self-absorption are qualities Altman discovers in many of his characters and most of the places they inhabit. He finds the idea of a successful community difficult to imagine and the smaller units within communities—conventional romantic couplings and domestic unions of the kinds celebrated by American film—impossible.[41]

Kolker knows, as is clear in his discussion of *McCabe and Mrs. Miller*, that this is not quite right, and it is indeed neither the whole story nor all of what we see. For while Altman does not project sustained, successful communities, more than any director since

Frank Capra, he does create and reveal groups of people whose structural relations allow for the possibility of community. At times, these characters do achieve a moment of communal action. The whores and the miners do, after all, work together to put out the fire in Presbyterian Church; Hot Lips overcomes her outrage and ends up a cheerleader for the "team" in *M*A*S*H;* Popeye conquers the tax collector and thus unites and strengthens the vulnerable citizens of Sweethaven. Conventional romantic couplings are, at most, brief interludes, but even Sueleen Gay is offered companionship by Wade, the one person willing authentically to acknowledge her.

There is danger in emphasizing the moments in these films when people are shown taking responsibility for one another, but there is also danger in ignoring such instances. Altman is not an American romantic; he neither applauds the individual pioneer nor imagines that the cities on our hills are what our literature once prophesied. What his films do is to confront both the absurdity and the lie in the roots of the nation: the society he projects is one that attempts to exalt the individual "doing it on his own" and yet sustain a fantasy of community. While his films reveal the illusions and corruptions of both premises, neither cynicism nor stupidity is the apparent attitude. The proverbial baby does not need to be thrown out with the bathwater; community might still be established on different premises than those initially asserted.

There is, then, an odd kind of faithfulness in Altman's films, despite and perhaps because of the acerbity of their wit and sad vacuity of the lives they enclose. Ironically, it is often the most isolate of Altman's characters whose roles point to such faith. For as much as these movies are distinguished by a dispersion of attention among many characters, they are also repeatedly identifiable by their inclusion of a type of character who remains vividly outside the significant group. The presence of this type, a role I am tempted to label as the voyeur but who is more accurately described as the commentator, is frequent to theater but relatively rare to film. The circus emcee, Shakespeare's Ariel and Puck, and the narrators of Thornton Wilder and Bertold Brecht and Tennessee Williams share the capacity to observe, comment on, and report the events of the play while remaining attached to its world. These are not choral figures; the Greek chorus, as Friedrich Nietzsche best understood, was separate from the central actors but expressed the voice of the community within the play. In contrast, the commentators of Altman's films and the modern theater are neither of the world of the audience nor of the community of the play. Although they sometimes wish to be and behave as insiders, they are distinctly outsiders.

Such a character appears overtly in three of Altman's films— *Nashville*, *A Wedding*, and *Health*—less distinctively or more tangentially in *M*A*S*H*, *Brewster McCloud*, and *Thieves Like Us*, and in exploded form in *Buffalo Bill and the Indians*. In its three most assertive instances, the role is played by a woman: twice by Geraldine Chaplin (as Opal, the BBC reporter in *Nashville*, and as Rita Billingsley, the wedding coordinator in *A Wedding*) and once by Carol Burnett as the White House representative at the convention in *Health*. In each of these instances, the commentator character is caught between the function of her role as an objective recorder and commentator and her desire for unmitigated engagement within the culture to which she is responding. The roles and social roots of these characters place them outside the community defined by the film; the dialogue, the *mise-en-scène*, the voices, physical gestures, costuming and color coding of these characters emphasize the separation of these women from the groups and subgroups with whom they share the frame.

There is a temptation to perceive these characters as a projection of the spectator onto the screen, to view them as the Athenian audience may have understood the onstage chorus as an extension of its community. Altman unmistakably thwarts such a temptation. Opal and Rita especially, but the White House representative, too, are the objects of our somewhat derisive laughter, not our empathy. They are models of vulnerability but also models of failure. They are persistently mistaken in their understandings and repeatedly indecorous in their behavior. Yet, they are not just a cheap butt of laughter, nor are they simplistic devices to establish our distance from other characters. These women arrive from the deepest traditions of comedy; their exaggerated errors follow us to laugh at ourselves and make us hesitate before committing similar stupidities in our judgments of those on screen. Most important, they point to the danger in a mode of interpretation that projects its own agenda onto the experience to be comprehended. To pretend to be like others, as do these characters, but to be at the same time unable to acknowledge the separate and distinct qualities of each other is to make community impossible.

That these commentators are women is neither coincidental nor misogynistic. All of the women in Altman's films are outsiders. The difference between the commentator characters and other women in his films is that the latter appear by role to be inside but define themselves as outside; the commentator characters are less astute and thus more distanced from us, but at the same distance from the center of the culture as any woman in an Altman film, If we compare Suzanne, a minor version of the Altman commentator, in *Brewster McCloud* to the Chaplin and Burnett characters, we see that the same essential attributes hold. Suzanne, played by Shelley Duvall, is a tour guide who is just outside of both Brewster's life and that of her other boyfriend, a political gofer. Brewster inhabits a hidden sanctum at the core of the Houston Astrodome; Suzanne guides tourists around the Astrodome, circling Brewster's space. She sees her boyfriend on dates; her contact with his political world is by phone or newspaper reports. Much like the Chaplin and Burnett characters, Suzanne is distressingly impetuous and frenetic in her attempts to penetrate both the male worlds with which she has some contact. In contrast to Opal in *Nashville* or Rita in *A Wedding*, Suzanne does reveal that she comprehends her exclusion, but that does not prevent her from attempting to be included. Opal's unawareness of her peripheral position protects her from pain and deflects our sympathy; Suzanne is neither as well-protected as Opal nor as vulnerable as most of Altman's female characters. She stands at some but not utter distance from us.

The commentator characters point to the paradox that is at the core of Altman's films. Over and again, and with increasing candor, women are revealed at the periphery of the society projected but at the center of the film's own interest. It is not only, as Kolker rightly argues, that "Altman is imposing peripheral action onto the center of the sequence,"[42] but also that Altman is imposing peripheral people—that is, women—onto the center of our attention. This is, in one sense of course, profoundly within the tradition of the movies. Stanley Cavell reminds us to remember, "how much of the history of film is a history of the firmament of individual women established there." Cavell also urges "that the movies' way of asserting community is typically through male comradeship (rather than, as in novels and the theater, through families); and that women are anti-community (because they interfere with comradeship)."[43] But this is as untrue of the men and women in Altman's films as it is true of most of the women and men we know from the silver screen. The women to whom Cavell refers were and are not peripheral but transcendent; they exist, precisely, in the firmament—not at the edges of a culture but untouchable by it.

Altman's women are fully of the worlds in which they are framed. They penetrate these worlds from its borders, attracting the camera by the awkwardness not the grace of their presence. Rather than thwarting community, they provide the catalyst and only resources for comradeship and society. It is the loneliness of women that is increasingly at the heart of Altman's films; in juxtaposition, we see and hear the solitude of men not as heroic but as dismal, and we see and hear the hollow in fraternal gatherings. Cast in a dramatized society, Altman's characters theatricalize the mundane and idolize the theatrical. Yet, in the company of women, Altman's camera discovers remnants of American rituals sustained in secret responsibility. None of this happens immediately or consistently or fluently in Altman's films. But it is this attempt to reorder the location of American women and men on film, an attempt that both initiates and requires imagining radical transformations of American culture, that merits further pursuit.

CHAPTER 2

POWER AND MORALITY:
THE FRATERNAL FILMS

We two boys together clinging,
One the other never leaving,
Up and down the roads going, North and South
excursions making,
Power enjoying, elbows stretching, fingers clutching,
Arm'd and fearless, eating, drinking, sleeping, loving,
No law less than ourselves owning, sailing, soldiering,
thieving, threatening,
Misers, menials, priests alarming, air breathing, water
drinking, on the turf or the sea beach-dancing,
Cities wrenching, ease scorning, statutes mocking,
feebleness chasing,
Fulfilling our foray.

Walt Whitman, "We Two Boys Together Clinging" (1860–67)

By the late 1960s, when Robert Altman began his cinematic odyssey through American culture, movies and moviegoing in the United States had taken a curious turn. Visually and orally, the movies had come of age. Wide-screen projection, the standard use of color, stereophonic sound, increased reliance on location shooting, and the sophistication of the zoom and of a wide variety of special effects made pre-sixties movies look like awkward adolescents by comparison. Every movie was now gorgeous, while at the same time televisions sat in almost every American household. A series of changes in the economic structure of the American movie business

48

had restructured production financing and distribution; "foreign" movies could now be seen regularly in every major American city. New discriminations were called for and quickly enacted. There were the movies and there were films. We could still just "go to the movies," but we could also scan the reviews or await the opening of the new Bergman vision. It was not long, of course, before many people stopped just going to the "movies." And at almost the same moment, perhaps because distinctions between "trash" and "art" in the movies seemed to defy both knowledge and pleasure, film books and film courses and the serious study of film emerged to establish their own cultural legitimacy.[1]

Among the other curious twists that characterized American movies in the late sixties and early seventies was an obsessive turn—or return—to the projection of worlds aggressively dominated by men.[2] Women appeared in *Easy Rider, Midnight Cowboy, The Wild Bunch,* and even in *2001,* but there is little distinction in these movies between the status of women and that of drugs, liquor, or food. Women appear in these films only as fleeting functionaries: they satisfy male lust on and off the screen and serve to mediate fraternal relationships while insinuating the superiority of fraternity to any relationships between men and women or between women and women.

It was not just that the movies of this era were about men—solitary antiheroes, buddies, and communities of men at work and war—but also that the values, traditions, and fantasies projected were assertively and almost exclusively male. The tales these movies told were of men in search of themselves, of journeys that could only occur in defiance of culture, law, family, home, and mortality. The acutely detailed depictions of sexual encounters and violence that characterized movies from *Bonnie and Clyde* to *Butch Cassidy and the Sundance Kid* were not gratuitous or cathartic or admonitory. Whatever initial responses of repulsion or pleasure or dread were evoked by the relentless images of flesh and blood that punctuated these movies, the meaning that emerged was clear. If these were the "now" movies, as reviewers and audiences claimed, then the "now" story in America was that the American male was on the move and on the make. If he were more lost and in worse straits than ever before—not just homeless and angry but dirty, drugged-out, and cynical—he was also more narcissistic, greedier, and more powerful. A female character could exit without guilt from these movie worlds, as one does in *Butch Cassidy,* but in contrast to earlier American Westerns, the absence of the woman neither transforms the social structure within the film nor diminishes the viewers' pleasure.

Movie reviewers and moviegoers were quick to pick up on the emergence of a recurrent motif in the "buddy films"[3] of the sixties and early seventies. It was not a "buddy film", however, but a movie about a single male rebel and his passage into adulthood, Mike Nichols's *The Graduate,* that most effectively synthesized the key elements of the story of the rebirth on film of the American male hero. The new college "graduate," Benjamin (Dustin Hoffman), and the camera share the same tunnel vision. Both are certain—and arrogant—in their confidence that they have penetrated the plastic surface of the American Dream and displayed its deception.

In another time and another drama, such knowledge meant pain and paralysis. But Benjamin is not Hamlet, nor is he an existential antihero. Witty dialectical montage employed with a classical Hollywood editing style complement the central character's verbal wit and antics to evoke delight in the process of rebellion against the older generation. At the same time, *The Graduate* avoids any serious opposition to the upper-middle class American values of Benjamin's parents and Hollywood movies. Like the easy riders and sixties' cowboys of other American movies, Benjamin is the latest version of the true American hero. His victory is in the taking of the woman (Katherine Ross) he desires, in much the same entreprenurial style that he loathes in his father's approach to business. His power is in our concurrence that such taking is admirable and is his right.

Dressed in the trappings of the counterculture, movie narratives like those of *The Graduate, Easy Rider,* and *Butch Cassidy and the Sundance Kid* reclaimed legends of American men defying or escaping "civilization" in order to define themselves. Natty Bumpo and Chingachgook; Huck Finn and Jim; Ishmael and Queequeg; Henry

Sutpen and Charles Bon—the buddy tradition is as old as American romance. From Cooper to Hemingway, Salinger to Mailer, violence, power, and the struggle of man against nature and society have been defining metaphors of American culture. (The absence or subordination of women in these narrative conflicts is inherent to the definition: American culture has most often been equated, without hesitation, to the culture of men.) The reproduction of these figures and their transcendent vigor in American movies of the sixties and seventies would hardly be remarkable were it not for the seemingly antithetical politics of the period—a countercultural politics associated particularly with the students, intellectuals, and young women and men who comprised the main audience for movies.

The irony comes full circle: the countercultural heroes of American movies sustained the traditions of American culture in much the same way that the countercultural political movements of the late sixties and early seventies reinvented Walden, the frontier town, and the extended family. The movies as well as some elements of the political movements of this era were ghosts of American Progressivism, that earlier uniquely American movement that Wilson Carey McWilliams describes as "an alliance of individuals seeking to escape themselves and one another, too insecure and lonely to accept themselves or fraternity with those who were most akin. They could not become one with America at large; they could only find a still greater alliance in war, when danger and death substitute for mind and emotion as bonds between men."[4]

In the sixties and early seventies, the Vietnam war provided the context for just such alliances, but on two different fronts. Those who actually fought in Vietnam surely were joined tightly, if incompletely, to one another, but those at home who fought to end U.S. participation in the Vietnam war also felt bound together by the threat of the draft, of jail or exile, and of violent law enforcement at home. Prior to the killing of the four Kent State students, only a small minority of my predominently male, white, lower-middle-class and working-class students at Newark College of Engineering (now New Jersey Institute of Technology) demonstrated any strong alliance among themselves over any issue or on any intellectual grounds; those who did so were those who passionately supported the Vietnam war as a battle for freedom against the "tyranny" of communism. In a strikingly dramatic moment, made possible perhaps by the fact that Kent State was not Columbia or Harvard, with the killings of the Kent State Students a substantial fraternal community emerged at NCE that vividly transformed a number of students there from the "lonely and insecure" individuals remarked by McWilliams to assertive, proud "brothers."[5]

Robert Altman's fraternal films reincarnate those ghosts, rendering ethereal spirits whole again by re-placing them in history. In the context of Robert Altman's production history, this endeavor was its own peculiar counter-cultural gesture: from 1957 through the mid-sixties, Altman had worked almost exclusively in television, directing and writing scripts for such programs as *Alfred Hitchcock Presents, Kraft Theater, Combat,* and *Bonanza.* He was repeatedly fired by television studios because of his unorthodox use of overlapping sound, his defiance of conventional plot sequencing, and his nonauthoritarian directing style. However, rather than denouncing the constraints of television production, Altman has suggested its value as a context that inspired his development of techniques to subvert dominant practices and meanings while working within the rules of the game:

> I was actually doing what the French critics praise the American directors for. I was making films under a system and trying to sneak my own personal message through all that veneer . . . In television, I learned how to say things without saying them directly.[6]

In 1968, Altman began to apply those lessons to feature films. *Countdown* (1968) and *That Cold Day in the Park* (1969) point to the terrains he would explore for the next ten years. *Countdown* confronts the one adventure of the sixties that united most Americans—the moon shot that John F. Kennedy had envisioned as a rebirth of the pioneering spirit. Produced a year before the first U.S. trip to the moon, *Countdown* projects the behind-the-scenes relationships and political forces that propel the jet-age journey of conquest. *That Cold Day in the Park* is equally a film of and to the "Now" generation, but in contrast to the public escapism and national insecurities that frame the world of *Countdown, That Cold Day in the Park* juxtaposes the private and sexual instabilities of a single, bourgeois woman with the self-satisfied hedonism of a young man on the loose who is complicit in his eventual imprisonment in the woman's apartment.

Both *Countdown* and *That Cold Day in the Park* exhibit the pitfalls of too much and too little directorial control. *Countdown* was removed from Altman's control before the film was edited, and the producer also reshot the ending—the monophonic sound track; conventional, chronological sequencing of shots; and the cliff-hanging triumph of American heroism that concludes the film are not Robert Altman's work. Nor are these the kind of collaborative interventions that would occur in many of Altman's later works; Warner Brothers' editing and reshooting of the ending of *Countdown* oppose Altman's original strategy and limit his responsibility for the film. *That Cold Day in the Park,* rather than fulfilling Altman's stated aim of "sneaking messages through the veneer," veers between placing labels on the veneer and trying so hard not to say something that little comprehensible is said. *Countdown* and *That Cold Day in the Park* do not challenge or subvert the traditional selectivity of American movies. They do, however, indirectly call attention to the distortions of that particular selectivity by the assertion of cultural dilemmas that had previously been excluded from the movie screen. Both films also display a distinctive consciousness of history and its intricate intimacy with the mythos of American culture. It would take twelve more years before any other movie (*The Right Stuff*) would dare to explore the illusions of fraternity, through the deceptions and gross irresponsibilities behind the scenes of the American space program. And it would take the oppositional efforts of women directors and Altman's own pursuit of understanding to get beyond the notable achievements of *That Cold Day in the Park* in turning a respectful, nonreductive filmic attention to American women and in confronting the enigmatic American historical consciousness.

Yet, by both omission and commission, even these early, awkward Altman films suggest what the off-screen politics of the late sixties was already claiming—that feminism and a transformation of concepts of gender keep available to Americans an authentic, far-reaching countercultural movement.[7] Appropriately, given his own gender, and perhaps necessarily in the context of the tenacious traditions of male dominance in American culture, most of Altman's films during the next several years approach the centrality of gender to film and to social relationships by exploring the ideals and limitations of fraternity in American society.

*   *   *   *

Between 1969 and 1974 (between *That Cold Day in the Park* and the release of *Nashville* in 1975), Robert Altman directed seven films: *M*A*S*H* (1970), *Brewster McCloud* (1970), *McCabe and Mrs. Miller* (1971), *Images* (1972), *The Long Goodbye* (1973), *Thieves Like Us* (1974), and *California Split* (1974). The issue in all of these films is how men and women make meaning in their lives as Americans and as men and women. Each of these seven films assumes—and many of them call attention to—the potency of stories of fraternity and of stories of the lone male pioneer. Each of these films also begins with the presumption of the marginality of women in American society. These films are thus in synchrony with what I have referred to as the "curious twist" from the late sixties on toward the assertion of male authority over and within the world viewed in American movies. *McCabe and Mrs. Miller* and *Images* are consistent with these interests, but because a particularly assertive consciousness of women as women in society empowers each narrative, I want to put these two films aside until I can return to them in the context of later works in which the feminization of Altman's films becomes more evident. In contrast, *M*A*S*H, The Long Goodbye, Thieves Like Us, California Split,* and, to a lesser extent, *Brewster McCloud,* isolate and emphasize the distinctive spaces and stories in which American men seek definition. They are fraternal films.

M*A*S*H, the first and commercially the most successful of these films, initiates the experiments with narrative structure and the thematic concerns with gender and power that will be recurrent issues in Altman's representations of the dislocations of men in American culture. Comprised of a series of plot episodes rather than a single narrative line, the movie traces the evolution of relationships among the army personnel stationed at a Mobile Army Surgical Hospital three miles behind the battlefront, in a place that is explicitly identified in subtitles as Korea but which was always intended to be Vietnam. The focal relationships in the MASH unit are fraternal. Captain "Hawkeye" Pierce (Donald Sutherland) and Captain "Trapper" John McIntyre (Elliot Gould) meet near the beginning of the film and become its key buddies; their equal competence, wit, and countercultural disdain for authority invoke the classic qualities of American male companions suggested by their nicknames. Their social relationships with each other, with women, and with other buddies on the base are repeatedly punctuated by strikingly vivid scenes in the base operating room where both the men and women of the MASH unit demonstrate their competence and grim wit as they attempt to heal and save the victims of war.

The first section of an Altman film has its own distinctive shape and import; it usually implies that which will follow and is rarely merely an entryway or teaser. M*A*S*H starts out as a film that locates the audience at an intellectually detached distance from its military context and at an illusory historical distance. In the first shots, two helicopters dance in the skies above a military base that suggests a stage on which these graceful mechanical birds will alight to perform. The dance is accompanied by a lilting song. The upbeat melody of this song carries the perverse message that "Suicide Is Painless" and goes on to declare:

> The game of life is hard to play.
> I'm going to lose it anyway.
> The losing card I'll someday lay,
> So this is all I have to say.
> The only way to win is cheat. . . . [8]

Biographical and textual evidence from the array of Altman's films suggest an initial reading of these lyrics as the enunciation of a gambling metaphor that is key to both the stories Altman tells and his manner of telling: life is a game that involves both skill and chance, but unlike other games, the victor, Death, is known from the start. To play is to accept defeat. Since only the fool, therefore, hopes for fairness or victory, the only chance to give this game some meaning is to take risks and attempt to subvert the rules.[9]

Gambling games do set the ambiance or contribute to the plots of several of Altman's films, including *M*A*S*H, McCabe and Mrs. Miller, Brewster McCloud, California Split,* and *Quintet;* the success of *M*A*S*H* as a television series can be attributed in great part to a set of simplistic variations on this theme. The heroes of the television series suggest the ultimate optimism of the gambler; they take chances of various kinds and they place their wits against the odds (or gods). But gambling is the wrong reading here. Life itself is a gamble in *M*A*S*H,* and living and game playing are not the same kinds of activities. Neither in the film *M*A*S*H* nor elsewhere, does Altman mistake the one for the other or conflate the two. Most evocatively in *California Split,* for Altman gambling is a metaphor for imaging the assertion of the individual will. In *M*A*S*H,* and throughout Altman's work, game-playing, and the freedom this allows within a set of known and unquestioned rules, is a metaphoric terrain for exploration of the limits and possibilities of fraternity in American society.

Removed from the context of the film, both the game-playing metaphor and the lyrics of "Suicide Is Painless" portend a descent to cynicism and truisms. In context, however, these verses lose their surety and have no separate authority. The visual images that combine with the song are as subtle and supple as the lyrics are blunt and rigid.

Oppositions abound in these initial moments, but, rather than colliding explosively, as in classical Eisensteinian montage, the variously interacting gestures of sweet music, mordant verses, muted earth colors, and erotic movement combine effortlessly. The camera returns twice to the most jarring image of the opening—that of a wounded man carried on the skid of a helicopter—but even this harsh sign of adversity is muted by the strong suggestion of nurturance in the gentle landing of the helicopter-bird and its symbolic cradling of the injured soldier.

No other scene in *M*A*S*H* achieves the lingering impact of this opening. This is not just a matter of the conjoined power of verbal irony and visual invention. It is more specifically a matter of the reestablishment of the integrity and fullness of film as a form of drama and as what I earlier described, drawing on M. M. Bakhtin, as a theatrically hybrid medium that functions most effectively when it also intentionally employs hybridization as a device for making meaning.[10] The opening exemplifies what Bakhtin argues is one of the essential attributes of deliberate hybridization: the constructed contact of different points of view of the world within a single utterance, a construction that serves to transform discourse and forms of consciousness by illuminating and ultimately redefining one form of representation through another.

The opening of $M*A*S*H$ reclaims film's theatrical roots: something is beginning; entrances are made; and matter, music, and dance welcome the spectator. Ironically, this once-traditional representation of dramatic temporality is, in this context, adventurous. "Something is taking its course," Clov announces in Samuel Beckett's *Endgame,* and critic Hugh Kenner suggests that it is to the inexorability and invulnerability of the projection of film that we owe this orientation toward dramatic time.[11] But it is precisely this assumption that Altman violates, offering instead a more dramatically traditional finding of a satisfaction to a desire made present in the moment.

At least for spectators who watched late sixties television news, the images of the helicopters signal the war in Vietnam.[12] It is not that we disbelieve the title references to Korea; we accept them in the tradition of such fictions. But the helicopter images, as well as numerous subsequent gestures and jokes in $M*A*S*H,$ unquestionably allude to Vietnam and call forth our feelings about that particular war. (Altman noted in a 1983 interview that in the original cut of $M*A*S*H$ there was not one reference to Korea: " . . . they said you have to put in the titles that it was Korea. That's when we put in the statement of Eisenhower's ["I will go to Korea."]."[13]) For Americans, at least, the knowledge of the war in Vietnam is inseparable from the knowledge of conflicting understandings of who we were and are as a citizenry.

Even if superficially disguised, the initial allusions in $M*A*S*H$ to the Vietnam war orient our viewing and identify the film's audience. Allusions are linked to constraining the world viewed to a particular community because allusions pierce the proscenium arch or the film frame without weakening the basic structure of the work. Allusions in any medium rely on and confirm a common set of beliefs and experiences; they are, however, not messages from authors to audiences but invitations from the makers of the work to the audience to participate in making meanings.[14] In theater, the presence of a live audience makes the allusionary activity vibrant; even in the numbing decorum of modern theater audiences, evocative allusions can effect an audible murmur in the audience, can elicit cheers or at least a serial passage of nods and nudges. The even more passive behavior of movie audiences combined with the absence of the world of the film from the world of the audience means that the effect of an allusion for the film audience is to leave it with history but with no world with which to interact. For the film audience, this may actually heighten the pleasure allusions can provide—the pleasure in knowing that we know something. The danger is that that knowledge may appear to be sufficient or may be taken as further evidence of our impotence in any world outside our own bodies.

Allusions in Altman can be intertextual (for example, Julie Christie's cameo appearance as the actress Julie Christie in *Nashville* that becomes a specific allusion to her role in *McCabe and Mrs. Miller* when an on-screen spectator in *Nashville* asks why the woman does not comb her hair), but, more significantly, they remark and delineate a social, historical context. In *Health,* for example, a variety of images and gestures (most memorably the hole in a candidate's shoe) allude to the presidential election campaign of the fifties between Adlai Stevenson and Dwight D. Eisenhower. One of the more aggressive allusions to Vietnam in *M*A*S*H* occurs in a sequence that displays the administration of a drug to a young Korean boy in an effort (eventually proven unsuccessful) to assure his failure of his army induction physical; the doctors and the boy are ostensibly Korean, but for moviegoers in 1970, the historical moment evoked is clearly that of the Vietnam War.

These allusions function in a way that is peculiarly elitist *and* democratic. For a sign to act as an allusion, the signifier (a word, phrase, sound, moving patern, visual image of an object) must have emerged from everyday life as an icon, and the spectator or reader of the sign must be a member of a particular community of knowledge. Such communities are exclusive, but ideally, anyone can participate. Anyone can participate by virtue of having "been there" or by making the effort to acquire the requisite knowledge, and if artistic allusions work, they encourage such participation. They do not, of course, guarantee it.

As an allusion to Vietnam, the helicopter images at the beginning of M*A*S*H call forth a whole set of beliefs about the United States and its role in Southeast Asia, but also specifically re-present the association of this particular war with this particular machine, a vehicle that is deceptively nonthreatening in appearance but without which the American military would have been impotent on this terrain. The narcotic ambiance induced by the soothing tones of music, color, and movement complements the visual emblem of the exotic but unstable helicopter; it re-collects the seductive stupor that was the other side of the period's protest movements and the logical extension of hallucinations and numbness in the epigrammatic refrain "Suicide Is Painless."

In addition to setting the historical arena of the film, this initial tapestry also locates and dislocates point of view. The tutorial eye that has woven this sequence cannot be the "I" that sings "Suicide Is Painless," if only because the zoom-in toward the bleeding body of the wounded soldier asserts itself as an intervention of a point of view that is literally moved by this evidence of human pain and vulnerability. The power of the singing voice relies on the assumption that the "I" is really a "we," but the zoom confronts us as spectators with knowledge that undermines our ability stoically to concur with the devaluation of life proclaimed by the singer and thus separates us from the "I." Both the song and the zoom call attention to authorial presence; whereas film conventionally strives to disguise its subjectivism by establishing a consistent and inclusive value system, the opening of M*A*S*H foreshadows the assertive multivoicedness and incompleteness that will become central to Altman's representations of American culture.

The voice projected over the base loudspeaker shortly after the opening credits, and repeatedly during the film, also reminds us of authorship, absence, and perspective. No one we see at the base responds in any way to the loudspeaker announcements of film screenings or missing articles, nor do we see any character whom we might suspect of being the source of either the voice or the judgments it implies. But someone is speaking, and as with advertisements, there is a set of values and an intention in these utterances even if there is no accessible agent.

The disembodied loudspeaker voice is one of several alternative "openings" to a particular set of historical moments; each of these elements orients the spectator to a particular way of watching the film. This orientation (perhaps, more aptly a form of disorientation) establishes and frames a space and place and our relationship to it. The "it" here is important. In $M^*A^*S^*H$, as in most of his films, Altman's approach to space and setting is, in conventional terms, ostensibly theatrical rather than cinematic: the dominant setting maintains the Aristotelian unity of place, and the world of the film is specified and inhabited by those who have some defined relationship to this setting. The world of M*A*S*H is the world of one Mobile Army Surgical Hospital unit, based a few miles behind the front in Korea; the word "Mobile" in the group's title is ironic because, from the first high-overhead shot of the base, the unit appears almost eternally fixed in one place.

If social and geographical mobility is an illusion within the military world depicted, however, it is deliberately discrepant with the authenticity of movement and the possibility of mobility in $M^*A^*S^*H$, the film. In contrast to our experience in the theater, where confinement to a rigidly limited number of settings (which can include several but not innumerable locations) is a necessary condition of the separateness and otherness of the stage world, the possibility of moving to and through an unlimited number of settings is essential in film. It is when this is not, in some gesture, acknowledged by the film itself, that we feel ourselves in the presence of film weakly imitating theater, of film imprisoned by space in a way that is inauthentic to what we know of its nature. Whether or not we experience filmed space as cinematic or artifically theatrical is not a matter of the diversity of locations actually shown or the extent of movement in and across space but of the presentation of the idea of space as open or closed. André Bazin saw this as inherent to cinema's "essence" as "a dramaturgy of Nature." While Bazin seems to me mistaken in claiming that film replaces the universe while theater *re-presents a part* of a particular world, $M^*A^*S^*H$, like all of Altman's films, instantiates Bazin's claim that "the screen cannot give us the illusion of this feeling of space without calling on certain natural guarantees."[15] The space of theater is closed—not as a segment or part of the natural world but as a perfect and complete world, constructed to be self-contained. The "open" space of film is not, in this sense, at all theatrical and is, in fact, "natural," in the way that the world itself is incomplete and without inherent parameters. And as Bazin went on to say, this "is less a question of set construction or of architecture or of immensity than of isolating the aesthetic catalyst, which it is sufficient to introduce in an infinitesimal dose."

Beginning with $M^*A^*S^*H$, Altman persistently experiments with diverse forms of "aesthetic catalysts" that will maintain an open filmic space within a unitary social setting. Only once, in *Streamers* (Altman's filmic rendition of the Broadway hit by David Rabe), does he fail to open a crack in the closed space of theatrical representation.[16] In $M^*A^*S^*H$, this acknowledgment of the peculiar incompleteness of filmic space and its implicit promise of mobility occurs in four segments: the opening shots of the arriving helicopters; the sequence, near the beginning of the movie, in which Hawkeye Pierce and Duke (Tom Skerritt) steal a jeep in a nearby town to facilitate their arrival at the base; Hawkeye's excursion to a nearby town with the young Korean Ho-Jon (Kim Atwood) for the latter's Korean army physical; and Hawkeye's trip with his buddy Trapper John to Japan to operate on the wounded son of an American congressman.

All four of these segments remind the American characters and the viewing audience of the displacement of American cultural forms and of the American misperceptions of those who are other. This is particularly evident in the third off-base segment, in which we witness the failure of the MASH unit's attempt to deceive a Korean doctor by giving Ho-Jon drugs that will temporarily debilitate him. The doctor makes clear that the ploy has been discerned, suggesting pointedly to Hawkeye and the American film audience that the Third World knows the tricks of the First World and is not as stupid as Americans may sometimes presume.

The fourth instance of a violation of the unity of place in $M*A*S*H$ is revealing in a different way. Hawkeye and Trapper's trip to Japan confirms the spectators' expectation of film but also calls this expectation into question. This sequence feels like a digression, an exception to the internal rules of this particular film, as it is an exception to the norm of immobility for most of the servicemen—and servicewomen—on the base. Much of the human behavior that is at the center of the film's interest is inseparable from the confinement of the men and women of $M*A*S*H$ to their remote base; Hawkeye and Trapper John can escape only because a powerful U.S. politician makes a special request.

Film can follow Hawkeye and Trapper John to Japan because it, too, is privileged, and privileged in a way that live theater is not. But this privilege does not necessarily make the world lived or the world viewed better. Hawkeye and Trapper's trip to Japan ostensibly asserts the unique flexibility of filmic space, but in violating the space-time focus previously established in $M*A*S*H$, the trip appears as a sideshow and ironically underscores the theatrical conceptualization of space in this film.

This ambivalent approach to space in $M*A*S*H$ recalls some of the early history of film in which claims of film's dependence on theatrical conventions were challenged by claims that the camera "liberated" drama from the artificial confines of the stage.[17] These claims were exemplified and instantiated by practice: studio-based movies appeared to confirm film as a stepchild of theater in contrast to films shot "on location" in which the physical world was infinitely expansive and "redeemed," as Siegfried Kracauer later argued. The geographical mobility of American social life and the illusion of social-role mobility at the heart of the American Dream, especially in the thirties, lent support to filmic representations of movement through space and from place to place as metaphors for the American experience: the cowboy on his horse, galloping across the frontier; the train transporting the innocent and the corrupt from East to Wast and town to city; the half-fictional sophisticates dancing their way from New York to Paris and back again, conjoined the freedom that centered American morality with the illusion of unfettered and fluid movement in American cinema.[18]

Unity of place in Altman suggests an alternative strain of American film—the exploration of community and of particular communities—that has recurred in American movies from Capra to Coppola. Even (and perhaps especially) in Westerns, it is the tension *between* a focused, single place and the promise of a vaster, unlimited world that is key to the coherence of the medium and its message. This second, less examined, inclination of American film toward a focus on one community, is elementally theatrical but is not thereby uncinematic. The "openness" of filmic space is less a matter of transportation from one location to another than of the openness of the world projected.

We can re-collect this distinction between the openness of filmic space and the closedness of theatrical space by imagining ourselves in a theater for the first moments of a live performance and comparing this with the experience of the first moments of a film screening. In theater, the unveiling of the set, even when accompanied by suggestive music, precedes the drama; props, backdrops, lighting are elements of stagecraft and only partake in the making of meaning with the entrance of an actor as character. The stage reveals a world at the same time that it encloses a world. A stage space empty of actors or, at least, empty of some hint of a human voice, will rapidly make me claustrophobic.

My reading of the opening shots of $M*A*S*H$ suggests that film has a very different relation to the places it screens: on the stage, elements of setting orient the actors and the audience to the constraints of the staged world; they establish a context and simultaneously imply the subordination and separation of the context from characters. On film, objects, landscapes, and rooms can make meaning in the absence of animate characters and in conjunction with them; human voices and the space they penetrate play together dialogically. Context merges with point of view. In theater, a bare stage may have various meanings but does not disrupt the basic relationships of audience to characters and the world they inhabit because the stage space is always an abstraction hinting of no place. In contrast, the settings of film are always particular, and no frame is ever empty. The men and women who appear on screen are situated in both time and space.

In the first sequence of M*A*S*H, questions have been raised and contradictions revealed; no speaking characters have appeared on the screen, yet the world has opened before me. The only human being visible in the first moments of the film is the wounded soldier; his immobility contributes to the sense of a world removed from human will. Even after the one helicopter lands with the wounded soldier, all that we are shown is the rush of several uniformed bodies toward the victim; no human faces are yet revealed, and it is barely evident from the shape of one hip and a glimpse of hair that one of the soldiers is a woman. In its first moments, M*A*S*H hints of a threatening relationship in which we will be led to acknowledge the frailty of our attachments to any point of view. Now, even more than in 1970, the emphatic absence of controlling points of view is a discomforting reminder of the actual absence of most Americans from the war in Vietnam.

The subsequent introduction of the central characters of M*A*S*H and of their relationships to each other, diminishes the threat to the audience while maintaining the distance established in the credit sequence. Overlapping sounds—of male voices, the announcer on the loudspeaker, and a marching band—establish the ambiance of a military base. Almost immediately, the screen is split, displaying on the right the figures and objects of the world to be viewed in this movie and on the left graphic verbal commentary on that world. The first title, "and then there was Korea," locates M*A*S*H within the overlapping genres of newsreels and war movies; it implies, as well, that the Korea projected on the screen is one episode in a longer narrative. In the next shot, Hawkeye Pierce makes his entrance, carefully placed to the right of the frame in an internal montage with a new title that displays to the left of the frame the words of General MacArthur after he was recalled from Korea: "I have just left your fighting forces in Korea." Aptly enough, Eisenhower's "I will go to Korea" concludes the historical indexing while also serving to further theatricalize

Hawkeye's entrance and to alert the viewer to the ironic interplay of points of view that will continue throughout the movie.

Given the publicly available but little-known information that Altman's producers forced him to add this and subsequent titles that would locate the film in Korea, there is a critical temptation to dismiss these graphic interventions as irrelevant to any discussion of Altman's work and, less convincingly, as irrelevant to the "real" text of $M*A*S*H$. To do so, however, would be to betray my own arguments about the complexity of authorship in film in general and in Altman's work in particular. It is not only that we need to keep in mind the economic and political conditions that inform and constrain film production and distribution (which is not to deny the importance of these conditions); reminders of the multiplicity of voices that speak in a movie are also to be treasured. The titles included in $M*A*S*H$ are gems because, even without the external evidence that they represent an "other" point of view, the appearance of such written texts in movies is at once an appeal to legitimacy and an admission that dramatic settings are selected from history and are always partial.

The selection of these particular quotations is a typically Altmanesque double entendre, positioning those for whom the citations recall the historical drama of the fifties inside the frame of reference while placing those with no prior knowledge of the words of MacArthur and Eisenhower at the entrance to this particular corridor of history. The contradiction between the image of American soldiers in Korea presented to Americans at home by MacArthur and the distinctly nonmilitary image of a soldier projected by Hawkeye Pierce is blatantly contrived. The shot is more resonant, however, if you know that Eisenhower dismissed MacArthur from his command of the American forces in Korea because the President did not want to risk war with China and judged the general to be overzealous in his anticommunism and mistaken in his plan to invade North Korea.

The segment focusing on Hawkeye's entrance also introduces the viewer to the film's interest in gender-based relationships. Hawkeye moves into the center and foreground of the frame; he locates an empty jeep and awaits the driver he presumes will take him to the

MASH base. Another man, who subsequently introduced himself as Captain "Duke" Forrest (Tom Skerritt), enters the frame above and behind Hawkeye; Duke is riding with several uniformed women in an open military vehicle. He leaps from the van and moves toward Hawkeye, whose proximity to the jeep Duke misinterprets to signify that Hawkeye is the jeep's driver. Misinformed by his own misinterpretation, Duke commands Hawkeye to take him to the MASH base. Hawkeye does not correct the mistake but exploits it, declaring to Duke, "I'd follow you anywhere, Sir." With few words exchanged, both men take off in the jeep, and there is no doubt from the viewer's perspective that they will be buddies henceforth. A fraternal relationship is established, and we know from the long tradition of the American male hero and his sidekick—from Huck Finn and Jim to the Lone Ranger and Tonto—that the loyalty promised in Hawkeye's response to Duke's command is authentic, even if, in context, his words conceal a different truth and are deliberately misleading.

At the same time and in the same shots that present the entrance of Hawkeye and subsequently establish the comraderie between Duke and Hawkeye, fully in focus but situated behind the jeep and in the upper periphery of the frame are the group of women soldiers who arrived with Duke. Each woman descends from the van; the first woman's exit is mostly hidden from view by the images of Hawkeye and Duke in the foreground, and the others clamber out with a notable awkwardness that calls brief attention to their legs and the tight, straight skirts that impede movement. Nothing the women do or say is remarkable, and they are deemphasized by their position in the frame. I would venture a guess that few viewers of *M*A*S*H,* including those who have seen the movie more than once, will remember the presence of women in this scene. Nonetheless, Altman and his colleagues chose to include this group of women in the segment when there were numerous other ways to fill the frame, and, with movies as with dreams, we have nothing to lose by wagering that god and the devil are in the details.

There are two obvious and not mutually exclusive functions that the presence of women may play in this early segment of *M*A*S*H.* Given how much of the history of film is not only "a history of the firmament of individual women established there,"[19] but also a history of the decoration of the world with women and representations of women, the slight emphasis on the legs of these uniformed women may serve simply to ornament the picture. And because images of women so often serve this function in film, they can be relied on to fill the frame pleasantly without distracting the viewer's attention from the men who are the apparent focus of attention. Additionally, or alternatively, the presentation of these women at this point in the film informs us that the world of $M^*A^*S^*H$ does include women, something we could not have previously assumed from either military history or film history. (War movies and movies about the military exclude women or include them only minimally far more frequently than any other genre of film.) This information prepares us for the presence of women in the next scene, when Hawkeye and Duke arrive at the MASH unit's base.

I am not satisfied by either or even both these explanations. While in many films of the late sixties and seventies a commonplace gesture or icon signifying the presence of women may suffice to decorate the picture, Altman's camera does not here indulge in the familiar, objectifying close-ups of women's faces and bodies, nor does the camera isolate a particularly pretty woman from her companions. This leads me to look at the shots again in what I might call an ordinary language reading of the text. Starting from this point, let us suppose that the primary function of this segment is to introduce one of the main characters of the film—Hawkeye Pierce—and, simultaneously, to orient the viewer to a way of seeing this character and his relationship to the world of the film. What, in seconds, I understand about this character is that he is a man, a member of the U.S. military, presented first as a lone, independent individual. He is then centrally delineated in relation to an automobile and, next, in relation to a bonding of instant trust with another man. His character is also immediately decorated with wit.

In the context of what follows in $M^*A^*S^*H$, and in the context of Altman's other films, I take this to be a declaration that this film is interested in and informed by a consciousness of men as men. Who Hawkeye is, why we should be interested in him, and what meanings he makes and we make of him in the world are deeply and importantly defined by his gender. The presence of a group of women, behind Hawkeye and in a subordinate position in the frame, is, then, not trivial or conventional, but a way of stating from the beginning that a consciousness of men as men is inseparable from a consciousness of women and the relationship of men to women. More specifically, the film defines this relationship as one in which the presence of women, as a backdrop, not as individuals, is central to the cultural meanings of male gender and of a man's consciousness of himself as a man.

In a sense, this is not to say anything different than what I described as the "obvious" explanations for the inclusion of women in these scenes. The camera's maintenance of distance from the women and the stability of their location behind the men and the jeep, in the upper periphery of the frame, do deemphasize the women's presence, and this is an efficient way of informing the viewer that Hawkeye and Duke are central figures in the story and that the women are relatively peripheral. By slightly altering the accent or practice of the conventional, however, by capturing the women's legs in a necessarily awkward gesture rather than in a glamorous pose, the habitual has been reaccentuated and enlivened in a manner similar to that by which certain modern philosophers, linguists, and playwrights have reinvigorated the language of clichés by sounding an utterance so that it again says what it means.[20]

I will readily admit that the meaning I make of this segment is infected by what follows in the film. Most obvious, this shot of these women's legs foreshadows the first images displayed of the film's central female character, Major "Hot Lips" Houlihan (Sally Kellerman). I do not, however, take this "backreading" as a flaw in my reading but rather as one of the conditions for my reading, a condition urged by the text and by the many persuasive examples available to contemporary readers of readings that demonstrate how language recovers meanings when encountered consciously in context. (This recalls the inherent resistance in Altman's films to the dominant cultural assumption that movies make all of their meanings available in one screening.) Because (not just in the subsequent introduction of Major Houlihan but throughout the film) discourse is comprised of at least two different understandings of gendered behavior, it seems to me likely that there is more rather than less going on in these first shots of women and men together.

What "more" is going on in $M*A*S*H$ is a cluster of understandings of men and women that emerge from a set of stories linked not by causality but by the common culture shared by the figures who tell and participate in these tales. From the arrival of Hawkeye and Duke at the base, the remainder of $M*A*S*H$, like its beginning, ignores the conventional narrative structure of movies, building its world, instead, by a series of vignettes that amplify, complicate, and elaborate the issues of human identity and relationship already raised in the entrances of the helicopter and of Hawkeye and Duke. Eschewing the device and metaphor of the journey that so often frames episodic storytelling in traditional prose or verse, the structure of $M*A*S*H$ is folkloric rather than epic in its ambiance, closer in form to the tradition of carnival than to the irrevocable unravelings of traditional drama and film.[21]

Four key tales unfold in the course of the film: the symbolic and physical deflowering of the woman in the story of "Hot Lips" Houlihan, the reclamation and reaffirmation of manhood represented in the trials of the dentist Painless Waldowski, the proving of male heroism in the Tokyo adventures of Hawkeye and Trapper, and the confirmation of community in the ritual enactment of tribal battles of the football game. Notably, each of these story lines stands alone and has neither temporal nor causal connection to any of the other narrative branches of the movie. The inclusion of Trapper and Hawkeye in each of these main episode clusters provides continuity from one story to another, but more than the presence of the two central male figures, what links these episodes is their participation in and representation of a common cultural system. Each of these story lines addresses an elemental issue that is problematic for any society and that is traditionally and repeatedly resolved in rituals created by the society to make sense to itself of itself and to confirm and transform its own values and practices.[22] In $M*A*S*H$, each of these stories draws on classical Western story structures to represent rituals of identification particularized by and in American culture.

The first of these narrative episodes introduces an ancient icon of Western culture and, specifically, of American movies—the woman as goddess and virgin.[23] Major Margaret Houlihan (Sally Kellerman) descends from the skies to the base in a helicopter identical to those we saw at the beginning of the film. For those on earth, inside and outside the film, Nurse Houlihan is first of all a pair of legs. The shot of Houlihan as she exits from the helicopter is a blatant set-up; the woman has been deliberately "framed," established from the start as a sexual object by the emphatic separation of a stereotypically sexual portion of her body from her face and voice. As Laura Mulvey notes of similar classical shots of Monroe, Dietrich, Bacall, and Garbo: "one part of fragmented body destroys the 'Renaissance' space, the illusion of depth demanded by the narrative, it gives flatness, the quality of a cut-out or icon rather than verisimilitude, to the screen."[24] The obviousness of the shot, however, and its association with numerous other movie shots of women's legs (or breasts or buttocks) frames the frame-up, and while it does not settle how we will subsequently see Nurse Houlihan, we may henceforth be hesitant to separate our knowledge of the character from our knowledge that she is being watched and sexually objectified.[25]

Interpreted in isolation from what follows in the story of Houlihan, the initial zoom in to this woman's legs may still be understood as objectifying; it does, after all, exhibit the fragmenting, tyrannical attributes of what has been described as the "loathsome zoom,"[26] confirming the dangers of the zoom as a weapon in the hands of patriarchal filmmakers. At least, one might argue, in Frank Capra's famous "leg shot" in It Happened One Night (1934), the woman (Claudette Colbert) chooses to expose her leg, to present it as an object of desire, in order to exploit male fantasies to satisfy her own needs. (At this point in Capra's film, Colbert and Gable are penniless, hungry, and, prior to the extension of Colbert's leg, unsuccessful in their attempts to hitchhike.) Capra does not appear to be using Colbert against her will; this is the one scene in It Happened One Night in which the woman takes command of the action.[27] In contrast, the camera's approach to Major Houlihan appears to be unabashedly voyeuristic, understandably unleashing the wrath of such feminist critics as Joan Mellen, who finds M*A*S*H to be insistently demeaning to women and a prime example of the misogyny of the Hollywood movies.[28]

I do not now read the first image of Major Houlihan or the subsequent treatment of women in M*A*S*H as misogynistic because of the ways in which subsequent scenes reorient my seeing.[29] After establishing, visually and aurally, that Houlihan is "a damned good nurse" (as Trapper John eventually informs her), that she is unswerving in her adherence to U.S. Army regulations, and that she is unreflectively patriotic, naive, and prudish, an omniscient camera captures her in the preliminary stages of a romance with Major Frank Burns (Robert Duvall). Burns is a Christian zealot and a less than virtuous doctor who is so dishonest that he transfers his own responsibility for the unnecessary death of a wounded soldier to Boone (Bud Cort), the youngest and most vulnerable member of the MASH team. A late-night sequence comprised of cross-cuts between Houlihan's quarters and a tent where most of the MASH men are gathered around a makeshift tape recorder and amplifier quickly reveals that the omniscient narrator-camera is not alone in its awareness of the budding Houlihan-Burns affair. Utilizing the technical knowledge and acquisitiveness of the always resourceful Corporal "Radar" (Gary Burghoff), the men have bugged Houlihan's tent, and we watch them and listen with them as the sounds of Houlihan's and Burns's mutual lust are broadcast throughout the base.

Neither the film audience nor Houlihan is ever allowed to forget this scene, not the least because it is Houlihan's own plea to Frank— "Oh, Frank, my lips are hot. Kiss my hot lips"—that establishes her new name, "Hot Lips." But for Trapper John, Hawkeye, Duke, Radar, and their pals, their broadcast invasion of Hot Lips's intimate moment with Frank does not suffice, despite the fact that this mischief drives Frank crazy, as is efficaciously revealed in a shot (soon after the late-night assignation) in which we see Frank in a straitjacket being literally driven away from the base, with "Sayonara" playing over the base loudspeaker. Well after Frank's departure, and several segments later, we find the men of M*A*S*H renewing their efforts to humiliate the woman now known as Hot Lips.

The context is that of the women's shower time. Before our eyes, the men of $M*A*S*H$ literally transform the setting into a theater, complete with stage, house seats, and refreshments. Accentuated by a disconcerting quiet that is particularly noticeable in contrast to the ambient noise and overlapping dialogue that has prevailed until this

Hot Lips Houlihan (Sally Kellerman) attempts to shield herself from the on-screen audience that has set her up to be humiliated by hoisting the shower tent in *M*A*S*H*. (*The Museum of Modern Art/Film Stills Archive, New York City*)

Hot Lips (Sally Kellerman) hurries away to find the colonel after being humiliated by her voyeuristic peers during the shower scene in *M*A*S*H.* (*The Museum of Modern Art/Film Stills Archive, New York City*)

point in the film, the "performers"—several women in bathrobes—appear on screen. A close-up shows a man turning a sign that reads "Men—Off Limits" to read "Women—Off Limits." Each of the women except Houlihan is withdrawn from their entrance parade by some trivial appeal from one of the men—"look at the photos I just got of my kids." The camera turns its close attention to Hawkeye, Trapper, Duke, and a dozen other men who have established themselves, with several of the women, as an audience in front of the curtained platform that is at once the shower area and the stage. In the mode of sixties' and seventies' improvisational theater, one man, seated in the audience area, plays a guitar, and another creates a percussion accompaniment on an overturned oil drum.

On Trapper's cue, clearly attended to by the camera, the "shower" curtain is drawn, revealing Hot Lips, in profile, naked under the shower, her hair frothy with shampoo. She instantly attempts to conceal her breasts with one hand and her pubic area with the other, then grabs her robe and deliberately crumples belly-down to the stage floor, screaming furiously and squirming gracelessly offstage. Responding to calls of "applause" and "author," the camera returns its attention to the spectators, only to show them removing themselves and their chairs somewhat awkwardly and joylessly from the audience area. The vignette ends with Hot Lips bursting into the tent of the colonel (Roger Bowen), who is tranquilly sitting in bed with his mistress, another army nurse. The colonel appears nonplussed by Hot Lips's shaking body and shrill cry that "This isn't a hospital, it's an insane asylum," nor is he troubled by her parting threat to resign her commission. "Well, goddamn it, Hot Lips, resign your goddamn commission," he tells her, then dismisses her by turning to the woman beside him with the supercilious query, "A little more wine, dear?"

These and other supporting scenes that constitute the humiliation of Hot Lips Houlihan—what I earlier called her defloration—are, transparently, *about* the ritualized degradation of women by men. The male heroes of $M*A*S*H$ set out to disarm and control Major Houlihan; they achieve their victory by assaulting her where she is most vulnerable—in her knowledge, and ignorance, of her own sexuality. There is no ambiguity in what is done to Houlihan: rigid, remote, protected by her uniform and moral convictions when she alights from the helicopter at the beginning of the film, Nurse Houlihan enters the world of $M*A*S*H$ as a Valkyrie, but by the end of the shower scene, her male colleagues have succeeded in recasting her as a debased angel.

What story is this string of episodes telling the viewers, what meanings are we to make of these events? One available reading of these sequences would emphasize the triumph of honesty over hypocrisy, of imagination over rigid regulations, of sexual liberation over sexual repression. In each of these paired attributes, the men, represented most vividly by Hawkeye and Trapper, are on the side of virtue and victory. Whether in the operating room, the mess, or the "Swamp" where they bed down, Hawkeye and Trapper persistently and ruthlessly scorn the pretensions and delusions of army decorum and rhetoric; they "tell it like it is." Ardently embracing Lieutenant "Dish" (Jo Ann Pflug), the attractive married nurse who is blatantly torn between her desire for Hawkeye and her vows of marital fidelity, Hawkeye refuses to romanticize his intentions but tells her, "If my wife were here, I'd be doing this with her." When Hot Lips wonders aloud how someone as uncouth and disrespectful of military rules as Hawkeye could have been accepted in the army, the deflating retort from Dago Red (René Auberjonois), the Catholic chaplain, is, "He was drafted." Trapper wins our applause when he punches Frank Burns, because we have just witnessed Burnes falsely blaming the death of a wounded soldier on young Private Boone (Bud Cort).

Almost always in M*A*S*H, candor is framed by wit, and wit, whether articulated by characters or by the directorial voice evident in visual and aural gestures, repeatedly penetrates the world of this movie. It is the film's prevalent form of play. Truth, imagination, and sexual freedom are thus all apparently lined up on the same side of the barricades in M*A*S*H, and in 1970, there was little question for those of us who identified with the counterculture (or who, more narrowly, were opposed to U.S. participation in the war in Vietnam) that this was the side to be on. This means that we would find ourselves—women as well as men, as the film provocatively insists— right there in the audience with Hawkeye and Trapper, applauding as the shower-curtain scene reveals Hot Lips, fallen and furious, before us. We might then take this scene, along with those that precede it, to suggest that by a conjoining of our wits and imaginations, and by determined, coordinated, but "nonviolent" resistance to authority and convention, including rigid codes of sexual behavior, we could reveal and render impotent the hypocritical behaviors of those who held power in our society. We could overcome.

Joan Mellen offers a similar reading of M*A*S*H with an alternative conclusion or judgment of what this means, or should mean, for the viewer. Her telling of the plot and the story of M*A*S*H is consistent with the interpretation I have just presented, but for her, the "we" who can and will overcome are strictly men, and their important foe is not the North Koreans (or North Vietnamese) or war itself or the general social conditions of hypocrisy, authority, and repression but women. "Director Altman," Mellen writes, "is interested only in depicting the cool machismo of his heroes, toward which he demonstrates not the slightest irony."[30] For Mellen, M*A*S*H is wholly consistent with other buddy films of the period and provides "further evidence that these buddy films are made in conscious hostility to the women's movement."[31]

Altman does present woman as "other" in M*A*S*H (as, I will argue, he does consistently in his films), and my own reading of these and other episodes of M*A*S*H insists, too, on the importance of the film's association of men with power, integrity, sophistication, sexual aggression, and comraderie. But where Mellen sees "not the slightest irony" in Altman's depiction of his heroes, I see irony, parody, and contradiction at most key moments of the movie, and I take these to make an alternative story at least as available to the viewer as those which I have just described.

I find this alternative story most available in the shower scene. Repeatedly, in this episode, my expectations are thwarted. The earlier visual insistence on Major Houlihan's containment of her body—she wears her tight-buttoned army uniform like a shield and opens it like armour in her love-making scene with Frank Burns—and the narrative implications that Houlihan is not what she appears to be, seduce on-screen and off-screen viewers to anticipate pleasure in her unveiling. There is not, however, a single full-frontal nude shot of Houlihan in the film; nor is there pleasure for the viewer in the profile shot of Houlihan in which we see her for a brief moment undressed on the shower-stage and then watch her crawl offstage. Her desperate, flailing gestures and her facial expressions of fear and humiliation destroy any sensual appeal we might have anticipated. What I understand, watching her, is that she is a terribly vulnerable human being under assault, not a sex object.

The failure of this scene to fulfill my expectations also points me in the direction of the meaning of those expectations. I am uneasy, to start with, in my conviction that women as well as men anticipate experiencing pleasure in the unveiling of Hot Lips. I can resist this conviction and argue that, as with most movies (and one could extend this to much of Western painting), both the creator of the image and the imagined viewer are male. But while it is obviously the case that most movie directors have been men, and it may be true that these men have usually given little thought to the differences between the points of view of men and women spectators, I find it unlikely that the large and continuous female movie audience has for sixty years or more quietly accepted the irrelevance—or offense—of the images of women projected before them. Women may be passive, but they have always had the option of not going to the movies.

Nor does it assuage my anxiety to recall periods—the Hollywood thirties, for example—or particular films that created more complex and less demeaning images of women than was the case in the late sixties and early seventies. Compare, for example, how we feel about Hot Lips in the shower scene with our experience of Amanda Bonner (Katherine Hepburn) in George Cukor's *Adam's Rib* (1949). Few films better satisfy my desire to see the world from a woman's point of view than does *Adam's Rib*, but the finding of that satisfaction in no way diminishes my desire for intimate knowledge of Amanda Bonner, the particular woman whose point of view about women's points of view is one concern of Cukor's film. And it would be foolish as well as false to say that my interest in Amanda is focused solely on her mind or spirit or soul, as if these were somehow separate from her body. Indeed, the relentless concealment of Hepburn's body—we might think of her as the most fully dressed female movie star ever to appear on the screen—instructs us as to the difference between prudery and modesty. The high-cut necklines that are as much a part of the Hepburn signature as are her determined gait or daring gaze do not signify sexual denial or repression; they are signs of the respect for authentic female modesty with which the actress endows her characters. This modesty is not a matter of social decorum (the screen characters that Hepburn has created, Amanda Bonner supreme among them, are among the least concerned of movie women with adherence to conventional social practices) but of what French critic Sarah Kofman describes as the ability "to hold oneself to appearance, to interrogate oneself indefinitely on the infinite riddles of nature/Sphinx, without seeking—perhaps it is only prudence—to 'unveil' the truth."[32]

It is to just this issue of the relationship between female modesty and "naked" truth that Cukor's *Adam's Rib* addresses itself and to which Altman turns, first in *M*A*S*H* and later, with biting poignancy, in the striptease sequence in *Nashville*. *Adam's Rib* begins with breakfast in the bedroom of Amanda Bonner and her husband, Adam. Shortly after their unfinished breakfasts, Amanda and Adam retreat to their separate dressing rooms, off-screen, left and right, while the camera remains in the mostly empty bedroom. The camera's position increases our intimacy with the couple and remarks the particular and peculiar intimacy with others with which film provides us. Neither in this scene nor in our culture is the undressing and dressing of a woman the same as the undressing and dressing of a man, and from the tantalizing promise of Amanda's nightclothes (in contrast to the baggy, almost clownish noneroticism of Adam's pajamas) to her eventual appearance in her day clothes, we are held not only by the "invisible and pervasive" presence of the couple in their intimacy but, specifically, by our awareness and incomplete knowledge of this woman's body. It is our knowledge that she is naked *and* hidden that fixes our attention, as is made transparent at the end of *Adam's Rib* when the two return to each other and their bed behind the curtains of their four-poster. While it is accurate to say that what is hidden from us is their love-making and *both* their naked bodies, there is, as Adam reminds Amanda and us just as they retire, an important difference between him as man and her as woman. Although Adam does not verbally articulate the nature of this difference, he has just shown Amanda and the viewer something of what it is about. He has nothing left to hide, or nothing he considers important to hide, having already displayed his half-fake tears and, more important, his anger and pain. His sexuality has been uncovered in front of the curtains. But hers remains to be seen and will only be seen, as she intimates, and he requires, "behind closed doors," or curtains, as it may be.

The line of connection I am attempting to trace between *Adam's Rib* and *M*A*S*H* is drawn from the link made in both films between the idea of "woman" and the idea of "truth." Not uniquely, but more explicitly than in other media, women in movies are mistresses of appearances. Since its origins among the ancient Greeks, Western drama has been obsessed with the artifices employed by women to transform how they appear to others; at least half the history of Western drama might be written as the history either of accusations against the feignings of women (Clytemnestra, Desdemona, and Maggie in *Cat on a Hot Tin Roof*) or revelations of women's transformations as vehicles of power (Medea, Portia, and Martha in *Who's Afraid of Virginia Woolf?*). Movies continue this tradition and extend it, perhaps because their art and technology is inevitably conjoined with magical manipulations of appearances—a skill, ironically, associated with women and, in our times, primarily transferred into the hands of men. And in the movies, as in their ancestral dramatic forms, truth is as much or more a woman than she has ever been. Whether, in their inalterable embrace of appearances, the movies and the women they project are in the service of good or of evil is a question that cannot be settled as easily as some have claimed.

   M*A*S*H makes no secret of the liaison it suggests between the unveiling of woman and the grasping of truth. The shower sequence is set up by Duke's bet that Hot Lips is not a real blond. As if to attest to their interest in truth, Duke, Hawkeye, and Trapper contrive the shower prank as a show because "We've all gotta see it together." For any one of them to see "it" alone would risk turning the seeing into sex or, conversely and simultaneously, might be sex rather than truth. Truth, notably, cannot be achieved by one person alone; in this vision, fraternity shares with science a skepticism about uncorroborated evidence that makes collaboration not only desirable but a necessary condition for the integrity of either enterprise.

   Altman's refusal to provide the knowledge that Duke, Hawkeye, and Trapper seek is not then simply a gesture of opposition to the conventional sexism of the movies. The shower scene is an Edenic movement; female sexuality mediates the more dangerous temptation toward perfect knowledge, and it is this desire to know what lies beyond and beneath the veil that tempts both women and men. In thwarting the fulfillment of this desire, Altman instructs us in the errors of such pursuits. His warning echoes Nietzsche's, as interpolated, at least, by Kofman: "The will to strip woman naked is a sign of a lack of virility and of instincts insufficiently strong and insufficiently beautiful to love appearance and the veil."[33]

What I begin to understand in $M*A*S*H$ is that my vulnerability to the seductive appeal of the shower scene and to the subsequent discomfort it evokes, complicated as it is by the intersection of my disdain for Hot Lips's misplaced attachments and my anger at the male characters' exploitation of women, is a matter in part of the frailty of my commitment to my own convictions. Having argued in *Feminist Theatre* that the recognitions that are the fruits of the traditional unveilings of drama delude us to believe that we have found some valuable truths and lead us to a dangerous delight in our own prisons, I find myself impressed, and troubled, by the tenacity of the illusion that there is a truth worth seeking behind the veils of appearance. Perhaps we will only begin to understand—and challenge—the power of phallocentrism when we women celebrate our half-admitted knowledge that when we lift our own skirts we remain hidden also from ourselves.

Watching the shower sequence, I perceive that the men who have set up this spectacle are callous, mean, and selfish. As Vincent Canby suggested in a review of $M*A*S*H$, "Hot Lips is a good deal more vulnerable than the men who torment her. . . . " He goes on to note his "odd and disturbing suspicions that $M*A*S*H$'s good guys are essentially bastards."[34] I share his suspicions, and there is ample evidence that we are disturbed not in spite of but because of the movie's own strategy. Temporally and spatially, throughout the shower scene most of the attention of the camera is on those who set up and subsequently watch the drama. These viewers do not appear to us as lecherous monsters; to the contrary, the on-screen audience is a motley group of ordinary people, more disturbing because of their casual cruelty than they might be were they imaged as grotesque male chauvinists. That some of the $M*A*S*H$ women join the men in the audience makes a discomforting kind of sense.

The story told in the earlier sequence that amplifies the love making of Major Burns and Houlihan is also more critical of the viewers than the viewed. We see Radar peering through Houlihan's tent window, then placing a microphone under a cot; much more of the subsequent footage in the sequence is comprised of images of the listeners than of the lovers' coupling. As in the shower sequence, the charm, wit, and playful cynicism of the voyeurs may lead us to associate our point of view with theirs, but to do so is to become complicit in their thoughtless violation of others as well as their power and their mistaken pursuit of "truth."

*   *   *   *

The sequence that intervenes between the two episodes concerned with the degradation of Hot Lips is foreshadowed, not coincidentally, by yet another shower scene that tells a story of voyeurism. Here, all that we see is a line of men queuing up to peer into what, for the moment, is the "Men Only" shower tent. Overlapping, often mumbled remarks and an exchange between Father "Dago Red" Mulcahy and Hawkeye inform us that the person inside the tent, "Painless Pole," the dentist who is famous for the size of his penis, now is the object of the soldiers' gaze and interest. Not surprisingly, we do not see any more of Painless's celebrated organ than we will see of Hot Lips's genitals.

But the meanings of these concealments differ considerably. Hot Lips's shame and Altman's authorial intervention hide her sexuality from our view, confronting and opposing acceptable cultural and epistemological practices both in the realm of movie making and in the world within the frame; within the film and outside it, anyone is free to watch the anticipated unveiling of Hot Lips's naked body, and the inclusion of women in the internal audience makes clear that there are no cultural rules that exclude anyone from gazing at the female body. In contrast, while the acknowledgment of the idea of the male body as the object of sexual scrutiny is unusual, not only is the Hollywood taboo against male nudity maintained, but there is no question of assault on Painless's dignity because all of him remains hidden. Furthermore, the society of viewers within the film is obviously limited to men, and the film makes no attempt to question this exclusivity or to explain the ritual being enacted. It, indeed, succeeds so well in sustaining the viewing of Painless's penis as an exclusively male ritual that in my first several viewings of *M*A*S*H,* I took the men to be lined up for tooth extractions. Smile, Freud, wherever you are.

I admit to this blindness not to flaunt my naiveté but to point in the direction to which this brief moment orients the viewer, male or female. The plot line that begins with Painless's sideshow exhibition in the shower unravels to reveal that this man, whose self-definition has been structured primarily by his sexual prowess, has decided to kill himself because in several recent sexual encounters with women, he has been impotent. His despair has been intensified by his own research on male impotence, research that he has interpreted to mean that his current impotence is a sign that his prior sexual prolificacy was a "cover-up" for latent homosexuality. Unable to dissuade Painless from his conviction, his buddies create an elaborate pre-funeral rite, including a parodic Last Supper. Painless takes his place in his coffin, surrounded by offerings (including a bottle of Scotch) from his friends and swallows the black capsule "suicide pill" that is, in actuality, a tranquilizer. In the end of this episode, Painless is resurrected by Lieutenant Dish who agrees to Hawkeye's plea that on this, her last night at the base, she make love with Painless as an act of charity.

Painless's impotence and suicide attempt provide a narrative frame for a story of the resurrective power of the fraternity of men. The energy that invigorates this fraternity derives from two main sources—competition, as evidenced in the Painless shower scene, and empathetic support. After trying to convince Painless that his occasional impotence is something that happens to everyone, Hawkeye, along with all of the other men of $M*A*S*H$, proceed to provide a double support system for their friend: they conveniently prevent him from committing suicide while they preserve his dignity by appearing to facilitate his self-destruction.

The visual images tell much of the story in this sequence: from the saintly white medical garb in which the men of $M*A*S*H$ are costumed for Painless's last supper to the ethereal light source that glows from above during their meal together, every detail suggests a constructed, theatrical event that these men have together invented for their friend—and for themselves. The memorable images of this episode are of the group of men, seated in a parody of the Last

Duke (Tom Skerritt) makes a last toast to Painless (John Schuck) during the "Last Supper" attended by Ugly John (Carl Gottlieb), Vollmer (David Arkin), Hawkeye (Donald Sutherland), and Trapper John (Elliott Gould). Painless plans suicide; his coffin is in the foreground. The shot is from *M*A*S*H*. (*The Museum of Modern Art/Film Stills Archive, New York City*)

Supper, and, later, parading past Painless's coffin to present him with gifts and to say a final word in parting. Neither the camera nor the dialogue lead us to care particularly about Painless; the scene mesmerizes and delights as a ritual display of wit and shared knowledge. No one man is the hero of this sequence; each contributes what he can. Thus, while others say their farewells to Painless in his coffin, a young black soldier sings a repeat of the opening song, "Suicide Is Painless," accompanying himself with a guitar; he sings in a traditional gospel style but grins and addresses the camera spectator with the manipulative brilliance of the skilled performer.

Each man who participates in the ritual knows the rules and

knows his own part. Within those borders, each has the freedom to play and to mock the relics of traditional culture (the Last Supper image both undermines what Walter Benjamin has called the "aura" of uniqueness in art and deflates the cynical use of this image in the earlier war film *The Dirty Dozen*). There is pleasure in pretending and pretending well. The success of this scene, both as a segment of a movie and as a constructive response to Painless's woes, depends on the perfect cooperation and consistent performance of all the men involved. The one moment of near exception proves this rule: when the chaplain, Father "Dago Red" Mulcahy (René Auberjonois) resists the performance of last rites, on the grounds that it would be sacrilege to perform this sacrament when he knows that Painless is not about to die. Hawkeye retorts: "We're not dealing with an act, we're dealing with an intention." This claim and Father Mulcahy's acceptance of it return the situation to theater, where, as in the institution of fraternity, the maintenance of fragile illusions depends on the perfect cooperation of all who participate. (That an intention is not an act is also a complicated claim that might perplex Father Mulcahy and us long after this "Last Supper" is over.)

No other moment in Altman's work achieves as shimmering and appealing a representation of fraternity as does this one. At once harmonious and polyphonous, somber and comic, good-willed and intent on doing good, these men and Altman's representation of them recall the inspiration of the idea of community in America. Discomforted by the knowledge that these bonds of men rely in part on their empathy with Painless's terror of homosexuality, I am still seduced by the playfulness of the sequence and its reassurance that our ties to each other rest not on our virtue but on our acceptance of each other with and even because of our common frailties. The ritual and its imaging in *M*A*S*H* deflate Painless's argument for suicide. He claims that he is impotent—he is, "therefore," gay—and this means he is no longer a man; if he is not a man, he does not want to live. His buddies demonstrate to him, as the framing of Painless encircled by his fraternity demonstrates to us, that, to the contrary, he remains a man among men. Therefore, he has no good argument for suicide. Curtain down. Story ended. And the lesson might be no different, only more confident than in other movies.

But the story, in M*A*S*H, is not quite over, and, in an odd fashion, the "movies' way of asserting community,"[35] does not suffice in this particular movie. In a cutaway, isolated from the communal rites, we discover Hawkeye in the act of persuading Lieutenant Dish to make love with Painless. Hers will be the noble sacrifice, she is told, that will save Painless's life. "There is no defense against the charitable gesture," Beckett's Molloy once reminded us. Perhaps neither for the giver nor for the recipient, or so it would seem as this episode of M*A*S*H nears its conclusion with shots of Painless's funeral bier accompanied by heraldic music, and a coda the morning after, in which we see Lieutenant Dish wistfully half smiling, then grinning as she departs from the base.

Why is this woman smiling? Not because she is a saint who has taken a martyr's pleasure in sacrificing her body for a more worthwhile cause than marital fidelity; we have seen enough of her amourousness with Hawkeye to disallow such a reading. There is no hidden grimace in her smile, and the shadow of pain transcended seems to emanate from her ambivalence about leaving the base, not from any sense that she understands the previous night to have been sordid. She forgets her hat and then her travel orders, stares fixedly ahead as she initially departs in a closed jeep, then gazes wistfully down at the base as she ascends from it in the helicopter. Is this, then, simply the smile of the sexually satisfied woman? Perhaps. It is certainly at least that. Then how are we to react to this smile, especially since it is finally directed emphatically and disconcertingly at the camera and, thus, at us? What does Lieutenant Dish's smile mean in relation to what has preceded and what follows? Maybe we are not meant to think about happy endings in movies; most often, when we do, they leave us less content than we might wish to be. But not to think at this moment requires acceptance of the most obvious and worst of sexist clichés: in a word, all that women need is a "good fuck," and the larger the penis, the more satisfied the woman will be. And what men need is the penis that empowers them to provide that pleasure.

To think just one step beyond this stereotypical response is to recognize the invocation of woman's instrumentality in this scene; Lieutenant Dish not only has been exploited as a sexual object but also is complicit in her own exploitation. It is her complicity that makes her virtuous in the eyes of those beholding her within the film and, if all goes as it seems to be intended, in the eyes of those watching the film. "If you think that your virtue is more important than Painless's life . . . ," Hawkeye challenges Dish. Then what? I am tempted but not meant to ask. For the movie not only makes authentic consideration of this possibility unnecessary but also provides us with evidence of what Hawkeye and Trapper might do (in the name of transcendent moral claims) to Lieutenant were she to say no to the request that she go to bed with Painless. What they did to Hot Lips might look benign by comparison. Then, we should take the more troubling next step and imagine our responses as spectators had this woman refused the call. What of our image of her had she been portrayed "the morning after" not as woman-well-fucked but as a distraught, adult person in physical and emotional disarray from a night spent with a reborn sexual athlete with whom she had neither ties of friendship nor lust? Overtly directed at the spectator, Lieutenant Dish's smile confirms a common morality and aesthetics; who among us would be so ungenerous or so cold as to refuse such powers and pleasures?

We are, or course, not meant to think about what might have happened in the movies. It is they who are telling us what might have happened. But what does happen in $M*A*S*H$ is as perplexing and disconcerting upon reflection as what might have occurred. Community is asserted through male comradeship but is then announced to be insufficient to its own claims and cause. One way or another, by the rules established in this film, it is the woman who prevents the pre-funeral ritual from becoming a disaster: without her, either the man would have died, proving the impotence not only of the individual but of the community to protect its own members from harm, or the man would have decided not to take his life, proving the irrelevance of the ritual enacted by his comrades.

This sequence affirms a process that Raymond Williams has called "selective tradition"[36] Key and contradictory elements of conventional images of woman are retained from past and still-dominant cultural notions of gender: she sacrifices her purity and honor for the larger needs of the preservation of the (male-dominated) community, and she is finally persuaded to do so after she lifts the sheet covering Painless's presumably naked body and sees for herself the famed giant penis. Lest we doubt that this organ merits its reputation, the extraordinary penis is symbolically represented in the triangular shape of the sheet, held erect by Lieutenant Dish. The symbol is reiterated in an external shot of the tent that images the same shape in black. But the representation of woman simultaneously inverts conventional notions by showing woman to be specifically necessary to the preservation of fraternity. In *M*A*S*H*, as in traditional American society, women are outside of and other than those who participate in fraternity. Fraternity, in *M*A*S*H*, is the basis for community, but fraternity is mediated by women. It is therefore difficult to maintain the usual position of movies, a position that situates women as *anti*-community.

*   *   *   *

The presence of an emergent cultural element here, a practice and value that provides an alternative to dominant cultural values and practices,[37] becomes more vivid when we arrive at the final two major episodes, the excursion to Tokyo and the football game. The first of these sequences is more fully in the mode of the buddy films (and the American literary tradition of male comrades) than any other episode in *M*A*S*H*. Trapper John and Hawkeye in Tokyo are initially presented entering a hospital; decorated in tropical golf clothes, like flamboyant birds-of-prey, they appear center-screen, isolated for nearly the first time from the noisy visual and aural ambiance of the base. (*Nearly* isolated because there is a prologue to this scene in which we witness these two, alone, playing golf on a small hill on the periphery of the MASH base.) Their repartee and perfectly coordinated role-playing suggest that these two men were born into the manner of the American buddies. The arrogance of their physical presence and of Trapper's immediate commands and demands for medical equipment, staff, an operating room, and a steak conquer the hospital personnel and seduce the audience simply because, together, there appears no question that they know who they are and what they are doing. If in the suicide ritual there was no defense against the charitable gesture, here there is no defense against male competence; the only defense is that of the nurse who asks, "How do you want your steaks cooked?"

The Tokyo hospital scene is the counterculture's vision of bliss. Putting golf balls in the office of the officious colonel who administers the hospital, Trapper and Hawkeye are free men, unfettered by the authority of the army, the officer, or the rules of social decorum. They have their own rules and, within those, are at liberty to play. Lest we doubt their unspoken claims to be on the side of virtue, they are put to the test. Asked by another doctor, who claims their attention on the grounds of previous fraternal bonds, to operate, illicitly, on a critically ill baby born to a Japanese mother and fathered by an absent American G.I., Trapper and Hawkeye protest, then take on the challenge and with it the right to wear the robes of heroes.

There is one flaw in these scenes of joyous and virtuous fraternity, and as with previous episodes, the leak in the system appears at the end of the sequence. Caught by the Tokyo colonel in their illegal efforts to save the life of the Japanese baby, Trapper, Hawkeye, and their old-new pal, Me Lay[38] Marston (Michael Murphy) covertly anaesthetize the colonel. The last frames of the Tokyo episode are filled with semipornographic still photographs of the colonel, who appears undressed and entwined with several Japanese prostitutes. Trapper and Hawkeye had ensured their liberty by hoisting the rigid officer on his own petard of orthodox notions of vice and virtue. Once again, their point of view and the film's narrative voice coincide, as they do at the end of the suicide sequence, and once again, this occurs only through the instrumental exploitation of women and their sexuality.

*   *   *   *

The persistently submerged problem with $M*A*S*H$ that now appears is that it is caught between its desire for a dialogic perspective and its groundings in the univocal folklore of male fraternity. Every joke in the film has its costs, and Altman knows it; the sense of humor that binds these men to each other and informs the movie's celebration of community occur, repeatedly, at the expense of the other's pain. The multiple views of the world represented in the movie's visual and aural emphasis on groups of people, most effectively dramatized in the operating-room scenes that punctuate the entire film, strain in two opposing directions—toward the harmonies and common understandings of fraternal community and toward inchoate understandings of an imagined community that includes women as well as men and new meanings for each. These are two very different views of the world, and nowhere is the film's awareness of its limits in acknowledging this difference more striking than in the final football-game sequence. The values and practices of male competence and teamwork, competition and mutual support, prevail in this blatant allegory of American visions of war as a football game. What appears from the distanced view of the camera to be chaos and violence is, on closer view, a triumph of common understanding and an embrace of freedom within unquestioned limits for those who play the game. The confused and confusing position of outsiders, especially of women, in relation to this game, is succinctly conveyed by Hot Lips, now transformed into a cheerleader for the MASH team. "Kill, kill, kill," she screams with the other women cheerleaders. But, when the half-time gun goes off, terrified, she screams, "My God, they've shot him."

Football, the American general informs the MASH commanding officer near the beginning of this sequence, has been declared by the big guns in Tokyo to be "one of the best ways we've got to keep the American way of life going here in Asia." But *M*A*S*H* suggests that there is an even more effective way—the movies we make and screen for ourselves and others. Despite its insistent critiques of American culture, including the parodic advertisements for American war movies that blare from the base P.A. system throughout the film, the gloss and gleam of American movies is no place more evident in its seductive and distracting appeal than in *M*A*S*H* itself. The cost of *M*A*S*H*'s success at the box office and among the cults that made it a television ritual was the virtual obliteration of its own, tentative alternative perspectives. Success with *M*A*S*H* was a kind of failure, and this paradox was to inform all of Altman's subsequent films. Altman took no chances that *Brewster McCloud* (1970), his next movie, would be glibly accepted or dismissed as yet another Hollywood entertainment. From its demystification of Hollywood's greatest myth, *The Wizard of Oz*, to its carnivalesque, curtain-call finale, *Brewster McCloud* invigorates the almost clichéd simile of American culture as a circus, a multiringed spectacle in which the limitless powers of magic have been replaced by the limited powers of technology. *Brewster McCloud* was Altman's first fully developed experiment with achronological narrative structure, and, whether because of its disorienting form or its barely oppositional critique of American culture, it was a commercial failure.

*   *   *   *

I will return to *Brewster McCloud* in the context of the theatricalization of Altman's films. More pertinent to the issues of gender and fraternity that I wish to continue to pursue are three Altman films of the early seventies that, more deliberately perhaps than *M*A*S*H*, scrutinize the relationships of men to men and suggest the power of earlier American movies in informing the rules and recipes in these bonds. Together, these films—*The Long Goodbye* (1973), *Thieves Like Us* (1974), and *California Split* (1974)— define an "anti-buddy" theme. Like the "buddy" films to which they are counterposed, these movies place women at the peripheries of their narrative and visual interests, but in contrast to the dominant mode of the period, *The Long Goodbye, Thieves Like Us,* and *California Split* deflate the romantic representation of male comraderie as an idyllic form of human relationship.

The object of much commentary as an "anti-genre" movie,[39] Altman's first film in the "trilogy," *The Long Goodbye,* immediately situates itself in the history of American movies by its opening (and closing) music, "Hooray for Hollywood," and by its lingering introduction to Elliot Gould's interpretation of Philip Marlowe, classic American detective and Hollywood archetype. An initial camera pan discovers Marlowe at three o'clock in the morning in bed; the camera then shifts its interest to Marlowe's cat, which Marlowe quickly determines will not let him sleep until it is fed. From the start, the camera establishes its and our relationship to Marlowe and his world as hesitantly voyeuristic, shooting through a doorway to Marlowe's kitchen as he attempts, unsuccessfully, to satisfy the cat with salted cottage cheese; the fixed distance of the camera and the fragmented glimpses it provides of Marlowe's culinary efforts imply the inappropriateness of our presence in the intimacy of Marlowe's kitchen. As if determined to fulfill its minimum obligations to provide introductory information to the audience, the camera next captures a series of quick images that incorporate most of the rhetorical figures of filmic device: a pretty but eerie shot of shadows on the wall outside Marlowe's apartment signals trouble ahead; blurred visions of Marlowe's diaphanously clad young women neighbors, identified more clearly by their vocal request for "hash-brownie mix" than by their physical presence, establish the Southern California youth scene and hint of a remote sexuality; a shot of Marlowe donning a tie to go the all-night supermarket in search of cat food appears to utilize another of film's conventional devices for establishing character. The harsh fluorescent lights of the supermarket further establish a location and life-style, as does the half-exchange between a black clerk and Marlowe, as the latter searches in vain for Curry-brand cat food:—Clerk: "What do I need a cat for, I got a girl." and Marlowe: "He's got a girl, I've got a cat. . . . "

This beginning, is accentuated and complicated from the time Marlowe leaves his apartment in his late-forties vintage Lincoln Continental by parallel cuts to the man we will come to know as Terry Lennox, driving his obviously newer car. *The Long Goodbye* announces itself, at the least, to be a mixed commentary on the mixed genre of the detective film and the gangster film. It is not to be a pure gangster film like *Scarface, The Public Enemy,* or even *The Godfather I* and *II,* in which the inner-urban world of the film comprises a distinct community articulated by its opposition to the dominant urban society and by its own rigid rules; nor is it to be a pure detective film, in the mode of *The Maltese Falcon* (1941) or *Murder, My Sweet,* movies in which the centers of morality and visual interest are lone individuals who, much like the reader, reconstruct apparently disparate elements of character and event such that they reveal already enacted plots. *The Long Goodbye* is, as many critics have noted, similar in many of its story elements to *The*

Big Sleep, a film that, in fact, combines its interest in a "hard-boiled detective" with its exploration of the dark, murky world of organized crime. That the integration of these genres is, in fact, more central to American film mythology than either "pure genre" is made manifest in *The Long Goodbye.*

At the center of this mixed-genre film, and key to the mixture of points of view that perturb the viewers' relationship to the world of the film, is the legendary American private eye Philip Marlowe. The disparities in judgments of *The Long Goodbye* by reviewers can be accounted for almost entirely by critical responses to Gould's portrayal of Marlowe and to Altman's presentation of the relationship of Marlowe to the world he inhabits. Reviewers agreed, with what I continue to find perplexing consistency, that Gould's Marlowe differed fundamentally from previous incarnations of the type—both in Chandler's fiction and in the movies, but most particularly in Bogart's enactment of Marlowe in *The Big Sleep* (a portrayal that is often described as if it were simultaneously Chandler's written presentation and Hawks's filmic projection). The gist of these reviews was that Altman-Gould's Marlowe was a weak, effeminate, unattractive anachronism who had little in common with the handsome, sexy, witty man of the world (more accurately, man of his world) created by Bogart.

Both men might be marginal figures in relation to the societies they investigated, but as Robert Kolker notes, critics began with the seemingly common assumption that Bogart's Marlowe (and usually by extension Chandler's Marlowe) was quietly in control of the "closed, dark and curiously stable world" that employed him in contrast to Gould's Marlowe who appeared to be floundering in a world in which he could be easily manipulated.[40] The basic differences among initial critical judgments of *The Long Goodbye,* then, rested on the degree to which reviewers were offended or pleased by what they agreed was a lack of fidelity in Altman's film to the original (meaning "real") Marlowe.

Kolker's detailed discussion of both movie Marlowes in the context of his examination of *The Long Goodbye* reassures me that my own finding of essential similarities between the two interpretations of the type is not merely eccentric. It seems to me obvious, for example, as Kolker suggests, that "the Hawks/Bogart Marlowe becomes, despite himself, deeply entangled in the world he enters, caught in the very morass he attempts to clear up."[41] But then Kolker joins those whose readings of this movie befuddle me, claiming that "Altman and Brackett [the co-screenwriter for *The Big Sleep* and screenwriter for *The Long Goodbye*] merely strip away the security of the Bogart persona: his wit and his ability to stand back from a given situation in a posture of self-preservation."[42] To the contrary, my belief in the dignity and self-assurance of Gould's Marlowe is centered in his wit—meaning both his cleverness at detection and his ability to appreciate discrepancies in the world around him, an ability I deem to be essential to a sense of humor or the appreciation of the comic. And, in turn, it is Gould-Marlowe's reliance on his wit that allows me to be secure in my relationship to him, that assures me, throughout *The Long Goodbye*, that he should and will endure.

I find abundant evidence of Marlowe's wit in *The Long Goodbye*, but given the apparent lack of companionship in this reading, let me begin at the beginning with a few recollections. There is, first, Marlowe's query to his cat, in response to the cat's rejection of the offering of cottage cheese: "Why don't you think of all the tigers in India they're killing who don't get enough to eat?" A few moments later, as he departs for the supermarket, Marlowe responds to the grateful "You're the nicest neighbor we ever had" from one of the girls next door with the accurate dismissal, "I'd better be. I'm a private eye." Who among us is as quick with an apt retort when awoken at three a.m.?

Nor is Marlowe's affable acuity only applicable to mundane moments. Taken into police custody after he has driven his friend Terry Lommax to Tijuana, Marlowe diplays his awareness that he performing in front of a one-way mirror by blackening his face with fingerprint ink and singing "Sewanee," conforming to the "smart ass" label attached to him by the police. Marlowe gets across the double message that he has nothing to tell the police and that he perceives their questioning as a vaudeville routine. Marlow's blackface routine also reflects back on the black cop's pointed query, "You know a white guy named Terry Lennox?"

This Marlowe, like Bogart and the Chandler original can put two and two together and make five and a half. And like his predecessors, Gould's wit is the key tool of his trade. Employed by Eileen Wade to rescue her writer-husband, Roger Wade, from the clutches of a corrupt psychiatrist, Marlowe locates Roger Wade with remarkable efficiency and chooses the precisely right moment to extricate Wade from the exploitative Dr. Verringer. The morning after fulfilling this assignment, after a sleepless night that included not only the rescue of Wade but a brutal encounter with the gangster Marty Augustine and his thugs, Gould's Marlowe is as intellectually agile and ironically cognizant of others' games as he was in the police station. Leaving his apartment undetected by Harry, the "tail" assigned by Marty Augustine to follow him, Marlowe not only gives Harry the address of where he is going but suggests that he will win the favor of the security guard at their destination, the Malibu Colony, if he asks the guard to impersonate George Raft. Harry is befuddled and intimidated; we, at the least, are amused if not impressed because Marlowe has not simply out-witted Harry but has demonstrated both the absurdity of and the mythology inherent in Harry's task without placing Harry unnecessarily in harm's way. In addition, there is a more subtle link among *Scarface, The Big Sleep,* and *The Long Goodbye* made here by Marlowe and Altman. In *The Big Sleep,* Marlowe forms an attachment to Harry Jones, whose death, at the hands of the gangster Lash Canino, Marlowe witnesses;[43] in *Scarface,* George Raft plays the kind of cool tough guy that Harry imagines himself to be. Marlowe's direction to Harry conjoins and naturalizes the reflexivity of the contemporary Marlowe character with that of the directorial reminders of cultural context. Marlowe's daily work requires that he perceive connections between superficially separate details; it is clever and appropriate that he associates his Harry with Raft and himself with Bogart and that he notes the irony in these associations.

These and other examples of Gould-Marlowe's mental agility are more whimsical and less heroic than the gestures of wit we find in Bogart's or Chandler's Marlowes. But then, that is precisely the nature of wit. Like decorum, wit is not ahistorical but rather is inseparable from and defined by the users' appropriate application of their intelligence to a particular cultural moment. Authentic wit also requires an astute understanding of that moment as both distinct from and continuous with cultural history. The terse sarcasm of the Bogart-Marlowe shields and separates the detective from others, reinforcing the recurrent American mythos of the solitary male hero, a projection, perhaps, of what Michael Wood calls the longing of Americans to be lonely. In the sixties and early seventies, that longing, displaced by the alternative desire for community suggested that the character had problems rather than answers. Gould-Marlowe's wit is deployed most often either to make connection with another or to name his pain in his isolation, as appropriate to his own culture as Bogart's was to his.

This relationship between the necessary and peculiar sagacity of the detective hero and a participant cultural context is central to the argument of Raymond Chandler's celebrated essay on the fiction of detection, "The Simple Art of Murder." Chandler's praise for realism in detective stories and his contention that most detective stories are not realistic are grounded in the notion that the most powerful stories of murder are those that take place in and of a particular social world. In his case, this means "a world in which gangsters can rule nations and almost rule cities, in which hotels and apartment houses and celebrated restaurants are owned by men who made their money out of brothels, in which a screen star can be the finger man for the mob, and the nice man down the hall is a boss of the numbers racket."[44] For Chandler, the stories of murder that merit our attention are not those exemplified by Agatha Christie's ten men and women who happen to find themselves isolated with a corpse in what could as easily be a Victorian resort as a Santa Monica hotel. The story (as Wallace Stevens once urged of modern poetry) must "speak the language of the times" and the hero, Chandler urges, must talk "as the man of his age talks, that is, with rude wit, a lively sense of the grotesque, a disgust for sham, and a contempt for pettiness." Chandler's ideal hero is a decidedly American hero, not a person whose style denotes an upper-class background and academic education, not a clever logician or man of the world, but a man of a particular world, "a common man or he could not go among common people." What separates Chandler's ideal hero from others' is not a glamour or sophistication that removes him from the ordinary world but a sense of his integrity in his particular world: "He has a range of awareness that startles you, but it belongs to him by right, because it belongs to the world he lives in."

It is this voice, Chandler's voice, that we often hear in *The Long Goodbye,* not in contrast to Altman's or Gould's or Marlowe's voices, but as a point of view that animates and makes dialogic a text that superficially appears to be more monologic than any of Altman's movies.[45] Only two of all of Altman's other films— *Quintet* and *Secret Honor*—even appear to be as narratively and perspectively limited to one character as does *The Long Goodbye,* and since, as I will eventually argue, *Secret Honor* is finally one of Altman's most multivoiced movies, the singularity or multiplicity of perspectives in *The Long Goodbye* is not a trivial matter.

It is, however, a somewhat deceptive aspect of this film and a matter that takes us back to the questions of genre and movie types. In his solitary individualism, the American movie detective is much like his derivative, the spy-hero, and obviously similar to his counterpart in the Western, the cowboy. American literature, of course, has its own ample share of self-sufficient male loners—from Billy Budd to Gatsby and Hemingway's old man—but it is on film that the solitary man has found his heaven, has most effectively filled his world. Stanley Cavell locates many of the mythic qualities of this figure in the "dandy," as described by Baudelaire, and because this description so precisely names some of the common characteristics of the heroes projected by the male stars of American movies, it is worth reciting several lines:

> ... Dandyism, an institution above laws, has laws to which all its representatives ... are subject. ... The dandy does not make love his special aim. ... What then is his ruling passion? It is, above all, a burning need to acquire originality, within the apparent bounds of convention. ... It is the delight in causing astonishment and the proud satisfaction of never oneself being astonished. ... The characteristic beauty of the dandy consists above all in his air of reserve, which, in turn, arises from his unshakeable resolve not to feel any emotion. It might be likened to a hidden fire whose presence might be guessed at; a fire that could blaze up, but does not wish to do so.[46]

Pointing to Bogart and the Western heroes as "our most brilliant representatives of the type," Cavell suggests that such heroes are "outside society," because they have chosen to so situate themselves, not because "they have been pushed out." Almost echoing Chandler, Cavell stresses the "strength and purity of character" of this figure, what others, including Chandler, have called his sense and obedience to honor. But in his discovery of this hero "outside society," Cavell would appear to be opposing Chandler's insistence that this hero must walk the "mean streets" of ordinary society, must be "a complete man and a common man" among common people even though he is an "unusual man." Cavell, I think, would respond by calling our attention to his discussion of *The Man Who Shot Liberty Valance*, a conversation in which he defines the position of this hero as mediator between privacy and society, between lawlessness and civilization. As the one who "marries" privacy and society, the American hero cannot partake in the world he preserves or creates. He remains outside society as long as society is not founded on justice, the creation of human beings together, but rather on force, the assertion of one man's power.

This is a good enough answer for the Western and its frontier hero, but it does not suffice, I believe, to explain the position of the gangster or the hard-boiled detective, and in Cavell's conflation of these types and Chandler's separation of the one from the others, we find the source of their difference. Cavell and Chandler point to a utopian vision that projects a just society as one in which, in Chandler's terms, "If there were enough like him [the detective hero], I think the world would be a safe place to live in, and yet not too dull to be worth living in."[47] In such a world, for Cavell, a world of citizen-Marlowes, men would live together, "each granting the other a certain right over his own autonomy."[48] This democratic utopia is not created, even imaginatively, in Westerns, but on the frontier it is possible, perhaps necessary, for the hero, once he has done his work and ensured the survival of some form of society, to move on and outside the civilization he has enabled.

The city, especially the American city, is a different sort of world, not just because it is a jungle where, as Chandler details, every institution and situation is susceptible to the diseases of greed and malice, but also because it has no "outside." A man can be a cowboy, or claim the genealogy of the frontiersman, like Trapper John in *M*A*S*H*, and be from "nowhere," but he cannot walk the mean streets of the city and simultaneously be outside its society. Americans have found a place for those who are not frontiersmen but who wish to escape or reject the city; we call it "the suburbs." But no American would mistake the suburbanite for the city-dweller, and even in Los Angeles, we know that there are sidewalks where the private eye and the gangster stride, and they bear no tint of suburban blush.

The hard-boiled detective and the gangster figures of American movies are more profoundly American male heroes than the cowboy, as Robert Warshow probably understood better than anyone. Each of these types exhibits what Warshow calls "the queer and dishonest skills" and "terrible daring" that signify not just knowledge of the city but the success we Americans most covet—the success of the person who has been one of the crowd and emerged from it, distinct and notable, but able always to return to the crowd when he (and occassionally she) so desires.[49] The skill of the city-dweller, epitomized in the hard-boiled detective, is, in part, that of the dandy; the flux of city life within its unmapped but known borders fans the flame of the dandy-detective's essential hidden fire. But the American hero of the city also has another kind of skill. He is the man of perfect common sense, and he knows this common sense, as Clifford Geertz has elaborated, to be the fundamental grounds of any cultural system.[50]

Altman's Marlowe does not possess perfect common sense, but, like Altman himself, it is exactly that skill, the skill of making one's way about a culture, perhaps the only kind of knowledge one can have of a culture, for which Marlowe strives. In the changing world of the United States in the early seventies, and especially in the urban threshold of this culture in Los Angeles, this is not an easy task. For Marlowe to play his role well, he must know and live by the unstated rules of his culture, and he must know when and where to negotiate when the rules he lives by clash with or are ignored by others. Our admiration for Bogart's Marlowe is rooted in our confidence in his common sense and in the model he provides of the possibility of perfection of the skills and knowledge necessary to negotiate the culture we inhabit. Altman and Gould's Marlowe has more skill than we, but he makes us uneasy because he confirms our suspicions that some of the neighborhoods we once knew are now so unrecognizable that even our mythologized hero cannot find his way around.

No matter how much the façades changed in the city neighborhoods of Chandler and Hawks, the Marlowe of the forties could count on some structures remaining stable. And what the old Marlowe most counted on was the structures of his relationships to other men. Chandler's Marlowe, and Bogart's, can emerge from the crowds of the city, can, for example, choose to be a private eye and not a police-department detective, because he knows what to expect when he deals with certain men and he know what the rules are with others. Chandler's Marlowe knows which reporter to call when he wants something printed in the one independent newspaper, and he knows how to put down a doctor and keep him there. Women offer more surprises to the old Marlowe, but, even with women, there are limits to the possibilities, and besides, they are, essentially, outside the cultural system.

In contrast to the old Marlowe, Gould's Marlowe repeatedly discovers the instability of his relationships to other men. Questioned by the cops who pick him up after his trip with Terry Lennox to Tijuana, Marlowe attempts some of the same savvy lines used successfully by Chandler's Marlowe: "This is where I say, 'What's this all about?' and you say, 'We ask the questions.' " In earlier times and movies, Marlowe's knowledgeable composure and resistance to police attempts at intimidation gained him the unspoken respect of at least one officer in every police station; at every such station, Marlowe could count on the presence of one man of a sensibility similar to his own. In the world of *The Long Goodbye*, however, the gestures of male bonding made to Marlowe at the police station come not from one of the policemen but from two other men under arrest: the black supermarket clerk who remembers Marlowe's search for Curry-brand cat food and Marlowe's cell mate, whose storytelling and complaints—"they've got people in here who smoke marijuana—they get people on possession—

possession of noses, of everything. . . . "—may amuse us but form no grounds for friendship with Marlowe. Persistent camera movement, including short pans, zooms, and numerous cuts between the two sides of a one-way mirror destabilize our relationship to Marlowe as well as his to others. And a disruptive sound track mediates voices such that what we hear half of the time sounds filtered through a bad tape recorder, further diminishing the possibility of even covert acknowledgments of others.

The most promising new man-to-man relationship for Marlowe in Altman's *The Long Goodbye* occurs with Roger Wade, the Hemingwayesque writer whom Marlowe rescues from Dr. Verringer's live-in clinic. From the start, however, the friendship that Wade seems to seek is doomed by the dependency structure of the relationship. During the rescue sequence, Marlowe's position outside the room where Dr. Verringer is attempting to manipulate Wade dominates and controls the scene, accentuating Wade's weakness. Movie reviewers may, as Kolker suggests, be attracted to Wade as the perfect imaging of the romantic, he-man American writer, but Marlowe never appears drawn to this form of American nostalgia and stays aloof from Wade throughout their acquaintance. Their relationship fails not, I think, because, in Kolker's terms, Marlowe cannot see Wade but because Gould's Marlowe has seen too many Wades in the Malibu Colonies of Southern California. Both men may embody key types of American manhood (Wade calls Marlowe the "Marlboro Man"), but when Wade invites Marlowe to drink with him the day after his return home and initiates gestures of fraternity, Marlowe politely agrees to Wade's beverage of choice but remains unengaged.

A routine, steady pattern of crosscuts between one-shots of Wade and of Marlowe and of occasional medium shots that include the two emphasize the unaltered distance between them. When Wade makes a further stab at bonding, telling Marlowe that the detective has "a pretty good face," Marlowe queries Wade about his thoughts on ladies' faces. Marlowe's retort is clearly not intended to establish male confidences. It is a nasty reminder that Terry Lennox's wife, Sylvia, was found dead with her face bashed in and an equally nasty probe to discover how much Roger Wade knows about Marty Augustine, who, the night before in Marlowe's presence, had smashed a coke bottle across the face of his mistress.

Marlowe has emerged from the crowd of the city in part because he is a man with a cat, and this detective, who cares about the cat when it is lost, has little in common with Wade who owns loud Doberman dogs. Marlowe does not differentiate between men like Roger Wade who proudly associate themselves with violence but are apparently on the side of the good and men who behave similarly, like Marty Augustine, but do so in the name of greed or other labeled evils. For this detective, and in this movie, fierce dogs do not signify the virility of the owner but rather suggest his weakness.

Marlowe's most important relationship, his friendship with Terry Lennox, is the least visible of Marlowe's associations and yet the source of the meaning and plot of the film. Structurally and narratively, this relationship frames the film. The parallel editing of Marlowe's trip to and from the supermarket and Lennox's trip from the Malibu Colony to Marlowe's apartment ends, conventionally, with the two men coming together. In usual filmic practice, the device of parallel cuts emphasized the temporal simultaneity of two actions that occur in different spaces; the meaning of both the simultaneity and the spatial separation is almost always related to a plot and character context that has been previously established. Altman reverses this process, using the convention to establish a relationship between two men whom we have no other reason to associate with each other at this point in the movie.

The brief encounter between Lennox and Marlowe in Marlowe's apartment confirms the point of the editing device: the fraternal bond between the two men not only resists explanation but exists outside of explanation. Despite the odd hour and the signs of trouble in the bad scratches on Lennox's face, the exchange between the two men is primarily a ritual of mutual recognition. Their comparison of serial numbers on dollar bills and naming of the three Dimaggio brothers are obvious reenactments of games they have played before and will presumably play again. Lennox says that his scratches resulted from a fight with his wife, Sylvia, and Marlowe requests no elaboration, instead, asking only and rhetorically if he should fix up the couch for Lennox. Marlowe, after all, also has a scratch on his face, from his cat. "My cat scratched me" would seem an obvious lie in most circumstances, yet, in this case, we know it would be true. It is not naive for Marlowe to accept Lennox's mininal explanation. Trust is not only the ground of friendship but of common sense. Without it, all knowledge is suspect. With this established, when Lennox says that he wants Marlowe to take him to Tijuana, there is no need for discussion or demand for reasons; we know Marlowe's response, and our expectations are simply confirmed by the follow-up shot of Lennox walking across the border.

Terry Lennox haunts every subsequent moment of the film, but neither we nor Marlowe see him again until the very last sequence of *The Long Goodbye*. Lennox's disappearance and the various explanations thereof motivate the plot and Marlowe's involvement in it: Lennox may or may not have killed his wife or stolen a large amount of money from gangster Marty Augustine; Lennox may or may not have committed suicide in Mexico out of guilt for one or both of these crimes. Since Marlowe was the last person to see Lennox, both the police and the gangsters turn to Marlowe to provide missing material and answers. Marlowe's interest in the Wades is, in turn, motivated by their prior acquaintance with Terry and Sylvia Lennox.

Lennox's absence is essential to the story of the illusions and delusions of fraternity that is at the center of this movie's interest. In a world where no other relationships are predictable or operate on rules and codes of honor, Marlowe insists on the integrity of his bond to Lennox. The camera captures the distress in Marlowe's face when the police tell him that Sylvia Lennox is dead; where other hard-boiled detectives may provide signs of their "hidden fire" in relation to a woman or to gross injustice, this Marlowe's expressions of caring are repeatedly attached to his bond to Terry Lennox. Like Chandler's Marlowe, Gould's (Altman's) Marlowe refuses to believe that Terry Lennox could commit murder, especially the kind of brutal murder that occurred in the case of Sylvia Lennox, and like the Marlowe of the novel, Altman's movie character has only his faith in which to ground his disbelief. Chandler's Marlowe, however, seeks support for his fidelity to his friend in an uncovering of history, and through that history, he comes to know that he is right about Lennox's innocence. Altman's Marlowe refuses to question his friend's past but rather focuses his attention on seeking evidence for alternative explanations of the murder. Altman's Marlowe finds that he is, in fact, wrong, that in this story, Lennox did participate in the murder of his wife. This does not show a stupid or inept Marlowe, but a man whose ethics are out of joint with his time. The ethics of Altman's Marlowe are fundamentally those of Chandler's Marlowe. The dominant values of American culture in the thirties and forties are not the same, however, as in the seventies. Altman is making a pointed comment about what has happened to our society over the last forty years.

Altman's Marlowe (like Chandler's) suffers humiliations and physical beatings as a result of his loyalty to Lennox, and it is in the difference between the character's and the film's attitudes toward Marlowe's pain that the ironic tension of *The Long Goodbye* is situated. Gould's Marlowe displays hurt more than the Hollywood heroes of old: when one of Marty Augustine's thugs kicks Marlowe in the groin, Marlowe moans and writhes in expressions of pain that the traditional dandy-detective would surely have hidden. But his stoical silence about Lennox and his flippant remarks each time is assaulted convey the character's conviction in the noble and enduring value of the buddy relationship. As represented to the audience, however, there is no hint of either a cathartic value or test of heroism in any of these scenes of violence and degradation. Robert Warshow was probably right in his equation of brutality in the classic gangster films with both "the means of success and the content of success."[51] The notion of the "hard-boiled" detective was, then, always a misnomer because the heroism of the detective who was the unflinching subject of or witness to brutality was attributable not to a tough shield that separated the detective from evil and aggression but to participation in this world of power and achievement. By his presence in contexts of violence, the traditional detective demonstrated his virility and the comparability of his commitments to those of his foes; by our watching, we give evidence of our own toughness and acknowledge what we see as our world, too.

The most awful scene of brutality in *The Long Goodbye,* the scene in which Augustine gratuitously destroys his girlfriend's face, neither ennobles Marlowe's commitment to Lennox nor allows us the satisfaction of knowledgeable safety. Augustine conceives of his gesture as a dramatic threat to Marlowe: if I would do this to someone I love, he tells Marlowe, think about what I might do to you. But the threat does not even have a horrid logic to it; grotesque as it was, the bloody horse's head placed under clean sheets in the intended victim's bed in Copolla's *The Godfather* is appropriate to the characters and the situation as both threat and revenge, whereas the punishment of Augustine's girlfriend is wholly disproportionate to her infringement of the minor rule that she stay in the car. Her punishment is also irrelevant to the concerns of either Marlowe or Augustine. Augustine's brutality, rather than demonstrating what Warshow called the "unlimited possibility of aggression" articulates these limits; the absurdity and crudity of the gesture define Augustine's brutality as outside the limits of effective aggression; even symbolically, this particular violence signifies stupidity and impotence of aggression, not the means and content of success.

Altman's filming of this sequence maintains our distance from it and disallows the appeals of either suspense or empathy. Augustine's sexist sweet-talk to his mistress Joanne does not anticipate his sudden brutality toward her, unless, of course, we are familiar with the gangster genre, in which case we will not wonder but know that something awful is about to happen. The similarities between the beginning of this scene and the one in *The Big Heat* where the gangster eventually throws boiling water in his woman's face raise expectations of horror for those who recall the earlier film. Even if we know *The Big Heat,* however, we are disoriented by the dim lighting and the camera positions in the *The Long Goodbye*'s comparable scene, positions that suggest the perspective of one of Augustine's thugs, crowded into Marlowe's living room. The camera is either too near to and at a slightly wrong angle from the faces of Joanne and Marlowe to capture their emotions as sources of empathy or zooming counter to the coded pattern of camera shots that we expect to interpret such a moment. Just before Augustine breaks the coke bottle on Joanne's face, the camera zooms out; conventionally this would signal an end to intimacy, an easing of tension, and a return to the central issue of Marlowe's relationship to Lennox and the money the latter stole from Augustine. Thus oriented by the reverse zoom, Augustine's brutality authentically shocks; we will be stunned even, I think, if we have the memory of *The Big Heat* in mind, because we will read the zoom-out as a sign that the moment, and its historic possibility, has passed.

Because the overwhelming sense of this scene is its meaningless suffering, Marlowe's cause itself is called into question. If Lennox has left Marlowe in a position of danger, without any warning to his friend, then Marlowe is a fool to remain faithful, and Joanne had been hurt for a fool's cause. It becomes increasingly difficult to admire Marlowe's principled loyalty to Lennox, especially since Lennox's continued absence from the world of the film contributes to our sense of the hollowness or mistakenness of Marlowe's bond. In a novel, and, in fact, in Chandler's novel, a character like Lennox can be absent from the present of the plot but present in the stories others tell, recall, or uncover. In a film, however, a character who is absent from the screen is not present in the world of the film, and verbal allusions to such characters, rather than replacing their direct speaking presence, are understood vividly as calling attention to absence, not substituting for presence.

Given minimal reason to be interested in Terry Lennox when we did, briefly, see him, we can only remain interested in him through Marlowe, and even he cannot maintain that interest on our part while Lennox becomes increasingly remote. Thus, we begin to wonder at Marlowe's continued concern, and any investment we might once have had in Terry Lennox and in the buddy relationship between him and Marlowe diminishes rapidly as the movie progresses. The bond between the men becomes an abstract principle for which what is sacrificed increasingly seems out of proportion with the cause.

When Marlowe's reencounter with Lennox does finally occur at the end of *The Long Goodbye*, it should not be a shock to the spectator. It is, indeed, the logical transformation of the ending of Chandler's novel, given that the context and events *are* different in the forties' story than in the seventies'. Chandler's Marlowe tells

Lennox, in their final encounter, that he will not drink with him because the two friends who once drank gimlets together exist no more. In the novel, this is only a half-truth; Lennox has become another person, but Chandler's Marlowe is not changed from the man who appears at the beginning of the tale. Since the novel is told in the first person, the speaking voice has already arrived at the point of view of the Marlowe of the end of the narrative.

Altman's Marlowe, however, has changed. The structure of belief in the fraternity of men that shaped his view of the world has been deconstructed, and the only way he can acknowledge that the world is different is to destroy the image of its sameness. Marlowe goes to Mexico at the end of *The Long Goodbye* to reveal the falsity of Lennox's absence—both from the plot and the movie screen—and to transform that absence into truth. Chandler's Lennox, created with words on paper, can proclaim his absence by noting that he is just "an act." In the movies, however, where every character is only an act, both the character and the image must be killed to ensure the absence of the character from the world of the film. Altman pointed to this fact of film rhetoric at the end of *Brewster McCloud;* borrowing from the similar gesture made by Antonioni in *Blow-Up,* Altman "kills" the character of Louise, Brewster's guardian angel, by obliterating her image from the frame as she walks out of Brewster's life.

Marlowe's killing of Lennox, like the coke-bottle scene earlier, avoids the conventions of ominous music, parallel cutting, stark lighting contrasts, and close-ups to key characters that usually prepare the audience for such a moment.[52] Marlowe discovers Lennox, relaxing in a hammock in sunflecked, tropical Mexico. Alternating zoom-ins to each man emphasize their separateness and the uncommon grounds of the dialogue: Marlowe accuses Lennox of using him, Lennox responds that "that's what friends are for." Lennox declares the situation to be simple and resolved; he is free because "nobody cares." But Lennox is mistaken, as the camera reveals, zooming in to a tight shot of Marlowe's tension-lined face as Marlowe counters, "Yeah, nobody cares but me." The banter that once articulated the bonds between the two men, that echoed their own earlier word games and the similar, more extensive word games of

$M*A*S*H$, no longer works because each man now plays by different rules. As the camera remains on Marlowe but zooms out, showing Marlowe pulling a gun, the rules of this game are still ambiguous. Only after we are shown Lennox, fallen into a pool of water and dissolved into thin air, do we know that this endgame is being played with real bullets.

At once lyrical and grotesque, the shooting of Lennox is notably similar in style to the shooting of the young cowboy in *McCabe and Mrs. Miller,* which Altman had directed three years before making *The Long Goodbye.*[53] The two killings carry very different moral weights, however. The horror in the cowboy's death is in the triviality of the motivation, like the coke-bottle scene in *The Long Goodbye;* Marlowe's killing of Lennox, in contrast, is meaningful both in terms of social justice (Lennox gets the punishment he deserves for killing his wife) and the integrity of the structures of fraternity. The bonds between men that Marlowe has revered throughout *The Long Goodbye* and not without their structures; by killing Lennox, Marlowe remains a responsible player in the game of fraternity, while raising the possibility that this is the last time he, at least, will play. Marlowe's responsibility is to the *idea* of fraternity: trust, loyalty, and shared values that do not need to be spoken, and the knowledge that the players accept common rules. But one cannot participate in a game or a ritual without another; fraternity may no longer make common sense.

It is, therefore, appropriate and important that whereas Altman lingers on the death of the cowboy in *McCabe and Mrs. Miller,* as if unable to take his or our eyes from the sight and unwilling to admit this death, the shots of Lennox's death are remarkably brief. The camera cuts quickly to Marlowe, spitting and then walking away, playing the miniature harmonica given him in a previous sequence by his heavily bandaged hospital roommate. I do not take this to signify either Marlowe's callousness or the sweet taste of revenge; I understand the harmonic to represent Marlowe's dignity, earned by his holding fast to the rules that shaped his relationship to Lennox throughout. Not unlike the bittersweet hymn to anarchy and narcissism that will sound at the end of *Nashville,* Marlowe's music, played on the harmonica he received as a gift from a fellow-sufferer, simultaneously declares his survival and reminds us that gestures of human relationship are not entirely obliterated, although they may be more likely to come from a mummy, from someone with some attachment to the past, rather than from those who sit well in contemporary society.[54]

The end of Altman's *The Long Goodbye* has provoked lengthy and intensely engaged discussion from everyone who has written about this film; in large part, I think, because it is in the end that we are least able to escape this movie's essential dialogism. Unlike many Altman movies, *The Long Goodbye* unravels a plot in a basically chronological sequence of events, and this plot constantly focuses on one familiar Hollywood type who is more present on-screen than any other Altman character. Until the end of the movie, it is relatively easy either to ignore the directorial point of view that repeatedly interacts with Marlowe's or to accept Altman's point of view as one that consistently re-mediates Marlowe's demystifying the type along with the blurred genre.

My sense of the end of *The Long Goodbye* is that many spectators find it troubling precisely because it brings forward the conflicts among world views that have been disturbingly present but somewhat resistible throughout much of the film. It is, after all, consistent with the detective genre that various versions of a story be possible until a final moment when everything is configured into a logical, inevitable pattern. With *The Long Goodbye,* however, significantly varied readings persist after the movie is over. This suggests to me that Altman's concern is not so much with the demystification of the hard-boiled detective type or the movie genres he inhabits but with the authority of film itself. The Los Angeles setting, the numerous references within this movie to other movies and movie stars, as well as the introductory and concluding projections of the song "Hooray for Hollywood" remind us that this is a movie and that the story within the movie takes place in a culture shaped by movies.

The three most celebrated sequences in the film—the quarrel between Roger and Eileen Wade during which Marlowe is sent out to the beach, the death of Roger Wade, and the killing of Lennox— all employ devices that call attention to cinematography and to the

director's presence. The zooms and their counterdirectional movement are part of this strategy; so are the numerous shots through
windows. Virginia Wexman, whose remarks on the reflexive gestures in Altman's films are especially cogent, argues that Altman's
proclivity in *The Long Goodbye* and elsewhere for shots through
glass and similar surfaces suggests "that we are seeing not an un-
adulterated vision of the world but rather one that reflects the prism
of intellectual constructs through which we, and the director, view
the universe."[55]

The Long Goodbye, like almost all of Altman's films, partakes in a
modernist sensibility in that it calls attention to its createdness and
reminds us, in particular, of its relations to movies as a cultural form.
One attribute of the movies to which these three shots call attention
specifically, as Wexman notes, is the selectivity of the directorial eye,
particularly evident in the most celebrated shot of this film, the quarrel between Eileen and Roger Wade. Altman creates a complex visual
image that conjoins an interior view shot through a window and a
view through the reflection in the same window of Marlowe on the
beach; the visual images interact with the intermittent projection of
the sounds of Roger's and Eileen's argument. The explicit complexity of this filmic construction, the striking condensation of points of
view, and the simultaneous display of the window as aperture and
mirror all claim the director's position as storyteller. Altman's approach, however, distinguishes his position from that of the omniscient storyteller. The self-consciousness of points of view and of
visual images and the partiality of sound (much like the overlapping
sounds and words elsewhere in this and other Altman movies) point
to the incompleteness of any witness's record or construct, including
that of the filmmaker.

Yet, *The Long Goodbye* is not typically modernist in its sensibility (nor are any of Altman's other films) because it is not really
concerned with film form or with the movies as form. Instead, *The
Long Goodbye* wishes our acknowledment of movies as creations
that mediate our understandings of our culture, and it urges our
examination of the kinds of values and practices movies encourage.
Altman's invocations of movie history recall Bertolt Brecht's concept of the alienation effect more than they do other devices of

The relationship among Marlowe, Eileen Wade, and Roger Wade in *The Long Goodbye* is framed by the windows that function as both mirrors and transparencies. (*The Museum of Modern Art/Film Stills Archive, New York City*)

modernism because they seem intent on reinstating our attention to the world in which we live rather than suspending our disbelief in the world projected. And here, as with Brecht, but unlike much of the post-Brechtian deployment of alienation devices, Altman's point is not to make us just sit back and think, for the sake of the knowledge that we are thinking, but to make us think about certain, particular elements of our cultural history.

✻   ✻   ✻   ✻

The particular issue to which *The Long Goodbye* draws our attention is, I have been arguing, the grounds of our relationships to each other, and especially, in this case, the grounds of relationships between men. Altman seems more certain in *The Long Goodbye* than in *M*A*S*H* that the buddy relationship is a dangerous delusion, that beneath the appeal of the games men play together there is no

longer the common worldview that gave authenticity to such relationships. The buddy relationship separated some men from others
and was played by its own internal rules, but its viability, especially
in the city, depended upon the stability of other relationships among
men. *Thieves Like Us*, Altman's next film, takes up this topic again,
and both the fact of its recurrence and the distinctiveness of the
exploration of men's relations in *Thieves Like Us* suggest that fraternity in America is not a topic easily concluded or dismissed.

Bowie (Keith Carradine), Chicamaw (John Schuck), and T-Dub
(Bert Remsen) are the buddies of *Thieves Like Us,* three escaped
convicts bound together by a common history and by their inability
in the present to satisfy their financial and social desires within the
mainstream culture of thirties America. The fraternal terrain of the
film is established in its opening shot of two of the men, Bowie and
Chicamaw, in a boat—an invocation of what is likely the most
recurrent image of male identity in American culture, from Melville
and Twain to Crane and Hemingway. The initial, overheard dialogue follows suit with a sick joke about a boy who painted his
turtle and a man who puts the turtle in syrup. The effervescent
energy of male comraderie then continues as Bowie and Chicamaw
connect up with T-Dub who awaits them with a change of clothes
and a car; the men change clothes by the roadside, leaving their
prison garb strewn beside the road, and take off in the car they have
just stolen from its driver to the cacophonous sounds of their own
laughter, the noise of the car's motor, voices talking over each other,
and the "Star-Spangled Banner." Discovering the car radio does not
work, they make their own music, together singing a school anthem, "Central High School."

The next several scenes continue the display of male bonding and
reveal the weak links in this particular fraternity. Taking refuge in a
barn, where we discover them similarly dressed—or undressed—in
long underwear, Chicamaw and T-Dub exchange stories of their
past escapades outside the laws and practices of conventional society. The appearance of the men counters the personae of hardened
criminals suggested by their stories; undressed, for the second time
within a few minutes, all three appear more vulnerable than threatening. Like the scene in *The Long Goodbye* in which Marty Augus-

tine commands Marlowe and then his own thugs to strip (with the implicit threat of the castration of Marlowe), this scene of the three men in the barn suggests that, in the movies at least, the undressing of men is a comic gesture, one that limits masculine power and sexuality. Whether in the tones of dark comedy or comic romance, such movie moments have not yet approached the eros of those involving their female counterparts.

While we look at the men and listen to the exchange of stories between T-Dub and Chicamaw, Bowie, blatantly and pathetically the youngest of the three, is separate and silent. His remoteness from his pals and his discomfort in his solitude are emphasized again the next scene, which finds him alone by a railroad track, only somewhat relieved of his nervousness and isolation by his chance meeting with a stray dog. The midwestern countryside, pastoral and appealing in previous shots, now appears threatening in its vast emptiness. Bowie uses the mutt, whom he identifies as a kindred "thief like me," as blanket, bodyguard, and companion, telling the dog what he could not tell his male companions: "I don't got no more folks, You know, that's the first thing the law does—look up the places a man can write to and watch them places. Goodbye, Mama. One thing about you, though—whatever I did was okay with you."

Visually and verbally, Bowie's uneasy night alone establishes his and our desire for others and names the grounds for relationships of both family and fraternity: those are the communities where your belonging is not called into question. These ties that bind rely not on what you do but on commonalities of history, blood, or belief. For Bowie, as for Robert Frost's hired man, home is "where, when you have to go there, they have to take you in," but it is also, in Bowie's understanding, exactly the place where you will not go when going there means trouble.

With desperate relief and out of necessity, Bowie therefore rejoins his buddies, who take refuge in the apartment of Chicamaw's cousin. The most telling shot in the film, a shot that will be echoed several sequences later, captures the three men in midground around a table, with the adolescent Keechie (Shelley Duvall) revealed in depth-of-focus puttering in the kitchen and then at the rear of the room, sitting in a chair, reading. Keechie penetrates what had been and attempts to remain an all-male world, but she does so while remaining emphatically in subordinate, sterotypical female roles (she fetches cigarettes and the newspaper for the men), and her position at the beginning of the film is much like that of the servicewomen seen at the beginning of *M*A*S*H:* at the peripheries of the frame and of the men's interests. While T-Dub and Chicamaw excitedly read a newspaper account of their prison escape, Keechie captures Bowie's attention and ours. What interests us in Keechie has little to do with the usual movie-star attributes of beauty, wit, or grace, but has something to do with her insistent, subordinate presence and the subtle opposition to the men expressed in her posture and movement.

From this point on, Keechie provides for Bowie an alternative companionship to that of T-Dub and Chicamaw. But the forms of interaction that work well among the men fail when Bowie attempts similar kinds of play with Keechie. At night, alone at the soda fountain in the small cluttered general store–gas station run by Keechie's father, Bowie tries to amuse Keechie with jokes: "You know what the Mississippi state animal is? [Pause] A squashed dog." Keechie does not laugh, but does express her interest in Bowie—and her wariness of him—in her own inimitably blunt way, asking if it were true, as the newspaper reported, that Bowie had killed a man. Bowie answers that "It was him or me," then immediately goes for another joke-riddle: the Mississippi state flower, he tells Keechie, is a weed. Keechie's response, "Pretty dumb," may refer to either or both Bowie's excuse for murder and his awful jokes, but there is no ambiguity in her judgment. The props of American adolescent romance are evident—the soda fountain; the awkward, ill-disguised, erotic small talk; the covert, nighttime meeting—but Keechie signals from the beginning that a world that includes her will require a different set of values and practices than the world Bowie knows, even if minimally, from his prison buddies.

The structure of *Thieves Like Us* is built on the tension and contrast between these two worlds. Bowie moves back and forth between foolhardy exploits with T-Dub and Chicamaw and periods of domestic respite with Keechie. The world of the men is noisy, mobile, and often, in Keechie's word, "dumb." About to rob a bank, the men bicker about roles, then pull straws to determine who will stay with the car; their symbolic instantiation of equality proves to be irrelevant because T-Dub cannot drive a car, and Bowie has no knowledge of how to rob a bank. In contrast, the little world created in separate moments and spaces by Keechie and Bowie is still, slow, and quiet, a world where the creaking sound of a rocking chair is at once reassuring and irritating in its incessancy.

The essence of this contrast and the tension between the two worlds lie in the appeals of mobility and stability, conflicting appeals that in thirties' America were transfigured by the economic depression that required new understandings of traditional American myths. Since its colonial origins, physical mobility, across the land and toward new frontiers, has been uniquely conjoined in American culture with economic "upward" mobility; in contrast to the worlds from which they came, those who settled the colonies and then the states understood movement and relocation to include and nurture family life. The mobility of the thirties was of a different order, a fleeing from as much or more than an adventure toward a particular way of life, an attempt to sustain the illusion of economic mobility through the literal movement so aptly emblematized by automobiles and the proliferation of highways to accommodate these machines. While some families, like the Joads in *The Grapes of Wrath*, journeyed together, the mobility of the thirties, actual and illusionary, was more often represented in the movies through the quests of men who bore no signs of family connections. Sometimes these men, like Capra's John "Doe" Willoughby, had a sidekick; at other times, in such gangster movies as *Scarface* and *Little Caesar*, a group of men surrounded a male leader in a constant pattern of motion within the confines of the city; Charlie Chaplin represented the dream of mobility in his own unique and solitary transformations of body and role.

Thieves Like Us rereads these thirties' associations of men with mobility, bringing forward what in most of the movies of the thirties were subordinate and often conflicting understandings of the falsity in the equation of movement with change. We do witness

Bowie (Keith Carradine), T-Dub (Bert Remsen), and Chicamaw (John Schuck), "three boys together," rob a bank in *Thieves Like Us*. (*The Museum of Modern Art/Film Stills Archive, New York City*)

transformations—call it growing up—of character in *Thieves Like Us*, not in the interactions of the men but in the series of domestic scenes between Keechie and Bowie. Both young people become stronger and abler to be responsible to another person during the period when Keechie nurses Bowie after he has been badly hurt in an automobile accident, and the self-confidence Bowie gains in his romance with Keechie is essential to his successful masquerade as prison officer in order to get Chicamaw out of prison yet one more time. In contrast, neither the bonds among the three men nor their individual or collaborative skills are strengthened by their shared endeavors.

Bowie cannot imagine any alternative, however, to continuing his outlaw career with T-Dub and Chicamaw. The choice before Bowie is clearly established in the dialogue that frames the last bank robbery the three men undertake together. When, against Keechie's wishes, Bowie agrees to join his partners in yet another theft, T-Dub celebrates: "Hell, we'll never get three boys like us together again—that's for damn sure"; after the robbery, which results in the death of T-Dub and the reimprisonment of Chicamaw, Keechie tells Bowie: "You took them. It was me or them and you knew it and you took them."[56]

Thieves Like Us ends with the visual correlatives to Keechie's verbal summation. Bowie succeeds in springing Chicamaw from prison, only to have Chicamaw betray him, first by the gratuitous murder of their prison-warden hostage and then by enraged accusations that Bowie is taking all the media limelight. Bowie finally turns away from his partner, and we last see Chicamaw alone and rooted on the deserted country road, shrieking Bowie's name into the wind. Bowie tries to go home again but, of course, cannot. Back at the motel where he has left Keechie with Mattie—T-Dub's grim, maternal sister-in-law—we watch a small army of state troopers approach the cabin that Bowie has entered, looking for Keechie. The camera stands as witness for us, watching the troopers bombard the cabin with gunshots. The camera also catches Mattie a few yards away forcibly holding Keechie in her own arms to prevent the younger woman from running to her lover.

If Stanley Cavell is right in his claims that the movies typically assert community through male companionship and that typically women are represented as outside community and interfering with it, then we might understand *Thieves Like Us* as both an acknowledgment and reversal of this tradition. T-Dub and Chicamaw, and to a lesser extent Bowie, make the claims for male community that speak for the tradition of the movies, and in the scenes that these men dominate, women are excluded, treated as sexual objects, or marginalized. This community of men is shown, however, to be hollow, lacking in honor, and, in the end, the opponent of what in this film is the most promising if indeed fragile resource for community, the companionship of Bowie and Keechie. When the men of

Mattie (Louise Fletcher) holds back Keechie (Shelley Duvall) while both witness the machine-gun assault by state troopers on Keechie's lover, Bowie (Keith Carradine) in *Thieves Like Us*. (*The Museum of Modern Art/ Film Stills Archive, New York City*)

the film refuse the option of male-female community and insist on sustaining loyalties to the now-empty traditions of manliness and fraternity, they leave women to make what communities they can among themselves and with their children. This is a position Robert Altman will return to, most dramatically in *3 Women* and *Come Back to the 5 and Dime, Jimmy Dean, Jimmy Dean*, but to some extent in every film after *Thieves Like Us*.

The inevitable comparisons between *Thieves Like Us* and Arthur Penn's *Bonnie and Clyde*, made in 1967, tend, understandably, to focus on the similarities and differences between the endings of the two films. In both films, the agents of the law take their revenge on the outlaws with vehement assertion of violence and power. In both films, while the outlaw is the overt object of destruction, there is also an aural and visual assault on the audience through the noise of the gunshots and the similar, slow-motion, dissolved images of the victims' blood and gore. The most obvious difference between these ostensibly similar scenes is that in *Bonnie and Clyde*, both members of the romantic couple are killed, whereas in *Thieves Like Us*, Keechie is saved, notably by another woman. A second and perhaps equally clear distinction is that in *Bonnie and Clyde*, Penn's slow-motion photography dwells on the physical assaults on the bodies of the hero and heroine, while in *Thieves Like Us*, as in classical drama, the protagonist is not initially in view when attacked, and the slow-motion photography focuses on Keechie's agonized witnessing of the attack on the cabin. The subsequent image of Bowie's body wrapped in Keechie's bloody quilt is secondary in our knowledge of Bowie's death.

The significance of these differences is apparent in what follows in each movie. *Thieves Like Us* ends with a careful, delicate, and brittle coda that finds Keechie in the grimy waiting room of a train station. In one of those inappropriately intimate revelations that embarrass most of us, Keechie tells a woman stranger that she is pregnant, that the baby's father died of consumption, and that, although she believes the baby is a boy, she will not name him after his father. As Keechie rises, moves up the stairs towards a train, and merges with the crowd, the camera transforms its shooting to slow motion, as if reluctant but nonetheless determined to let her achieve the anonymity she desires.

Almost nothing happens after the killings of *Bonnie and Clyde* in Penn's film. Robert Kolker's reading of the emptiness of that ending merits quoting in full:

> The very last shot of the film is from behind the car, observing through its window the police moving about the scene of carnage in quiet and awe. The camera almost cowers in reaction to what has happened. And what has happened is not merely the death of the characters in the film, but the destruction of the point of view that has been so carefully forged. The car violated, its inhabitants dead, we have no one to look at or look with; no secure and mobile isolation. We are alone and lost. The bad guys have won, and the film has nothing more to tell us about our heroes. Since there is, as

far as Penn is concerned, nothing more to see, the screen unceremoniously and anticlimactically goes black.[57]

The difference this points to is not just the difference between something and nothing, or even that, with Keechie still alive, we still have someone to look at and with. As Kolker implies in the passage cited and elaborated elsewhere, Penn's strategy in *Bonnie and Clyde* depends on his successful association of the spectator's point of view with that of his hero and heroine. *Bonnie and Clyde* is not, of course, a first-person point-of-view film. (With a few notable exceptions, such as *The Lady in the Lake* and *I Am a Camera,* very few narrative films even attempt first-person point of view for more than a short sequence or a single shot, and when they do, it is usually to express an altered state of mind, as in *Nine to Five.*) *Bonnie and Clyde* is, however, obsessively devoted to establishing the world as viewed by its two central characters, to establishing what Pier Paolo Passolini calls indirect subjective point of view,[58] and it is equally intent on attaching the audience to those characters and their points of view. Finally, as Kolker also notes, from the time Bonnie meets Clyde, Penn unites their points of view in what I find to be a complicated kind of doubling that even allows Clyde's anguish over his impotence to be mirrored by Bonnie.

Altman, in contrast, retains the autonomy of Keechie's and Bowie's points of view, even in their most intimate and loving moments. Bowie not only resists Keechie's pleas and judgments but is never really able to understand how she sees the world. This becomes painfully evident when, long after their relationship has passed its initial gropings, Bowie tells Keechie yet another "Mississippi state" joke. (This one is about the Mississippi state tree, which Bowie declares is a telephone pole.) Keechie still finds such jokes dumb. We often see Bowie and his world separated from Keechie, and although we see Keechie alone less frequently, by the end of the film she has established her voice sufficiently that it is not inappropriate for us to continue, briefly, to follow her, and, indirectly, to perceive the world as she sees it.

This separation of points of view in *Thieves Like Us* contributes to the antiromantic ambiance of Altman's film and makes the highly romantic tone of *Bonnie and Clyde* even more striking. If *Thieves Like Us* is in part a critique of *Bonnie and Clyde,* the importance of its reinterpretion of the sixties' version of the mythology of the outlaw lies in its historicization of the questions it raises about the kinds of heroes and heroines our movies screen for us. Altman's critique, deliberately aimed at *Bonnie and Clyde* or not, is cogently framed in *Thieves Like Us* by voices from history, represented in the film by injections of music, drama, and news commentary conveyed most effectively by the radio, the medium of the thirties. In the absence of a musical sound track, these voices situate *Thieves Like Us* in a particular moment in history. Whereas musical sound tracks covertly attempt to manipulate our responses to characters and their relations to the world, the snatches of Big Band music, radio melodrama, news reports, speeches by Franklin D. Roosevelt, and commentary on *Romeo and Juliet* in *Thieves Like Us* overtly allude to specific cultural products of the thirties that mediated the cultural consciousness of Americans in that time. Bonnie and Clyde, despite and perhaps because of their highly stylized costumes, appear as ahistorical figures, incarnations of the timeless American mythos of free spirits become stars, the American woman and the American man pursuing the American Dream and liberated from the boundaries of class, place, or race. Keechie and Bowie, T-Dub and Chicamaw, Mattie and Lula, in contrast, are rooted in and bound by time and place; their language and their fantasies, their relations to work and to family, are inseparable from the towns and practices of poor, rural Mississippi during the economic depression of the thirties. These relationships, in turn, are complicated by the fragments of possibility transmitted on the radio and by newspapers. The stories, sounds, and political rhetoric that punctuate the lives of these characters bind them to other anonymous Americans, who, like the folk of *Thieves Like Us,* may find some relief from their own troubles in the knowledge that outside, beyond danger for them, there are ganglands and lynchings, and outside as well, there is a President promising a "new deal" for the little people listening.

The thirties in America were pivotal years in American social, economic, and cultural history. Before the thirties, despite the ravagings by European-born settlers of the lives and lands of native Americans, despite the outrages of slavery and post-slavery racism, despite industry's exploitation of workers, despite the inequality of women and man, it was possible for most Americans to believe in a vision of individual progress and success, grounded in an amalgamation of Puritan Calvinism, nineteenth-century transcendentalism, and, subsequently, social Darwinism. The promised land held out for all the chance to become whatever they wished; opportunity was limited only by one's own initiative and industry. In Hollywood's terms, anyone could become a star; all one had to do was wish and try hard enough. In the thirties, for the first time fully, Americans had to acknowledge economic and social limits that could not be altered by individual will and desire. Families could disintegrate even in the presence of love. For the most part, American mass media resisted the changes in consciousness this history required. The accomplishment of *Thieves Like Us* is that it relocates both the thirties' characters and its contemporary audience at the nexus of those peculiarly American contradictions of historical conditions and cultural productions that have forged our subsequent confusions.

*   *   *   *

Altman's next film, *California Split,* returns us to these confusions in their more contemporary manifestations. *California Split* continues Altman's examination of the limits and possibilities of community, focusing again, but with a difference, on the ways in which gender and class consciousness (or its absence) provide the structures of meaning in American lives. *California Split* takes and extends the buddy theme to its natural and unnatural limits. The entire film is concerned with the development and dissolution of the friendship between two men, Charlie (Elliot Gould) and Bill (George Segal), and when the two men separate at the end of the movie, it is with a note of finality that suggests an exhaustion of the topic; this is not apparent in the contemplations of fraternity we find in *M*A*S*H, The Long Goodbye,* or *Thieves Like Us.*

California Split appears at first to begin where *Thieves Like Us* left off. The first strong voice emanates from a video monitor in a gambling casino and provides instructions not only on the rules of the available gambling games but also on the rules of social decorum appropriate to the setting. The video tape situates us in time and place, but in a notable stylistic change from the persistent use of audio projections in *M*A*S*H* and *Thieves Like Us* and the visual manipulations of *The Long Goodbye* (or *McCabe and Mrs. Miller*), this is the first and the last time in this movie that we will hear or see either the obvious hand of the director or the intrusion of other media. More than in any of his previous films, with the possible exception of *McCabe and Mrs. Miller,* Altman in *California Split* isolates the distinctive powers of the voices of the film's main characters to assert the multiplicity of points of view that make meaning in its particular world.

A visual metaphor introduces us to Charlie and Bill, the two central characters of the film. In separate but similar establishing shots of the main room of a casino, we see Charlie (Elliot Gould) cross from screen right to left and then watch Bill (George Segal) cross from left to right. These entrances, as is so often the case in Altman's movies, are theatrical; the main characters are not discovered in the world but come into it. Like the base in *M*A*S*H,* the casino in *California Split* is framed from the beginning as a world unto itself, a theatrical space that provides the specific boundaries and liberties for playing. The long opening sequence of *California Split* and the even longer closing sequence are both emphatically contained within casino settings, while the many locations screened in the middle of the film are doorways through which Bill and Charlie pass.

At the same time, by introducing Charlie and Bill in two separate shots Altman reminds us that, unlike the theater, film's power lies in its control of points of view. Like the photographically stylized window and mirror shots of *The Long Goodbye,* the separate shots remark the narrator-director's voice in the telling of this story. The more conventional introductory setup would be a single shot that captured Bill and Charlie blindly crossing paths; such a shot would have aimed to seduce us to the illusion that we are voyeurs of chance events. True to the paradoxical nature of montage, Altman's

Charlie (Elliott Gould) and Bill (George Segal) become buddies at the bar in the casino where they first meet in *California Split*. (*The Museum of Modern Art/Film Stills Archive, New York City*)

juxtaposition of these shots of Charlie and of Bill reveals both the director's control of meaning and the audience's responsibility to make connections. The two separate shots of Charlie's and Bill's crossings also orient the viewer's relationship to each of them and their eventual relationship to each other: each comes from an opposite direction to the other and inhabits his own space or frame; each is not only present in the same arena but has sufficient presence as character and as movie star to attract the audience's attention as he moves through a crowded room.

With no further preamble, Charlie and Bill take hold of each other and of our interest at a card table where Bill coolly defends Charlie's honesty and honor against an accusation of cheating from an oafish loser at the table. The enraged loser then insists that

Charlie and Bill are partners, thus ironically fabricating their relationship. The scene that follows, in the casino bar, joyfully details the fulfillment of the loser's prophecy. Initially emphasizing the space between Charlie and Bill at the bar, the camera's rambling shots complement Charlie's awkward overtures to Bill; it is only after Bill decides to play along with Charlie that the visual focus narrows and stabilizes. And play together is exactly what they do. From a safe distance at first and then on adjacent bar stools, Charlie and Bill begin to make music together, beating out rhythms on the bar and eventually adding snatches of song. Drunkenly exploring the terrain they share, the two men move on to a challenge reminiscent of Marlowe and Lennox's ritual naming of the Dimaggio brothers in *The Long Goodbye:* the superior man will name all seven of the seven dwarfs. Neither man, however, is able to meet this challenge alone, and finally, they seal their bond by pooling their knowledge. Helping each other, working as a team, they can name the seven dwarfs.

The efficiency of this scene is stunning. The displays of wit, the humor, the acts of competition, and the accomplishments of cooperation that are revealed for two hours in *M*A*S*H* and concealed for a comparable time in *The Long Goodbye* are here compacted in a single encounter, a single space, a perfectly contained unit of film. We endure the long, claustrophobic bar scene near the beginning of *McCabe and Mrs. Miller* because in making us work to see and hear something that makes sense, Altman gradually alters our orientation to sound, time, and space, gradually adjusting our point of view closer and closer to that of McCabe. The bar scene in *California Split* makes no such demands on viewers, yet positions us in an equally appropriate place in relation to the men on the screen. With far fewer people to look at and not a hint of character mystique or latent violence, this almost equally long and dimly lit bar scene inebriates the viewers as much as it does the characters. Bill and Charlie work through a catalogue of clichés of male comraderie: one upholds the honor of the other, gratitude is never expressed explicitly but only implicitly, they talk about sports, they neither ask nor tell about past histories or present circumstances, they play games and make music together with unquestioned understanding of rules, and they locate their common cultural grounds inspirationally rather than logically. Finally, as they leave the casino, they are physically assaulted by a common enemy and retreat to the apartment of Barbara (Ann Prentiss) and Susan (Gwen Welles) two professional call girls whose door is always open to Charlie. At Barbara and Susan's place, Bill and Charlie nurse each other's wounds. They are American buddies, pure and simple.

At this point, *California Split* looks a lot like other buddy films of the period and especially evokes comparisons with *Butch Cassidy and the Sundance Kid*. I would be dishonest, or mistaken, in ignoring the pleasure I experience watching either the scene of Bill and Charlie's bonding or the comparable scene of the recovery of a buddy relationship in *Butch Cassidy and the Sundance Kid*. Both movies arouse my desire for the freedom from explanation evidenced in relationships between the leading men; they also recall the value and the pleasure of loyalty, of adventures spontaneously conceived and shared, and of the finding of time and space for laughter in the absence of need or lust or power. I am attracted to these qualities. At the same time, I recognize their dangers; even in historical contexts where commonly held beliefs allowed such fraternal behavior to have its own integrity, the costs of these pleasures were high. In its most authentic instances and representations, fraternity has required the exclusion and denigration of women, a deceptive and safe eroticism, and a resistance to change that have contributed to the arrogance, ignorance, and self-satisfaction of American culture. In the opening sequence of *California Split*, however, it is relatively easy to forget these changes when in the presence of the apparently pure pleasure of fraternal play.

Charlie and Bill never fully recover or transform that exuberant pleasure in each other's company, that pleasure that has much in common with the delight Cavell discovers in the male-female couples of thirties' and forties' comedies who waste time together wonderfully (and for whom, therefore, no time together is wasted).[59] But it is because Altman has allowed us the appeal of that comraderie that we can also take seriously the subsequent reflections in *California Split* of the particular fragility and harmfulness of the buddy relationship when the performance of fraternal rituals becomes a form of distraction from narcissism and resistance to responsibility.

Buddies in other American films sustain their relationships by constant movement away from ordinary society and the mundane demands of daily life or by escape to a relatively stable marginal world. Butch Cassidy and the Sundance Kid go to a remote town in Latin America; Ratzo Rizzo and Joe Buck of *Midnight Cowboy* inhabit the grim corners and holes of Manhattan; and Billy and Wyatt of *Easy Rider* ride their motorcycles through the Southwest, perversely traveling against tradition from west to east. Bill and Charlie move from the special space of the casino to the stable but transitional space of Barbara and Susan's apartment. Because both the apartment and the two women are immediately comforting and accessible, and because casual comments quickly reveal the women's marginal occupations as call girls, Charlie and Bill are able to sustain their own relationship for a while, exchanging rounds and rubbing shaving cream on each other's bruises. But even in this supportive, unquestioning place, they soon separate: literally, when Charlie retires to "his" room and bed and Bill attempts to sleep on a living room couch, and symbolically, when Bill displays his discomfort with the disregard for privacy and other non-bourgeois practices of the two women.

The series of vignettes that follow and fill the middle of *California Split* further isolate the two men in space and in values, as they return to their ordinary lives, attempting, each in his own way, to continue the friendship and incorporate it into his life-style. Bill's preppy sweater and well-groomed appearance on the night of his meeting with Charlie signaled something of the world he was from, but we are not allowed the escape of vague imaginings of the conflicts between that world and a cultural space that would sustain his relationship to Charlie. Altman's camera invades Bill's tight and demanding office, where we are, again with notable efficiency, shown that his charm is not sufficient compensation for the advertising copy he is supposed to produce. Charlie succeeds, by phone, in seducing Bill away from the office, but while the phone conversation reconnects the two men, it simultaneously calls attention to their separation and the disparateness of their worlds. They no longer occupy the same frame.

Altman allows us a moment to admire Bill's escape from the tyranny of his office, but we are prohibited by each man's subsequent behavior from drawing the simplistic conclusion that contemporary middle-class life is the single and solitary barrier to authentic human relationships. Apparently unencumbered by a job or family ties, Charlie continues the practices of his nomadic life-style, and when he returns from an unannounced excursion to Mexico, he fails to comprehend Bill's accusations of betrayal. Charlie's absence from the screen, like Lennox's absence in *The Long Goodbye*, detaches him from us as it detaches Bill from him. Their discord is aptly signified in a rapidly paced montage that juxtaposes Bill's activities to Charlie's as each prepares for a final joint gambling venture. Bill moves little within any frame, but each shot discovers him in a different location, intent on raising gambling funds by selling his possessions to appropriate buyers; Charlie stays in one spot but moves all over the screen, playing basketball with street kids whom he eventually cons into betting on baskets.

In the end, Bill and Charlie are only able to return together to the casino setting (albeit a different casino, where the stakes and the ambiance are no longer casual) because both have agreed to a partnership in which Bill sets the rules and Charlie obeys. It is sad but not surprising that Bill's main rule for their final gambling partnership is the exclusion of Charlie from any game that Bill plays. We are haunted by the memory of their contagious pleasure playing together in the opening casino scene. The series of shots inside this second casino of each man in his separate place allows us to grieve for what is lost but resists any sentimental hope that we may harbor for their reunion. Bill wins enormous amounts of money, but finds no pleasure in the winning or in the glee and devotion of his partner. Bill's magical wins continue even when he eventually changes the rules to allow Charlie to play with him, albeit in roles Bill explicitly defines, but the magic of their companionship is unrecoverable. In the end, each man exits the casino alone, the money evenly divided. Where buddies were, now partners shall be.

The Long Goodbye, Thieves Like Us, and, finally, *California Split* each tell stories of men who try and fail to attain community and meaning in their relationships to other men. Marlowe, Bowie,

Charlie, and even Bill cling to a model of male fraternity that proves to be destructive, deceptive, and profoundly disappointing. In *M*A*S*H*, Hawkeye, Trapper, and Duke could thrive on their fraternal relations because they shared a common understanding of the world; they could count on each other's competence and loyalty in the operating room as well as on the golf course, and they could assume that they shared a common judgment of Hot Lips's convictions and hypocrisy. Their certainty and the virtue of their actions were only called into question by the penetration of their world by images and comments that reconfigured the way others saw them. For these interjections, however, they had neither responsibility nor knowledge.

Marlowe, Bowie, Charlie, and Bill attempt to fulfill the buddy roles that American cultural productions encourage, but fail in their attempts because they misinterpret signs they assume of common understandings where there are none (or few), and their interactions with others are mediated on these faulty grounds. Circumstantially or socially remote from women, or mystified by evidence of women's otherness, each of these men is seduced by the familiar gestures of fraternity to risk harm for the benefits of companionship. Altman images these men as lonely people, who are weakened and perplexed by the failures of empathy and mutual acknowledgment they encounter. Marlowe and Bill finally choose to reject opportunities for fraternity, but each does so only after confronting the absence of any authentic and secure grounds of commonality. Bowie and Charlie are willing to accept the semblances of fraternity but are unwilling or unable to grapple with its real requirements.

California Split is a definitive and mournful yielding to its grave of the American myth of fraternity. Perhaps, in part because of this, it is also a story of the painful, hidden, and disguised isolation from each other of contemporary American men and women. The relationship of Charlie and Bill fails because they are unable or unwilling to make the effort to understand each other and because neither man is ever accessible to the other. They are not entirely alone in the world of this film, however. The two women who occupy a small but precise space in the center of *California Split* provide a resource for Bill and Charlie that neither man is able to give the other. For

Charlie, and for a brief time for Bill, they are the people who provide a reliable refuge: when you have to go there, they will always let you—and a friend—in. The women share what they have and ask nothing in return except respect and the freedom to continue their daily activities without adjustments. There is no word that accurately names the relationship between the two women and the two men. It lacks the mutual knowledge of the other that distinguishes friendship and love from other relationships, yet some of its attributes make it difficult to distinguish from love.

Barbara fulfills the responsibilities of friendship when she bails Bill and Charlie out of jail on the night that the two men meet. Later in the film, when Charlie and Bill arrive at the women's apartment unannounced, demanding that Barbara and Susan share their celebration of winning at the track, both women reveal the dependence of their own dignity on a sense of responsibility to others, especially those who are weaker than they. The "other" in this episode is a transvestite with whom Barbara and Susan have an appointment for an evening on the town. The unexpected invasion of Susan and Barbara's apartment by Charlie and Bill occurs just before the scheduled arrival of the transvestite client. Empowered by their success at the track, Charlie and Bill command Barbara and Susan to dress up immediately for an evening on the town. Bill and Charlie explicitly promise an extravagant indulgence; their implicit promise of community is, however, a far more difficult temptation for Susan or Barbara to resist.

Each of the relationships we have seen before this night has been significantly constrained, by defenses against vulnerability or by the monetary basis of the association. Bill and Charlie alter the terrain of possibility for any and all of the relationships among them by attempting to recapture the original pleasure they found in each other's company and by choosing to share that pleasure with Barbara and Susan. For the audience, whose position outside the frame provides a broader if not deeper knowledge of the loneliness of all four characters, the unanticipated but imagined transformation of these four isolated souls into a community of four is a seductive scenario.

Barbara and Susan's planned date with "Helen" Brown (Bert

Remsen) is the sole barrier to the fulfillment of Bill and Charlie's plans. Reluctantly but firmly, Barbara announces the women's fidelity to the prior engagement. Charlie and Bill are unmoved and uncomprehending of the fundamental betrayal they are requiring Barbara and Susan to make. The two men arrogantly ignore Barbara's unambivalent refusal and Susan's more hesitant resignation to the prior date. Charlie and Bill exploit the powerful appeal of their collaborative performance: they fill the frame with manic, relentless play and an exhibition of the indomitable male ego that overwhelms Susan because it so perfectly matches the image of her desire. In the wake of previous scenes that tersely delineated Bill and Charlie's separateness, the wild reunion of the two men is also intoxicating for viewers.

Barbara does not yield to the continuing seduction, however, and with the full attention of the camera now on her, she asserts her authority over this space and time. Gently but forcibly she pushes Bill and Charlie out the door. When she reopens it just a moment later, we expect to see Bill and Charlie, whose noisy frolicking can still be heard outside. Instead, framed in the doorway is Barbara and Susan's client "Helen" Brown, whose appearance is surprising, less because he is in full drag than because his simple pride in the careful composure of his costume prevents us from seeing him as grotesque. As if to ward off any further ambivalence on the part of the spectator, Altman insistently holds a full shot of "Helen" Brown standing between and visually supported by Barbara and Susan; rather than appearing comic or macabre, there is an appropriateness to this threesome and an underlying challenge to the rigidity of our perceptions and categorizations of sexuality. It is a moment that will come back to haunt us in later Altman films.

Persuaded of the rightness of Barbara's position by Altman's treatment of this scene and by the irresistible performance by Bert Remsen of the character of Helen Brown, the sudden reintrusion of Charlie and Bill, is more disturbing than it is welcome. We now see them gleefully engaged in getting rid of Helen by representing themselves as the vice squad. Their histrionic threats succeed in scaring Helen away, and Barbara and Susan are freed, although not without the shadow of their silent complicity in Charlie and Bill's manipula-

The opposition of women and men and the authenticity of cross-dressing are framed in a scene from *California Split* in which Charlie (Elliott Gould) and Bill (George Segal), pretending to be members of the vice squad, confront "Helen Brown" (Bert Remsen), who is notably supported by Susan (Gwen Welles) and Barbara (Ann Prentiss). (*The Museum of Modern Art/Film Stills Archive, New York City*)

tive antics. That complicity, combined with the childlike self-interests of Bill and Charlie, shifts our position in relation to the four. When their evening's pleasure is blatantly undermined by a holdup on the street and more substantively by the tendency of each of the four to play in parallel rather than with the others, our sense of loss is not as great as it might have once been.

We are to learn, soon enough, that nothing really was lost. Reading a book alone on the couch one night following the frustrated celebration evening, Susan is interrupted by the unannounced arrival of Bill. Our first glimpse of him watching her through a window establishes Bill's voyeuristic relation to Susan, but the desperateness of her desire for a romantic relationship with Bill obscures her understanding of him. For the spectator, this is the moment of unambiguous truth. Wistfully gazing at Bill after he tells her he enjoyed their "real" date, Susan mentions that she and Barbara are about to go to Hawaii for two weeks with two men she has never met. Bill's unthinking blurt, "How can you take that kind of chance?" is ironically revealing of an awful truth in the conjoining of narcissism and paternalism. From what we have seen, he not only takes repeated chances with his money, his job, and even his life but finds great pleasure in his obsessive gambling. His inability to at least perceive the structural parallel between the chances he takes and those Susan takes speaks both to his unquestioning assumption of a distinctly other honor in the possible violation of a woman's sexual sanctity, and to his particular lack of empathy for Susan as a person. Susan's answer is less and more than it should be: "Those are the chances you have to take," she stoically tells Bill. Narratively, it takes Barbara's sudden arrival to prevent Susan and Bill from making love, but it is now clear to the spectator that for Bill, the reciprocity of authentic lovemaking was never a genuine possibility. Our loss here, and theirs, extends beyond the moment's pleasure: there is little hope for male-female relationships grounded in respect as long as the terrains of risk-taking for men and women remain so foreign and unknowable one to the other.

California Split does not end here in part because one of the tasks of the long final sequence of Bill's extraordinary good-luck streak in Reno is to instruct the viewer in rereading the scene between Bill and Susan. I was angry at Barbara's interruption of Bill and Susan's embraces when I first saw the film, and while I understand its meaning to be the impossibility of wholeness in any of the relationships that I had viewed, I suspected Barbara of insensitivity to Susan's needs and to Bill's self-consciousness, and additionally, I condemned her apparent desire to control Susan's life and affections. That remains one available reading of *California Split*'s penultimate gesture of deflation of romantic illusions.

Alongside that reading, however, is a more profound despair that arose out of a second viewing of *California Split*, a viewing that was mediated by my foreknowledge of the final sequences of the film. Inherent in every movie, and acknowledged and nurtured in Robert Altman's movies, is the potential explosion of a new way of seeing, kindled by the movies' dialogues among overtly different points of view. The utopian methodology of movies rests in the knowledge that there is a potential new understanding of the world in the viewers' recognition of the nexus of their voices with those heard and viewed. *California Split* reminds me of this vision, but it also warns me that cacophony is as likely as harmony in worlds where men and women are unwilling or unable to attend carefully to each other's voices. The common understandings as well as the genuine interest in the differences among us that are requisite to the makings of new meanings in the world must be sought and worked for; they are not gifts. For different reasons, and with varying degrees of responsibility, the four men and women of *California Split* are resigned to wishing and unable to make the community they desire. Or, perhaps they and I mistake wishing for desire. It is to that distinction and the cultural encouragement of that confusion that Altman turns next in *Nashville*.

CHAPTER 3

NASHVILLE: NEW ROOTS

FOR THE NATION[1]

If there is a most important film of the 1970s, it is *Nashville*, Robert Altman's gleeful vision of an American landscape perpetually exploding upon itself. More than any film of the seventies, *Nashville* releases us from our most recent mythical entropy and frees a constrained public to admit new matter to its dreams. Projected on a screen those emphatic rectangularity strains at its frame, *Nashville* recognizes our peculiarly American compulsion toward heroes. Since the entire film appears to be a series of parenthetical expressions, we must either refuse the whole or pay attention to that which both stylistically and socially we usually overlook.

Nashville's ideal spectator is naive and vulnerable *and* observant. Our engagement in the film is that of the "participant observer";[2] like the anthropologists from whom V. F. Perkins drew the filmic notion of participant observers, we are placed by Altman in a position of at once partaking in spectacle and reflecting upon it. Altman articulates our stance as participant observer in the unforgettable *Nashville* scene of the highway pileup. A sofa falls off a pickup truck; a nearby car swerves to avoid the sofa but in so doing hits still a third car, and from there begins an accumulation of collisions too numerous to count. The careless driver of the pickup truck goes obliviously on his way as hundreds of others are impeded by a virtual barricade of cars. Our vantage point is markedly similar to that of those actually on the highway. As the camera notes by shooting from the interior of a car through the windshield, most of the riders on that highway have witnessed fragments of an event in which they have participated by virtue of their presence and the degree to which they have been observant. Like us, they are safely separated from the accident itself by a screen; like us, they had no control over the event itself. Those delayed on the highway may later report that they were "in" a highway collision, but as Altman's camera also observes, their engagement in the crash itself may actually be less than ours. This is not to deny that we are privileged: those on the highway are wholly impeded in their progress and left to their own resources to fill their unexpected waiting time, while the magical mobility of the camera continues our journey about the scene. We can laugh because we are not physically there and because we took our seats as spectators and they did not.

As important as the fact that Altman disturbs our passivity are the ways in which he accomplishes this. He neither humiliates nor enslaves us by the activity that he provokes. As Pauline Kael suggests we do not "recoil" watching *Nashville* as we might in response to the strategy of a film like *Blow-Up* or in a number of instances of participatory theater.[3] Instead, Kael continues, "When you get caught up in his way of seeing, you no longer anticipate what's coming, because Altman doesn't deliver what years of moviegoing have led you to expect."[4]

Somewhat paradoxically, once we learn to *listen* to *Nashville,* we overcome much of the difficulty we might have with the unorthodoxy of the film's narrative structure. As noted in Chapter 1, the events of a film are usually most readily grasped when presented in chronological syntagmas—autonomous contiguous segments that are temporally consecutive within the world of the film.[5] The predominance of achronological syntagmas in *Nashville* (as well as, subsequently, in *A Wedding, Buffalo Bill and the Indians,* and *Health*) suggests that Altman is deliberately constructing barriers against our penetration of the world of the film. However, while *Nashville* does undermine our groundings in consecutiveness and thus limits our reliance on plot, on superficial relationships of cause and effect, it is also transparently eager to tell us a number of stories and to make us care about the world it projects.

To achieve these ordinarily contradictory effects, Altman relies heavily on blatant but unconventional pairings of filmic signs when he cuts from one syntagma to another. Within the usual conventions of film, continuity, whether in chronological or achronological syntagmas, is most frequently established by information connected by the semantic content of verbal dialogue, by the repetition of some aspect of the visual image, or by some combination of these elements in which the linkage is clearly narratively based. Such conventional linkages do occur in *Nashville*, but Altman's film is also powerfully propelled by a mode of montage in which the key connecting elements present themselves initially in metaphoric rather than syntactical relationship to each other. In a cut mentioned earlier, Altman remarks the consanguinity of grief and delight by juxtaposing the sob of one character to the laughter of two others; in another of many such instances, we cut from a diatribe in a junkyard on the color yellow to a yellow phone located in an ostensibly unrelated house. We might speak about such cuts as examples of Eisensteinian montage, but Altman has at the least extended Eisenstein's vision of the collision of images for the collision is so frequently not simply of images but of images and sounds, and even more precisely, a phonic sound and musical sound, or phonic sound and graphic tracings. Perhaps more important still, Altman's montage is rarely didactic because its components include depth-of-focus photography and what I described in Chapter 1 as depth of focus in sound. Even when the montage in *Nashville* is momentarily didactic, specific pairs of signs are almost always absorbed into more extensive codes of meaning and in these larger contexts become resonant. Each editorial gesture in *Nashville* adds a detail to at least one of the stories being told, and *Nashville* finally tells its most vivid story not by any single series of incidents but by the accumulation of pairings of signs which become codes and then evolve into meaningful patterns.

Nashville is not, then, a film where we are meant to "figure out" the plot; rather, we are meant to sense what is happening—to both the characters within the world of the film and to us. It is not a matter of gradually coming to understand or expect that Kenny Fraser, the young man who "looks like Howdy Doody," will kill Barbara Jean, the virgin queen of country music, even though when seeing the film a second time we are apt to discover a variety of clues that may appear to tell us just that. Our experience of seeing Barbara Jean posed (alive) in her hospital bed in an oddly unnatural position may suggest a corpse, just as the sound and image of the release of Kenny's overheated car radiator may connote the release of some frustrated energy, but more than this we neither can nor should know until the world of *Nashville* is complete. We thus acknowledge *Nashville* before we fully know it, and that acknowledgment increases with the knowledge that comes with repeated viewings.

This is not to say that Altman deliberately withholds information so as to achieve suspense and keep us in the theater. To the contrary, Altman is generous with the information he gives us, but it takes us time to know how to sort out what we know. Even the opening credits serve as an abundant resource for understanding the film. In contrast to many contemporary films, which use the credits (or a scene prior to the credits) as a teaser to the plot of the film, *Nashville*'s opening, which includes its credits, serves as prologue to the film in a fashion that is classical in the context of both film and theater. The credit sequence introduces us to the characters and actors, their visual images, their names, and their sounds. But this sequence also initiates the strategy and style of *Nashville*. Images move simultaneously in three directions: vertically, circularly, and, in the center of the frame, in a rapidly paced montage of stills. Three kinds of sounds are heard: music, lyrics from songs we will eventually hear in full, and the barking of an announcer's voice, which calls forth both a country fair and the hard-sell pusher of late-night television. We are clearly being thrust into the world of show business, into a three- or twenty-five-ring circus, but we are also being told from the very first moment that we must pay attention to more than one gesture at a time. As we have come to expect of movies since the sixties, the credits are thus not isolated from the film itself but are stylistically coherent and integral to what follows. Yet this first moment of the movie remains a prelude, not unlike those older movies whose credits were displayed on what appeared to be pages of a book. The credits are neither a deception nor seduction into the narrative; even those that continue through the first sequence of the narrative appear as distinct information. The function of the credits, as it always was, is to reveal the stars in their particular filmic context, and this is exactly what occurs in *Nashville*.

*   *   *   *

When the story itself begins, it does so quietly with a reminder that films' origins, this film's especially, are in silence and in theater. The curtain literally rises with a dissolve from the isolated title, *Nashville,* to an opening garage door on which the title at first appears superimposed, then becomes part of the physical world of the city. A campaign van, displaying the name "Hal Phillip Walker" emerges and moves slowly down a deserted street. As the truck arrives in urban traffic, we begin to hear music that has no obvious source. Steady drumbeats resound and give momentum to the movement of the campaign truck; their heavy undertone is an eerie reminder of the coincidence of the sounds of politics and funerals in our recent history.

For a moment, we take in this music as a conventional filmic device to both comment upon and characterize the emotional intent of the visual images. The camera shows us a large red sign passed by the truck. The sign reads, "The Bank," (with the *T* half hidden, thus reading "he Bank," suggesting the male dominance of banks), and the music now changes into the lyrics of a song that begins, "My mother's people came by ship / And fought at Bunker Hill." Then in the midst of our amusement and complacency about the film's rhetoric, Altman catches us unawares and cuts to the actual source of the music—a recording studio where Haven Hamilton, whose very name embodies both the myths and history of old America, is laboriously recording his new hit. The curtain has risen, not to reveal the glitter of the stage, but to penetrate the hard, cold grindings of the star at work. We *should* be disoriented.

The visual images of the campaign truck and the recording studio are connected neither by characters nor by location; in the language of montage, they "collide." The problem with such collision in many films is that the new synthesis of perception it intends is often either so obvious as to be discomforting or so obscure as to be meaningless. By initiating Haven's song in one visual sequence and continuing it in another, Altman both carries our emotional response from one place to another and allows the intellectual link to be present but not ponderous. We take the song's lyrics to be a comment on politics, but what could be a simplistic reflection of the popular wisdom apparent in country music becomes an ironic comment on the recording industry itself as the camera pans the studio, revealing its manipulative technical devices, its "star" enclosed in a glass box, and its human faces tense with boredom, impatience, and arrogance.

This first song introduces us not just to Altman's wry comments on America, not just to the context of a country-music recording studio, but to Haven Hamilton himself. Haven's song is a soliloquy; it gathers our interest in the character; we hear it unmistakably as *his* song. (That most of *Nashville's* music was written specifically for the film and was written by its actors is important to what the movie does to an audience and not just an interesting note about Altman's rehearsal process.) After the opening credential of his Puritan heritage, Haven's song continues:

> *My Daddy lost a leg in France*
> *I have his medal still.*
> *My brother served with Patton,*
> *I saw action in Algiers.*
> *Oh, we must be doing something right*
> *To last two hundred years.*[6]

The transition from "I" to "we" in this first stanza of the ballad is carefully achieved. Haven provides his credentials as a typical American and a heroic figure; by confiding in us his own personal history, he achieves the legitimacy of a "we" which is at once his particular family and all Americans. That endurance may not be ample evidence for rightness does not occur to Haven.[7]

In *Nashville*, Altman's camera and editing tell us how to listen. The camera immediately cuts through the sentimentality of the song by its own and the editor's technical virtuosity—one of the first shots in the studio is a triple superimposition—and by what it focuses on.[8] Haven's own isolation in a sound booth is one overt device to distance him from us, but equally strong and amusing are the intermittent shots of his audience, the members of which are quickly identified as family. Through the glass of the sound booth, we witness Haven's family besieged by an invader with a microphone. With no semblance of tact, Haven dismisses this woman from the studio, an action that Altman instantly exploits to again disrupt our narrative assumptions. We expect the camera to yield us more of Haven's world and character, but, instead, we exit with the distracting woman, Opal (Geraldine Chaplin), and suddenly find ourselves in Studio B where an entirely different recording session is occurring. Haven's song is silenced and replaced by the intense projection of a group of black gospel singers led by one white woman. As if the question were genuine, they sing, "Do You Believe in Jesus?"

Here Altman arranges a trap to play to our assumptions that the movie will focus on a star, if not a movie star than surely a character who is a vocal star and self-acknowledged hero. In Studio A, everyone and everything is focused on Haven Hamilton, and we naturally assume a similar situation for Studio B. (That this is our conventional perspective will be eventually evidenced by the walk-ons of Julie Christie and Elliot Gould, who are ignored until recognized *as* stars.) With the cut to Studio B, we are on uncertain ground, divided in our attention between Buddy, Haven's son; Linnea, striking because of her white presence in a black singing group; the group itself; and Opal, the intrusive reporter, whose startling, mobile face and abrasive comments pull focus no matter what the competition. We tend to be drawn to Opal, but her nervous energy and obvious pretension do not make her pleasant to watch, despite her photogenic beauty and claim to our attention as the offscreen daughter of a star. In affirmation of our discomfort, Opal speaks her most outrageous line of the scene, "Do they carry on like that in church?" Buddy's answer, "It depends on which church you go to," may not be attended to at the moment but will be recalled later in the film.

This first sequence of *Nashville* concludes with an acceleration of parallel editing and the introduction of still another character, Frog, the piano player. Haven is not pleased with Frog's performance, and announces his displeasure with authority: "When I ask for Pig, I want Pig." Exiting to the unheard round of our laughter, Haven continues, "You get your hair cut. You don't belong in Nashville." Haven's pronouncement is a double cue: this is a movie that intends to make us laugh; it is also a movie unabashedly conscious of itself as a film, in which the relationship of characters to the world of film will have something to do with belonging in Nashville. Haven's lines themselves are only half of the comedic routine that sets up such a response. The other half, a sign reading "Welcome to Nashville," is projected immediately after Haven's line and initiates the next sequence of the film.

*   *   *   *

The "Welcome to Nashville" sign appears for a second as an arbitrary editing gimmick but, like Haven's song in the previous sequence, is quickly justified by the new context, the Nashville airport. Witnessing this second transition, we should acquire an alertness to the film's efficient wit. Such alertness is vital to our reception of the complicated information and tonalities of the airport sequence itself. *Nashville* is replete with pointed jokes articulated not by characters but in the montage; they are the director's jokes, integral to the performance for which we are the audience.

The airport sequence serves the traditional function of an exposition scene while orienting us to the unconventional structural pattern of the film. We are introduced to most of the characters of *Nashville* as well as to the two events that unite these characters: the return to the city of its grandest vocal star, Barbara Jean, and the arrival of a political machine whose purpose is a rally for the presidential candidate, Hal Phillip Walker. These introductions are not chronologically or causally linked. We are bombarded, both within shots and from shot to shot, with images and sounds whose only apparent connection is that they exist in and around the Nashville airport. The "construction of images" in this as well as almost all of the subsequent sequences of *Nashville* coheres with Metz's basic concept of the "bracket syntagma."

> Definition: a series of very brief scenes representing occurrences that the film gives us as typical samples of a same order of reality, without in any way chronologically locating them in relation to each other, in order to emphasize their presumed kinship within a category of facts that the filmmaker wants to describe in visual terms.[9]

Yet, despite the congruence of this definition with the syntagmatic structure of the film, Altman's structuring of *Nashville* also transforms this filmic convention. In part, the transformation lies in Altman's assertion of the equality of aural with visual terms, but the more important distinction lies in the use Altman makes of the bracket syntagma. Metz's experience of the bracket syntagma is that:

> None of these little scenes is treated with the full syntagmatic breadth it might have commanded; it is taken as an element in a system of allusions, and therefore it is the series, rather than the individual, that the film takes into account.[10]

Altman's strategy in *Nashville* is to employ the series as a means to take many "individuals" into account. In Metz's description, each element stands in service to the system of allusions; in Altman's film, the system establishes a context in which we can become engaged by an exceptional number of individual moments as well as individual persons. After three or four shots in and about the airport, the context is sufficiently established to allow us to assume a principled selectivity: a relatively few images are needed to inform us that the substance of the kinship is in politics or show business; once we know the nature of the kinship, we are freed to ask more particular questions of each projected image. As with the learning of any language, once we have absorbed the rules of grammar, our attention is loosed on the semantic content of each assertion.

Perhaps recognizing that we are being asked to be quick students, Altman assists our penetration of his work by ordering the series of images at the airport into an accessible pattern of interior and

exterior shots. He first establishes the opposing exteriors of the
airport through a rapid series of cuts from the "Welcome to Nashville" sign to a reporter at an outdoor gate, to the airport parking
lot, and then to the arrival of a plane on the runway. The interior of
the airport is first known in an extended vignette in the airport
coffee shop. The film then cuts to the airport lobby, back to the
arriving plane, and then again to the lobby. Characters, too, are
presented as either insiders or outsiders in relation to the town of
Nashville. The tension between outside and inside is first made
apparent in the coffee-shop scene where we meet Sueleen Gay
(Gwen Welles), a waitress with aspirations of becoming a country-
music star. Here we also encounter Wade (Robert Doqui), Sueleen's
black friend whose ascerbic humor and graceful bearing arouse our
instant trust. Dialogue reveals that both Sueleen and Wade work in
Nashville; they are both, then, insiders, but because Sueleen is not
the star she wishes to be and because he is a black man in Nashville,
they are ironically—spatially inside but on the outside of Nashville
society—not on the runway awaiting the arrival of Barbara Jean,
the real star. And outside is where the real insiders, like Haven and
his family, are.

Also in the coffee shop, we briefly meet Delbert Reese (Ned
Beatty), the lawyer for all the big shots in town and the rising
political entrepreneur of Nashville. Delbert initially appears to be
one of the inside powers of the city, but as the film unfolds, his
authority is persistently undercut, and he is increasingly shown to
us as the destroyer of community rather than its center. With
Delbert, as with the inside-outside code itself, Altman presents the
cliché and allows it enough space to self-destruct. Eventually, we
perceive that distinctions between outside and inside, while conventional to film rhetoric, when situated at an airport are both ambiguous and ironic. Similarly, while Delbert strides in and out of the
airport with the officious air of a man who belongs with the stars,
the Hal Phillip Walker truck warns us of the danger of lawyers
running the country. Later in the film, we see that even at home his
ignorance of the sign-language used by his deaf children makes him
an outsider. Partially because of his wife's association with the
black gospel singers seen in the recording studio, Del appears able

to move fluidly between the political world and the show-business world of Nashville, but he is, in fact, tangential to both worlds. And despite his appearance of masculine self-confidence, he is deceived by his wife and rejected by Sueleen.

Two other outsiders appear "inside" in the coffee shop—Mr. Green (Keenan Wynn), an older man waiting at the airport to fetch his niece for a visit with her ailing aunt; and an unnamed hirsute young man who persistently haunts the film, appearing most frequently riding the "Easy Rider" tricycle. Mr. Green truly belongs in Nashville, both in the city and in the film. He lives in Nashville and owns a house there but remains outside its politics and its country-music business. He exists at the emotional core of the film; it is his genuine pain as he struggles with his wife's illness and eventual death that gives us access to our own distress and that of others in Nashville. Mr. Green's involuntary participation in the chaos and violence of these five days in Nashville prepares the way for an intimacy with a world presented in epic scale.

Altman juxtaposes the inside scene in the coffee shop to two strikingly different airport locations: the gate where Barbara Jean is arriving; and the passenger area where a collection of ordinary people, including Mr. Green's niece, musicians, would-be stars, and politicians, meet and fail to meet each other. The key moment in the passenger area is easy to miss, perhaps deliberately so. John Triplette (Michael Murphy), the advance man for presidential candidate Hal Phillip Walker, has arrived in the airport, oblivious to the homecoming of vocal star Barbara Jean. Triplette's line, as he knowledgeably picks Del Reese out of the crowd, "You looking for me, I'm John Triplette," is undercut by the noise of the by-standers and overwhelmed by the outrageously sexual presence of a young woman whose travel outfit of short shorts and halter can only be appreciated by being seen. This young woman, Martha, or L.A. Joan (Shelley Duvall) as she prefers to be called, is Mr. Green's niece. Martha actually shares the frame with Triplette and Del, but here, as throughout the film, her function and concern is to draw attention to herself. In a film, Altman reminds us, characters reveal themselves not only within the structure of the plot but within the structure of the frame. Altman accentuates the moment with a filmic pun by turning his camera to an airport sign which reads, "All persons entering concourse are screened."

*   *   *   *

Altman's willingness to allow us to laugh with him relieves the potential gravity of his rhetoric. This is not to say that *Nashville* simply records the world that unravels before the cameras; nor is it the case, as Leonard Quart would have it, of purely "aesthetic" reflection, devoid of any social or historical intent.[11] Any doubts we might have about the deliberate construction of the world projected should be dispelled by the end of the airport sequence, if for no other reason than that almost everything we have seen for half an hour has been limited to the colors red, white, and blue.[12] Most vividly in the costumes of the cheerleaders and band who greet Barbara Jean with their gun-shaped batons; more subtly in the clothing of everyone else including music stars and politicians; unobtrusively in the decor of the opening street scene and of the airport itself, Nashville the city and *Nashville* the movie are painted in the colors of America. What is surprising is that those colors of American patriotism never feel arbitrary or distract us from the activities they tint. Certain aspects of American life, it would appear, are so natural to us that even when waved as a banner before our eyes, they go almost unnoticed. Altman enjoys such perceptions and shares his pleasure with us. When an enormous American Airlines jet crosses the screen from left to right, proudly displaying its red, white, and blue, we grin, not only because the image is hyperbolic but also because we might have missed it without Altman's assistance.

Altman captures and relishes a world that is often absent from us because of our absent-mindedness. Certainly, the combination of red, white, and blue exists as an iconographic sign of the United States in our daily "real" world. Without this societal signification, the colors would function differently in Altman's film, even if he created a red, white, and blue code for Nashville that, by its pattern and context, came to be understood as representing the United States or loyalty to the United States. But while Altman has chosen a world where the preponderance of red, white, and blue is more plausible than it might be in another location, it is not "natural" that all of the decor and clothing is limited to these colors. Even the Goo-Goo candybar commercial at the Grand Ole Opry is red, white, and blue. Outside the world of this film, red, white, and blue have a more limited and yet less-controlled signification; the range of our response to the linkage of these colors in daily life can extend from dismissal (because they are a cliché) to obliviousness, to pleasure or anger if emblems and rituals of patriotism are important to us. Within the film, however, these colors function in at least two ways that cease once the film is over: they serve to suggest a relationship between the world viewed in *Nashville* and the entire United States, thus making it difficult for us to dismiss the ambiance and events of the film as either purely fictional or only possible in Nashville; and they serve to make connections between the worlds of show business and of politics, a conjoining which is key to our experience of this film.

With his use of color, as with his use of sound, Altman risks taking what are most frequently the repressed or hidden conventions of film and placing them at the center of his work. Umberto Eco's comments on two related shots from Fritz Lang's *M* here become relevant to the persistent activity of *Nashville*:

> The film is playing a risky game between the coded and the uncoded. It supports daring suggestions by coded connotations. Culture acts as a glue to amalgamate the invention of unheard-of relationships. In all this, nothing is really "natural." Semiotic laws are at work at every level. A movie is the meeting point of many semiotic phenomena.[13]

To assert that "semiotic laws are at work at every level" is not to imply that Robert Altman overtly uses such laws to construct his movie, but nor is it synonomous with saying that semiotic laws are at work in every sentence we speak, despite the speaker's ignorance or indifference to such laws. Any work that is of art is made and structured with some specific intentions toward an audience. While a sentence, too, is articulated to act toward another, that the making of a movie is both a less ordinary and more public action than the making of a sentence (even for a prolific filmmaker like Altman) must evoke a greater consciousness of gesture and meaning, of signifier and signification, than is true in daily conversation. With some films and filmmakers, including ones we are apt to take seriously, addressing systems of signs could be useful but might distract us from the experience of the film itself. With *Nashville*, however, we are in a territory where the film itself calls attention to the process of signification. Even though he may be unaware of the semiotician's vocabulary, Altman knows that he is playing " a risky game between the coded and uncoded," and he goes further than Eco or Lang because he confronts us with the risky process itself.

Among the least disguised efforts to make us aware of his use of specific and repeated filmic gestures is the Sunday morning sequence that culminates in Opal's discourse on the color yellow. It is the middle of the long weekend we spend in Nashville and more than halfway through the film. Altman's cameras have just taken us on a brilliantly montaged tour of Nashville's churches, where we have witnessed most of the characters in the film in their various forms of worship. Only the rock trio of Bill, Tom, and Mary; and Triplette, Hal Phillip Walker's advance man, are not in church, and their absence from a place of worship emphasizes their roles as rebellious outsiders; their rock music, their politics, their transience connects them to Frog, the piano player who early in the film was told by Haven that he did not belong in Nashville. When the camera discovers Opal wandering around a junkyard, it is clear that she does not belong in Nashville either, but unlike Bill, Tom, and Mary; or Triplette, she is attempting to penetrate, with embarrassing intensity, the meaning of the city through its garbage.

As the camera follows Opal through the piles of discarded auto wreckage, we see and hear that she is speaking into her microphone, desperately making metaphors of the garbage around her. She calls the location a "grave yard," which leads her ever-fertile mind to thoughts of the color of dried blood and then to an analogy between this heap of junk and "an elephant's secret burial ground." She is startled by the sudden appearance of a man carrying a music case and is momentarily distracted from her reflections, only able to comment inanely, "You're a musician." After two quick cuts to Mary and Bill's motel room and then to the Walker campaign truck, we return to Opal who is now contemplating the meaning of a herd of yellow school buses she has come upon in her wanderings. Opal is struck less by the fact that these are school buses than by their color. "Yellow," she begins, "yellow is the color of. . . ." Groping for the "correct" connotation, she suggests that yellow is the color of peril, caution, cowardice, sunshine. But yellow is also the color of ordinary objects, like the telephone to which Altman cuts in the middle of Opal's search for signification. The cut is both whimsical and laden; while undermining Opal's attempts to uncover symbolic truths, Altman adds another image to his own series of yellow allusions. The yellow phone to which the film cuts is not just any yellow telephone but one situated just outside the rented room of Kenny Frazer, the young man who will eventually shoot the star Barbara Jean.

As is persistently true of her, Opal is only slightly, if sufficiently, off the mark. The color yellow has taken on significance in the movie; it has been manipulated such that increasingly it connotes danger and death. Repeatedly in the film, Altman uses a broad stroke of yellow to contrast to red, white, and blue; the color appears vividly in the hospital scenes: Barbara Jean's hospital room suffuses yellow, from flowers to bedsheets. Because Altman's yellow glares at us (as it will again in *3 Women*) and consistently seems unnatural, it draws our attention to the red, white, and blue, which are oddly more subtle; because yellow is the focal color of the hospital and the junkyard, we can readily associate it with death and destruction. We should therefore be uneasy when Kenny picks up a yellow telephone; in *this* film, yellow is ominous. Yet the color maintains a paradoxical quality, a tension between its common usage as a cheering color (that is assumedly why Barbara Jean has yellow bedsheets and why Millie's apartment is plastic yellow in *3 Women*) and its isolated occurence in the film at moments that foreshadow death.

The color yellow thus serves a double function in *Nashville*. As a narrative device, its cumulative effect is to inform us that death and danger lurk somewhere in the unfolding of the film. In addition, as a symbol whose meaning is arbitrary and enclosed within this film (in contrast to red, white, and blue), yellow demonstrates to us the different modes of signification possible within film. At least two different kinds of distinctions can be ascertained from Altman's uses of color in *Nashville*. There is, first, a difference between the connotative values we discover in the daily world and those placed in the world of a film. There are also distinctions to be made among the kinds of symbols that work in films. Drawing from Charles Sanders Pierce, Peter Wollens argues that in film we can usefully distinguish between icons, signs that represent their objects mainly by their similarity to them; indexes, which assert an existential bond between sign and object; and symbols, which signify through an arbitrary or contractual relationship.[14] The abundance of all three types in *Nashville* stands as good evidence for the accuracy of these distinctions and also affirms Wollens's secondary argument: that identification of the different kinds of signs in a given film assists our understanding of both filmic signification and our understanding of the continuous transformation of every mode of symbolic activity. The gun-shaped batons twirled early in *Nashville* are initially icons; they clearly bear a physical resemblance to a gun. Yet these "harmless" symbols carry an existential relationship to death, and in the course of the film, this relationship is extended both by the final events and by Opal's observation that the real danger lies in the unchallenged diffusion of guns among the "innocents" of the society. Wollens's claims become politically significant in Altman's hands: signs that begin as arbitrary symbols within a language or work of art may become transformed before our very eyes into dangerous weapons.

Opal's problem, not just limited to her relationship to colors, is that she misses the important issue because she repeatedly ignores the context of the object or quality on which she focuses. In her search for meaning, Opal does not or cannot allow herself to perceive incongruity or to acknowledge complexity and thus is unable to laugh at herself or the world around her. She is Altman's foil and fool, but she is also the character who best shows us how to look and hear because of the persistence with which she confuses the trivial with the significant. While Opal is reflecting on elephants' burial grounds and yellow buses, there is a man rummaging in junk at the side of the frame who merits Opal's and our attention. When this man, Kenny, shoots Barbara Jean at the end of the film, we will have a difficult time recalling when and where we saw him previously, and Opal's documentary on Nashville will have missed him entirely.

Opal is not, then, so different from us, although her function, like that of many characters out of the comedies of manners, is to teach us to be unlike her by allowing us to laugh at her. We may delight in the number of embarrassing errors Opal commits while stranded on the highway during the collision sequence, but we too, are likely to overlook the one incident in that syntagma that carries crucial symbolic and narrative weight. Although the highway sequence gives us, as well as Opal, a chance to know better many of the characters we glimpsed at the airport, we are likely to take little account of the shot of a young man who removes the radiator cap from his car, creating a geyser image of release, then takes his music case from his back seat and walks away. Before the young man, whom we come to know as Kenny, can withdraw, he is approached officiously by Delbert Reese, who asks him "where he got that car." Kenny's response is, "I stole it." In the cacophony of noises, irritated exchanges, and visual cuts that comprise this sequence, neither Kenny's stance nor his music case nor his words appear especially remarkable, but in retrospect, we can acknowledge how sufficiently Altman has introduced the character who will become the assassin in the final scene. Kenny maintains his anonymity despite the film's attention to him.

The key on-the-scene witness to this event is, or should be, Opal. Traveling in a car with Linnea, Del Reese's wife (notably ignorant of her husband's presence a few yards away), Opal is astute enough to declare that she needs "this"—meaning the accident scene—for her documentary. But Opal, unlike Altman, has missed all of the important action and proceeds to destroy some marvelous opportunities for interviews. Opal's first missed chance is with Linnea herself. We can guess that Opal has latched onto Linnea at the studio in order to explore the role of this white woman who sings with a black gospel group. But as Linnea starts to chatter, Opal either misses every cue or responds so tactlessly that she impedes genuine revelation. Even when Linnea mentions that she has two deaf children, Opal responds with clichéd sentimentality that avoids the very access to Linnea's world the reporter would supposedly seek. When

Opal then dashes from Linnea's car to a van that advertises its attachment to the star singer Tommy Brown, she removes any remaining doubt that she might be a reliable reporter of Nashville. Happily ensconced within Tommy Brown's van, Opal's assumptions about blacks and whites—especially in the South—obscure her ability to see and hear what is around her. She quickly hides her astonishment when introduced to Tommy Brown's black wife with mumblings about how liberal the singing star must be, all the while missing the barely repressed smile of the star himself, whom Opal neither sees nor interviews because she assumes Tommy Brown is white.

Opal misses her opportunities, here on the highway and persistently throughout the film, because of her own narcissism and because both personal and cultural qualities lead her to focus narrowly and hurriedly on what appears to be the heart of the story or the ostensible dramatic center. She is, thus, not simply Altman's foil because he is clever and she is dumb, he sophisticated and she naive, but also because her documentary is conceived on a conventional structure. The highway sequence, like the airport sequence, neatly coheres with Metz's description of a bracket syntagma, but used a second time so quickly, the device should begin to perplex us. The concept of a bracket syntagma is after all of a parenthesis—of material, as Metz argues, that "confirms the viewer's impression that the sequence must be taken as a whole, and that he must not attempt to link the partial scenes so directly to the rest of the narrative."[15] Yet half an hour into *Nashville,* most of what we have seen and heard has been enclosed in such brackets, and we will soon discover that the remainder of the film is almost wholly comprised of such series. At most, as in the exodus from the airport, a brief phrase will link one bracket syntagma with another; frequently, one closing bracket will bump against the next opening bracket. We are not being led astray from the narrative by those bracket systems; they enclose the pieces of the narrative itself.

*   *   *   *

By the end of the highway sequence, it should be evident to the spectator that Altman's is a Whitmanesque vision of the world, in which not only the camera but also the audience is asked to contain multitudes. Altman presents this world as transient, contradictory, disjointed, and unpredictable in its rhythm, and we must therefore pursue with unaccustomed concentration and willingness to select and judge.

We are, I might say, cruising. Initiated in the introductory sequences in *Nashville,* the promiscuity of camera and characters becomes central in the audience's relationship to the film and the characters' relationships to each other.[16] Promiscuity is a relationship that can only occur between those who know each other and refuse commitment to any one person or image. For the promiscuous, intimacy is difficult but not impossible.

To establish some measure of intimacy with each of the twenty-five characters who are important to our understanding of *Nashville,* Altman animates his frames with the songs that are the heart of both the city and the film. The music that engages the inhabitants of *Nashville* also establishes continuity for us. Altman counters the exhaustion we might experience from being moved through dozens of locations by the aura of leisure he evokes in allowing each of his characters to fully sing his or her song. Altman whirls us through Nashville at a pace no single person could endure, and we may forget some of the locations we pass through, but the persistent urge to sing that permeates all of these spaces will pursue us to the end of the film and beyond.

The songs of *Nashville* punctuate and please; people sing in *Nashville* to entertain each other, to make a living, and to acknowledge each other. That Altman allows most performances, whether they be secretly discovered by the camera or intentionally public, to be heard in full, suggests respect for each person who sings, and, in turn, commands our attention to those voices and the words they project. We frequently hear fragments of conversation in *Nashville;* we rarely hear *fragments* of songs, and this gradually teaches us to listen to the lyrics as we might listen to a soliloquy in the live theater. These songs are the self-conscious attempts of persons to tell us who they are.

The country-style music that is prevalent in *Nashville* lends itself remarkably well to such a scheme. The temptation to dismiss country music for its sentimentality has at its source the naked willingness of the composers and vocalists of this music to be narrative and confessional. The lyrics of country songs tell the stories of ordinary people who are made special or heroic by the singing of their names and deeds. The theater actor takes on a persona—a mask—in order to speak and thus is only peforming when he has become other and speaks as an other. Singers, especially country-music singers, achieve their power partially from the sense they convey of personal, autobiographical investment in the songs they sing. It is no coincidence, then that many country singers compose their own materials. Mistake though it might be to conflate fiction with autobiography, to confuse the consciously composed gesture with the spontaneous, it would be a greater error in this context to deny the singers' intentions to associate themselves with their words or our desire to imagine that the songs are these people's confessions to us.

From Haven Hamilton's "200 Years" to the last refrain of "It Don't Worry Me," *Nashville* is replete with such chanted confessions. The harmonies of the Rocky Mountain Laurels, who sing in one of the first clubs we visit, are as coherent with their visual persona as is Sueleen's awkward deportment with her off-key rendition of "Let Me Be the One." It is difficult to watch or listen to Sueleen, and the lyrics of her song make the process only more painful. We believe how much it matters to her to be "the one," and we know how much the undisguised desire will itself defeat her. We endure a similar pity for a character's humiliation a bit later when, at Haven's party, his son, Buddy, hesitantly sings his own song to Opal. Buddy's private performance for Opal makes clear that he is no undiscovered star, but both the lyrics and the music of the song, "It Comes from the Heart of a Gentle Woman," reveal his own sweet gentleness and his need for tender affection. When Opal abruptly cuts off Buddy's song because she has sighted a "real" star, Elliot Gould, we are angry at her callousness and regretful that we have not heard Buddy through.

By the time, then, that we arrive at the Grand Ole Opry for performances by the major vocalists, we are prepared for the revelatory quality of this music, and we expect performances that are more powerful, more skilled than those of the amateurs we have been witnessing. Tommy Brown, the first star to sing at the Opry, does not disappoint us or his on-screen audience. His song, "One More Dollar, One More Day," tells the story of a man who has been from coast to coast punching time clocks and working bars, never freeing himself from the relentless need to go out tomorrow and earn another dollar to make it through another day. The song enviously compares this man to the bluebird who flies freely over the rainbow, answering to no man or time clock but only to the wind. We do not equate Tommy Brown with the "I" of the song; Tommy Brown is vividly no working-class man, but we can believe that money slips through Tommy Brown's fingers, that his belief that "life was for livin' " is appropriately articulated in the past tense, and that his search for the pot of gold at the end of the rainbow has never been as easy as it seems to be for the bluebird. The pleasant, yet undistinctive melody and rhythm combined with the conventionality of the image of the rainbow also affirm the accusation made the night before by another black man that Tommy Brown is "the whitest nigger in town." Tommy Brown's song will offend no one and be remembered by few; it tells us as much about the singer's need to hide behind a façade of competence and respectability as Sueleen's raw discourse names her vulnerability.

During Tommy Brown's song, the camera is also establishing our privileged position, our separateness from the audience at Opryland. We glimpse the crowd outside as well as inside, but more important, in contrast to Winifred, a Nashville hopeful trying to sneak backstage, we are admitted to the backstage area and witness much of Brown's performance from upstage of him. We remain onstage during the Goo-Goo commercial as Haven is preparing to sing; this initially appears to deflate Haven's position as the eminent star, since the privileged onstage are moving and talking as Haven's performance begins, but Triplette's snide mockery of Haven's small physical stature is so inappropriate and mean that it ironically refocuses our emphatic attention on Haven.

The first of Haven's vocal selections—"For the Sake of the Children"—seems a curious choice. The song presents an epiphanic moment in which a man is telling his lover that he has suddenly changed his mind and will not leave his family for her because his children are too needy of his love. My initial experience of the song is irritation with the cliché and disappointment in the self-indulgent martyrdom it describes. The visual image of Haven in shining blue, white, and yellow affirms his lack of taste and of imagination. Nor does the camera help to entertain us; it remains remarkably still, often in close-up, simply recording Haven's performance; only occasionally and briefly does the camera shift its focus upstage or to the house. Yet as Haven continues, I become increasingly engaged, despite my knowledge that bored condescension would be a legitimate response. Part of the effect is accomplished by Haven's own control of tone and phrasing; his is not a beautiful voice, but he knows how to work his music. Haven Hamilton is vividly a professional, and there is a relief for the audience in this context in that mutual acknowledgment of professionalism. We have earlier seen and heard that Haven Hamilton is an obsessive, domineering father with an unspecified relationship to a woman named Lady Pearl, and we know that he is separated in some also unspecified fashion from the mother of his grown son. In this context, Haven's song of the toll of adultery on children reveals some courage and candor. If we hear Haven's song not as a sermon but as a confession, if we hear the naming of the children as metaphors for his own sources of pain, the song remains mundane as a piece of music but gains considerable interest as a way of seeing this character in this film.

While the lyrics of Haven's next song, "Keep A' Goin'," are often even sillier than those of the first selection—"Ain't no law says you must die, keep a' goin'." It is not surprising that this is Haven's theme song. Each of the songs we have now heard him sing embraces a clear and coherent set of values: he respects endurance, loyalty, personal fortitude; he abhors cowardice and passivity. The persona that Haven invokes is the frontiersman—tough, stalwart, relentless, and proud to bear the banners of God, Country, and Family. He is the obvious descendent of Altman's McCabe in *McCabe and Mrs. Miller.* We lack evidence as to whether this is the true Haven or the persona he believes will please his audience; what cynicism exists resides within us. Haven clings to the old roots of the nation, and if, like Hal Phillip Walker, we seek new roots, Haven reminds us that some will resist the upheaval.

Connie White's appearance after Haven extends Altman's gallery of portraits but also serves to articulate what is missing in each of the performances we have thus far witnessed. Connie is conspicuously *not* Barbara Jean, and her own posture and the voices of those around her persist in apologizing for that fact. What is missing is Barbara Jean, and while we do not know exactly what that means, we are provoked to imagine. Sueleen's songs are failed imitations of Barbara Jean's, Connie White is a "good friend" and stand-in but certainly second best, and Haven's competence only whets the audience's appetite for the potency of the grandest star. As the film progresses, we as audience for these vocalists and as spectators of the film have a double interest in hearing Barbara Jean perform: we want to share the pleasure in the special talent that those in the film hail, and we want to know Barbara Jean. The film repeatedly signals us that such knowledge is only possible if we hear Barbara Jean sing.

When, more than halfway through the film, we do hear Barbara Jean perform, both the context and the gesture are surprising. It is in the hospital chapel that the camera first discloses Barbara Jean, the vocalist. We arrive at this chapel in the midst of a filmic tour de force, during which Altman has cut from a Roman Catholic church, to an Episcopalian church, to a black Baptist church, and then to the ecumenical hospital chapel. Each place of worship is peopled with characters from the film (providing further information for us about who they are) and is resonant with the particular music of the religious sect. This archetypical bracket syntagma is achieved through classic montage: each individual take in each church is altered and enlarged by its juxtaposition to the next series of shots in another church. Altman magnifies and unites the whole montage by filling these spaces and the movie theaters with music that, while carefully differentiated, seems to flow from one church to another. Continuity is further established by the consistency with which the colors red, white, and blue again prevail.

Each of these churches asserts itself on the screen as a community, as a place where, even in Nashville where music is power and money, the democratization of song occurs. Altman calls attention to the pattern by jarring it when he first discovers Barbara Jean in the chapel. We see her first in a medium close-up, singing, "And He walks with me, and He talks with me"; we are confused as to where we are and about whom she is singing. Then the camera slowly withdraws, revealing that Barbara Jean is in a wheelchair in a simple chapel. The few other occupants of the chapel—Barbara Jean's husband, Barnett (Allan Garfield); a soldier who worships Barbara Jean; and Mr. Green, whose wife is a patient—identify the location as the hospital. Here, both the choice of song and the fact of singing augment our sense of who Barbara Jean is. Having previously witnessed Barnett's concern with his wife's public relations, we may distrust the sincerity of Barbara Jean's piety and generosity in singing in this paltry context, but nothing in Barbara Jean's face or voice hints that this is a calculated or ambivalent gesture. This church service is a contrast to the other services we have glimpsed in its focus on the isolation of each member of its congregation, but it is coherent with those others in momentarily returning singing to the daily world from its elevated status in the worlds of commerce and politics.

Barbara Jean's first "performance" links her to other stars singing in each of their churches but also emphasizes her separation in an unnatural context. She, whose hospital room it was a privilege to enter and whom the public in *Nashville* as well as its stars might see as the key insider, sings unprotected and "outside" the cloak of audience and caretakers. (Throughout the film, Barbara Jean is noticeably without genuine friends.) The song she sings accentuates our impression of her fragility and solitude. As with most of the songs in *Nashville,* the first person is emphatically present in this hymn and evokes an impression of personal testimony. Others might sing of the presence of God at their sides and go unnoticed or appear discomfortingly mystical, but given Barbara Jean's husband's references to her previous "breakdowns," we may readily hear this song as affirmation of all that we have previously inferred about this woman. She is desperately lonely while rarely alone; she strains to fulfill the expectations of others. Barbara Jean has created a separate world for herself to escape to, a world where, among other things, God talks to her because she has difficulty maintaining the requisite public image of the virgin princess.

To the extent that such thoughts occur to us during the chapel scene, we begin to know and care about Barbara Jean, but it is not until her first public performance later that day that our suspicions of Barbara Jean's distress are confirmed. When she does finally appear at the "outdoor" Opry, it is with all the fanfare and ornamentation anticipated by the first shots of her at the airport. Costumed, as always, in bridely white with pink ribbons in her hair, she parades down a red ramp (perhaps not an allusion to *Agamemnon* but surely a remarkable coincidence) escorted by four handsome young men. Her first piece, the "Cowboy Song," is less compelling in its lyrics than in the sheer force of the energy with which she sings. Altman again asserts the complementarity of sound and visual imagery: as Barbara Jean sings, the camera moves back and forth from her to the audience, gradually coming closer and closer in on Barbara Jean, until we are confronted with a close-up of her face. The intimacy of the camera and the passion of the voice conjoin to press Barbara Jean's presence upon us.

As if in recognition that we can only bear such intimacy in brief intervals, at the end of the "Cowboy Song" Altman cuts quickly to the audience where the camera appears to single out a soldier whose recurrence begins to feel ominous. In fact, however, the important narrative content of the frame is not the presence of the soldier at the Opry but the arrival in the front-row location of Kenny, the young man whom we first saw abandoning his car on the highway, later glimpsed in the junkyard, and then spotted again at Mr. Green's house where he rented a room. The shot of Kenny and the soldier, like the earlier one in the airport where L.A. Joan stole focus from the meeting of Del Reese and Triplette, is a warning to the film audience that the impatience we may experience is due not to the absence of persistent narrative development but to our own limitations as participant observers. In the post-Vietnam 1970s, the uniform of the soldier carries negative symbolic weight for many spectators; we thus pay wary attention to the soldier whenever he appears while ignoring the accumulating cues that Kenny is a more threatening presence.

The most transparent of these prophetic cues to Kenny's behavior occurs when Barbara Jean resumes her singing. The song, "Careless

Disrespect," is immediately painful for Barbara Jean to sing and for us to hear. We have little reason to separate Barbara Jean from the persona as she croons, "It hurts so bad, it gets me down, down, down / I wanta walk away from this battleground." During these lyrics, the camera alternates between Kenny and Barbara Jean, zooming into a close-up on each. Lines like "You've got your own private world" simultaneously express Barbara Jean's anguish and her Cassandra-like knowledge of Kenny. Altman extends the conventional filmic device of shot-reverse-shot employed to represent dialogue between two persons; the camera establishes a very specific connection between Barbara Jean and Kenny, in which the constrained tension on Kenny's face reveals and reflects the pain expressed in the lyrics of the song. A moment later Barbara Jean interrupts herself to ramble out of control. We believe Barbara Jean's words, "Writin' it down makes me feel better / Keeps me away from the blues," and recognize that singing it out is not "Writin' it down."

It is no accident that Altman now cuts to Linnea, the white gospel-singer wife of Del Reese and mother of two deaf children. We find Linnea in the process of silently agreeing, over the phone, to a rendezvous with Tom, the young stud of the rock trio, Tom, Bill, and Mary. Both the meaning and pervasiveness of promiscuity in this world become more pronounced. The camera's unwillingness to make more than temporary and tentative commitments to each space and each character is a reflection of the characters' own choices. This does not mean that genuine intimacy and significant gestures cannot or do not exist along the route or that the mobility of the camera is arbitrary. When Altman cuts from Barbara Jean and Kenny to Linnea, he picks up the thread of one of many "subplots," but he also clarifies Linnea's actions by association with Barbara Jean's despair.

The increasing prominence of the "promiscuous style" in *Nashville* is in itself provocative but specifically calls attention to the gradual dominance of women, both in this film and in Altman's subsequent work. Nashville the city is at least ostensibly controlled by its men, but *Nashville* the movie is made whole and compelling by its women. This is never more apparent than in the scene that follows Linnea and Tom's phone call in which these two meet in a club where Tom is singing.

Paradoxically, the promiscuous *character* in the "Exit" club is Tom, but the promiscuous camera illuminates the women present with such splendid insight that our image of Tom is literally over-shadowed. From the very beginning of this scene, the camera seems regendered; it is as if the camera were one of the many women gathered at this club to adore and seduce Tom, the nubile folk-rock hero. She, this female camera, is seated first at a crowded table with Opal, of BBC fame; Bill, of the trio; and Norman, the trio's chauf-feur. Shortly after Mary enters and sits down, Opal creates the occasion to announce, too loudly, that she has been to bed with Tom. So, too, as we know from an earlier scene, has Mary, despite the fact that she and Bill are a "couple." And so, too, more than likely, has Martha–L.A. Joan, who seats herself next to Tom just as Linnea enters the club.

The camera is now focused on Tom, but it maintains the women present in the periphery of its eye. Asked to sing, Tom abashedly recalls that he was or "is" part of a trio and suggests that Bill and Mary join him. The song the three sing articulates the pain they have inflicted on each other, which none of them has previously been able to address. As they sing lyrics like "Since you've gone, my heart is broken one more time," Mary turns blatantly to Tom, but Tom is looking elsewhere.

The camera pans from a relentless medium close-up to Mary, to Linnea, back to Mary, and then to Norman and Opal. Still placed within the club, we overhear Norman seducing Opal with an offer to give her the "real dope" on Nashville. Opal's demeaning put-down of Norman, "I make it a point never to gossip with the servants," serves both to affirm Opal's pretentious callousness and to set up the scene to which Altman now intercuts. We suddenly find ourselves disoriented again, located in another club of a wholly different demeanor. The context is a smoker for Hal Phillip Walker. It is a men-only occasion with the exception of Sueleen Gay, who is being lowered on an elevator stage to entertain the guests as the camera arrives on this location. We already know from Sueleen's earlier audition that she cannot sing, but her tasteless, loud green

Sueleen Gay (Gwen Welles) in *Nashville* sings "I Never Get Enough" at a political fund-raiser at which she is meant to perform a striptease, although she does not yet grasp this expectation. (*The Museum of Modern Art/Film Stills Archive, New York City*)

gown and her choice of song, "I Never Get Enough," only makes more awful her attempts to sound and look sexy. Despite the awkward set of relationships in the club where we left Tom, Bill, and Mary singing, we are glad when the film returns to them and Linnea because Sueleen is now out of our sight.

Back in the nightclub, Tom is about to sing a solo that he dedicates to "someone who might be here." The instant Tom speaks his dedication, the camera resumes its previous role and does what any woman in the crowd would do—it seeks out the object of Tom's affection. The difficulty the camera now faces is terribly funny and wonderfully sad. As we look first at Mary, then Opal, and then L.A. Joan, each woman's eyes for a moment acknowledge the dedication and take it as meant for her, but each woman in turn recognizes that

Tom's eyes are elsewhere. With that recognition, each of Tom's lovers turns her head to discover the true object of his desire, and finally, each, including the camera, locates Linnea at the back of the room, staring straight ahead, with no look of pride or conquest but an aura of taut composure. Each woman's illusion and then disillusion, each woman's acknowledgment of the truth is captured in the camera's slow sweep from one turning head to another. We are told a story in the changings of these faces and the movements of those heads, and it is a story that only moving pictures could tell. We might imagine from the still image of any one of these women's faces captured during this scene that she had suffered the loss of a love, or the loss of a fantasy of love, but the moving camera captures the transformation itself, and that, as Altman will again verify in the final sequence of the film, is what the magic of movies is about.

The magic of movies is also, however, about the camera's ability to disclose secrets, to capture spaces and actions that are more conventionally impenetrable or disguised. If we feel disquieted by our witnessing of these women's relevations, our anxiety at being voyeurs is relieved by our knowledge that while their nakedness is present to us, neither we nor anyone else is consciously present to them. We are also reminded by this sequence that Tom, a man, is and can be a sex object, but he, unlike women in comparable positions in and out of movies, has control. He is where he wants to be.

This is not the case in the private club where Sueleen has continued to perform, and Altman now returns us to this more overtly voyeuristic occasion. In the public club we could take pleasure and insight from being shown where to look; back at the smoker, where we discover the men demanding that Sueleen strip, we are reminded that our point of view as movie spectators is coincident with that of the men at the smoker who desire something arousing to look at. But Altman does not leave us in this position. Instead, much as he did in the Hot Lips shower sequence in *M*A*S*H*, Altman turns his camera on the audience of hooting, growling, and squawking men, men who throw their money and stomp their feet, demanding that Sueleen remove her clothes. Unwilling to acknowledge Sueleen's shame and vulnerability, these men appear obscene. In contrast,

Altman's camera focuses on the men at the political fund-raiser for Hal Phillip Walker as they ogle and laugh at Sueleen Gay who has come to the smoker to sing but has now reluctantly agreed to strip. The scene is from *Nashville. (The Museum of Modern Art/Film Stills Archive, New York City)*

when Sueleen finally does strip, persuaded to do so by a promise that she will be able to sing the next day with Barbara Jean, her removal of her clothes is made entirely unerotic by the awkwardness of her movements and the deliberate obstruction of our view of her body by the camera placement. We are shown the pain on Sueleen's face, and we see the moment she steps on her own dress as she removes it; we see her stoic gesture as she removes her underpants, and we see the slump in her thin shoulders. But what we do not see is equally relevant. Situated behind a pole and the piano, at a respectful distance from and behind Sueleen, the camera protects her from our gaze. We see her breasts from a side angle when she removes her bra, and we see her entirely naked from the rear, but what we see is de-eroticized by our intermittent witnessing of the vulgarity of the audience's behavior and by the expression on her face and her gestures of humiliation. Her nakedness is so blatantly demeaning and pitiful that the camera seems unable to follow her as she finally runs from the center of the room and the frame. We feel the obscenity of the occasion as an unmistakable act of violence.

The exposure of Sueleen's vulnerability juxtaposed to the conglomerate vulnerability of the women who desire Tom justifies the promiscuous camera of the final sequence of the film. We are defenseless because the parallel syntagmas refuse to allow us to complete one emotional response and replace it with another. Had Altman intended only to make the point that women in different contexts are treated by men as objects and that women often acquiesce to such treatment, he might have successfully edited these scenes sequentially. The accumulation of evidence would have sufficed. But, in addition, and perhaps more important, we learn from the experience of witnessing this sequence that we are able to care about more than one person at a time, to care deeply, and to care differently. There is no finite quantity of love or pain in the world of the film—or in us. Altman's *Nashville* extends our ability to feel, as he increases our agility at hearing and seeing. The better we are able to hear and see, the more he places in front of us; he challenges us to be better than we think we are, and he gives us the tools to accomplish that.

*   *   *   *

The broadest challenge and its difficult reward leap to greet us in the final sequence of the film. Tenacious to the end in his desire to surprise, Altman begins the sequence with the image of a Hal Phillip Walker ticker tape proclaiming the logo, "New Roots for the Nation." A familiar voice-over issuing from no apparent source is describing the Walker phenomenon. It is a few seconds before the camera draws back, revealing that we are watching Howard K. Smith on television and that the television set is situated outdoors on a wide expanse of grass, complete with picnickers and watermelon. The image of the TV set is made particularly absurd as the camera widens its focus to include a building that bears a remarkable resemblance to the Athenian Parthenon. Incongruity is further emphasized by Smith's serious contemplation of Hal Phillip Walker's question, "Does Christmas smell like oranges to you?" Yes, Smith responds, it does smell like oranges to him. So much for Howard K. Smith. He must live in Southern California.

The vaudeville joke completed, the conclusion to *Nashville* now announces its ritual self-conception. To the steady beat of drums, not unlike those heard at the very beginning of the film, but more deliberately funereal, we witness a parade of darkly colored limousines and police cars slowly moving in behind the Nashville "Parthenon." The slow pace and aura of caution, combined with information conveyed throughout the film, leaves little doubt that we are witnessing the preparations for the political rally at which Hal Phillip Walker will appear, boosted by the collection of entertainers we have come to know in the previous four days, including, and especially, Barbara Jean. The approach of these formal vehicles is accompanied by the one song in the film that is not associated with a particular figure. The song, "Wonder What This Year Will Bring?" in its ponderous rhythm and eerie lyrics embellishes our impression that we are witnessing a memory, not a new event. We now expect to see and hear Hal Phillip Walker, whose campaign truck and advance man have haunted *Nashville,* but the camera pulls away from Walker's limousine, allowing us only to hear what *may* be Walker's voice telling Triplette he wants to continue working on his speech. The figure of power remains invisible.

While Hal Phillip Walker remains hidden, the setting of his stage accelerates. This is no neutral site for a campaign rally. As Del Reese tells Triplette, the building that stands as stage and backdrop for the rally is not only called the "Parthenon" but was deliberately erected as an imitation of the Parthenon. The Nashville community was so enamored with this edifice that they have maintained it permanently. Nashville, Del informs Triplette and us, has consequently seen dubbed the "Athens of the South." If the audience sees resemblances between this occasion and a Dionysian festival, with all of the congruence of politics and theater that such a tradition calls forth, it is not hallucinating.[17]

John Triplette (Michael Murphy) and Barnett (Allen Garfield) argue on the stage at the Parthenon in *Nashville* about Triplette's violation of their agreement that there would be no signs advertising the candidacy of Hal Phillip Walker on the platform where Barbara Jean, Barnett's wife, is to sing. (*The Museum of Modern Art/Film Stills Archive, New York City*)

Altman maintains firm control of the reins of his imagination and ours. He quickly deflates the allusion by focusing on a quarrel between Barnett, Barbara Jean's husband-manager, and Triplette over the "rules of the game." Barnett had agreed to Barbara Jean's appearance at the Parthenon on the condition that there would be no overt, public connection between Barbara Jean and Walker—no statements of her support, no signs or banners. Triplette has blatantly broken these rules by hanging an enormous banner with Walker's name and slogan, "New Roots for the Nation," directly upstage of where Barbara Jean is to perform, and Triplette is no longer in the stance of the seductive compromiser. He plays his political cards coldly. If Barbara Jean's announced appearance does not occur, after the humiliating debacle at the outdoor Opry, it will do more harm to her than to Walker. The Replacement party is ironically true to its name; political expediency smoothly and relentlessly substitutes for the moral force of upholding a covenant. (This is not, of course, a replacement for the ethics of American political parties outside the film, but for the avowed morality of the "Replacement party.")

This exchange would be trite if it were not for its public exposure. We assume such manipulation occurs behind closed doors, but here, not only the audience in the dark of the theater, but bystanders and reporters in front of the Parthenon are witness to Triplette's display of power. At this moment, and repeatedly throughout the final sequence of *Nashville,* Altman remarks the peculiar transparency of our recent political history by filming someone photographing each sordid gesture. To make present the unresolved distress we experience in relation to the assassinations, conspiracies, and corruptions of the sixties and seventies, it is necessary to remind us that we were persistently presented with pictures—still and moving—of what happened. Our memories of John Kennedy's assassination, of the Vietnam war, of the Watergate hearings, are inseparable from our recollections of seeing photographs, of watching televised projections of these events.

We are told by Walter Benjamin that "for the first time in world history, mechanical reproduction emancipates the work of art from its parasitical dependence on ritual."[18] The reverse is also true. Mechanical reproduction allows both the artificial imitation of ritual—as in the reconstruction of a Parthenon for a festival occasion—and the spontaneous eruption of spectacle. Watching films of those fated cars passing through the streets of Dallas had the aura of ritual in its first instance, and subsequent viewings have not altogether lost their ritual momentum.

In *Nashville* Altman unshrouds a myth and renders it into aesthetic form. *Nashville* makes the myths of our recent past knowable by asserting the pedestrian details of their context. Altman shows us the squabble between Triplette and Barnett, then immediately cuts away from the Parthenon to the cemetery where Mr. Green's wife is being buried. The cut is jarring because wide-screen, distance shots of the Parthenon and the green surrounding it have emphasized expanse, and the camera now shifts to a contained, conventional composition; the cut also frustrates our desire to arrive at whatever events will fulfill the presentiment established by the initial sounds, music, and visual images of the sequence. Yet the short scene at the cemetery is key to the final unfolding of the story and to the way we respond to the world before us. Mr. Green's grief is ordinary and profound; so is the anger he displays at his niece's ostentatious disrespect, at her failure to appear either at Mrs. Green's bedside or her grave site.

Hearing—and looking at—Mr. Green's anguish exacerbates our sense of our own helplessness as spectators. The difficulty we have in consoling another whose pain can be known but not shared is doubled by our absolute inability to affect the characters on screen. Even in theater, where we are also powerless before the tears of an onstage character, there always remains that strange hope that the desire expressed in our silence, our laughter, or our tears will arrest the hurt before us. In theater, we await and deny the moment where our applause will make Tinker Bell live; with film, such hope is wrong and foolish.[19] It is thus with relief that we watch Mr. Green propel himself out of the inertia of his own grief. He is able to act. His fury at his niece's absence from the funeral suddenly thrusts him away from the grave site and draws him and the camera back to the rally at the Parthenon.

In others of Robert Altman's films the hollow or obscure moments sometimes threaten our ability to sustain our belief in the importance of the world projected. In *Nashville*, the fragility of the feeble gestures of the cemetery scene seem only to make the grandeur of the film's conclusion more eloquent. A quick cut back to the Parthenon erases impatience and satisfies our greed for extravagant sounds and images. The perfect duo, Barbara Jean and Haven Hamilton, sing "One, I Love You" before a "capacity crowd" that includes everyone we have come to know in *Nashville*.

Our pleasure in the performance by Barbara Jean and Haven Hamilton is only partially a matter of their artistry. We also feel the delight of completion in the reunion of this pair who, although not lovers in a conventional sense, were clearly meant to be together. Because its moments of desperation and destruction are so stark, it is easy to forget that the structure of *Nashville* follows closely the pattern of classical comedy. Early in the film, in the airport sequence, the arrival of Barbara Jean provides the context for a vision of the community as a whole; the group is then fragmented and separated by the necessities and accidents of their own lives. In the end, Barbara Jean, who has been separated from the rest, is returned to her "natural" place and role center stage at the side of her artistic equal, Haven Hamilton. Nor have we wholly relinquished our adulation of the stars. The promiscuous camera, the cast of twenty-five "main" characters, the humorous appearances of Elliot Gould and Julie Christie (as Elliot Gould and Julie Christie) call into question the hypnotic power in which the stars of film generally hold us, but Altman has still tantalized us and the *Nashville* audience with the promise of Barbara Jean's magic. When, after the untainted completion of their duet, Haven turns the stage over to Barbara Jean, we greet her as a long awaited gift.

From the moment Barbara Jean takes the stage alone, we are at the mercy of the director and the camera. We are vulnerable because despite the dispersal of our attention, we have become increasingly attached to this woman before us, and the nature of our attachment is complicated. Always costumed in white, often with ribbons in her hair, Barbara Jean is frozen in the role of the virgin bride, a child about to become a woman. But unlike the virgin bride and despite the attempts of her husband, she is unable to wear a veil; her face and her personhood are always present and revealed. In vivid contrast to Hal Phillip Walker, Barbara Jean will not hide behind masks or symbols. And we know that her candor has taken its toll; we are as much attached to her fragility as we are to her power as a performer. As Triplette reminded her husband, Barbara Jean is now utterly dependent on the audience. This is obviously true in terms of her "career," but we also sense that Barbara Jean is personally dependent on her audience, that she needs its acknowledgment of her as a person and not just as a successful star.

Left alone on stage, Barbara Jean fills the frame and satisfies our eyes and ears, yet is strikingly unprotected by her power. Haven's exit from the frame accentuates her majesty and her helplessness. The song she sings, "My Idaho Home," at first seems nostalgic and sentimental, a stereotype of maudlin country music, but her obvious investment in the lyrics, the integrity in her voice as she sings "I still love Mom and Daddy best, my Idaho home," penetrates our cynicism. The lyrics of this, her last song, confirm what she has previously told us. Pressured into adulthood by stardom, she remains a child in woman's dress, longing for the comforts and small pleasures of her too-remote past. The camera zooms close up to that face, allowing us no distance between her longings and our caring.

Still, the camera has another story to tell, and, in the midst of Barbara Jean's song, it begins to do so. In a gesture that recalls Barbara Jean's earlier performance, the camera now switches its focus to the audience, and quickly singles out Kenny whose look of consternation is, at least, puzzling.

The camera lingers just long enough on Kenny to allow us to see him remove a key from around his neck and begin to open his music case. A shot of the American flag intercepts the return of the camera to another close-up of Barbara Jean. The image of the flag warns us that the link between Kenny and Barbara Jean is not coincidental. The red, white, and blue that has colored the surface of this film from its beginning is now returned to its customary cloth. The symbol that has gradually lost its power to thrill in the culture becomes ominous in this context; rippling in the breeze, the flag fills the frame and transforms the screen into a three-dimensional banner.

The film now becomes increasingly and unabashedly prophetic; the accelerated activity of the camera is no longer promiscuous but deliberate and efficient in its arrival at the right place at the right time. As Haven reenters the frame to present flowers to Barbara Jean, the camera zooms away from the Parthenon platform, giving us a distance shot of the triumphant pair of stars. A quick cut to Kenny reveals his possession of a gun; we automatically link his fixed stare to the next shot of the American flag. It is from a distance again that we hear sudden gunshots and witness Barbara Jean crumpling abruptly to the stage. The sequence of shots just prior to and during the shooting cut borders on the fabric of the film while distinguishing the threads of which it is woven. Kenny's target is at once the woman who remains dedicated to her parents, the virgin bride who stands as a sacrificial victim to the power that remains invisible, and the nation that raises its banners high. (It is not for nothing that Hal Phillip Walker's platform includes a derisive attack on the national anthem.) We can distract ourselves forever piecing together the clues to Kenny's motivation; we can propose political, psychoanalytical and aesthetic interpretations of his action and intent. All analyses will be insufficient, however, not because the evidence is contradictory but because knowledge of what and why and how only turns us away from acknowledging the wound to Barbara Jean.

Altman recalls but does not repeat the mistakes of our history. He refuses to linger on Kenny and instead turns his camera to the world that is disrupted by Kenny's blow. Many of the reactions we witness are predictable: Opal asks, "What happened?"; Triplette, hurrying to escape, shoves his way through the black gospel singers and crosses paths with Del Reese, who is moving rapidly onstage to remove Linnea from the scene; the caravan of funereal limousines encasing Walker unhesitantly withdraws from the area. Yet there are heroes in this crisis. Haven Hamilton's first reaction is to throw himself over Barbara Jean to protect her, despite the fact that he, too, is wounded. That this is not an isolate or falsely heroic gesture is impressed upon us by Haven's subsequent actions. He dismisses the attempts of others to aid him and makes certain that Barbara Jean is removed. He then turns his attention to the chaotic crowd. Immediately recognizing the danger in a large, frightened gathering of people, he calls upon what he knows can transform a crowd into a community—singing. Since he is aware of his own wound, he thrusts the microphone into the hands of someone—anyone—on stage who can perform and commands that she sing. And she does. Feebly at first, and then with the command of a star, Albuquerque-Winifred, the "unknown" singer who arrived in Nashville in her husband's pick-up truck, belts out "It Don't Worry Me."

The oddly static chaos projected on the screen after the shooting of Barbara Jean is not new to us. We have known that sensation at least since the sixties. In another context, without *all* of this context,

Haven Hamilton's outburst, "This isn't Dallas, it's Nashville," would be chauvinistic and didactic. It is neither. Throughout the film, the legend of Kennedy has been evoked *as* a mythology repeatedly: Haven's exclamation is only an epitaph. Haven's shock and incredulity call forth our own belief and disbelief; through his momentary selflessness, limited as it is, we are led to question how and where we look for virtue and evil, for the images of power and for the potency of imaging.

Throughout *Nashville*, the audience has been repulsed by Haven's mannerisms and arrogance. In the absence of this arrogance in his last moment on stage and on camera, we are asked to reconsider our judgment. We are also asked to participate in the birthing of a new star, the woman to whom Haven passes his microphone and Barbara Jean's mantle at the end of *Nashville*. None of the women who sought to imitate Barbara Jean will replace her; in her stead appears Albuquerque about whom all we know is that her commitment to making it as a singer has led her to leave her husband and to try to be in the right place at the right time. Her perseverance has been repaid, and it now allows her to transcend herself and the moment. Fragments of the song she hesitantly begins to sing have been heard recurrently during the film; the lyrics of its refrain are pointed to this moment: "You may say that I ain't free / But it don't worry me."

There is something crazy in this final song of *Nashville*. What we hear in the lyrics of "It Don't Worry Me" is not the delirium of the sixties that has been remembered throughout the film and re-imaged in the political rally and the sacrificial ritual of the assassination of Barbara Jean. *Nashville*'s last song, which we have already heard in fragments as the song that everyone in town is singing, expresses the particular craziness of the seventies. It is a response to violence and confusion, but a response characterized by a public contract of inertia. The refrain of the song, "You may say that I ain't free / But it don't worry me," is at worst a suggestion that the desire for freedom is not an appropriate motivation and at best the claim that freedom does not lie in the empirical contingencies of everyday life. What we have at the site of this reconstructed Parthenon is the mimetic, modern expression of the Dionysian state. We may be perplexed by the lethargy that so quickly after the slaying of Barbara Jean permeates the crowd, but this may be the paralysis of what Nietzsche taught us to call nausea rather than the inactivity of indifference. Perhaps it is knowledge, not stupidity, that kills action at the end of *Nashville.* As Nietzsche warned in *The Birth of Tragedy:*

> For the rapture of the Dionysian state with its annihilation of the ordinary bounds and limits of existence contains, while it lasts, a *lethargic* element in which all personal experiences of the past become immersed. This chasm of oblivion separates the worlds of everyday reality and of Dionysian reality. . . . [A]ction requires the veils of illusion: . . . true knowledge . . . outweighs any motive for action.[20]

In this context, other lyrics in this final song are less foolish—and less dismissable: "Economy's depressed, not me / My spirit's high as it can be. . . . Cause in my empire life is sweet / Just ask any fool you meet / And life may be a one-way street," (as we witnessed at the beginning of the film), but "It don't worry me."[21] If life is a one-way street, there is nothing the crowd in *Nashville* can do to change it; precisely the knowledge gained in the sixties makes action for the crowd of the seventies impossible. For as Nietzsche also reminds us, "they feel it to be ridiculous or humiliating that they should be asked to set right a world that is out of joint."[22] It is that crowd who unite only and finally through this song that should worry *us.* And if Albuquerque is thus for the moment more Bacchante than she is Winifred, she is also no more or less than leader of this chorus.

As Albuquerque's voice loses its falter and begins to belt its way through the audience, Altman's camera pans the crowd. Inscrutable faces transform only as they begin to sing with their leader. Albuquerque does not lead the crowd to escape either the event or the scene; she transports those before her while leaving their bodies in place and intact.

A friend of mine, a true and old-fashioned film buff, claims that this is why he goes to movies—not to escape but to be transported.[23] The conclusion of *Nashville* makes eloquent the importance of this distinction. Even as the camera withdraws from the scene, we are held transfixed by what it reveals, by how it reveals, and by the song that accompanies its movement. Pink flashes of a balloon rising to the sky recall the frivolity with which the day and the film began. A shot of Sueleen Gay, frozen forever against a pillar of the Parthenon, tells more than we wish to know of what she now knows and reminds us—still photographs force us to create our own narratives. When the camera turns upwards to fill the screen with a sky so devoid of color and motion that we are uncertain if we are in fact seeing sky or only the silver screen itself, we resist the emptiness and search for the shadow of a cloud to define that space.

We do not escape to or from *Nashville*. As Altman's last shot suggests, we are carried over the Parthenon and carried through a period of our history by a film that envisions a city as a world and hears the music not of the spheres but of our clanking souls. Long after the final credits are completed, when we must accept with certainty that no more images will appear on the screen, Albuquerque's voice pursues us out of the theater. It takes an effort to refrain from singing—"It Don't Worry Me."

CHAPTER 4

THE UNCONQUERED:
THE FEMINIZATION
OF ALTMAN'S FILMS

As the credits begin to roll in the opening moments of *McCabe and Mrs. Miller*, we hear the chilling sound of a relentless wind, and behind the graphics, the camera pans a blue, cold, rocky terrain. The perfectly formed head of a white horse enters the frame. On the sound track, the familiar voice of Leonard Cohen drones, "I told you when I came I was a stranger," introducing us to McCabe (Warren Beatty), who enters the frame and the film on the back of the horse whose head we first saw. McCabe pauses, dismounts, removes the heavy furs that encase his body, and mumbles something incomprehensible. Suited in notably eastern apparel, he tips his hat, and near him we note the brilliant glow of a fire that blares despite the icy challenge of the wind. From McCabe's point of view, we take in a crudely lettered sign that reads "Hotel" and an equally crude footbridge that lies between the man and the dwelling beneath the sign. Cohen's ballad about a gambling stranger continues:

> For you've seen that man before. . . .
> And he wants to trade the game he plays for shelter . . .
> Like he was giving up the holy game of poker.[1]

Casually, yet disruptively, the point of view shifts. We are now looking out at this "stranger" through a window from the interior of a space in which faces and furnishings are barely discernible as they mingle with each other and pass through the brown and ochre haze that seems to envelop them. From this vantage, we witness the arrival of McCabe in a place metonymically called Presbyterian Church—a hole in a mountain about to give birth to a town. While we watch him dismount from his horse, leave behind the forest from which he has appeared and cross the planked bridge, Cohen's ballad repeats its refrain, "He was just some Joseph looking for a manger."

We are told almost everything we need to know about the film in these first few seconds. The classic landscape and carefully framed arrival of the long stranger on a white horse establish the Western genre. The contrasts of ice and fire, of crystal-clear single figure and the murky images of the interior group of men, of the vestments of the civilized East and the informal, ramshackle surfaces of the new West, of vast exterior space and claustrophobic interiors, all reaffirm the binary oppositions that are among the central conventions of the Western. We also learn from the opening footage that this Western is self-conscious about itself and its form; the church that so often visually emphasizes the Western town now *is* the town itself and the ballad that Cohen sings is reminiscent of the songs that accompany John Ford's *My Darling Clementine* and *She Wore a Yellow Ribbon*. But unlike the more traditional Western ballads in those films, Cohen's song calls attention to both the nature of the genre and our experience of it. The first line of the song emphasizes and names one of the primary characteristics of the Western—the hero's initial identity as a stranger—and the second line of the song presumes our acquaintance with the genre and implicitly urges us to compare this hero, McCabe, with others whose screen lives we have witnessed. During the brief moments in which we watch McCabe's approach on horseback to Presbyterian Church we also glimpse a church, a traditional symbol for the humane, eastern, and civilized forces in the frontier town; this church, however, like the church in *My Darling Clementine*, is unfinished. In both films, the image of the church in the process of construction reminds us that the settings are on the frontiers of American society.

There is a notable absence in the initial sequence of *McCabe and*

Mrs. Miller. No women appear in these opening shots. It is, of course, conventional to the Western genre that the presence of the hero and the ambiance of the male world of the town and plains be established prior to the introduction of female characters; traditionally, women are intruders in the West, whether they arrive by coach or train from the East or descend into a saloon from their unseen upstairs quarters. *McCabe and Mrs. Miller* is consistent with this tradition, and through this consistency sets up our anticipation of the eventual invasion of the frame—and Presbyterian Church—by women or at least one woman.

What is missing at this point in my account is the weight of the title of the film. We do, after all, know the names of the movies we see before we enter the theater; the title of a film is usually one of the first sources of knowledge of the film we have. (There are instances, of course, in which what we know first is the name of the director or a lead actor or actress, but the occasions on which we do not also know the name of the film before we see it are rare.) And although the specific strategies behind the titles of films vary considerably, the primary function of a film title is to attract an audience.[2]

The title *McCabe and Mrs. Miller* should attract us to this film, at the least because its denotative lucidity is countered by its connotative complexity. A brief deconstruction of the title suggests further that the connotations of the title do not replace the denotions, but both stand in a signifying relationship of difference to each other, thus creating what Roland Barthes calls a "second-order semiological system." The most literal, or first-order reading of the title, *McCabe and Mrs. Miller* tells me only that there is a person named McCabe, another married female person named Miller, and that these two persons are in some fashion connected to each other. However, as with Barthes's example of the Latin grammar exercise in which the phrase *quia ego nominar leo* ("because my name is lion") has a simple meaning but also signifies "the presence of a certain agreement of the predicate,"[3] this film title infers a number of readings that are immediately suggested by the particular combination of words. We might read the words in the title as meaning, "This is a film about McCabe; it is also about Mrs. Miller." But such a reading is unlikely, given our expectations of film and of

Westerns in particular. It makes more sense to understand the words of the title as signifying that this is a film about the relationship between a single person named McCabe and a married, female person named Mrs. Miller. In addition, there is significance in the absence of a title before the name McCabe and the presence of a title before the name Miller. Since in the United States it is far more common to refer to a man than to a woman by a last name alone, we are likely to infer that McCabe is a male. Our experience of movies will suggest that a title that contains a man's name, a woman's name, and the connective "and" will be a movie about a romantic or erotic relationship between these two, but in ordinary use of language in the United States, an association in which the woman was known as *Mrs.* Miller and the man addressed only by his last name would not signify intimacy or romance. Finally, a reading of the title may include a recollection of another contemporary Western, *Butch Cassidy and the Sundance Kid,* made just a few years earlier than *McCabe and Mrs. Miller.* If so, the title of Altman's film might signify partnership to the reader, but attention will then be called to the rarity of a partnership between a man and a woman.

I have made much of the meaning of the title, *McCabe and Mrs. Miller* both because I think that it is intended to signify much and because a careful reading of the title illuminates the process by which signification occurs in many of Altman's films. If the meanings of the title that I have remarked are read by the spectator, more than usual attention will be paid to the absence of Mrs. Miller in the first moments of the film. As with other self-referential gestures at the beginning of the film, the title redresses the convention of the absence of women from the original society of the Western. The imbalance and peculiar modes of naming in the title also provoke our desire to see Mrs. Miller and to see her in relationship to McCabe.

Our expectation of the imminent arrival of Mrs. Miller—whoever or whatever she may be—is adamantly frustrated for the first half hour of the film. For what seems an almost unendurably long time, McCabe plays cards, drinks, and attempts to negotiate a business deal with Sheehan (René Auberjonois), the owner of the saloon, and,

McCabe (Warren Beatty) returns to Presbyterian Church with three prostitutes to start a whorehouse in the tiny mining town in *McCabe and Mrs. Miller.* (*The Museum of Modern Art/Film Stills Archive, New York City*)

until McCabe's arrival, the big man in town. Especially in the context of the Western genre, this is a scene remarkably devoid of what we would normally call action; there is conflict—over a chair, over a card game—and there is tension generated by the very presence of this stranger McCabe, but the absence of light, of bright colors, and of sustained interaction among the men in the saloon suggests passivity within the world of Presbyterian Church and confuses our notions of how to relate to this world. While the camera works from inside the space of the saloon, it seems as unable as we are to find a focus for attention. The world that is being established is the primary society of Presbyterian Church, the society of men, but instead of the terse, epigrammatic talk and explosive actions customarily associated with the men of the West, we hear fragments of mundane conversation, and nothing of any apparent import occurs. This is the community of Presbyterian Church; these are men who work together, drink together, play cards together; but this is a community of men without fraternity. As Robert Kolker notes, we see no eye contact between any two of these men,[4] nor do we hear words spoken or witness gestures of affection or connection that would establish the interdependence of these men. Anyone of them could depart, and neither those within the scene nor we would be affected.

It is with the arrival of women in Presbyterian Church that more vibrant activity occurs and genuine contact among persons is first seen, but the women who first arrive do not include Mrs. Miller. The women who alter the ambiance of Presbyterian Church and who disturb the lassitude of the camera and the world it captures are three bedraggled people whom McCabe has brought to town to employ as whores. For a moment, the filmic presentation of these women seems to be both comic and a demeaning gesture. All the women are unkempt, their facial features and bodies are either jarringly angular or blurred by excessive fat, and they are led on pack horses like an ungainly load of supplies. If anything, these women present antierotic images; they are the antithesis of the glowing plastic prettiness that usually glues our eyes to the screen. Yet the camera and the town's men treat these women with chaotic and intense attention. The men immediately grab at the women, creating conflict among themselves and between them and the women. For these men, the women are objects to be purchased and used. The camera responds to the women as it usually responds to women; it zooms in on their faces, pulls away, takes in the reaction of McCabe and the men, and returns to the faces and bodies of the women. But in this context, the same camera gestures that so often objectify women on the screen as aesthetic objects here serve to make us acknowledge these women as people. The close-ups of the women's faces reveal masks, but because there is no facile beauty in these masks to distract us, we are confronted with our inability to know just what these women are thinking in this situation. These are not masks created by the actresses, the makeup artists, and the lighting designer; they are masks donned by the characters to protect some measure of their selves. In contrast, the movement of their bodies and the words of one of the women suggest discomfort. We are not allowed to see these women as simply and only whores whose feelings and ordinary needs are dismissable. When one of the women tells McCabe that she has to go to the potty and does not think she can hold it, the camera pays close attention to the woman and to McCabe.[5] He and the audience are not allowed to avoid the essential humanity of these women.

When Mrs. Miller (Julie Christie) does finally arrive in Presbyterian Church, another filmic gesture of affirmation and confrontation greets her. Altman sets up her arrival carefully. In a quick but complex sequence, McCabe is interrupted in his dismissal of the saloon-keeper Sheehan's overtures toward partnership by a violent encounter between one of the whores and a customer. From the visual and aural chaos that ensues, we infer that the man has terrified and humiliated the woman and that she has responded by stabbing her "client." The camera draws our attention to the woman's hysteria and then to McCabe's bewilderment and incompetence with this business he has brought to Presbyterian Church. With an eloquent irony, similar to the editorial wit that he would later exploit in *Nashville,* Altman now cuts to the smoke and squeal that precedes the steam engine bearing Mrs. Miller and Ida, a mail-order bride (Shelley Duvall). Like most Western heroines, Mrs. Miller makes her transit from the outside world to the film's town on a vehicle that reminds us that there is an outside world, but the engine that bears her and Ida is a whimsical distortion of the conventional train or stagecoach, and Mrs. Miller's own persona is an even greater alteration of the expected type. Her fair skin and hair and her fragile, graceful body fulfill some characteristics of the type of the Western lady, but there the resemblance stops. Her most immediately startling feature is her hair; in contrast to the prim bun we expect of this type, Mrs. Miller's hair is a puff of tangles and curls that appears never to have known the discipline of a brush. We recognize in looking at her that hair style is a potent signifier. The tightly drawn, carefully pinned blond hair of the female stars of Westerns has often been used to signify the cultured, mannered, Anglo-Saxon, repressed eroticism of the good, virginal woman in contrast to the dark, buoyant, unrestrained locks of the dance-hall girl (implicitly the whore), the loose woman who loses. But Mrs. Miller defies and combines the two types. The meaning we attach to her hair is clear. She looks like she has just arisen from bed and wants to assert just that part of her identity. (That this hair is a blatantly disturbing gesture to the audience will be remarked in *Nashville* when Julie Christie makes a brief appearance—as herself—with Mrs. Miller's hair.) Yet she is *Mrs.* Miller, and her every movement reveals confidence and control; there is nothing of the vulnerable, self-effacing dance-hall girl about her. Her voice confirms our confusion. She speaks in a wonderfully jarring Cockney accent that instantly cuts through stereotypical assumptions about class. In the genre of the Western, the signs of eastern origins, usually, automatically mean middle or upper class. But here is a working-class, married English woman who carries herself like a lady but looks like a whore. Her first words are as direct and as undermining of our assumptions as is her appearance: "You got anything to eat? I'm bloody starvin'," she demands.

From the first instant of her arrival to the last frame of the film, Mrs. Miller is in command of our attention and of the attention of all who come in contact with her. In itself, the fact that a female character, played by a star, is the main attraction of a film is not usual: as Stanley Cavell reminds us, "A woman has become the whole excuse and sole justification for the making and preserving of countless films; in many of Garbo's films, or Dietrich's, next to nothing may be memorable, or even tolerable, but these women themselves."[6] But while the presence of Mrs. Miller in some sense does justify the existence of *McCabe and Mrs. Miller*, the film generates attention to her through gestures that consistently defy our expectations of the treatment of women on film. The compelling face, the tensely erotic body, the rippled voice of Julie Christie are never enough. It is not the presence of a female star but what the character, Mrs. Miller, says and does that engages us. With Garbo or Dietrich, Monroe or Bacall, we could, with some accuracy, presume to know, even before the particular movie was projected, what these women wanted. Whatever the particular needs and desires of the characters they played, what these women wanted—and received—was the adoration of the men within the film and the men and women in the theater audience. Mrs. Miller explicitly refuses John McCabe's adoration—and ours. What she wants when he and we first encounter her is four eggs, stew, and strong tea, and what she wants next is for McCabe to become her financial partner in the establishment of a "proper sportin' house with high-class girls and clean linen." While we watch Mrs. Miller consume her eggs and conclude her business proposition, a violin off-screen ironically hums the opening bars of "Beautiful Dreamer"; despite every assumption we might bring to the film, there is no ambiguity in the reference of the song's title. McCabe, not Mrs. Miller, is the beautiful dreamer of this movie, and Mrs. Miller wishes neither to be the object nor the perpetrator of anyone's dreams.

Like the title of the film and the opening sequence, the series of shots that introduce us and McCabe to Mrs. Miller expose the world framed by this movie but also remark and unveil the myth-making capabilities of film itself and of this film in particular. In contrast to Godard or Bergman, Altman's reflections of and upon the film's process of signification do not interrupt the narrative but are embedded within it. The title, *McCabe and Mrs. Miller,* and the initial absence of the woman named in that title, the white horse and the lone male figure, the church, the terrain, the men in the saloon, and the identification of the women as whores, might in another film be simply symbols; one could argue that even in *McCabe and Mrs. Miller,* in the very first instant of our recognition of these signs, they maintain a symbolic status. But the context and arrangement of these words and images immediately empties them of their symbolic content; there is no longer the direct, nameable, repeatable relationship of signifier to meaning that we presume of the symbol. In place of that symbolic content is an over-abundant presence, which, as Barthes explains such activity, is "tamed, put at a distance, made almost transparent; it recedes a little, it becomes the accomplice of a concept which comes to it fully armed, . . ."[7] When images and words are thus transformed (Barthes would say deformed) a myth-making process is occurring. The function of that process in *McCabe and Mrs. Miller* and in most of Altman's films is at least what Barthes urges is true of all myth: "it points out and it notifies, it makes us understand something and it imposes it on us."[8]

The claim I want to make in this chapter is that Altman's films take an additional vital step. They cannot escape the filmic process of myth making, but rather than obscuring this process, which is the implicit task of most films, they call attention to it. By re-invoking signs, such as the American flag of *Nashville* (discussed in Chapter 3) in a context that calls attention to the myth function of these signs, Altman's films attempt to demythologize these images. Myth, as both Barthes and Nietzsche remind us, functions in such a way as to make its process of signification and the signs and their meanings it employs seem to us natural, inaccessible to questioning.[9] In contrast, Altman's films take signs that initially appear to be natural and unassailable and remark their fabrication. This is especially true in the context of an overtly established genre. The most coherent of Altman's films, *McCabe and Mrs. Miller* among them, also attempt what might be called a third-order semiological system; they disrobe the filmic signs of their myth concepts and allow the denuded signs to function anew within history and politics. Altman wants to give them back to us, as ours in our ordinary lives.

Once acknowledged as both partaking of and confronting myth, *McCabe and Mrs. Miller,* as well as most of Altman's films, become more accessible. Analogies between films and dreams are dangerous, essentially because we tend to forget that a film is not the dream of the spectator but of the director (and/or of the screenwriter, performers, and cinematographer); but Barthes's claim that the Freudian process of decoding a dream can be aptly applied to the decoding of myths is useful in approaching the signs and codes of these films. The manifest content of *McCabe and Mrs. Miller,* like the manifest content of a dream, tells us a story, yet we know after seeing the film that its most readily repeatable tale is not sufficient to our experience of the film. We need to recognize the latent content of the film's signs and codes, but we also must pay attention to what Barthes calls the "functional union" of latent and manifest material.

As in dream analysis, part of what we can discover in tracing over the path from manifest to latent content and back again to manifest signs is that images, sounds, and words that we overlooked in an initial recounting appear from the shadows of obscurity. This is especially true of Altman's films, both because his movies are extravagant in the quantity of signs they project and because Altman so often distorts or avoids the filmic conventions that we rely upon to sort out the trivial from the significant content. One of the resonant images in the opening sequence of *McCabe and Mrs. Miller,* that of the suspended footbridge, is so casually photographed that it is unlikely we will immediately grasp its mythic function in the film. More precisely, in its first appearance in the film, the bridge functions only in a first-order semiotic system.[10] The first function of the bridge in *McCabe and Mrs. Miller* is as symbol for connection, much as the word "and" functions in the film's title.

Shortly after the first sequence of *McCabe and Mrs. Miller,* again shooting from the inside of the saloon out through a window, the camera captures the town preacher crossing the bridge. At this point, the bridge becomes marked for us as the passageway into the community; its signification has been augmented, yet it remains a simple symbol. But in the middle of the film, the semiotic function of the bridge changes radically. It serves not only to link the outside world with that of Presbyterian Church but also to connote the tension between them. For while our attention and that of McCabe and Mrs. Miller have been focused on the construction of the town and the relationships among its men and women, forces from the outside world, from big business, have crossed the bridge, quietly penetrated Presbyterian Church, and asserted their power. These forces appear first in the characters of Eugene Sears (Michael Murphy) and Ernie Hollander (Anthony Holland) of the M. H. Harrison–Shaugnessy Mining Company. Exuding the arrogant sophistication of corporate America, Sears and Hollander offer to buy McCabe's business interests in Presbyterian Church. McCabe is unable to hear that this is an offer that will not accept "no" as an answer. He rejects their proposition and attempts to locate his position by repeating a riddle he had previously used with Sheehan, the saloon keeper: "If a frog had wings, he wouldn't bump his ass so much."

But whereas Sheehan was duly mystified by the riddle and thus overpowered by McCabe, Sears and Hollander appear only to be confirmed in their judgment that McCabe is a fool. The two businessmen leave town abruptly. Only later, after McCabe fails to renegotiate the deal in the nearby "big town" of Bearpaw and after the company's three henchmen—Butler, Breed, and the Kid—arrive in Presbyterian Church, does McCabe grasp that their departure does not signify his victory but theirs. It is McCabe who is the frog, and since this is a movie and not an animated cartoon, he will continue to bump his ass.

With the threat of harm from the mining company's gunmen looming over McCabe, the movie appears to be well on its way toward a conventional Western showdown between the bad guys and the good guy when our attention is distracted by a young man, known only as the "cowboy" (Keith Carradine), who is reluctantly taking his leave from the group of women employed as prostitutes. The cowboy has resided with the women for a prolonged period of rest and recuperation. When, early in the film, we first glimpsed him, he was an archetypally gawky, gangly, adolescent whose virginity was emblazoned on his façade as undeniably as Hester Prynne's adultery was embroidered on her chest. Brief shots of the cowboy with the prostitutes have previously suggested that he was thoroughly enjoying passage into adulthood; as he kisses each of the women good-bye, his postures and demeanor reveal a transformation into graceful manhood.

As if to allow the cowboy a moment of privacy in his leave taking, the camera cuts to another adolescent, the Kid, who is standing on the town side of the bridge, attempting to shoot and sink a container of syrup in the water. The youngest of the three men who have been hired to kill McCabe, the Kid is a defensive punk; in contrast to the Cowboy, the Kid attempts to demonstrate his virility to the town men by an ostentatious—and unsuccessful—display of his skill with a gun. After repeatedly failing to hit the container, the Kid declares, "I wasn't tryin' to hit it. Trick's not to hit it but to make it float." It is embarrassing even to laugh at the Kid's defense of his impotence. He might just as well be saying, "The trick is not to have an erection but to keep your penis limp."

At this point, the cowboy enters the frame, and begins to make his exit from the town over the bridge. We watch the cowboy almost complete his crossing, turning and walking backwards to wave and catch a last glimpse of the little world that has brought

The "Kid," one of the gunmen hired by the mining company to kill McCabe, attempts (and fails) to demonstrate his skill with a gun, while one of his partners looks on. The shot occurs in *McCabe and Mrs. Miller* just before the "Kid" mounts the bridge (indicated by a rope in the foreground) and deliberately kills the naive young cowboy. (*The Museum of Modern Art/Film Stills Archive, New York City*)

him strength and pleasure. Suddenly the Kid starts taunting the cowboy, commanding the latter to take off his boots and show him the socks that the cowboy has remarked were worn out during this stay at the whorehouse. As the camera focuses on the cowboy, whose own eyes naturally descend to his boots, the vulnerability of his position is evoked for the spectator by the camera's visual attention to the bridge. Although he appears more abashed than threatened by the Kid's command, the image before us contains sufficient information to arouse distress. The bridge on which he is caught is an ominously weak structure, a set of loose narrow planks precariously suspended over rushing water. And the Kid is not about to relent. He begins to move across the bridge, toward the cowboy, quickly escalating his demands, "What are you wearin' that gun for? Well, let me see it?"

The compression of visual space, created repeatedly in the film by use of a telephoto lens and the Panavision screen, is here aptly exploited to emphasize the tightness of the situation.[11] Like the men on the riverbank who appear to be immobile as they witness this confrontation, the camera seems paralyzed by the encounter unfolding before it. The images subsequently projected are at once as vivid and as implausible as the fragments of a poorly remembered dream: the cowboy naively reaches for his gun to show it to the Kid; the Kid immediately draws his gun and, from a distance of just a few feet, shoots the cowboy, whose body appears to fall in slow motion toward the water below. From the location on the bridge that the cowboy has now vacated, the camera watches the Kid's back recede from its eye; then, slowly and agonizingly turns its gaze to the waters into which the cowboy is gradually sinking. This last shot is relentless in its focus and duration; the waters suck the body under until the cowboy wholly disappears from our vision. The absence of the image of the cowboy is inseparable from his death.

Throughout this sequence, the manifest signification of the bridge as link or connector has been gradually removed from the signifier. Traditionally a sign of hope, transcendence, of the ability of human beings to make connections, to overcome the obstacles of nature, the bridge now becomes an ominous sign of vulnerability and disassociation; we will not be able to see it again in the context of this film without a sensation of fear or suspicion. And our readings of previous glimpses of the bridge must now be rethought. It is not that the bridge has become a different kind of symbol. It is no longer a symbol, yet history as it has occurred within the film has endowed the bridge with conceptual value. This conceptual resonance is no longer limited, specific, or confined; in this intermediate stage, the bridge functions as a myth sign; but it is almost instantly a weak myth because we are witnesses to its creation and because it quickly becomes questionable. An analogous process has simultaneously occurred in the deconstruction of the gun as a filmic sign.

By enclosing the Kid and his gun in the same tight space as the cowboy and his present but concealed penis, the gun relinquishes its power as a phallic symbol. The differences between a gun and a penis become transparent, as do the temptations of substituting one for the other or confusing them. What remains here is the knowledge of a gun as an instrument of death and separation. Barthes's assertions on such knowledge are illuminating: "In actual fact, the knowledge contained in a mythical concept is confused, made of yielding, shapeless association. One must firmly stress this open character of the concept; it is not at all an abstract, purified essence; it is a formless, unstable, nebulous condensation, whose unity and coherence are above all due to its function."[12] It is only in transition that the bridge and the gun exist as such signs in *McCabe and Mrs. Miller;* each is quickly reinstituted as a conveyor of meaning.

Both the process by which Altman transforms the signification of the bridge and the gun and the concepts to which each now points are central to our experience of *McCabe and Mrs. Miller.* The reorientation accomplished by Altman's appropriation of the bridge and the gun is contiguous with and analogous to Altman's assault in this film on a much more intense, more irresistible symbol: the image of woman in film. In order to accomplish the goal of this assault, that is, in order to project an image of woman or women that is disturbing, open, and unstable, Altman empties this image of its traditional symbolic meanings, much as he works and reworks the image of the bridge. But the bridge and the gun as reactivated signs are also part of the process of transformation of the signification of women on film. The various movements in the film on and over the bridge gradually arouse our distrust of the stability or possibility of relationships that we might otherwise assume to be natural or easily fabricated. The minister whom we first see crossing the bridge might typically be understood as the bearer of charity and organizer of community in Presbyterian Church; we come to know by the end of the film that he serves not to link but to separate. The gun that we might expect to reestablish male potency in this world becomes for both us and Mrs. Miller simply a threat to human life; its continued presence in the film leads us and Mrs. Miller to avoid investment in relationships with those who associate with a gun.

John McCabe and Constance Miller, who, within the conventions of most films and certainly most Westerns, would seem destined to mutual dependency and the permanent ties of love, are more isolated, one from the other, at the end of the film than they were when we first saw them meet.

By filmic tradition, the "hero" of *McCabe and Mrs. Miller,* John McCabe, should forge a union with the "heroine," Constance Miller, that transcends the turbulent rush of life in the town that they both inhabit and that defeats the forces of evil, here represented by the mining company. Should this union be prevented or broken, it would be because the male hero had "things he had to do" that were deemed by the hero to be of a higher value than the activity of loving a woman; such things in the conventional Western would be a stronger sign of virility than making love to a woman. But the story of McCabe and Mrs. Miller tells us not of a union of two souls but of a tenuous partnership between two people, two "citizens" of Presbyterian Church, and the precariousness and final severance of this partnership has everything to do with Constance Miller's refusals to forge the expected romantic bond and little to do with McCabe's ostensibly heroic attempt to do the right thing. We may regret the failure of connection between these two, but it is precisely that failure that allows Mrs. Miller to survive and that frees the image of woman in the film from the usual servility. Neither Mrs. Miller's life nor her pleasure are dependent on her relationship to a particular man; although she repeatedly tries to tell him this, McCabe never fully understands what this means. In contrast to gender stereotypes, Mrs. Miller is also a pragmatist who recognizes the inalterable power of the mining company. It is McCabe who is the naive dreamer, as we saw and heard earlier in the film. It takes the entire film to impose the possible recognition on the audience that the failure of a relationship is also the achievement of the liberation of the image of woman—and of man—from the various myths of women and men.

As is true in many of his films, and most successfully so in *Nashville,* Altman's narrative structure conjoins with the aural and visual content of the frame to undermine the anticipated story and call into question assumed understandings. The scene between the cowboy and the Kid that is set on the footbridge structurally "bridges" two syntagmas that each reveal McCabe and Constance Miller in her room. Each of these syntagmas illuminates the increasingly caring but tenuous relationship between McCabe and Mrs. Miller. In the first sequence, McCabe relates to Constance the advice he has been given by lawyer Clement Samuels, whose aid he sought to fight the mining company. As he quotes Samuels back to Constance, it is clear that he has embraced Samuels's romantic vision that "Until people start dying for freedom, they ain't gonna be free." But Constance is not interested at this point in the principle of freedom. For the first time, she reveals some genuine concern for McCabe: "They'll get you, McCabe, and they'll do something awful to you." McCabe responds to her warning with gentle delight, hearing only in her words that she does care for him. But the moment he manfully tells her, "Don't worry, little lady," she retreats from the intimacy and declares that all that concerns her is retrieving the $1500 she has invested in their mutual business.

In her withdrawal from McCabe, Mrs. Miller attempts to disguise her distress; less self-interested than McCabe, the camera penetrates Mrs. Miller's display of cold anger and allows us to see and hear the uncontrollable distress in her body and voice. In its continuing fidelity to Mrs. Miller's integrity and dignity, the camera now immediately cuts away, retreating from its momentary intimacy as she retreated from her moment of vulnerability to McCabe. As it exits to the outside world, it discovers the cowboy at the beginning of his farewell scene.

In terms of conventional filmic narrative structure, this cut is inexplicable and initially frustrating. Neither parallelism nor consecutiveness clearly link the syntagma in Mrs. Miller's room with that on and around the bridge. There is no causal connection between the two scenes, nor is there information or reason to know whether the scenes occur consecutively or simultaneously. Yet the juxtaposition of these two syntagmas and the addition of the subsequent scene that returns us to McCabe and Mrs. Miller, is strategically loaded and efficient. The bridge sequence serves first to assault the credibility of McCabe's epigrammatic quote from Samuels, "Until people start dying from freedom, they ain't gonna be free." Nothing in the murder of the cowboy substantiates such a romantic vision, and everything in his death suggests that freedom has nothing to do with dying. Greed and power destroy the cowboy and, we can infer, will similarly defeat McCabe. Of equal import to our experience of this film, the bridge sequence stands between the two most potentially intimate interactions of John McCabe and Mrs. Miller. Without the intervention of the bridge sequence, the relationship between McCabe and Mrs. Miller would be sustained before us, and even if the content of such a sequence revealed distance and disjuncture between the two, the fact of their continuing presence, together, before us, would challenge our acceptance of Mrs. Miller's resolute solitude. With the interjection of this scene, our experience of their relationship is as fragmented as is their experience of the relationship.

The bridge sequence thus functions to separate and refute, to diminish our investment in the erotic and romantic relationship between McCabe and Mrs. Miller, not simply by distracting us from that relationship but by creating a structural barrier between the moments of their intimacy. Here, as in similar syntactical instances in *M*A*S*H, Brewster McCloud,* and *Nashville,* a narrative structure that initially confuses our impression of a coherent story actually clarifies a complex thematic pattern. We are disconcerted because neither chronology nor the necessity of descriptive information motivate the sequence of syntagmas, yet as *McCabe and Mrs. Miller* progresses, connections of meaning manifest themselves repeatedly. The difficulty for the viewer of Altman's films arises in part because understanding is provoked by accumulation and the gradual disclosure of a pattern, not by any single shot or juxtaposition of shots. From shot to shot, what we perceive in these films is often not linkage, but exactly the kind of collision that Sergei Eisenstein extolled as the primary source of power in film. Eisenstein's image for this process corresponds remarkably well to my experience of *McCabe and Mrs. Miller:*

> If montage is to be compared with something, then a phalanx of montage pieces, of shots, should be compared to the series of explosions of an internal combustion engine, driving forward its automobile or tractor; for similarly, the dynamics of montage serve as impulses driving forward the total film.[13]

Such explosions occur, both within shots and between them, with increasing rapidity as *McCabe and Mrs. Miller* races to its conclusion. When we return to Mrs. Miller's room, after the cowboy is shot on the bridge, what we see collides repeatedly with what we hear; John McCabe's naiveté collides with Constance Miller's knowledge; and our desires as spectators are determinedly set in conflict. This is the last scene that we witness between McCabe and Mrs. Miller. Early in the scene McCabe tells Mrs. Miller, "You're the best looking woman I ever saw and I ain't never tried to do nothin' but put a smile on it. I guess I haven't been this close to any one before." We know, however, that McCabe's efforts to put a smile on Mrs. Miller's face are irrelevant if not futile. She achieves a smile from the opium she smokes, not from McCabe's gestures of desire or affection. McCabe weeps quietly, and Mrs. Miller urges him under the covers and cradles him; the intimacy McCabe believes he has achieved is countered by her obviously maternal role and by the Cohen song that begins to drone over the sound track, "I'm just a station on your way, I know I'm not your lover." McCabe does not, in fact, know this, nor does he know as he sleeps that Mrs. Miller has quietly crept out of bed, onto her balcony, and down the stairs through the snow. McCabe sleeps, content in his assumption of Mrs. Miller's companionship; we know the opposite is true as we watch her separate herself from him. To confirm this dissonance, the final shot of the scene emphasizes the juxtaposition of the cold white snow falling rapidly outside with the warm red light that still glows from the interior of Mrs. Miller's house.

When McCabe awakens to the grey light of an early morning blizzard, he collides instantly with the vision he half dreamt and the reality of the world before him. His utter solitude and total separation from Mrs. Miller become undeniable to him and to us in the series of shots that now press the film to its end. The camera focuses for a moment, as McCabe emerges from Mrs. Miller's room, on the red girders of the bridge against the snow. The visual design of crossed bars and the contrasts of color evoke a conflict and tension parallel to that among the characters; the design of the setting reflects the relentless opposition within the human society.

This single shot explodes into a series of contrasting images, as the world within the film and the structure of the film itself now divide before us. In the church, McCabe seeks knowledge of and refuge from his gunslinging pursuers; instead, he finds a hostile preacher who moralistically takes McCabe's gun and commands him back into the snow. But McCabe's gun is an even more potent source of destruction in the minister's hands. Butler, the head gunman, enters the church after McCabe's exit, sees only the gun, shoots the preacher behind the gun, and thus initiates a fire in the church. The minister is ironically consumed by the blazes of his own misplaced passion, and the film returns its attention to the safer, colder world outside.

Altman exploits parallel editing in this final sequence with a grace and understanding that reveal the vast, authentic potential of this traditional device. Most parallel editing belies the geometric construction; two or more intercut lines of action in film are usually temporarily separated only to intensify our interest in their eventual connection. In *McCabe and Mrs. Miller,* however, three lines of parallel action are intercut, only two ever meet, and those that do meet collide within the frame. Reminding us once more that this film has its roots in the Western, *McCabe and Mrs. Miller* appears now to be seeking its resolution in the conventional gunfight. After the exodus from the church, the camera cuts between McCabe and glimpses of the gunslingers who seek to kill him. Altman employs a number of point-of-view shots in these sequences, not so much to reveal what McCabe is thinking as to replicate for us McCabe's dislocation in the world before him; the camera quickly moves, and cuts are made from buildings to barriers to fences—places where "they" might be. The effect is to disorient us; to see the world from McCabe's point of view at this moment without being of that world, as McCabe is, is to make us less sure of where we are than he is.

Our focus is even more disrupted, however, by the third line of action projected. While the customary battle between the hero and villains is being waged in the rapidly falling snow and a few desolate interiors, in town and around the church, the struggle has commenced to save the church from the fire started by Butler and the preacher. In this final episode, Altman manages to consume two of

The town of Presbyterian Church after the slaying of one its citizens. The scene is from *McCabe and Mrs. Miller*. (*The Museum of Modern Art/Film Stills Archives, New York City*)

the most evocative American Westerns ever made—John Ford's *My Darling Clementine* and Fred Zinneman's *High Noon*. The allusions to these films are not gratuitous. The church fire and the necessary (although not obviously consequent) desertion of McCabe by the community that rallies to put out the fire serve to rectify the incomplete significations of church and community in the two earlier Westerns. In *My Darling Clementine*, the half-finished church needed only to stand there on the edge of town to assure the arrival of civilization; in *McCabe and Mrs. Miller*, the church is a hollow, meaningless structure until the community acknowledges it with its attempts to put out the fire. In *High Noon*, as Robert Warshow argued, "The technical problem was to make it necessary for the marshall to face his enemies alone; to explain *why* the other townspeople are not at his side is to raise a question which does not exist in the proper frame of the Western movie, where the hero is 'naturally' alone and it is only necessary to contrive the physical absence of those who might be his allies, if any contrivance is needed."[14] But in *McCabe and Mrs. Miller,* the solitude of McCabe is not natural or satisfying but a fabrication of the society and the game imposed on the man. It is not the internal necessity of the character or the myth that makes McCabe fight the gunslingers alone. Altman avoids the inappropriate question and mythologizing of McCabe by presenting a perfectly reasonable explanation for why the townspeople are not at McCabe's side; they are at the fire. Whether they would be with McCabe had there not been a fire is part of, not beside, the point; the fire is, after all, initiated within the pursuit of McCabe.

The church fire enhances the collisions of images and articulates the conflicts of interest within the film. Silence penetrated only by McCabe's labored breathing surrounds McCabe and the gunslingers; the carnival sounds of the ancient fire engine and the noisy shouts of the townspeople embrace the fire at the church. The community assaults the hot red fire, while McCabe and Butler stalk each other in the cold white snow. McCabe and each of the gunmen are repeatedly discovered in empty spaces with little to fill the frame; shots of the community rushing to water down the fire stuff the frame with detail. McCabe and the gunslingers move slowly or hold still to protect themselves; to protect their church, the community must move madly about. The two worlds—of isolated individuals and of people gathered in society, of murder and of salvation—exist in the same space but never connect one to the other. The productive collision of these opposing images must occur in our heads if it is to occur at all.

Poignantly, and unquestionably, the worlds of McCabe and Mrs. Miller will remain distinct, too, at the end of the film. Severely wounded after shooting all three of his pursuers, McCabe pushes his body through the snow toward town and stops a few feet short of shelter. In his death, McCabe finally becomes a filmic convention: the man freezes in the snow and his image becomes a still photograph, a study in black against white. If film seduces us, in part because its mobile images suggest eternal movement and thus eternal life, the still photograph should equally trouble us in its ability to stop, to freeze, the very movement that signifies life. That the camera arrives at an arrest exactly when McCabe can no longer move might be seen as a potent conspiracy of ontology and aesthetics to demystify both death and the Western hero.

If there is such a conspiracy in *McCabe and Mrs. Miller,* it works equally well to threaten our understanding of the role of woman in the Western and in American society. From the motionless shot of McCabe, frozen in the snow embraced only by the howling wind that recalls the film's first moments, we are taken to Mrs. Miller, half reclined, lost in a stoned dream; the camera seeks the answer we want in Mrs. Miller. Finding none, no matter how closely it observes Mrs. Miller's face, the camera returns as if in anger to an image of McCabe's head in the snow. Only his blood relieves the starkness of the black and white field. McCabe can yield no more understanding, and so we move back to Mrs. Miller, whose eyes are fixated on a small pottery jar. The camera zooms closer and closer until it has achieved an extreme close-up on one of Mrs. Miller's eyes; finding nothing it can grasp there, the camera changes perspective, and the film ends with a point-of-view shot of the slowly turning jar. Both the extreme close-up and the point-of-view shot are self-consciously unsuccessful; they tell us nothing we did not know before of who Mrs. Miller is, of what she is thinking at this moment, or of why she is where she is. We can try to interpret the symbolic meaning of the turning jar, but all that we are, in fact, given by this last shot is an abstract maze of lovely mobile color.

In *McCabe and Mrs. Miller,* as in *Nashville, That Cold Day in the Park, Images, 3 Women, Come Back to the 5 and Dime, Jimmy Dean, Jimmy Dean,* and *Fool for Love,* the final images are not so much symbols—they do not resolve into symbols—as they are reminders of the pregnancy of the minutiae of everyday life. What we see at the end of *McCabe and Mrs. Miller* is a woman who endures. This is not a simple or facile consolation, nor is it unimportant. For none of the women who end these films, and certainly not for Mrs. Miller, is endurance mere survival, nor has the daily struggle to continue been easy. We do not know the precise cost to Mrs. Miller's psyche of the battles she has won; we only know from the external indications of her opium smoking that there has been a price, that pleasure for her does not come easily from the world but must be induced by a drug. Altman's film does not say that this is as it should be, nor, importantly, does he demean her by the exhibition of her drug habit. We have every reason to respect Mrs. Miller at the end of the film: she has treated well the women she employs, she has made a successful enterprise out of a disorganized business, and she has given McCabe what she could, including warnings against his self-destructive romanticism. And she refused to be a martyr to a hopeless cause in which she had no way of intervening.

This is not to say that we are not or should not be perplexed by our relationship to Mrs. Miller at the end of the film. Her business is whoring, and the film makes undeniably clear that she partakes fully in that business. The film does not, however, allow us to judge her as a person for that whoring, nor does it indulge our fantasies of proximity to Julie Christie, the star. We see McCabe undressed, not Mrs. Miller; the camera caresses his body, not hers. Her behavior reveals neither pleasure nor dismay at her work. In other films, and not only in films, the spectator can dismiss the prostitute either from pity or dismay. Even in a challenging film like *Klute*, Jane Fonda as the whore can be finally ignored because she is deeply neurotic and because she hates what she does. Fonda's whore is a "female grotesque" in the terms of M. C. Kolbenschlag's tempting argument that the female characters of many contemporary movies are "freaks."[15] But despite her unruly hair, Mrs. Miller is not a freak. We have no evidence that Mrs. Miller turns to prostitution because of obsessive, neurotic needs, and in the absence of such evidence, it is we who err in condemning her or dismissing her for her occupation. In Presbyterian Church, the only roles available to women are those of wife or whore; we see when Ida, the mail-order bride, loses her husband early in the film that the role of wife is unstable and not necessarily less demeaning than that of whore. If blame is to be placed, it is on a society in which these are the only two roles open to women. To say that Mrs. Miller did not have to come to Presbyterian Church is a foolish excuse for false consciousness; neither McCabe nor the other men in town had to come either in an ordinary historical sense, but we accept their presence as part of the mythological framework of the film, and we must do the same with Mrs. Miller and her colleagues.

Altman's troubling success in *McCabe and Mrs. Miller* is that he has allowed the women in this film, and especially Mrs. Miller, to be characters. They are not stars or titillating objects of our visual lust; they are complicated, opaque human beings whose lives can only be known through their demonstrations of the roles they play in society. We expect nothing more or less of male characters in films; even when their physical grace is in itself appealing, the men whom we adore in movies sustain our attraction to them by their constructive manipulations of the societies in which they dwell. In turn, the relationship of the camera to men on the screen is usually determined by the relationship of the *character* to others and to the place he inhabits, whereas with women, the relationship to the camera is usually one of the actress's and the camera's mutual flirtation.

Even in Altman's early films, this usual relationship of camera to actress is reconsidered and eventually violated. In *M*A*S*H*, Hot Lips is in a customary object-voyeur relationship with both the men at the camp and the camera until the theatrical scene in which the men blatantly become voyeurs while she is totally disrobed before us; once that relationship has been named and exploited, she is treated as a character, like any other person on the scene. In *California Split* only the verbal evidence and the "date" with Helen, the female impersonator, indicate that the two women, Barbara and Susan, are call girls; the camera overtly refuses its opportunity to shoot from a lascivious angle or linger on the particularly female aspects of the female body. (The one scene in which the camera does begin to focus on the woman's body in a conventional shot is the pre-love-making scene between Susan and Bill that is interrupted and undermined by Barbara's entrance.) The framing, timing, and angles of shots define the characters of Barbara and Susan and their relationships to others but do not present us with object-images of woman. In *Nashville*, Sueleen Gay's strip is photographed to maintain respect for her body and capture her pain and humiliation, not her breasts or buttocks or thighs; we know that she is entirely naked at the end of the scene because we see her throw her panties, but we only see her nude from the rear in a distance shot, and we never witness the frontal nudity the men in the film's internal audience demand. In each of these instances, rather than the actress and her body determining the relationship of the camera to the character, it is the character and her desires that organize distances, angles, and focus.

*   *   *   *

The relationship of film to women is an issue in all Altman's films. But in four instances—*That Cold Day in the Park, Images, 3 Women,* and *Come Back to The 5 and Dime, Jimmy Dean, Jimmy Dean*—the relationships of women to their contexts, including the context of film are insistently explored. *McCabe and Mrs. Miller* presents a town divided socially, and a film divided structurally, into a world of men and a world of women. In the four films that might be called Altman's "women's films," a sexual paradox is expressed: all of these films focus on women who are peripheral to the societies they inhabit, and men in these films are peripheral to the films' attention. Unlike the earlier genre of American "women's films" of the thirties and forties, which were so called because they appeared to be strategically conceived to appeal to a female audience, Altman's women's films are *about* women and are equally accessible—or inaccessible— to any presumed responses of men and women. To be about women is also not, in this case, only to make the stories of women of central importance; it is an engagement in a struggle toward knowledge, acknowledgment, and change.

Such large claims rest on ample but often enigmatic evidence. Frances Austen (Sandy Dennis) of *That Cold Day in the Park* appears to fit neatly Kolbenschlag's description of the female grotesque. Frances seduces a boy half her age, locks him in a room, solicits a prostitute for him, and finally murders this same prostitute. She is, as Kolbenschlag suggests is true of many grotesques, "both victim and victimizer—a perfect object for sadism, a masked form of vengeance and self-hate."[16] The interest of the film, however, is not in provoking our sadistic pleasure in Frances's neurotic sufferings; it is in drawing our attention to the complexity of her behavior within the framework of an ordinary life.

Despite its familiar chronological narrative and its climactic plot, *That Cold Day in the Park* is a dialectical film that actively judges and quietly challenges the assumptions of its audience. Frances Austen manages her life—her money, her household, her social relations—competently, yet reviewers consistently referred to her as a "spinster" (a creature not very far removed from a wicked stepsister), and others within the film are openly troubled that she lives alone "at her age." The film quickly shows us that Frances is lonely, but that is neither extraordinary information nor does it make her odd or grotesque. Is it, then, bizarre that she asks a strange boy into her house, a boy she knows only from seeing him sitting in the cold rain on a park bench? Would we find her behavior strange if she had instead met a man her age in a bar and invited him home?

More disturbing than anything Frances does (until the end of the film) is the purposeful silence of the young man she befriends. From the moment the boy enters Frances's apartment, he speaks not a word in her presence. She appears to assume that he is mute, as we also assume until we see him during a visit to his sister and her boyfriend; with them he speaks freely and naturally. The boy's sister reveals that since childhood, he has used an artificial silence as a manipulative weapon, which is precisely what he is now doing with Frances. The boy is not, therefore, the "first of Altman's passive characters"[17]—anymore than is Frances—as Robert Kolker claims. At the least, the boy is a passive-aggressive, someone who consciously uses silence to maintain control, even while he appears to be under Frances's domination.

The boy's aggressive silence transforms Frances's world. One remembers this film with an uncomfortable recollection of Frances's constant chatter; what we may too easily forget is that her apparent logorrhea is not a simple expression of her loneliness but a means of adaptation to the boy's muteness. For us, the boy's silence calls attention to the persistent presence of Frances's voice. In the few scenes where we see Frances without the boy—in the opening sequence with her older friends; in a doctor's office; with Michael Murphy, when she is seeking a prostitute for the boy—there is no indication of someone neurotically inclined to incessant chatter.

If, then, *That Cold Day in the Park* is to be understood, as it generally has been, as the study of a woman going mad, then we must include in our interpretation the knowledge that she is driven mad; further, she is not driven mad by the world in general or by her own "grotesque" unconscious but by the deliberate actions of a self-indulgent, manipulative young man. This is one reason why the camera's repeated movement away from Frances and the boy toward objects that are potential sources of light feels incoherent and self-consciously directorial. The blurred focus shots of windows, lamps, and a shiny coffeepot signify the lack of focus in Frances's mind, but this code is arbitrary and inconsistent with the rest of her behavior. In contrast, visual images in the film associated with water—the rain, the boy's bath, his sister's bath, the hot-water bottle—are less ostentatious and more threatening to us because they reinforce the boy's disruption of Frances's life and the assaultive power of silence. Water, in each of these instances, initially signifies nourishment and comfort; its sounds relieve the aural chill of the filmic space. Water also works somewhat tritely as a sexual sign in the film, but at least here, in contrast to the light images, Altman plays a bit with predictable significations. When the boy and his sister take a bath together in Frances's over-elegant tub, regression and incest are all too apparent, but Altman does relieve the glare of this information by allowing us to enjoy the banter between siblings and by intercutting to scenes of Frances at the doctor's office, where she has gone to be fitted for a diaphragm. These scenes are linked by more than a voyeuristic invasion of private sexuality. In both instances, it is the women, the sister and Frances, who take the sexual initiative; and in both instances, the men respond conventionally and demeaningly to the women. The boy rebukes his sister's sexual invitation and is more worried about using up Frances's bubble bath than about his sister's vulnerability; the doctor exploits the occasion of the gynecological examination to proposition Frances.

If, then, we carefully unpack both the direct narrative elements and the visual and aural codes of *That Cold Day in the Park,* we discover that the facile, Freudian story of the film's immediate surface is undermined by a set of signals that tell another tale. The most accessible story projected is that of a lonely, repressed single woman, who seduces a mute young man into her apartment, forcibly imprisons him when she recognizes that he cannot be held by her personal charm or desire, and finally entraps the boy by setting him up as an accomplice to her murder of the prostitute whom she has ostensibly brought home to him. For this story to be plausible, we must believe early in the film that Frances is quite crazy and that the motivation for her entrapment of the boy and the murder of the prostitute must be found in events that precede the time frame of the film. In this case, we must accept the narrow cultural perspective of Frances's upper-class friends at the beginning of the film: she is to be pitied for her solitary life-style, and her gesture of charity (whatever its other motivations) in bringing the boy in from the cold park bench is to be seen as madness.

Read in this way, the film is both misogynistic and frustrating. Either we must accept Frances's solitary social state as sufficient motivation for her violent behavior, or we must respect as an ontological gesture the film's apparent unwillingness to reveal motivations; in many of Altman's films, and most effectively in *McCabe and Mrs. Miller, The Long Goodbye* and *Nashville,* a persuasive argument can be made for the latter. In these other films, either the presumed conventions of the genre or structural and formal aspects of the work make adamant the incapacity for and disinterest in psychological motivation. But in *That Cold Day in the Park,* both focus and perspective direct us toward the revelation of Frances's character. Not only is it her voice that provides most of the oral information of the film, but for much of the film, the camera is static and relentless in its full and medium shots of Frances or the furnishings surrounding her. The visual ambiance is of the television melodrama, and the expectation is of the epiphanic close-up in which Frances's unconscious past is suddenly made manifest.

Fortunately, but incompletely, there are countersignals that tell another tale almost from the beginning of the film. We do not need to hear the boy talk to his sister to know that he is not mute; we hear him sigh as he slides into his first bath at her apartment. Early in the film, on the boy's first night in Frances's apartment, the camera breaks from its routine proximity to Frances and captures the boy, naked, in a sustained depth-of-focus shot; he is suddenly perceived as more a threat than a passive victim. The next day, when the boy is alone in her apartment, the camera again finds him at a distance and naked; the discovery asserts his arrogant complicity in his presence in this space. There are moments, too, when the camera seems unable to maintain its invisible, stoic presence around Frances. While the boy and Frances play an intense yet ultimately innocent game of blind-man's buff, the camera plays, too, and captures their shadows on the wall. At the end of the game, the camera zooms away from Frances as if disconcerted by her passionate pleasure.

The difficulty for the spectator with this film is that neither these differing stances nor the disparate stories being projected ever comprise a coherent world. There is potentially a second and more interesting story in this film: that of the contained, self-assertive woman who rationally acts to alter her life and then rationally takes vengeance on a man who exploits her. But this narrative neither collides with nor sufficiently complements the story of the disinte-grating crazy lady to allow the spectator a clear point of entry and participation. In Stanley Kubrick's *Barry Lyndon,* the tale told to us by the film's narrator is so consistently a misinterpretation of the images and conversations projected that we are deliberately led to distrust the narrator and, in turn, become more active interpreters ourselves. Only once in *That Cold Day in the Park*—during the sequence that cross-cuts between Frances at the doctor's office and the boy and his sister in Frances's apartment—do we feel confident that our activity as specatators is worthwhile. It is in this sequence that Altman employs the depth-of-sound technique that engages us so effectively in most of his other films; the bits of conversation we hear from the women in the doctor's waiting room are mundane, but the dramatic irony of an overheard line like, "If more girls would come to a place like this before they got into trouble," is seductive and provocative in the context of Frances's present and future actions.

While coherent in itself, this sequence is set apart from the rest of (and not in opposition to) the film, not only because of its narrative discontinuity but more crucially in its approach toward point of view. When Altman uses parallel editing, or explodes that technique into the bracket syntagmas that structure *Brewster McCloud, Nashville, Health,* and *A Wedding,* point of view becomes either omniscient or obliterated. Or, more accurately, when Altman is most under control of his montage, the key point of view, as Eisenstein predicted would occur, is that of the audience.[18] In the sequence noted above, each of the characters whom we see—Frances, the boy, his sister, the women in the doctor's office, the doctor—has a narrow and distinctly partial view of the world, but the world we are led to piece together is whole and complex. In the preceding and subsequent portions of the film, however, the camera unmistakably vacillates between subjective point-of-view shots from Frances's perspective, indirect subjective shots that include Frances in a world imaged as she might see it, and voyeuristic shots that suggest a corrupt, inappropriate and invisible presence, not unlike that of the boy. The problem is not simply that of the combination of omniscient shooting with point-of-view shooting or of direct point-of-view shots with indirect point-of-view shots. Indeed, it remains one of the special curiosities of film that instances of entire movies shot from one character's point of view are not only rare but are less persuasive than films with multiple points of view.[19] The central difficulty is that we are asked, at random, to switch our perspective from that of identification with Frances, to voyeuristic intrusion of Frances's space and life, and then to that of participant observer of the society that Frances inhabits. To ask such arbitrary transformations of attitude from us as spectators is not only to demand of us a near-impossible emotional flexibility but to thoroughly confuse any sense we might have of how to know this world.

Obstacles to understanding similar to those present in *That Cold Day in the Park* occur elsewhere. In the body of his filmmaking, one finds several other films that do not quite work but that contain provocative experiments in the rhetoric of film in association with illuminating glimpses of the society projected. These films—*Brewster McCloud, Images, A Perfect Couple, Quintet, Beyond Therapy,* and *A Wedding*—are like a painter's sketches; at least occasionally, as in the relationship of *Brewster McCloud* to

Nashville, these sketches are the hypotheses from which vast and coherent canvases derive. The riddle that faces Altman with *That Cold Day in the Park* has no magical solution: if, as all of his films evidence, he wants to pay particular attention to the roles of women in American society, how does he do so while maintaining the integrity of both male and female points of view? The difficulty is not simply that Robert Altman is a man attempting to make films about women. (Although well intentioned, Kolker seems to me to put each of his feet in a different quagmire when he asserts that "It is impossible for a man to explore feminine consciousness from anything but a male perspective. . . ." and then goes on to hesitate on grounds of insufficient evidence concerning the reverse claim about women making films about men.) In the first place, I oppose the claim that a person of one sex is unable by definition to fully acknowledge and represent a person of another sex; to do so implies that there are essential impenetrable, and inescapable male and female perspectives and also leads to the aesthetic absurdity that no one (actor, painter, filmmaker) can justly portray a person who is remarkably other. I am unconvinced that there is a significant difference *in kind* between the issues before a white male director making a film about eighteenth century men or about twentieth century black people and the issues before a man making a film about contemporary women. In addition, we are only beginning to grapple with the attributes and sources of male and female consciousness, and the degree to which these are distinct and unrelenting is yet to be determined.

Equally enigmatic, but perhaps more soluble, is the paradox that Altman encounters of the male director who wishes to pay emphatic and resonant attention to women while sustaining the presence not only of men but of a male perspective as a social reality and political force. Male directors, including Altman, are vulnerable to accusations of illegitimacy if they attempt to present the world projected from a subjective and female point of view. But if, as Altman does in *McCabe and Mrs. Miller*, the women are imaged either from men's points of view or in relation to men, the argument can be made that the interest of the film is still not in women (or women *and* men) but on men and their perspectives on women. The latter is in itself not an unimportant or uninteresting terrain, but it still places the aesthetic and social emphasis on men.

*   *   *   *

That Cold Day in the Park may thus be more generously appreciated as an attempt to grapple with the difficulty of making a film that brings to the fore the complexity of a woman while maintaining the authenticity of a world in which male and female consciousnesses exist side by side and have political implications. In 1972, immediately after completing *McCabe and Mrs. Miller,* Altman made another attempt to confront these issues in his film *Images.* As with *That Cold Day in the Park, Images* could be described as a narrative of a woman's evolving lunacy, but it is ironically the weakness of *Images* that in this instance such a description is accurate. *Images* is less about the central figure Cathryn than about how the world appears to her. In contrast to *That Cold Day in the Park,* the contradictions and incoherences in the world framed by *Images* are not a matter of the film's shifts in points of view but of Cathryn's "images" of the world as she constructs it. *Images* is structured by the contradictions in the projected narrative. Cathryn's husband, Hugh, comes home late one night and suddenly transforms into her dead ex-lover René; out at their country house, Cathryn sees herself shoot their neighbor Marcel in order to repulse his tenacious advances toward her; she views his dead body and then encounters an unscathed Marcel a few moments later. Altman's camera makes no attempt to categorize any of these images as "real" or "unreal;" light, color, and clarity are all consistent, sharp, and naturalistic.[20] The chronology of the editing suggests what has actually occurred as separate from what Cathryn has imagined, but while the "real" is sometimes supported by substantiating reports from other characters (Marcel's daughter, Susannah, talks about her "live" father after Cathryn has seen him dead), the camera's perspective is so consistently associated with Cathryn's that there is no absolute certainty for the spectator as to what has actually occurred.

In its assertive imaging of events that are implausibly contiguous, as in many less interesting aspects, *Images* is blatantly derivative of Ingmar Bergman's *Persona.* But only once in *Images* does the double entendre of the concept of projection engage the spectator as it so consistently does in *Persona*. Cathryn has accompanied Hugh to the top of a hill where he has gone to shoot birds. (An instance of Altman's delight in in-jokes here: Hugh is played by René Auberjonois who, two years earlier, had played the bird-loving, gun-hating professor in *Brewster McCloud*.) The scene at first appears to by idyllic, the setting for a moment of romance and reconciliation in a tension-ridden marriage. Hugh, however, is not interested in Cathryn but in shooting birds—or at least, we see no evidence of his romantic interest in Cathryn. What follows is a series of shots that makes most sense as a projection of Cathryn's isolation and terror. We see Cathryn separated from Hugh, and we see Hugh focusing his "shot," perhaps at a bird but perhaps at Cathryn. We see their house off at a distance, below in the valley, but then we also see a shot from the house that captures Hugh on the distant hill. The camera shots are incongruous; Cathryn cannot be both looking down at her house and looking up from it in such a short time. The conventions of film lead us to expect some transitional shot that would indicate her movement from one spot to another. The most coherent reading of the sequence, given that the camera angles are consistent with Cathryn's point of view, is that she has "projected" herself safely separate from Hugh and back at her house but also sees herself as the victim and object of her husband's shooting.

With its play on a double meaning of "shooting"—Hugh's two apparent pleasures are shooting quail and shooting still lifes with his camera—*Images* recalls and provokes comparisons not only to *Persona* but also to another film made the same year (1966), Antonioni's *Blow-Up*. All three films exude filmic modernism; that is, they are self-conscious about their own processes and call into question the activities of shooting, of performance, and of projection. In each of these films, too, events that are perhaps imagined by a character within the film, events that could not be confirmed or would be denied by other witnesses within the film, are undifferentiated from "real" events; thus for us, as for at least one character within each of these films, the dream life of a character has equal status with that character's conscious, public life. Notably, in each of these films, the most disturbing and contextually plastic images are those concerned with sexual and violent events. The appearance of Elisabet's husband, near the end of *Persona*, might well be understood as a fantasy of either Nurse Alma or Elisabet; guided by Elisabet, he makes love with Alma; indications that he is blind are of more symbolic than literal interest. The film, however, contains no stylistic signal that this scene is more or less actual than the preceding or subsequent interactions between Elisabet and Alma. In *Blow-Up*, after "discovering" a corpse in a photograph, photographer David Hemmings returns to the park setting where he took the picture and confirms that indeed there is a man's body hidden in the brush. But when Hemmings comes back to the park once more a few hours later, there is no sign that this corpse was ever present. Here, as in *Persona* and in *Images*, film exploits its capacity to project *everything* with equal authority. "The little flashlight in the dark" does not need verification to betray.

Given these common ontological surroundings, what is remarkable is not Altman's indebtedness to either or both Bergman and Antonioni but the ways in which *Images* is distinctive as a film. Most obviously, Altman resists in *Images* that assertive self-reflective stance found in *Persona*, *Blow-Up*, or any number of other contemporary films. No projectors, cameras, or microphones are ever revealed in *Images*; nor does the film contain any gesture equivalent to the transformation of illusion in the mimed tennis game that concludes *Blow-Up*. Perhaps this is why it is a less striking film than either *Persona* or *Blow-Up*, but *Images* is neither terrified of nor arrogant about its own potential power.

This discussion still fails to satisfy the sense I have of the strangeness of *Images*. Despite the interruptions and obscurities of narrative in *Persona* and *Blow-Up*, I remain attracted to the people in these films in a way that is common to my experience of film: Elisabet and Alma, and even David Hemmings and Vanessa Redgrave (notably, the characters in the one instance, the actors in the other), become objects of my desire. Whatever questions these characters and actors provoke about the complexities of their psyches or their relationships to the world are subordinate to the fact that first

I am attracted to them as erotic presences. I do not want to *be* any one of them, any more than I ever wanted to be Cary Grant or Marilyn Monroe, but what I want first, before I think about them, is to make love to them.

I have no such longing toward Cathryn in Altman's *Images* or toward any of the men in that film. And this is not because these characters, or the actors who play them, are physically unappealing. The difference is that these characters' presence on the screen is neither flirtatious nor seductive. My intimacy with the human images on the screen is not the intimacy of eroticism but of social and political knowledge. *Images* is a key work in the Altman canon because its very limitations in subject and style bring forward an elemental version of the absence of the erotic that characterizes much of Altman's work. In many of Altman's other films, a variety of factors contribute to blur the potential recognition that the people on the screen are distinctly, significantly nonerotic in their presence to us: sexual interactions are rare and when they do occur are undermined in some fashion; the multiplicity of characters reduces our attraction to any one character; or the landscape appears to substitute for the sensual body. *Images,* however, is a film about one woman's relationships—and especially her sexual relationships—to three men, a young girl, and to herself. Yet, in contrast to a dozen other films with similar configurations of relationships, this woman remains throughout the film undistinguished by her charm, her beauty, or even her eccentricities. What distinguishes her is her struggle against the oppressive, self-indulgent paternalism of her husband and the unsought lecheries of her husband's friend. And what the camera captures is not the way her hand brushes an imagined strand of hair from her brow or the haunting luminescence of her eyes but rather her fumblings as she tries to maintain control of her life and the images of her fear and disgust as she loses that control. When Cathryn takes her shower at the end of the film, what we see is a deeply disturbed person cleansing herself. The image is wholly emptied of its erotic message; only the symbolic signification of cleansing is asserted. The allusion to Hitchcock's *Psycho* is a gesture of ironic contrast, for although Hitchcock has been more willing than most film directors deliberately to eliminate the erotic from images of women on film, in *his* shower scene, all is Eros.

*   *   *   *

That Cold Day in the Park and *Images* are good texts from which to discern the distinguishing features of Altman's images of women, but in retrospect they are exercises that do not have the force or clarity of vision to stand firmly on their own. *3 Women*, the next film in the "women's" quartet, more than encompasses the works that precede it. Like *McCabe and Mrs. Miller* and *Nashville*, *3 Women* is immediately disconcerting, assertive of its territory, unhesitant about the world that it includes and disallows. Its washed out pinks and ambers and surreal yellows articulate this world as precisely as do the red, white, and blue of *Nashville* or the black and white of *McCabe*. Like *Nashville*, *McCabe and Mrs. Miller*, *Buffalo Bill and the Indians*, and *Come back to the 5 and Dime, Jimmy Dean, Jimmy Dean*, *3 Women* exploits the signs of one cultural myth and sets the terrain for an alternative.

In one sense, *3 Women* begins where *Images* lets go. The first shots of the film are of women and water, and as with the shower in *Images*, the visual context that frames the women is emphatically erotic. *3 Women* begins with the frescoes that persistently punctuate the film—and with a glimpse of Willie (Janice Rule), the woman who is painting these icons on the bottoms and sides of various swimming pools. The iconography is classical and grotesque. Colored in florid pinks and blues are images of bulls, mazes, and threatening creatures who appear only half human. Despite the inclusion of breasts and female bellies in some of the figures, the dominant symbol of these frescoes is the phallus; the dominant tone is hostility; vaguely Greek and early Renaissance allusions are evoked. In contrast to the challenging physicality of the painted images, the woman creating these icons is oddly ethereal and placid. What could be titillating is made intimidating by the intensity of the woman's attention to her work and by the harshness of both the pictures and the glaring light that floods the scene.

This same white light drains color from the next image, a shot of an old woman's fat rippled thighs and hips moving laboriously through the water of a swimming pool. Imperceptibly, the camera retreats slightly, capturing other pocked and fleshy legs underwater and then tilting up to discover, from the waist up, in a simple tank suit, a slender younger woman whom we will come to know as Millie (Shelley Duvall). Immediately, the camera returns to water level, and deliberately and unabashedly shoots directly at the crotch of Millie and other old, heavy people whom Millie is leading through the water; the movement through the pool is so tedious that the water seems to have the viscosity of thick oil. From the sound track, we hear ponderous string music interrupted at random by percussion chords; the movement of the music complements the tension evoked by the movement of bodies and distracts us from the constant mobility of the camera, which has been gradually expanding its frame of reference. On the pool deck, the camera reveals more elderly people, all swathed in stark white sheets. Then, behind a window, the camera discovers another young woman, staring out at the pool with a face devoid of any expression. Pinky, as she will shortly be identified, is appropriately dressed in a childish pink blouse. Her freckles, blond braid, and demeanor convey the ambiance of a girl of thirteen or fourteen. Immediately, the camera returns to Millie, the assured young woman in the water; the connection between Pinky and Millie is established. Extremes of light and languor connect the two opening scenes of 3 Women and enunciate the tension that is the emotional chord of the film from its very beginning. But whereas the opening shots of Willie and her icons are covert and enigmatic, it is the emphatic aura of exposure that characterizes our introduction to Millie and Pinky at the desert health spa. Not only does the film stock appear to have been overexposed to light, but the bodies captured on that stock seem to have too much flesh for the camera's eye. And the gesture of exposure, as we always half know, removes the objects of exposure from our desire. We are infinitely more covetous of those other "Pinkys" of American film—Spencer Tracy and Katherine Hepburn in Adam's Rib—when they exit off-camera, leaving us only an empty hallway to view, than we are of any of the figures who appear in full daylight-exposed flesh in these opening moments of 3 Women.

Nor is the film content to only expose the bodies of the people it projects. With notable efficiency, given the continuing ambiance of lassitude, the textures of the daily lives of two of the "three women" are laid bare. From every corner of the health spa and the cafeteria where "the help" adjourn for lunch, we hear the grating jabbering voice of Millie, the young woman whom we first glimpsed in the pool. By continuing the sound of Millie's voice, even when she is not on camera, the film informs us of an essential quality of Millie's relationship to the world: the audience she imagines for her monologues is rarely present, yet she sustains her role despite evidence that her exertions go unappreciated. And each moment she plays in this unapplauded part exposes her more violently to us. In one voice-over we hear her saying, "You know, the Breck girl, well they're having a contest to find the new one. I'm gonna send in my picture." Without a glimpse of her face (or her hair) as she says this line or of the reactions of others to her pronouncement, she has made herself as vulnerable as did Sueleen Gay when she was forced to strip in *Nashville*. And, as with Sueleen Gay, there is no allure in this vulnerability because the exposure is so complete.

It is Millie's fate, however, suddenly to find herself with an unexpected audience. Pinky, the young girl of the pink blouse and blank face of the previous scene, has been assigned to Millie as a trainee. The glimpses we are given of Pinky during the lunch break confirm our first impressions. Like a little girl, Pinky delights in blowing bubbles in her coke and later mischievously fools around in a vacant wheelchair. This is, she tells Millie, her first job in California.

As transparent as Millie and Pinky are in their presentations of themselves, Altman manages to establish almost whimsically the fated complexity of their relationship. One of Millie's first responsibilities is to find Pinky a bathing suit from the health-spa supply. "You're little like me, aren't you?" Millie inquires rhetorically of Pinky, calling attention to their physical similarities and their potential sisterhood. For those who remember, the line has a resonant allusion; in *McCabe and Mrs. Miller*, at a comparable moment, Mrs. Miller initiated Ida, the mail-order bride and then widow, into her work as a whore. Mrs. Miller, too, reassuringly told Ida that she was "little like me." That Ida was played by Shelley Duvall, who now takes on the role of the *older* sister, is at least an amusing in-joke and, by the flights allowed critics, an assertion of the extended sisterhood of Altman's women.

The foreshadowing of the sororal relationship as well as of the film's key events become more manifest once the two young women enter the pool for Pinky's training. Secure in the older sister's protection, Pinky becomes a mischievous child in the water. Told by Millie that she must pretend that there is "something wrong with her" in order to learn how to assist the spa patients, Pinky immediately exaggerates and exploits the game. At first, it is all in good fun, but when Millie tells Pinky that she must go all the way into the water, Pinky chooses childishly to interpret Millie literally and drops totally under the water—for just a moment too long. The suggestion that Pinky is drowning herself is treated lightly here, but in retrospect the gesture is a classic sign of dramatic irony. When Pinky does, later, actually attempt to drown herself, we will recall this moment as a warning.

That the film intends to allude to if not imitate a classical pattern of elemental, unavoidable event and relationship is underlined in the very next filmic sign. As Pinky emerges from her pseudo-drowning, she stares at two other health-spa therapists—two young women who are unmistakably identical twins. In the next scene, the twin motif is made directly applicable to Millie and Pinky. As Millie is touring Pinky around the individual hot tubs, Ms. Bunweill, the authoritarian co-director of the spa, appears. In a condescending effort to acknowledge the new "girl" she remarks to Pinky and Millie, "Don't you two have something in common, aren't you both from Texas or something?" They do, indeed, both come from Texas, as did Shelley Duvall, who is playing Millie. Almost immediately, the film cuts again to the twins who are now outside, leaving the spa after the day's work. The end-of-day exodus is staged as a recessional: the twins lead the line, followed by Pinky alone; after a definite gap, Millie appears alone, again jabbering to an audience only she perceives, and followed by the bosom friends, Doris and Alcira, walking together.

Like the epilogue in *Nashville*, the entire opening sequence at the health spa is at once plausible and even pedestrian as an actual event, yet is staged and structured to evoke its ancestral origins and ritual signification. The central motif in the sequence is that of twins, named most explicitly in the repeated image of the biological twins Polly and Peggy, but already suggested as well in the pairing of Millie and Pinky. When Pinky first sees the twins, she stares so fixedly, that Millie is led to ask, "What's the matter? Haven't you ever seen twins before?" Millie's reaction is appropriate to daily life in a modern society, but Pinky's apparent terror of the twins has a cultural and mythical legitimacy. Both ethnology and mythology remind us that twins often have a special place in a society. Whether the root cause of the special status of twins is in the problem of classification they cause a society (as the structuralists would urge) or of what René Girard calls their "baleful aspect of the sacred"[21] remains a matter of dispute, but it is certainly known that "In societies where their very existence is considered dangerous, the infants are 'exposed'; that is, abandoned outside the community under conditions that make their death inevitable."[22] Twins are threatening to a society because they present problems of identification; they confuse others. Dramatists have exploited twins as a source of laughter, but those who laugh are always those who are privileged to have some means of distinguishing what those within the society cannot. It is common, for example, in productions of Shakespeare's *The Comedy of Errors* to employ conventions of costuming and casting such that we accept that those on stage see exact likeness where we in the audience do not. Girard argues that twins inspire terror because in the absence of differences "violence threatens," but it is also the case, as the myth of Romulus and Remus relates, that twins inspire the creation of new cities on the hill. How much of such knowledge Altman assumes of his spectators is unclear, but there is no ambiguity in the early sequence of *3 Women* about the centrality of twins as a sign. Like the red, white, and blue of *Nashville,* or the gun of *McCabe and Mrs. Miller,* the twins as sign are quickly established in a "natural" context, only to be later emptied of one kind of signification and filled with another.

As he does with so many conventional cultural signs, Altman renders the image and notion of twins potent by thwarting our expectations of relationship. The two most important twins of *3 Women* are not Polly and Peggy who are physical duplicates, but

Millie and Pinky, whose resemblances either develop or are initially hidden. (It comes as much of a surprise and a threat to Millie as it does to us to discover that Pinky's "real" name, like Millie's, is Mildred. This information is only revealed after the film has established the distinct identities of each woman and the apparent attraction of Pinky to Millie.)

Just after the recessional from the health spa, Millie and Pinky are separated both spatially and behaviorally. Millie moves toward her enamel yellow Ford Pinto. She unlocks the door, seats herself with the assured aura of the proud owner of a flashy car, and promptly slams the car door, leaving a conspicuous portion of yellow dress hanging beneath the door frame. As Millie drives off, oblivious to the yellow skirt that remains outside the car, we—perhaps especially women—are caught by our own embarrassment at her ineptitude and lack of self-awareness. Millie's passage from spa to car reads as an advertisement for a car dealer—or for the carefree life of the chic young career woman—until she undercuts the message by the most vernacular of gestures. The moment is funny and painful but not, as some would argue, condescending toward Millie, both because it undermines the cliché of the codes of the commercial ad and because too many women have had an analogous experience.

Pinky's path at this point contrasts vividly with Millie's. Pinky catches a bus, and the film then cuts to the four walls of the little space in a rooming house where she is staying. While the light that surrounds Millie has been (and will be) fluorescent and glaring, the light inside Pinky's room is warm and glowing, softened by the flowered wallpaper of the room. There is a quick shot of Pinky washing her hands and her single pair of underpants, followed by two brief scenes of Pinky at work, where Millie is conspicuously absent. The camera then returns to Pinky's room, which we now see is colored in very dull yellows and earth tones, a complement but not a replica of Millie's plastic yellows. Pinky is now sewing with precision and with an aura of confidence in her work.

Our glimpses of Pinky at her sewing machine and on the next morning dressed in the skirt she had made the night before reveal more than her domesticity and competence. Though Pinky's space and behavior appear homespun and naive in contrast to Millie's veneer of sophistication, the other message conveyed is that Pinky is in the process of fabricating her character, of costuming and creating a self. The model for this new self is Millie, who has fabricated *her* identity and *her* space from the magazines whose business it is to sell images to those in search of a public identity.

Pinky, then, is becoming a twin. But she is also consciously seeking the other half of her twinship. Her state and her journey are remarkably, and I would guess coincidentally, like that of one of Shakespeare's twins, Antipholus, in *The Comedy of Errors*. Were Pinky half so articulate, she could speak Antipholus' famous words:

> *He that commends me to mine own content*
> *Commends me to the thing I cannot get.*
> *I to the world am like a drop of water*
> *That in the ocean seeks another drop,*
> *Who falling there to find his fellow forth,*
> *Unseen, inquisitive, confounds himself.*
> *So I, to find a mother and a brother,*
> *In quest of them, unhappy, lose myself.*[23]

Pinky, of course, seeks a mother and a sister, not a brother, but like Antipholus, her search for her twin is inseparable from her search for herself. Pinky, however, is not only a drop of water to the world but also to herself. She is publicly unnoticeable, and she is fluid and without form without that "other drop."

Throughout these introductory sequences, equal interest is evoked in Pinky and Millie, but it is Pinky's quest that inconspicuously determines the structure of the editing and the point of view of the camera. Throughout the first half of the film, the world that we are shown is the world that Pinky experiences. This is not to say that every shot is a subjective point-of-view shot; relatively few in fact are. Most of the shots exemplify Pier Pasolini's concept of "free indirect subjectivity," a representation of the world that emphasizes the distinct worldview of a particular character. Free indirect subjective shots, unlike conventional subjective shots, can include within the frame the character whose worldview is being imaged; such shots can also include objects or other persons that the key character could not actually see at the given moment but cohere with the way the character would see the world.[24] Pasolini's notion of "free indirect subjectivity" is particularly relevant to *3 Women* (as it is to *Bonnie and Clyde*) because it is a critical tool that calls attention to *style,* and style is not an unavoidable aesthetic issue in this film but is central to its subject.[25]

The intricacy of the stylization of *3 Women* is, in part, a matter of the overt presence of a style within a style. The overarching style takes its cues from the desert landscape that corresponds remarkably to Pinky's own initial ambiance. The key element of this style is color: pale greens, hints of rose, and yellows burnt toward brown permeate the desert locale in which the sun glares relentlessly, draining all vibrancy from the natural landscape. There is a barren quality, too, to the *mise-en-scène.* In contrast to *Nashville* or *A Wedding,* in which even the cinemascope screen seems too narrow to contain the cornucopia of detail within the frame, figures and objects appear isolated and detached in *3 Women.* The depth of sound that makes us work to hear and that so appropriately captures the aural textures of waiting rooms, mess halls, clubs, and airports in other of Altman's films is impossible here and is replaced by a consistent tension between silence and the too-loud sound of human voices. As in many of his films, Altman tends here to use close-ups sparingly, but there is an emphatic quality to the medium and full shots of the three women, accomplished by the length of the takes, that marks a deliberate withholding of intimacy. One can read this restraint as an admission on the director's part of the limits to his knowledge of these women, but that poised yet partial distance is also characteristic of the space between Millie and Pinky. Robert Kolker suggests that this style reveals a world that is not "fully articulated," and I think that is precisely right, but not because, as Kolker claims, the world of *3 Women* falls someplace between dream and reality.[26] Rather, the inarticulateness of the verbal and vocal imagery especially of the first half of the film is a correlative to Pinky's vague grasp of any world. Millie's world, a world that reflects the "style within a style," is overly articulate. Her hair, throughout the first sequences of the film, always looks like she has just given it the last stroke with a skillfully handled blow-dryer (despite the fact that she spends her day working in baths and pools); her dresses are perfectly hemmed and ironed; her mouth is sprayed with freshener after every meal. Even before we and Pinky see the domain Millie has created for herself, she has unabashedly displayed her style— part of her style is indeed the ostentation of its display.

As Millie tells Pinky, she plans out everything and has her preferences absolutely clear. Millie eats her lunch in the doctor's cafeteria, despite the ridicule this provokes from her peers at the spa; she breaks the rules and sneaks cigarettes on the job, even though her smoking appears to be less an addiction than a mannerism. When Millie takes Pinky home for the first time, to show her prospective roommate her apartment, she proudly prepares Pinky for the style she has established: "Purple and yellow are my favorite colors. I like flowers and food. Way to a man's heart is through his stomach." But neither Pinky nor we are fully prepared for the fullness of style that greets us at Millie's apartment. The purple exterior walls of the Purple Sage Apartments where Millie lives stand as a garish assault to the surrounding desert hues, and inside, Millie has so profusely indulged her preference for yellow that the color becomes a statement in itself. It is as if Opal's query into the meaning of yellow in *Nashville* has here found its answer, not in the verbal terms that Opal blunders through but in the vocabulary of the painter—or perhaps, more precisely, of the commercial artist. The yellow of Millie's clothes and car and apartment has cultural signification; the home decorating magazines that are the too-obvious resource for Millie's interior decor repeatedly use yellow, especially in kitchens, as part of the rhetoric of happy sunshine, cleanliness, order, and spaciousness; yellow will and does brighten your world. But in Millie's apartment, the abundance of color and the variations on the theme also become abstract. Much as the canvas in one of Morris Louis's "veil" paintings becomes one with the color of the paint, the objects and materials (and in particular the chintz's) in Millie's world become inseparable from their yellowness, and from Millie. Millie's tuna casseroles and canned pudding desserts, her recipe collection arranged by requirements of time, her self-consciously lilting walk, and her ladies' magazine vocabulary are all part of her mode, but all these become details in a style that is first and adamantly yellow.

At once connecting and separating Millie's yellow style and the complexion of the world framed around her are the intermittent shots of Willie's mazes and the mirage-like images that seem to appear out of water or float off the desert. The most straightforward reading of these images would urge that they are the third code in a set of styles and visions, each of which names the world of one of the film's three women. In this scheme, Pinky's world appears in the barren but bursting desert imagery that conceals its secret vitality; Millie's world asserts itself in gleaming yellow surfaces that would reflect before they could conceal; and before we even know her, Willie's world interrupts the screen with enigmatic visions that threaten the stability of both these other codes of understanding. Such associations are set up in the film but do not suffice, for even when the expressionistic style associated with Willie's silent presence is projected, Pinky remains as the constant observer. The appeal of the advertising for 3 Women, cited by Judith Kass,[27] was not false to the film: "1 woman became 2/2 women became 3/3 women became 1" does describe the relationship of styles in the film, even if it reduces what are genuinely complex relationships to movie voodoo.

The one style that is not absorbed in 3 Women, and the last to become manifest, is, not coincidentally, the code of arms presented by Edgar, the one significant male in the film. 3 Women is well on its way before Edgar appears for the first time; when he does make his entrance, it is with a grotesquely counterfeit bang. On their first trip home together to Millie's apartment, Pinky and Millie have stopped off at Dodge City, the local hot spot to which Millie wants to introduce Pinky. Set in the middle of no place, Dodge City is a bar and hangout where the guys come to roar around the surrounding brush on motorcycles and demonstrate their skill on a shooting range. The façade of Dodge City suggests a "B" movie set that will reveal three missing walls when you open the front door. Millie loves the place: "A lot of guys hang out here." Pinky is most attracted to a decaying miniature golf course. As Pinky and Millie are about to leave Dodge City, a car pulls up, and out of it appears a man who approaches the two women as if they are unquestionably his opponents in the gunfight at the O.K. Corral. As the man comes closer to the two women, he pulls a gun from the holster at his side; his first words are, "Never trust a dishonest man." The authenticity of this man's gestures is ambiguous; either he is a bad actor or a fool. We quickly discover that he is both—and more. The man is Edgar (Robert Fortier), Willie's husband; he was once the stuntman and stand-in for Hugh O'Brien, and as his display of gun twirling for Pinky demonstrates, he is the archetype of the "has-been" still living his remembered glory. Edgar's style and the style of Dodge City are one: under fake rocks are fake snakes, and what is truly frightening is the total lack of depth in man and context. The shot that follows this introduction of Edgar, a pan inside the Dodge City bar that slides along a tense, silent exchange of looks between Willie and Edgar, articulates a troubled relationship. (It is also rhetorically inconsistent as one of the few scenes shown in the first part of the film in which Pinky neither appears nor could witness the moment.) Edgar has already informed us that he is not to be trusted, and our glimpse of Willie's isolated pregnant body while Pinky and Millie were in the bar materialized the connection between this husband and wife but also suggested their separateness.

Even more conclusively than in *McCabe and Mrs. Miller* and *Nashville,* episodes spring ineluctably from the establishment of context and styles. Although Millie's exhibition of her apartment to Pinky is enacted as a seduction scene, there is no surprise for Pinky or Millie or us in Pinky's decision to become Millie's new roommate. The behavior of each woman that follows this new arrangement is also predictable. Pinky sews and Millie cooks; Pinky obsessively washes her one set of underpants after work each night, and Millie prepares with parallel absorption for a big date who eventually stands her up. That Pinky relaxes easily into her new home as Millie becomes increasingly tense about Pinky's invasion of her space is inevitable; Millie's world had everything in its place before Pinky arrived, and as long as there was no *other* to observe that world, it remained intact. Pinky's world was barren and could be most easily filled by a prefabricated life.

Yet the very ordinariness of the evolving relationship of Millie and Pinky is instructive because Altman treats the two women with respect. The film treats the people, institutions, and objects that

surround Pinky and Millie with disdain, but each moment that we
start to laugh at Pinky and Millie, the moments when their behavior
approaches parody of the media fantasies of single, American
women, the genuine despair and fear in each woman is acknowledged. The most eloquent of such gestures is the long sequence that
begins with Pinky and Millie's preparations for a "dinner party."
With the assumption that most of us recall a time before health
foods, for those who have neither been wholly deprived of the
tribulations of the kitchen nor have spent all of their years in elite
academic institutions, Millie's culinary concoctions cannot be too
remote to elicit a grimace of recognition. (I confess here to years of
tuna casserole and in a previous life to having served guests pre-
jarred shrimp cocktail.) But had Altman left this scene with Pinky's
awkward attempts to swirl canned cheese on crackers, we would
have been left only with a mockery of the culture. Instead, the image
of Pinky's ineptitude that lingers most provocatively is that of the
blood-red shrimp cocktail sauce that she finally spills over her party
dress. The unfortunate gesture signifies calamity: now, the dinner
party is short one shrimp cocktail, Pinky has nothing clean to wear,
and Millie must go to the market again and will not have time to
dress properly.

Altman's encoding exploitation of this minor disaster is indica-
tive of the dynamic process of the film. For Millie and Pinky,
Pinky's accident with the prefabricated shrimp cocktail is a genuine
calamity. The mess Pinky has created brings into unavoidably sharp
focus the difference between the two women and allows the repressed tension between them to explode. The accident disrupts
Millie's precisely planned preparations for the dinner party and
draws attention to Pinky's ineptitude with such preparations. Neither woman is able to laugh at the episode because there is too
much anxiety already invested in the dinner party and because their
relationship to each other is too precarious to acknowledge vulnerability. Nor can we laugh. In the presence of other domestic accidents
on film (or on stage) we can linger in our laughter in the face of the
despair of the wounded character; it is in the nature of comic characters to overcome or ignore such disasters—if only to provide the
space for new ones—and, more important, the messes they make or

Pinky (Sissy Spacek) and Millie (Shelley Duvall) put together their prefabricated dinner for two dates who never show up in *3 Women*. (*The Museum of Modern Art/Film Stills Archive, New York City*)

witness signify no more or less than a transient, physical chaos. When Stan Laurel attempts to help his friend Ollie Hardy clean house in *Helpmates* and instead creates ruin, we can laugh because the worst that can happen is what we have seen happen; neither their friendship nor their individual personalities are threatened. If anything, it is the messes they make together that name their relationship. And when Hardy, or an innocent bystander gets a pie in the face, we can giggle at the mess because the pie obscures the victim's dismay. But when Pinky gets her metaphorical pie on the chest, the camera does show us her face, and Millie's look of cold fury is the antithesis of the complicitous exchange with the camera that Vincent Canby remarks as a signature of Laurel and Hardy films.[28]

We might still laugh, however, at Pinky's accident, as we laugh at any mishap that concludes a series of overly-calculated steps, were it not for the immediate pressure of a second-order semiotic gesture. It takes only the few extra seconds in which the camera holds the image of Pinky with cocktail sauce all over her chest to transform that red sauce into blood. In almost any context, we are likely to mistake catsup and its equivalents for blood; in a theatrical context, we even accept the convention that we are to read catsup as blood. In this context, we are asked, as it were, to at once read from left to right and right to left. What we see is a pedestrian, commonplace domestic mess, but we also see a central character bloodied. The two significations conjoin, and the union is a warning. Genuine disaster can and will emanate from this relationship; real blood and the image of blood are one blurred sign. Just as Altman has earlier planted the image of twins in order to set up a particular conceptual structure for the relationship of Pinky and Millie, here he provides the ironic gesture of the splashed cocktail sauce to make us attentive to the violence that will follow. (The moment recalls the eruption of Kenny's car radiator during the highway crash scene in *Nashville*.)

Both Millie and the film itself now become noticeably more aggressive. As Millie is departing for the grocery store to replace the lost shrimp cocktail, she commands Pinky to put clean sheets on the roll-away bed; Millie thus effectively asserts her sexual projections and her vision that by the end of the evening she will be able to exclude Pinky from her space. *3 Women* then cuts to Millie passing the pool on her return from the grocery store; we hear the ominous music that accompanied Willie's icons at the beginning of the film. The pace of the editing accelerates. The evening's "company"— Millie's ex-roommate Deirdre and three male companions—pull up outside as Pinky is taking out the garbage; they inform Pinky that they are "really hot to trot" and are thus going to skip their dinner date and head straight for Dodge City. We can almost hear the collision of shots, as the camera cuts to Millie, now fully decked out in a special yellow dress with a yellow corsage on her bare arm. Millie's response to Pinky's news of the broken date is predictable. As quickly as the film transformed the situation, Millie changes her clothes and is on her way to Dodge City.

In this rush of small events, the relationships between Pinky and Millie and between the film and the audience have altered. Until this sequence, Pinky's vampirish mimesis of Millie and Millie's hostility to Pinky's sloppy, adolescent behavior have been unacknowledged by either woman; under Millie's relentless guidance, both women have hidden within the roles of good roommates. Because Pinky has known this to be a disguise, so have we. Like Pinky, we have been empowered by our knowledge, a kind of knowledge that discomforts some viewers and leads to the accusations that Altman is condescending to both women. Here, however, Pinky discovers the limits of her manipulations, and we are confronted with the limits of our knowledge. With loss of control of her relationship with Millie, Pinky also loses control of the film's point of view. In the shot after Millie's departure, it is dusk, and we see Willie sitting at the edge of the pool shaking water from a bottle (one of the many metaphors of Willie's pregnancy). In the next shot, it is dark evening and Millie is returning home with a figure who is initially obscure but who is revealed in the light of the apartment as Edgar. Millie has shed all patience and desire to accommodate Pinky; she unhesitantly opens the roll-away bed, wakes Pinky, and tells her to move to the roll-away. Millie's response to Pinky's horrified stare at Edgar is unrelenting and unequivocable: "If you don't like it around here, why don't you move out. Anytime suits me." Millie's slam of the bedroom door reasserts her style as forcefully as the cramped space in the tight interior shots and the rapid cuts enforce a change in the style of *3 Women*.

Outside the apartment, the dark blue world where Pinky and the camera now venture is not Pinky's world either, but Willie's. Pinky's slow movement around the balcony above the pool is intercut with shots of water, with reflections of her in the water. The visual motifs in this scene are as self-conscious as are Willie's icons. Mirror shots abound and recall an earlier shot at Dodge City in which the image of Willie was reflected in a window pane and was framed such that Willie appeared to us as posed between Millie and Pinky. The silence and stillness of this earlier mirror-image scene was made more notable by its juxtaposition to the scene of the "guys" tearing around the outskirts of Dodge City on motorcycles.

Here, at the Purple Sage Apartments pool, the same provocative stillness prevails.

Willie's myths are also reflected in the postures now assumed by Pinky. As Pinky stands poised on the balcony above the pool, she raises her arms as if she is about to fly; in the reflection we are shown in the pool, she resembles a Giotto angel, and like Giotto's seraph, the image is also that of the Christ figure. Pinky's martyrdom is announced for the second time, and like the catsup-splattered Pinky of a few moments before, the image is at once absurd and threatening. The film now cuts to the fresco figure awaiting Pinky in the pool; we see a grotesquely phallic creature who reminds us of Edgar's lustful proximity yet is also iconographically consistent with Pinky's pose. Engrossed in Willie's fresco, the camera seems almost to miss Pinky's bizarre plunge into the water, although afterwards, it is the oddity of the action itself that lingers. Pinky neither falls nor dives into the water; in another context, one might say she belly flops in. In this ominous context, however, her body appears to be possessed by a sudden rigidity, and she descends to the water like a statue of stone. It is as if the demon in Willie's fresco in the pool has possessed Pinky and drawn her to him.

Pinky has indeed been possessed, but the identity of the demon remains ambiguous and complex throughout the second half of *3 Women*. Not only is it Willie's creation who has greeted Pinky in the pool, but it is Willie who first appears, like a hovering spirit, after Pinky's plunge. Willie's scream for Tom, the neighboring playboy, is the first sound we hear from her, and one of the few sounds she makes in the entire film. Like Elisabet's muteness in Bergman's *Persona*, Willie's deliberate silence is never explained but is a vivid manipulation of her audience inside and outside the film. Also like Elisabet, Willie only breaks this silence in moments of violent crisis or after her role has been transformed. For Bergman, as Susan Sontag explains, "muteness is first of all a fact with a certain psychic and moral weight, a fact which initiates its own kind of causality upon 'other.' "[29] *3 Women, The Long Goodbye* and *That Cold Day in the Park* suggest that the psychic and moral weight of deliberate muteness is also intriguing to Altman, and in the corpus of Altman's work, which is so distinguished by its luxuriant use of sound, the presence of mute characters becomes particularly noticeable.

The omission at key moments in 3 Women of the ambient sound so characteristic of Altman's films serves to draw additional attention to Willie's silence. In part, this is a matter of the contrast between Millie's constant ineffectual talk—reminiscent of Frances's jabbering in That Cold Day in the Park—and Willie's reticence to participate in a verbal society, but it is also an issue of femininity and masculinity. If the heroic male in American film—and American culture—is typically the strong, silent type, then we are not mistaken in hypothesizing that Willie plays a male role in this triad of women. Such a notion is supported by Willie's apparent responsibilities as the manager of Dodge City and by the arduous physical demands of her fresco painting. Yet Willie is the only one of the three women who has fulfilled a role as a woman in the most obvious social and physical terms: she is wife to Edgar and visibly pregnant.

Willie's behavior thwarts facile sexual stereotyping, but that is accomplished at the cost of sustaining her role as the mystery woman. And the cost is significant, because from the moment Willie comes to Pinky's aid at the pool, her presence and her deliberately enigmatic style begin to take over the film. At the hospital, after Pinky's near drowning (I hesitate to call Pinky's plunge a suicide attempt since the visual information provided by the film discloses nothing of what Pinky had in mind when she stood poised at the edge of the poolside balcony), the camera informs us of Willie's new importance in the structure of 3 Women. The camera first finds Pinky in bed and unconscious, as she will remain for an indefinite period of time. Then, as if sensing her potent presence, the camera turns and captures a triple image of Willie, staring through a glass partition at Pinky: within one frame, we see Willie herself, and we see a doubled reflection of Willie's image in the window glass. In a trick of photography, if not of fate, one woman has become three women. In the manipulations of narrative, the lives of three women have become irrevocably intertwined.

The coma into which Pinky has descended as a result of her plunge into the pool transforms the relationship not only of the three women to each other but of the film's structure to us. Whereas doubles or twins characterized the first half of *3 Women*, the significant number in the second part of the film is three. Shortly after the projection of the triple image of Willie, we are presented with a comparable image of Millie, reflected twice in glass and once "for real" within one shot. But unlike Willie, who seems only to be visually multiplied by the experience of Pinky's plunge, the Millie who now appears to us at the hospital, is a woman transformed. Distraught but not hysterical, Millie has left her artifice behind; one can imagine her carefully practiced gestures of sophistication strewn like underwear on the bedroom floor and hurriedly left behind. The Millie we now see is oblivious to the bit of tobacco that a concerned physician gently wipes from her lip; an hour earlier, Millie would have been appalled at such tarnish on her façade. And the same Millie who pursued the male residents to their cafeteria now refuses a young doctor's offer to buy her breakfast. She is neither flattered nor repelled by the invitation; it is simply irrelevant. Millie turns away from the attractive doctor and weeps. This is no time for the erotic.

Millie's style has not been completely obliterated; indeed, it is her pace and her sense of order that structure much of the second half of the film. With Pinky in a coma, and thus temporarily functioning as a second Willie—silent and still—Millie now takes charge of both Pinky's precarious life and the indirect subjectivity of the film. Millie visits her unconscious roommate dutifully each day; she contacts Pinky's parents and arranges for them to visit their daughter; she arranges for the staff at the spa to sign a get-well card for Pinky. Millie's behavior is motivated by obligation, guilt, or a sense of propriety—or all of these—and is never examined by the film; what we see is a series of acts that identify Millie's sense of responsibililty toward Pinky. Altman allows neither probing close-ups nor confessional monologues to tempt us toward Millie's unconscious. We can only judge Millie as a citizen, not a soul. And we learn from Millie, more deeply than we did from Haven Hamilton in *Nashville*, that neither pretension nor vanity wholly exclude a person from responsible membership in a society.

Millie's citizenship neither arrives nor is maintained easily. From the instant of Pinky's fall, Millie's sense of responsibility toward others and her own strength are repeatedly tested. Even reaching Pinky's parents is a problem. The Roses have no telephone and Millie has no sense of how to send a telegram. But Millie figures this out, and, when the Roses do arrive, it is Millie who makes these American primitives accessible to us. In comparison to Pinky's parents, Millie is astute and sophisticated. Mrs. Rose has brought Pinky a crocheted motto for the kitchen; YR, Pinky's daddy, who gave his child her demeaning nickname, is so remote from the complexities of any society that at his child's bedside he can only ask, "What's wrong with her? Why doesn't she wake up?" The point is not, I think, what Kolker claims; that is, that "In 3 *Women*, everyone is trapped by clichés . . ."[30] but rather that our response to something as a cliché is a matter of context and relationship. What is a cliché to some members of the audience may not be to Millie, and what is a cliché to Millie may not be to the Roses. In her total absence of condescension to the Roses, indeed in her generosity to them, Millie teaches us about our lack of generosity to her.

At its most poignant, Millie's interaction with the Roses also reinforces Altman's persistent attempt to remind us of the unpredictability of human behavior. Millie has assumed that the Roses will stay with her. Accordingly, the night after their arrival, Millie pulls out the roll-away bed for herself and gives the bedroom to the elderly couple. Pinky's parents are vividly out of context in Millie's apartment, but both they and Millie appear oblivious to the jarring disjunction of style that we perceive. That night, despite the comforting convention of her yellow sheets and ritualistic diary writing, Millie is restless, and as if irresistibly drawn, she ventures toward her own bedroom and quietly opens the door. We see what Millie sees: the Roses locked in a tight embrace of lovemaking. Both Millie and the camera freeze, but neither indulges the temptations of pornography. The grunts and forceful, erratic movements of the two aging bodies are unquestionably erotic, and as the erotic should do, but seldom does in film, makes the image an extension rather than a substitution of our own sexuality. This is one of the rare erotic images in an Altman film, and it distinguishes itself unhesitantly from more conventional exploitations of eros in movies.

In good films, Stanley Cavell has argued, the relationships within a shot or a series of shots structure our relationship to the world of the movie.[31] Until Millie's encounter with the Roses, each of the central characters in 3 Women has inhabited a shared terrain but each has maintained a distinct distance from the others and the objects that surround them. Much as Millie and Pinky have managed to share an apartment and even a bedroom without genuinely gaining admission to each other's space, we have been kept at a calculated distance from the world of the film. Millie purposefully brings the Roses into her world, however, and then opens the door to their intimacy. Those gestures, in turn, give us entry into the world of 3 Women. The shot of Pinky's parents making love is neither gratuitous nor didactic, in part because it has been prepared for since the early shots of the bodies of the elderly at the spa. Altman, in 3 Women (as he also does in McCabe and Mrs. Miller and Nashville), provokes and establishes our presumptions, our automatic readings of cultural signs, so as to prevent us from facile dismissal of the new experiences he provides. When Millie closes the bedroom door on Pinky's parents' lovemaking, she includes us in her discretion. Here, in contrast to That Cold Day in the Park, there is no place for the role of the voyeur, but there is the privilege that theater has always provided of allowing us to learn from the nakedness of others while we remain modestly hidden.[32]

In one of the many paradoxes that Altman cogently projects, Millie's reward for her nonjudgmental generosity to the Roses is also the source of her most difficult trial. At the hospital, the day after the arrival of Pinky's parents, a nurse informs the Roses that after their initial visit, Pinky began to respond for the first time since her descent into coma. But when Millie and the Roses eagerly enter Pinky's room, it is not to the joyful reunion they expect. We are crowded into the tightly framed space of the hospital room only to discover that Pinky refuses recognition of anyone but Millie. When Mrs. Rose attempts to elicit her daughter's acknowledgment— "Pinky, it's Mama. Here's your Dad"—Pinky responds angrily, "I don't know you." Calling her identity further into question, the young woman also objects vehemently to being called Pinky.

From her immersion in water, Pinky, or Mildred as she now wishes to be called, has been reborn. The mythical pattern and the cliché are transparent, but the known explodes into unexpected fragments. Pinky-Mildred is neither simply innocent nor possessed of the Romantics' vision of a higher innocence derived from experience. The Pinky who returns to convalescence under Millie's patient care is a cruelly successful version of the female image for which Millie was so desperately striving in the first portion of the film. The new Pinky reigns as princess of the poolside parties; by day, she paints her toenails, drinks with Edgar, and merrily mocks Millie's naiveté. She aggravates Millie's sense of sexual inadequacy by remarking that she hopes she is not pregnant; she exploits her illness and Millie's subjugation to it by suggesting that she would recover more rapidly if she had the bedroom all to herself.

Ironically, abhorrent tyrant that she has become, the new Pinky, like the new Millie, gives us a mode of entry to the film we did not have in its first half. For the first hour of 3 Women, our gropings for access are repelled by Willie's muteness and physical remoteness, Millie's synthetic self-composition, and Pinky's vacuity. Now, however, not only Millie's tangible vulnerability, but Pinky's equally tangible arrogance engage us. Pinky's altered behavior evokes facile anger from us, but it is an anger that should provoke second thoughts. Finally, we have what we, and Millie, expect from women in the movies. The metamorphosed Pinky is pretty, sharp-witted and flirtatious. She drapes her barely bikinied body seductively in front of the neighborhood men and the camera, and the camera, for the first time, gives us warm alluring female flesh. She is the junior-high wallflower reborn as Gidget.

Pinky-Mildred also shows us Millie's unrecognized profit in her failure to become the model American woman. In her perfect occupation of the image Millie has sought, Pinky reveals the corruption of that image. Millie was (and to some extent remains) self-conscious; Pinky is now wholly absorbed. Millie groomed her body; Pinky cultivates hers. Millie used her sexuality; Pinky abuses the sexuality of others. Millie borrowed from the culture that surrounded her; Pinky steals not only Millie's car but the best pickings of Millie's style. Millie grasped at little free spaces in her job (a cigarette break here, a day off there); Pinky finds total freedom from work by letting Millie support her. If our chief discomfort in the first half of the film was with unaware ineffectuality, we must now confront what should logically comfort us. As many women eventually learn, even if they cannot themselves accomplish the trick, the art of being a "successful" woman in the context of dominant cultural values is to be sufficiently skillful to appear guileless; the success of the American film actress is the perfection of this craft. Millie embarrasses us because we are admitted to her failure, but in juxtaposition, and perhaps only in juxtaposition, Pinky's success becomes tainted.

This much, and more, 3 Women illuminates. Unfortunately, Altman seems possessed with the same self-conscious sense of inadequacy that undermines Millie's endeavors. Just as 3 Women gains control and momentum to bring it and us to its disorienting conclusion, it stops in its tracks for digression to a dream world that belongs neither to the characters of the film nor its fabricator. After still another eruption of conflict between Millie and Pinky, this time over the diary that Pinky has usurped from Millie, each woman retires to her bed. Without further preamble, the film dissolves into a rapid, disjunctive montage sequence that juxtaposes images of each of the three women and their worlds. The montage begins with an image of Millie sleeping, transforms to Willie sleeping, and then resolves to an image of Willie's face. Most of the shots that follow reiterate earlier shots from the film. We see the twins, Willie's frescoes, Millie visiting the hospital, Pinky in her hospital bed, a laughing mask, close-ups of Pinky's parents, phallic images from Willie's frescoes, Willie lying at what appears to be the bottom of a pool, Willie and Edgar dancing happily together, a knife, Pinky with the red stain of cocktail sauce (repeated twice), and finally the almost still shot of Pinky and Millie framed in the window at Dodge City looking out at the shooting range. Much of the montage follows the chronology of the film; in addition, a pattern of increasingly frequent images of violence emerges. Although I remember the montage as silent, it does contain characteristically Altman insertions of sound. Immediately after the first instance of the fresco shot, we hear a sound reminiscent of Pinky's cries just before she plummets into the pool; the electronic music we have heard intermittently throughout the movie also recurs here.

Unlike the initial or intermediate montage sequences in *Persona*, there is no ambiguity about the phenomenological nature of the *3 Women* montage. Pinky and Millie are in bed, preparing for sleep just prior to the montage. Directly afterwards, Pinky enters the living room where Millie is sleeping and tells her, "I had a bad dream." Consolingly but, of course, erroneously, Millie responds, "Dreams can't hurt you." But Pinky's fear is not assuaged. She asks, "Can I sleep with you?" and Millie gently takes her into bed and cuddles her.

What remains unconvincing and unclear is the source and motivation of this dream. The most available evidence—Pinky's assertion to Millie—informs us that the montage we have seen was Pinky's dream. Included within the montage, however, is material that is more appropriate to the latent mental activities of Willie or Millie. It is also difficult to imagine Pinky creating portions of the montage. The last two images of the dream sequence especially— those of Pinky with the catsup stain and of the reflection of Pinky and Millie—are not Pinky's dream material but ours or Robert Altman's.

A dangerous bit of knowledge can lead spectators, as it has Pauline Kael and others, to read the *3 Women* montage as a Jungian dream projection. The montage then presents the collective unconscious of the three women, and there is no problem in the fact that the dream is ostensibly attributed to Pinky; within a Jungian framework, symbolic activity, including that of the dreams of individuals, draws from not just one psychohistory but the psychohistory of a culture as well. The danger in reading the dream sequence as a Jungian vision is not in over-interpretation but in reduction of the film as a whole, a possibility to which *3 Women* is often vulnerable, and particularly so in this montage. It is all too easy to patch *3 Women* into Jung's *Psyche and Symbol*. Jung's triad of animus, anima, and shadow readily fits the structural triad of women and aspects of each. One could then dispute whether it is a failure or a success of the film that none of the women slides simply or fully into Jung's categories. Willie might be thought to be the personification of the shadow; like Jung's shadow she has a "kind of autonomy, and accordingly, an obsessive or, better, possessive quality" and could be said "to represent first and foremost the personal unconscious." The shadow, Jung relates, "can be realized only through a relation to a partner"; an explanation for Willie's marriage to Edgar thus appears. But the shadow is also "the negative side of the personality" according to Jung, and if one of the women is to represent the negative side of archetypes of female personalities, then surely it is Pinky, not Willie, who fills this function. To take this a step further, one could perceive Pinky and Millie as, respectively, representing anima, the "projection-making factor" and animus, the "mediator between conscious and unconscious"; Pinky's assumption of Millie's role would then suggest that she has absorbed her animus. Jung claims that between the anima and the animus "a feeling of inferiority makes mutual recognition impossible, and without this there is no relationship"; we could read this as the score for a good portion of 3 Women. If we add to this Jung's emphasis on water as the symbolic medium of transformation, his claim that mythologically the sacrificer and the sacrificed are one, and his proposal of Christ as a symbol of self, it becomes increasingly difficult to escape an eerie recognition of Psyche and Symbol as the original script for 3 Women. Indeed, I would wager that one could discover every laden sign of 3 Women in Jung's most well-known work: the uroboros, the tail-eating serpent, that figures so prominently in Willie's paintings is remarked in "Transformation Symbolism in the Mass"; in that same essay, Jung urges that "blood turns into cement in men, and in women into milk."[33]

My purpose in documenting these connections between 3 Women and C. G. Jung's visions is not to reduce a reading of this film to the game of sources and analogues. The problem before me is that I am faced with a film that at once presents the best and worst of Robert Altman's filmmaking. 3 Women is, as Pauline Kael claims, "a lovely, fresh sociological comedy about two working girls from Texas."[34] It is also a deeply disturbing examination and transformation of the cultural signs and roles that imprison American women while paradoxically providing their escape route. At its best, and certainly in the sequences that follow the dream montage, 3 Women transforms the sociological comedy of two working girls into a cultural epic of the interdependence of women and the upheaval and independence from men that might follow from recognition of the interdependency of women. At its worst, each of these women is not a type but an archetype, not a perplexed participant in contemporary American society but a floating soul or unconscious.

3 *Women* admirably attempts to unite the type and the archetype, to present a world that is at once historical and mythological. This is such a necessary endeavor and one so appropriate to both film and the study of women that I am tempted to ignore the flaws and simply applaud the struggle. The montage sequence is an assaultive mistake, however; it cannot be dismissed and therefore demands explanation. And the Jungian explanation makes double sense. As a worldview, it appears to accomplish just what Altman desires: it assumes that the individual psyche is inseparable from the cultural psyche. It also proposes that the world of the unconscious is a collective world, knowable not just by each individual but by the collective society. Within this framework, the presentation of the dream of one person is neither pretentious nor irrelevant but central to the revelation of a culture (a dream, in this context, is just one form of expression of a mythology). Secondly, the presentation of a dream reiterates and clarifies, makes manifest what was latent—in the film as in a particular personality. The insertion of the dream montage could then be understood as a gesture not of condescension and mysticism but of clarification and candor. In the montage, Altman identifies and synthesizes his framework; the presence of the montage prevents us from either ignoring the archetypes or dismissing them as unimportant. The dream sequence is then an explanatory and referential footnote; like any footnote, it interrupts the movement of the text, but in turn, we are supposedly rewarded by recognition of the nature if not the specific identity of the source, and what may have been obscure is made transparent.

In that very transparency, however, lies part of our difficulty. The dream montage is didactic, but the message is no clearer than it ever was in Jung—or in the first hour and a half of 3 *Women*. The condensation of images and sounds from earlier sections of the film weakens their potency because, edited rapidly in this ensemble, they create no new context or story but only remind us of the past. They therefore make us hesitant about the power and integrity of that past experience; if Altman does not feel that the world he has projected signifies sufficiently, why should we?

The montage sequence is also intolerable simply because it is so blatantly identified as a dream. In Bergman's *Persona,* and in many of Altman's films, our experience of shots that are parenthetical to the logical narrative is enriched by our inability to relegate the apparently incoherent material to a separate dream world. In psychotherapy or in daily life, to identify an experience as a dream may be to give it special importance, but in art it is a reductive convention. The student writer who concludes his or her theme with "and then I woke up" is making an excuse for the incoherence of the writing; the film director who does the same embarrasses and disturbs.

Yet through his mistake, Altman educates us. Pinky's dream is annoying because it is pretentious and uninteresting, but it is also aesthetically troubling. Film's power may be in its ability to transport us to otherwise inaccessible worlds, but that does not mean, as Altman seems to half know in most of his film, that all worlds are accessible to film. What we learn from *3 Women* is that the best film can do, like the best any of us can do, is to report a dream; it cannot replicate it. Films themselves may be the daydreams of their creators, but then all that is included within them has equal status as part of that daydream. Films may function for us, like dreams, as complex expressions of wish fulfillment, but in that case, we, not the characters, are being manipulated. The projection of a dream *as* a dream in film calls our attention to the nature and limits of film; we are reminded that with film, we usually suspend our disbelief. With dreams we must discover our belief. The crucial mistake of Altman's dream montage in *3 Women* is that in reinstating our disbelief it provokes us to reflect upon dreams and film, but not upon this dream and these three women. Altman may want us to believe, in a Jungian fashion, that the dream montage is at once a story told to themselves by Pinky, Willie and Millie, a story told to us by him, and a story we tell ourselves, but the obvious constructed ambiance of the sequence denies that very possibility. In some films, this might be a provocative assertion of the questions of modernism and post-modernism,[35] but in film that invites us to believe in the cultural and mythological presence of its characters, we are more likely to be confused by our mixed experiences of alienation and engagement.

Perhaps more threatening to the value of 3 Women than the aesthetic error of the dream montage is its implicit political confusion. If Altman actually does have Jung's worldview in mind, then, of course, he is immediately enmeshed in troubling assumptions. It is Jung, after all, who declares that "woman's consciousness is characterized by the connective quality of Eros" and men's by "the discrimination and cognition associated with Logos."[36] And Jung goes on to remind us that Eros "consists of opinions instead of reflections," which, "as everyone knows, can be extremely irritating" (with such assumptions, who needs archetypes?). I think it can be safely assumed, however, that few spectators will immediately connect the imagery of the film with Jung's image of woman. Nor is there any stretch of the imagination by which Edgar, 3 Women's dominant male figure, is recognizable as the model of "discrimination and cognition."

What must be accounted for is the effect of the dream montage on our relationship to Pinky. Pinky has become despicable since her transformation after her coma, but she has also become powerful and, at least internally to the film, attractive. As her dream, the montage serves to denigrate that power, to suggest not competence and ruthlessness but a fragile grasp of style peaking out from the mind of a lunatic. Then, in fact, she is a female grotesque and need not be taken seriously. As the dreamer of the montage, Pinky is pathetic and dismissible. Her regression to Millie's bed and soothing arms confirms this stance.

Pinky's regression can be read as setting up her role in the next, climactic sequence of the film, but here consistency is out of place. Nothing can or should prepare us for the scene of Willie's birthing of her still-born son, and, in fact, nothing does. The casualness with which the sequence begins contributes to its power. Having stumbled darkly into Pinky and Millie's apartment in search of a beer, Edgar first indulges his pornographic imagination with the sight of Pinky and Millie in bed together, then drunkenly informs the women that Willie is having her baby, that she is alone, and that she does not need him or anyone. The dimly lit scene is a far more powerful nightmare than was Pinky's; after the excessive white light of most of the film, it is difficult to recognize what we are seeing and hearing. Millie, however, sees clearly through the murk. Her body flashes past us, pulling Pinky with her to go to Willie's aid.

Like Millie, the film wastes no time in getting to Willie's labor, but unlike Millie, the camera mostly remains outside with Pinky, witnessing Willie's struggle from a distance. The perfectness of the camera's stance in this scene redeems the film's earlier mistakes, making an apt complement to the pure generosity of Millie's behavior within the narrative. We are returned in this sequence to Pinky's point of view, for Pinky, having been ordered by Millie to fetch a physician, ignores Millie's command and stands transfixed outside the open doorway to Willie's room. Standing in darkness, our attention is riveted on Willie's struggles to deliver her baby and on Millie's unsuccessful attempts to aid her. We are where film can place us; we are witnesses to the sounds and gestures of Willie's pain, and our anguish is in our helplessness. The tension of our position is made emphatic by Pinky's presence at the camera's side. We could scream to make Pinky move, but our cries would be of no use.

There is an integrity to the scene of Willie's labor that is rarely achieved on film. All movement is within the frame of the doorway. Nothing outside that frame is mobile, yet without Pinky as witness outside that door, a key pole of tension would be lacking. Our relationship to the film is precisely defined by the relationship within. We are voyeurs, but here we acknowledge that fact; it is not surreptitious. And the price we pay is that we can do nothing but watch. Because of this integrity, the death of Willie's baby and the horror of Willie's weeping, cuddling of the corpse cannot be denied or sentimentalized. And because we have witnessed the ardor of Willie's and Millie's struggle to deliver the baby, the male identity of the child signifies not an arbitrary destruction of men but a possible outcome of women's labor.

The shots of Willie's labor transform the sign functions of the film and also reveal a new relationship between Millie and Pinky. Having shown extraordinary strength and compassion during the delivery, Millie now allows her grief and fury to emerge. As she

Millie (Shelley Duvall) attempts to assist Willie in delivering her baby in *3 Women* (*The Museum of Modern Art/Film Stills Archive, New York City*)

stumbles through the doorway toward Pinky, Millie holds her still-bloodied hands in front of her, shaking; her pose suggests both her desire to rid herself of these ineffectual instruments and her desire to strangle Pinky. Instead, she slaps Pinky, and the camera closes the sequence with a lingering close-up of the bloody imprint of Millie's hand on Pinky's face. The image of blood no longer warns; it releases passion and identifies responsibility. Millie's mark is made on Pinky's face in a manner that Pinky can neither mock nor reject. As Kolker suggests, Millie's slap demonstrates "a hitherto unrealized sense of power"; more important perhaps, it signifies acknowledgment of both the separateness and the relationship of the two women. As was promised throughout the film, Willie finally serves her function as catalyst to this recognition.

Like *Nashville, 3 Women* has its epilogue, but in *3 Women* the final sequence serves not to conjoin the disparate elements of the film but to allow us to envision their restructuring. The setting and lighting of the epilogue of *3 Women* return us to Dodge City and the origins of the film, but roles have been significantly altered. Edgar, we learn from passing remarks, has met with a fatal accident (the implication is that he was shot, and since the film earlier showed us each of the women's prowess with a gun, any one or all of them may have contributed to this "accident"). In the absence of Edgar and any other significant men, the three women have formed a new family. The same elements of style from which we drew our first information about Pinky, Millie, and Willie now provide our knowledge of the women's new roles. The first of the women we see is Pinky, costumed again in a girlish pink blouse, hunched over the counter in the bar area of Dodge City. Her hunched shoulders and vacant visage recall the original Pinky, although the girl in front of us suggests no possibility of impending power. Pinky tells a Coca-Cola salesman that she will "Get her mother," and a moment later, Millie enters, visibly fulfilling the role of Mother. Millie's mother is the Pilgrim widow, her hair tied in a mature coil, her dress nondescript, pale-yellow efficiency, her face unadorned by makeup. We do not encounter Willie until Millie and Pinky have returned to the nearby house, the setting of Willie's birthing, to prepare dinner. Willie has let her hair down and her tongue loose. Her role, as it has

Millie (Shelley Duvall), imaged during a dream sequence in the maternal role she takes on toward the end of *3 Women,* cradles Pinky (Sissy Spacek) in front of one of the murals painted by Willie (Janice Rule). (*The Museum of Modern Art/Film Stills Archive, New York City*)

been throughout the film, is the most ambiguous of the three women; she at once functions as grandmother and older sister to Pinky and surprisingly, given the events we have witnessed, is protective of her. The last-heard words of the film are spoken by Willie to Millie about Pinky: "I don't know why you have to treat her so mean."

We are allowed to see these women in their new roles, but the persistent distance of the camera, and the renewed pressure of excessive light make clear that we will not be provided any intimate penetration of this new configuration. The epilogue informs us that the women have inhabited new roles, but the surrounding culture is static. The sequence begins with the image of a huge yellow Coca-Cola truck approaching Dodge City and ends with shots of carefully arranged piles of tires succeeded by a final glimpse of Willie's frescoes. The signs of the contemporary and the ancient culture endure.

The conclusion of 3 Women is unhesitantly ambiguous and oppressive. The zooms of the camera, the sparsity of sound, and the languor of internal movement keep us remote from the film's last moments and ask that we contemplate the scene. Robert Kolker concludes that Altman's final projection in 3 Women is the director's "most bitter observation of domination and passivity, of assent to ritual and assumption of cultural myths."[37] For Kolker, the end of 3 Women is a vision of a world in which only the sexual identities have changed; the structural patterns of power and domination remain.

Yet a world in which masculinity is no longer a source of power or key reference for identity is a different place from most of what we know on or off the screen. The only man seen at the end of 3 Women is the menial Coca-Cola delivery person. A film that began with three women, each of whom, at some important point, derived identity from men, ends with three women who have now destroyed the son and the father-lover. And they, the women, survive. Millie, Pinky and Willie own and run Dodge City, and it endures. Pinky and Millie no longer work as demeaned servants at the health spa. Power and domination may still structure relationships, but the key relationships now are among these women, and it is they who control the power and yield to each other's domination. Three women those lives were earlier connected by men and circumstance, by imitation, competition, and projection, now live together in distinct relation to each other.

The conflicts we witness in 3 Women do not resolve the dilemma of being men and women in society. 3 Women does, however, present a new sexual poetics for the expression of that society. The styles, the rhythms, the meanings of gender-laden signs are renegotiated in this film to form a distinct if faltering vision of a film language that gives space and control to women.

*   *   *   *

The final, silent images of the three women on their porch and of a pile of tires that conclude *3 Women* are sufficiently strong and ambiguous to suggest that this is all Robert Altman can say and is willing to say about women in contemporary American society.[38] But in the eighties, there was more to come. In *Come Back to the 5 and Dime, Jimmy Dean, Jimmy Dean (1982),* Altman returned to where he had ended with *3 Women,* to a dramatic world inhabited only by women, framed by a society dominated by men. Adapted from a theatrical script that Altman also directed for a Broadway production, *Jimmy Dean* had only one man in its cast, and he appears on screen only in memory segments. The six women in the movie come together in 1975 in a small town in Texas for the twentieth reunion of the Disciples, the James Dean fan club that they founded in 1955. One of the women, Juanita, owns the 5 and Dime where the other five women once held fan-club meetings and now reunite.

From the start, the world of the movie *Come Back to the 5 and Dime, Jimmy Dean, Jimmy Dean* asserts its origin in theater. All action is confined to one set, that of the interior of the 5 and Dime. The opening camera pan displays relics associated with James Dean—numerous photographs of the actor, a cartoon-like image of the house that was a key set element in *Giant*—and a huge banner that reads "20th Reunion—The Disciples of James Dean, September '55–September '75." Behind the banner are two American flags, cultural and political backdrops to this reunion and its meaning that recall Altman's iconic use of the American flag in other films, most notably *Nashville, M*A*S*H* and *Buffalo Bill and the Indians.*

On a second viewing of *Jimmy Dean,* the images captured in the first camera pan can easily be read as cues to the unveiling of the lives of the members of the Disciples. Perhaps more striking on a first viewing, however, is the ambiance of the 5 and Dime, itself a relic of pre-mall American culture; not only in small towns but also in numerous neighborhoods of Newark and Detroit and Atlanta, the 5 and Dime, with its cacaphony of goods and its seductive soda fountain, was, for many twentieth century Americans, the one site a person could count on for heterogeneous consumption. The handkerchiefs for aunts, the egg-beater for our mother, the toys for cousins and each other that my brother, sister, and I found at our local 5 and Dime when we did our Christmas shopping remain scattered on shelves and trays in this 5 and Dime in 1975.

It is a Proustian gesture, this first shot, one that simultaneously establishes a past and a present of American life. Like several major American dramas (Tennessee Williams's *The Glass Menagerie* is the obvious archetype), *Jimmy Dean* is a memory play; from the start, the past asserts its psychological indomitability and its material fragility. Seen always (except during the final credits) from inside, through a doorway or window, the world outside the 5 and Dime is vague and mythologic; bright white overly available light confirms the intense heat of the place and day and also washes colors that might otherwise distinguish one object from another. But inside, where artificial light has been plotted by the film technicians, colors and objects are distinct and appear vividly exposed.

Entrances make a big difference in *Jimmy Dean,* and as more frequently occurs on stage than on the screen, each character takes her first moment to reveal herself and to lay the first blocks in the construction of the world of this movie. (In classical American cinema, the camera discovers and reveals the stars. Our pleasure is akin to that of the astronomer but is also inseparable from the confirmation of our position as voyeurs.) Juanita (Sudie Bond), the owner of the 5 and Dime, appears on screen first, immediately turning on the radio to a station that plays religious music. As he did so precisely in *Nashville,* Altman uses song lyrics to introduce a quality of the characer and, in this case, a motif of the film: "Jesus knew . . . there's a cross for everyone and there's a cross for me." The cross that Juanita bears will be known soon enough, as will be the crosses of the other women who soon enter. In the meantime, what we see is a middle-aged woman whose frumpy, frowning appearance perfectly fulfills the type of the small-town working-class woman, a person whose face suggests the possibility of kindness and a lifetime without laughter.

Sissy (Cher) makes her entrance next, her constant theatricality announced by her flouncing, breezy stride to the radio, which she unhesitantly turns to a country-and-western station. Her white, off-

Sissy (Cher), in *Come Back to the 5 and Dime, Jimmy Dean, Jimmy Dean,* as she reflects in the present (1975) and is reflected in the mirror that transports her and us back to 1955. (*The Museum of Modern Art/Film Stills Archive, New York City*)

the shoulder peasant blouse and full skirt suit the music and a period style that was out of date several years before the 1975 setting of the film, except perhaps in isolated towns like McCarthy, Texas, and in Sissy's own timeless image of herself. Sissy's blouse also calls immediate attention to her character's signature, her "exceptional tits." Her opening claim that "it ain't going to rain" initiates the first of the film's intermittent transformations to the same setting twenty years earlier, when it did, indeed, rain. Using a shot of the mirror behind the soda fountain as the convention that announces the representation of a memory, we see and hear through the mirror Juanita chiding Sissy for her tardiness in words and gestures almost identical to those we have just heard exchanged in the 1975 "present" setting. This memory segment, like all those that follow, differs in hue and tone from the presentation of both the world outside the 5 and Dime and that within the store in 1975. Like the photographs on the wall and the *film noir* movies of the fifties, the segments from the past appear in a blue-tinted near black-and-white coloration.

Traditional film terminology would call these mirror shots flashbacks, meaning that they refer to a period prior to that in which the film is initially situated, but the term does not quite suffice here. In most instances, the flashback is explicitly a directorial gesture, a tantalizing gift from the *auteur* to the audience that establishes the discrepant awareness between viewers and characters that is key to dramatic irony. A classic example can be found in Sergio Leone's *Once Upon a Time in the West,* in which fragments of a sequence that depicts a grotesque hanging witnessed by a young boy sometime in the past provide the narrative motivation for the revenge sought by one of the film's male leads (Charles Bronson). While these images do represent pieces of the adult man's memory, those memories have been recollected and projected by another; they are projected to us as externally originated clues to the narrative, not as memories initiated and projected by the character. Flashbacks often are intended to exist in the realm of the unconscious of a particular character's point of view, but they are, nonetheless, symbolic; power in the relationship between sign and signifier, image and audience, is wielded explicitly, not by the character within the world of the film or by a dialogic text but by the director.

The mirror scenes in *Jimmy Dean* might be better described as imaginaries than as flashbacks. I am thinking here of the postmodern sense of the word "imaginary," a term that has its (not inappropriate) murkiness and confusions, but which usefully designates, to paraphrase Bill Nichols, "not the unreal, existing only in the imagination but rather pertains to views, images, fiction or representations that contribute to our sense of who we are and to our everyday engagement with the world around us. These signs are of social representation, the markers or bearers of ideology. . . ."[39] Although it is, of course, ultimately a filmic deceit, these imaginaries connote the director's absence rather than the presence asserted by conventional flashbacks.

If the mirror sequences of *Jimmy Dean*, seen, indeed, through a glass darkly, exist in the realm of the imaginary, then the world of the present, in the foreground of the soda-fountain mirror, remains in the realm of the symbolic, not simply in the sense that traditionally film functions within this realm but more precisely in the Saussurian sense of the indexical and arbitrary relations of signifiers to signifieds that Altman explores throughout his work. In the 5 and Dime of the present, signification is both ordinary and flexible; from the beginning, we understand what we see and hear but then are led to re-comprehend each image and sentence.

If we are to understand that not much has changed in this place in twenty years, Sissy's next recollected vision warns us that our perceptions of change depend on points of view. Within the mirror of Sissy's memory, we and Sissy discover a pleasant-looking crew-cutted boy identified as Joe (Mark Patton) revealing to a plain, shy-eyed girl named Mona (Sandy Dennis) that he is in love. Mona's refusal to hear this confession is interrupted, blocked by a quick cut of the camera (and of Sissy's desire) to a more pleasing image of Joe, Mona, and Sissy taking on the roles of the McGuire sisters singing "Sincerely." Theirs is a surprisingly precise and skillfully performed imitation.

The entrances of Stella Mae and Edna Louise, two more members of the Disciples, return Sissy and the viewer to 1975. Each of these women has traveled some distance for the reunion, and while both are immediately recognizable to Juanita and Sissy and may appear to us as additional relics of the fifties, both Stella Mae and Edna Louise quickly reveal that they have also traveled some distance from the girls they were in 1955. Although Edna Louise's sweet voice, uncurled hair, and clean-scrubbed face are those of a fifteen year old, she is pregnant with her seventh child, as she proudly announces. With her too-tight skirt, shrill voice, and cowgirl Stetson, Stella Mae's proclaimed wealth, acquired through her husband, carries with it an awkward arrogance that she further manifests in her put-down of Edna Louise, to whose quiet claim of good luck, Stella Mae retorts: "You ain't gonna be lucky until you get them tubes of yours tied."

The reunion has begun, but it is not until after another brief memory sequence in which Mona (still viewed in the context of 1955) first hears that Elizabeth Taylor, James Dean, and Rock Hudson will be shooting *Giant* nearby that Mona and then Joe appear, in what I have called the symbolic realm of the film, for the present occasion. While Sissy, Juanita, Stella Mae, and Edna Louise reencounter each other, they await Mona's return from a different reunion—that of the cast from the movie *Giant,* shot only sixty miles from McCarthy. It was as an extra in that cast that Mona took her heralded first step toward fame and glory. When Mona finally does enter, dragging a suitcase as if she had walked rather than taken the sixty-mile trip by bus, Stella Mae, Edna Louise, and Sissy have momentarily left the 5 and Dime. In the whiny voice that only Sandy Dennis can produce, Mona anxiously asks Juanita if anyone has come for the reunion, and Juanita, destroying what was meant to be a surprise, confides the arrival of Stella Mae and Edna Louise. Overcome with remembering and delight, it is now Mona who turns to the mirror, which, reflecting her reflections, reproduces the day Mona returned to the 5 and Dime after only one week at college because, she tells Juanita, her asthma proved to be too much for her. Back in the 1975 moment of this world, Mona anxiously inquires for "Jimmy Dean," a persona who her exchange with Juanita indicates is not entirely, at least, a figment of her imagination but her son. But Jimmy Dean is absent, as he will be throughout the film.

The only key character still missing, the Joe of the mirror segments, finally arrives after the re-entrances of Sissy, Stella Mae, and Edna Louise. But when Joe does appear, his identity at first eludes everyone. The person who appears is an elegantly dressed, beautiful woman who casually enters the store, vaguely commenting that she would just like to browse. This woman's graceful composure, flowing red hair, and subtly perfect makeup, as well as the yellow Porsche in which we are told she has arrived, delineate someone who is out of place in this world, a person who is as much a stranger to McCarthy, Texas, as McCabe was a stranger to Presbyterian Church. The woman's name, we come to learn, is Joanne; Jo for short.

Like almost all theater, the dialogue in *Come Back to the 5 and*

Joanne (Karen Black) exposes herself and other secrets to Sissy (Cher) and Juanita (Sudie Bond) at the soda-fountain counter in *Come Back to the 5 and Dime, Jimmy Dean, Jimmy Dean.* (*The Museum of Modern Art/Film Stills Archive, New York City*)

Dime, Jimmy Dean, Jimmy Dean is the action. And like Western tragedies since Sophocles' *Oedipus Tyrannus,* the dialogue moves relentlessly toward revelation and recognition. Soon after Mona's return from her other reunion and just before Jo's arrival, Mona admits to Juanita her disappointment in the *Giant* reunion, where, to her dismay, she found that the only remains of the set for *Giant* are stray fragments scattered like garbage. Even twenty years ago, she quickly adds, there was, of course, only the façade of the famous house, "but that's the way they do things in the movies," she notes. "Deceiving to the eye they call it."

This is the way they do things in this movie, too. For while *Jimmy Dean* embraces its origins in theater, it is simultaneously and self-consciously a movie. It is not present to us, in the way that live theater is;[40] it is always in the past, and thus the scenes that take place in 1955, while in a different ontological realm, are not in a different place (as they were on stage, where 1955 took place in the upstage playing area and 1975 occurred downstage) but always, as the movies dictate, on the screen. And where the deceptions to the eye on stage are presented to us as a mutually acknowledged accomplishment of the audience's collusion with the makers of theater, in most movies, the power intrinsic to the deceit appears wholly held by the screen and the fabricators of the images it displays. In contrast to our experience with many movies, however, in which, as Nichols claims, "our necessary act of collaboration in this deceit goes unnoticed and unnoted,"[41] in *Jimmy Dean* we are offered a form of knowledge and a consciousness of that knowledge that endanger our very position as movie spectators.

The knowledge offered, insisted upon, in *Jimmy Dean* also threatens each character's illusion of the stability of her own identity. From the moment of her entrance, it is the apparent stranger named Jo who is the on-screen source of this knowledge and who deploys its power. But even before Jo's arrival, Altman has initiated his collaboration with Jo/Joe in a memory sequence in which Mona recalls through the mirror Sissy's angry revelation that Sydney, Juanita's husband (who is deceased by 1975), has fired Joe, not because of the quality of Joe's work but because "of what he is." A repeat shot, still through the mirror, recaptures Joe, Sissy, and Mona imitating the McGuire sisters. Snatches of dialogue that refer, ambiguously, to "first what happened at the talent show and then the senior prom," followed by Juanita's assertion that "next thing, he [Joe] will turn into a Communist," begin to tell one story of how Joe was perceived by the townspeople of McCarthy, Texas. For Juanita, Joe "is a sick boy and should be treated. In the eyes of God, he does not belong." It is, stunningly, Mona who refuses this understanding of Joe: "Then God is wrong," she retorts. "God made him didn't he? If God doesn't accept him, then I don't accept God." In this movie, even God's point of view is only one way of seeing and telling a tale.

It is Mona, too, who initiates the recognition that the elegant woman stranger is, indeed, the Joe who does not belong. When the still-strange woman asks Mona if she is the mother of "his" son, referring to the highway sign that advertizes "See the son of Jimmy Dean. Visit Woolworth's 5 and Dime," what Mona hears is less the substance of the question than something familiar in the voice. If we perceive Mona from the start as odd, it is in large part because she insists on deconstructing many of the signs before her; for Mona, few signifiers are stably attached to significants. Hers is a world in continuous reconstruction and thus hers is a world in which a signifier, a tone of voice, can attach to unordinary meanings.

Informed further by the still unidentified stranger's claim that she used to find Sydney, Juanita's husband, on the floor, drunk, every Wednesday night when she came to mop up, Mona quietly announces, "I think I know. It's Joe." But what for Mona is a form of knowledge is initially approached as a frivolous deception by Sissy, Juanita, and Stella Mae. Sissy tells Joe/Joanne to "take off your wig and crap so we can see how you turned out." Stella Mae, more distressed, exclaims, "Shit! I didn't drive here all the way from Dallas to play who's a girl and who ain't" And when, a few moments later, Jo corrects Juanita's reference to her as "he," Juanita retorts, "Oh you're not a she—you're only pretending to be one just like you always did." Sissy, Juanita, and Stella Mae take Joe's appearance as Joanne as a form of play; he is pretending to be a girl. They want what they perceive to be a charade to end.

There are, of course, limits to what we can accurately call pretending, as J. L. Austin has shown.[42] Like the man in Austin's example who takes a bite out of another's leg, "pretending" to be a hyena, Jo's behavior does not strike Mona as a charade. For Mona, the moment is the dawning of an aspect. In her admission that she finds Joanne (and her sex-change operation) "disgusting," Mona ironically comes closer to acknowledging the complexity of Joe's change to Joanne than do the others at the reunion.

This leads me to wonder if Altman is here presenting Joe/Jo as something like the Gestalt figure of the duck-rabbit. I could say that Sissy, Juanita, and Stella Mae now "see" the figure before them as Joe, whereas Mona sees this figure as Joanne-who-was-Joe. This is not unlike one person seeing the Gestalt image as a rabbit, the other as a duck. That this is not a wrong way in which to understand Joe/Jo is suggested by Altman's immediate cuts to what I have earlier called imaginaries—to shots through the mirror of Joe twenty years before, after he had been brutally beaten and raped in the town graveyard by a male classmate, an event that was witnessed by a cheering mob of local folk who taunted Joe for being "like a girl."

By contextualizing Joe's transformation to Joanne, Altman enables us to comprehend Sissy, Stella Mae, and Juanita's initial way of seeing Jo as Joe. Context is not a magic word, however, nor is it singular or easily defined. We are still faced with the problem of the difference in Mona's response to Jo. If all of these women have participated in the same community, have shared the same community of discourse, why is Mona's point of view so different from that of the others?[43] Altman provides one kind of answer by further contextualization. Desperate to distract herself and her friends from the disturbance of Joanne's presence, Mona attempts to reestablish the ritual of the reunion by retelling her story of her participation in the filming of *Giant*. In highly romantic language, she brings both her on-screen and off-screen audience to the climactic moment in her tale—the night she spent with James Dean. She was "chosen," she relates, not just be an extra in the cast of *Giant* but to be James Dean's lover and, subsequently, the mother of his son.

Mona's story does provide another context, but it does not displace the context previously established; nor does it suffice. Near the end of Mona's narration, Jo begins to interrupt her and finally insists on telling her own story of the *Giant* shooting. As Jo tells it, Mona went with Joe to the *Giant* cast call for extras, and while Mona was selected to be an extra, it was Joe, not James Dean, who "chose" her to be his lover and who fathered her son. Although Juanita now admits that no one ever believed James Dean was the father of Mona's child, Joe's role in the story as related by Joanne is news to everyone present (except, perhaps, Mona) and serves to reorient the points of view of Sissy, Edna Louise, Stella Mae, and Juanita.

From the start, clued by the noted absence from the scene of Jimmy Dean, Mona's son, and by her nervous behavior, we, the audience, suspect something is untrue in Mona's story. We might, in fact, not even need these clues, since we are likely to share Juanita's sense (what we might call common sense) that it is unlikely that this

Mona shields herself from exposure of her own history behind the James Dean icons she has collected as she recognizes that Joanne was once her friend and lover Joe in *Come Back to the 5 and Dime, Jimmy Dean, Jimmy Dean*. (*The Museum of Modern Art/Film Stills Archive, New York City*)

ordinary, apparently timid woman would have attracted the great star James Dean. This is not, however, a simple or obvious response, because, at the same time, most American women, at least, will recognize in Mona's story their own fantasies of "making it" with a movie star. (I recall my mother and other women of her generation proclaiming that Clark Gable could park his boots under her bed any time.)

The discrepancy between what we now think we know and what Mona at least appears to know and believe follows the traditional pattern of classical tragedy, in which the true history of a central character is known or suspected by the audience and a restricted number of characters onstage, and the dialogue moves relentlessly toward the confrontation of the tragic hero or heroine with his or her "real" history. This does, indeed, happen in *Jimmy Dean*. Mona is not only confronted with the truth that not James Dean but Joe fathered her baby but also is led to know that all of the others present knew some of the truth and repressed it, in large part to protect Mona's fragile sense of self. In the terms of Altman's previous movies, Mona is left naked without ever having to strip.

The script of *Jimmy Dean* is thus structured on the basis of a traditional theatrical recognition scene, the anagnorisis that Aristotle defined as the central moment of tragedy. In the world of this drama, however, there is no bittersweet relief or catharsis—for characters or audience—in confrontation with the truth of the past. If anything, Mona is impoverished by the revelation of her delusion. No plague is relieved, no virtue restored by this revelation.

But there is something else that happens in the movie *Jimmy Dean*. The recognition scene here is dependent upon and intersected by what I have earlier called transformations. In the theater, transformations are gestures by which actors alter themselves in front of the audience; they take on another role or age or identity before us by blatantly changing their appearance before us. Much as actors project their voices, they *make* transformations in the theater. In film, however, it is either magic or technology that changes the world and its inhabitants before our very eyes. The disappearance of a character is not something we see the character do, but an act committed upon him. Transformations occur in the worlds of movies because they are possible, not because the actors make them happen.

The oddity of *Jimmy Dean* as a movie *and* as a drama is that it presents a situation in which not one but several characters are radically transformed, but it is the transformation of time and place not the key transformations of persons that occur in front of our eyes. Mona's recognition could not occur were it not for the transformation of Joe to Joanne, but Joe is already transformed into Joanne when we see the character. Dissolves from Joanne in 1975 through the mirror to Joe in 1955 are the most blatant instances of character transformations in the movie, but much like the dream sequence in *3 Women*, these are arguably gratuitous and are not key to our understanding of the changes that are a repeated refrain of the dialogue.

What we see and have to grapple with is Karen Black playing Joanne, who tells us that she, once, was Joe. Everything we see confirms that this person before us, projected on the screen, is a woman. We are led to ask ourselves what it would mean, then, to say she is "really" a man. Not the image but our imaging is thus transformed. Is gender a matter of sexual identity at birth or of the image one projects and the role one plays? Or is gender a matter of the qualities and projections we do not indeed understand, as we come to know that we do not understand our own viewing of Joanne?

These questions are not answered but further complicated by the story of Sissy begun by Jo but completed by Sissy herself after Mona's and Jo's tales are told. Once again, this story comes in various versions. At first, Sissy claims that her husband, Lester T., the man who had assaulted Joe, has been absent for two years only because he has a great job in another town. But as Jo tells of her own coincidental encounter with Lester T. in Kansas City, an encounter that included an attempted seduction of Jo by Lester, Sissy is provoked to admit that she has been deserted by her husband.

At the core of Sissy's story is her admission that her large breasts have been the basis of her attraction for Lester and, more important, her sense of self. Through the camera's due gaze, we repeatedly glimpse those breasts and Sissy's and her friends' attention to them. They indeed command attention. The camera repeatedly captures Sissy adjusting her blouse and glancing down at her breasts. Several verbal references are made to the size of Sissy's breasts, most poignantly, Sissy's own report that Lester T. had avowed that Sissy "had the biggest pair of melons in the whole state of Texas." Only after Jo's anecdote, however, does Sissy reveal that she has had a mastectomy and that these are not her real breasts but rubber substitutes.

Again, a conventional recognition scene is altered by the transformation of our understanding of what we see and know. A key attribute of what we have come to think of as the "female" is emptied of conventional meaning. Sissy is no less a woman than she was before we knew that her breasts were not "real." Indeed, she now appears to be a more complex person, and this may tell us something about what it means to be a man or a woman.

Just looking at Joanne and Sissy after each of their revelations of their operations is disconcerting. It is not only the object of our viewing, however, that unsettles, but the point of view from which we look. We are led to re-view each of the characters in this film by their own revisions of their points of view. Once she accepts that Joanne cannot simply remove a disguise and reemerge as Joe, Stella Mae is confused: "You know, I seen an amorphodite in a carnival once. They said it was a half man, half woman. Is that what you are?" In case anyone should ever ask? Jo replies, "Just tell them I'm a freak." Refusing that reading but demonstrating her own re-viewing of Joe, Sissy grabs Jo's hand and commands that they all go get a drink. Similarly, although the image of Sissy that we and the Disciples see remains constant (that is to say, the signifier remains constant), Sissy's admission of her double mastectomy and the fear of both death and rejection that accompanied the loss of her breasts effects a re-cognition of her by both her on-screen and off-screen viewers.

As an instance of a medium, *Jimmy Dean* exists at the conjunction of theater and film. This is to say that it is not a filmed play, nor is it a movie simply based on a script written for theater. Rather, it is a movie that embraces and swallows its theatrical parent. Knowingly unable to replicate the power of the voice on stage, the movie exploits the camera's ability to project and capture the speaking face. More like in conventional movies and unlike in much of Altman's other work, the close-up in *Jimmy Dean* responds to the characters' desires for intimacy or distance. In this movie, the close-up becomes a subversive gesture, a challenge to traditional film's conventional coding of the erotic. While viewers' potential pleasure in shots of Jo's legs or Sissy's breasts is eroded by the film's verbal revelations, close-ups in *Jimmy Dean* emphasize the positions of these women as subjects, and as subjects not with a singular "woman's" perspective but as subjects with disparate, only partially knowable and unstable points of view. Confined to the stage, like yet another actor, the camera moves and does what film can so strangely do—unselfconsciously and fluidly it constantly shifts point of view, marking the dialogic quality of any one's knowledge of the world.

This is yet another instance of Altman's deployment of what I have called a promiscuous camera, but used here in conjunction with the close-up, the promiscuous camera not only refuses to establish a star for this movie but also reminds us that part of what this movie is about is the destructive force of the worship of stars by many Americans. The close-up usually serves to iconicize particular actors, establishing their faces as objects of worship. But both by distributing close attention among the diverse faces of the women in *Jimmy Dean* and by capturing women's faces not as perfect objects of beauty but as subjects viewing each other, Altman avoids the fetishism associated with women that both critics and Altman himself have condemned in many movies.

Although I do not believe it is true of all Hollywood movies, critic Laura Mulvey is mostly right when she argues that "Women are constantly confronted with their own image in one form or another, but what they see bears little relation or relevance to their own unconscious fantasies, their own hidden fears and desires."[44] At the least, *Come Back to the 5 and Dime, Jimmy Dean, Jimmy Dean* is an exception to this rule. That the imaging of women in *Jimmy Dean* is relevant to the complex fantasies, fears, and desires of women is important in itself, as an act, let us say, of rectification, particularly so in a movie that revises and extends Mulvey's additional claim that "the message of fetishism concerns not woman, but the narcissistic wound she represents for man."[45] Fetishism is, after all, what the James Dean fan club is all about. And while I do not feel on sure enough ground to make an extended argument in this direction, were I to proceed along the Freudian path proscribed by Mulvey and others, I might make the case that the womb, not the phallus, is the true exhibit in this film and that the relics of James Dean that overwhelm the 5 and Dime and that objectify Mona's desire for pleasure and power represent the narcissistic wound *man* represents for *woman*. Stella Mae has, after all, spent fifty dollars on the picture of James Dean's penis that she brings as her contribution to the reunion, and all of the women except Mona greet the image with an awe and glee not unlike what women might project would occur in a men's locker room.

There remains a question of what to do with the knowledge that

Robert Altman, a man, is the director of this movie. It is he who stands behind the camera's gaze, directs its attention and ours. In at least one of his other films, *A Wedding*, Altman's camera becomes a participant in the activities screened, but always before, when looking at women has been the issue, the male point of view has been made problematic but not denied. Even, or perhaps particularly, at the end of *3 Women*, when the world has been reconfigured in terms of a family of women, the distance of the camera and the gestures of uncertainty of its interpretation of what it sees recall that this is, first, a man watching. When, however, the point of view in *Jimmy Dean* is not that, indirectly, of one of the characters viewed, as it sometimes is, it must/might be that of another woman. The stories these women tell, and the bonds they affirm and destroy are those established among women by women. They could not, would not, talk of breasts lost and desires thwarted in the ways they do in the company of men. Or could they, would they? They, after all, appear to have done so with Joe before his sex change. But then he was "too much" like a woman, and that was why he was despised by the men in town. So, perhaps what Altman is taking on here is a woman's point of view, but not necessarily the explicit identity of a woman. And this may provide an idea of what has been wrong and a model of what could be right about the movies we have seen and those we might see in the future.

In the end, then, the most important transformations made possible by *Jimmy Dean* are of the visions of those who watch and listen. But we must watch and listen carefully, as we learn from Edna Louise in the final moments of the film. Edna Louise does not become a new woman, as the dialogue suggests she might, when she puts on her party dress. But she, who works everyday as a beautician and is a mother of six going on seven; she, who appears to be the most pathetic and stable of the characters on screen, asserts calmly as she departs that she is not a victim but a happy woman.

We are shown examples of transformation in *Come Back to the 5 and Dime, Jimmy Dean, Jimmy Dean* so that we will encounter our own reticence in accepting the possibility of seeing women and men differently. If Juanita, the oldest and most ideologically reified of the women in this film, can depart telling Jo, "I hope you found what you came here looking for . . . Miss," then we, too, can change our ways of seeing. The latent message in *Jimmy Dean* is not that we can endure a world comprised only of women but that a world in which men must destroy the feminine and in which women are uncertain about what feminine means is a world that demands re-mediation.[46]

CHAPTER 5

DEMOCRATIC VISTAS:
SPECTACLES, SCREENS,
AND MONITORS

Exult each patiot heart!—this night is shewn
A piece which we may fairly call our own;
Where the proud titles of "My Lord! Your Grace!"
To humble Mr. and plain Sir give place.
Our Author pictures not from foreign climes
The fashions, or the follies of the times
But has confin'd the subject of his work
To the gay scenes—the circles of New York.
On native themes his Muse displays her pow'rs;
If ours the faults, the virtues too are ours.

. . . Should rigid critics reprobate our play,
At least the patriotic heart will say,
"Glorious our fall, since in a noble cause,
"The bold attempt alone demands applause."

From "A Prologue" to *The Contrast* by Royall Tyler,
first performed in New York City, April 1787[1]

Americans have always loved a good show. Many of the early Puritan preachers were charismatic performers, and it was not uncommon in seventeenth and eighteenth century New England towns for a parade to precede the annual election-day sermon. During the seventeenth century, several large pageants occurred in the southern colonies. Before there was an American Revolution, Philadelphia was already a theater center, and plays were being produced in

Boston, New York, and Baltimore, despite the misgivings of many of the town fathers. Buffalo Bill's Wild West Show may have radically changed American show business, as Bill (Paul Newman) claims in Altman's *Buffalo Bill and the Indians,* but it did so in an America already well disposed to an American "greatest show on earth" by numerous roving troupes of actors and burlesque artists, by increasingly elaborate parades in small towns and big cities, by rodeos, circuses, Fourth of July celebrations, and by dramas that explicitly demanded the presentation of distinctively American characters, issues, and settings.

About show business itself, we Americans have had fewer ambivalences than have most cultures, and we appear to be less anxious about the abundance of drama in our dramatized society than about most aspects of our lives. For more than two hundred years, the households in which most Americans have grown up have been replete with paradoxes. We are taught to be self-reliant yet to cherish community, to be pioneers while sustaining a sense of tradition. We are shown that mobility—geographic and economic—promises and carries high status in the culture, but we identify each other by the home towns from which we come. We herald the diversity of our ethnic origins, yet judge our success as Americans of distinct racial and ethnic roots in terms of our ability to assimilate the values and practices of an elusive yet recognizably dominant American middle-class white culture. We caution each other not to make a spectacle of oneself, while we reward and envy precisely those who make spectacles for us of their own lives and of our common histories. The spirit of Buffalo Bill and his Wild West Show not only haunts our national leaders, but was gleefully cavorting when the tall ships sailed in New York harbor in 1986 to celebrate the centennial of the Statue of Liberty.

At the core of the set of paradoxes that trace the contours of America as a cultural system is a schism between public and private life that has much to do with our infatuation with show business and our ambivalences about the forms it should take in contemporary society. Our most treasured documents and institutions attempt to protect the rights of the individual and to sanctify the individual's "private life," while ensuring that we are, in public as a public, responsible to one another. Perhaps because our heroes are, by our own cultural rules, ordinary people who have accomplished feats that might well go unnoticed were they not discovered and recovered by one or another form of media, we have failed as a culture to create the kind of "culturally totalizing" dramas we associate with the Greeks or Elizabethans or modern Europeans.

Instead, we have sought to represent ourselves and our accomplishments in public by transforming small but poignant acts into extravaganzas or spectacles. Self-consciously and deliberately separated from a consciousness of class distinctions, the desire for the upheavals and temporary social reversals of carnival that has penetrated many societies, a desire for occasions removed from history, has been replaced in the United States by forms of drama that transform history into spectacle and spectacle into history. More recently, with television as our major dramatic medium, we have attempted to obliterate distinctions between the spectacular and the ordinary, between spectatorship and audience membership, between audience as a commercial product of drama and audience as an integral element of dramatic discourse. We have become what English media critic Raymond Williams called "a dramatized society."[2]

*   *   *   *

Robert Altman began to make television and movie texts at a key point in American history—when the confluence or intersection of media was just beginning to redefine the discourse of all media.[3] From the start (or at least since the making of *M*A*S*H* in 1970), Altman's movies, theatrical productions, and television programs have acknowledged, parodied, and joined in the Faustian temptations of American show business. More than any contemporary dramatist, his moving pictures have also addressed the modern hybridization of forms of drama and forms of historical narrative and have reintroduced elemental conventions of theater into movies and television.

Brewster McCloud (1970), directed by Altman immediately after *M*A*S*H*, unabashedly announced this union with the theatrical devil, literally embodied in the film by Louise (Sally Kellerman), the goading and protective maternal angel who has apparently lost her wings (perhaps in a fall from grace) but is nonetheless able, magically, to transform an awkward adolescent, Brewster, into an Icarus-like superboy who can—almost—fly. Like *M*A*S*H* and most of Altman's subsequent movies, the setting of *Brewster McCloud* is confined to a limited, coherent space—the Houston Astrodome, a space that in *Brewster McCloud* is at once a "real" location and a theater. Early in the film, before and during a deliberately inept opening credit sequence, the public space of the Astrodome is the setting for a band rehearsal of the "Star-Spangled Banner," officiously directed, on camera, by Miss Daphne Heap. The band costumes are noticeably red; Miss Daphne's dress is notably red, white, and blue; the Astrodome is predominantly red with blue-green turf. Foreshadowing *Nashville* in its assertion of color as a cultural code, *Brewster McCloud*'s display of the red, white, and blue of American patriotism is one of the film's many explicit reminders that everything in theater (as in our dreams) means something.

In the meantime, backstage in his combined shop and living quarters (officially designated, with pun clearly intended, as a Fallout Shelter), Brewster, the adolescent dreamer and inventor, is obsessively constructing a set of wings—the key prop for the character he intends to play, the first human to fly on the basis of his own skill and energy. Later, we see him exercising, training his body for his role. That Brewster's faithful girlfriend Hope is sexually aroused by being in the same room with Brewster as he does his 250 pull-ups suggests the fine line between voyeurism and theater; it also recalls the deliberate confusion between rehearsals and performance that characterized much of the countercultural theater of the late sixties and early seventies. In this context, the MGM lion's announced inability to remember its line may be understood not as a threat but as an opportunity to improvise. And Miss Daphne's off-key attempts to sing the national anthem are no less comic because they occur during a rehearsal. The world before us is calling our attention to its fabrication as well as to its erratic control of the production of meaning.

As we are explicitly shown in its final credit sequence, *Brewster McCloud* is a filmic analogue to a circus. The lecturer, whose intermittent reflections on the relations of birds to humans serve to

introduce events and performers in the sideshows of the world outside the Astrodome, serves as ringmaster; our attention is dispersed
among these peripheral performances, Brewster's (and his guardian
"birdmother's") preparations for his flight, and the ringmaster-
lecturer's comments on these events. There is no "real" world outside this circus. Its resources and structures for meaning are confined to its own domain, the world of show business. The nasty,
overbearing Miss Daphne who sings the national anthem is played
by Margaret Hamilton, an actress who is fixed in American culture as the Wicked Witch of the West from the movie version of
the *Wizard of Oz*. When Miss Daphne's corpse is discovered
shortly after the opening of the film, the camera closes in on the
sparkling red shoes she was wearing at the time of her murder: it
is the wicked witch who coveted Dorothy's magical shoes who
dies, victim of the continuity in the created worlds of American
media, but evidence, as well, that Americans do share a specific,
common cultural base.

   Brewster McCloud is a sketch or preliminary model for Altman's
subsequent explorations of the values and practices of Amercia as a
mediated society. The recurrent punctuation of the film by radio
broadcasts continues Altman's exploitation of audio sources as key
elements in the reproduction of place and time; we see this convention used more precisely to specify a historical era in *Thieves Like
Us*. *Brewster McCloud* is amply sprinkled with vignettes that remark grotesque instances of racism and sexism; similar, but more
integral and subtler episodes appear throughout Altman's subsequent work. The achronological and often parenthetical arrangement of scenes, set up to evoke a metaphoric or metonymic association in the spectator,[4] initiated in *M*A*S*H* and now exploded in
Brewster McCloud, establishes the structural model that Altman
will use most emphatically in *Nashville*. The use of self-parodying
performances and blatant allusions to previous film types, actors,
and roles to diminish the aura of stars is exaggeratedly evident in
Michael Murphy's portrayal of the San Francisco detective, Frank
Stark, a parody of Steve McQueen's macho detective in *Bullit;* this
device, too, will be modified and complicated in much of Altman's

later work, especially in *Nashville, Buffalo Bill and the Indians, A Wedding, Health, Popeye,* and the television series *Tanner '88.* Reviewed in the context of Altman's subsequent films, *Brewster McCloud* provides a way of seeing the interrelationships among all the works that are properly associated with Robert Altman. Rather than the systematic exploration of diverse genres that initially appears to be the guiding principle in Altman's work, and in contrast to the patterns of thematic or stylistic continuities evident in the works of many *auteurs,* Altman's movies and television programs bear a geneological relationship to each other. I mean here to point not simply to a vague family-like resemblance among these films but to the specific Nietzschean concept that Tracy Strong has called "the logic of genealogy . . . by which the past lives on always to inform the present. . . ."[5] By this logic, when we turn to Altman's films of the late seventies and eighties, we do not do so with an expectation (satisfied or not) of linear progress or historical development but of climbing through a family tree in which the children are always the sons and daughters of their parents but are never necessarily better or worse than their ancestors. Reading *Brewster McCloud* as a "genealogical kernel"[6] that informs all of Altman's films, it is easier than it otherwise might be to comprehend why Altman, in public comments, persistently notes his special attachment to this film. The genealogical perspective also makes sense of Altman's claim that none of the movies he has participated in making has been a failure, that "all the films are what we set out to do."[7] Much as Nietzsche refused to describe human history in terms of developmental stages, Altman rejects a developmental view of his work. Not simply because he says so, but because it seems to me to be more accurate, we might better perceive the organization of Altman's work in terms of generational clusters or branches on the family tree.

In any genealogy, particularly striking resemblances can and do occur within and across generations. *Nashville* bears obviously similar markings to *Brewster McCloud;* it is possible, but more difficult to find traces of this genealogical kernel in *A Perfect Couple* (1979). One of the most remarkable characteristics of Altman's films is that, despite the consanguinity they reveal, each film stands firmly on its own bearings and definitions.

*   *   *   *

Among Altman's films, the best example of a work that is at once intimately related to other portions of the Altman "text" and yet singular is *Buffalo Bill and the Indians, or Sitting Bull's History Lesson*, the movie Altman made in 1976 after completing *Nashville*. Based loosely on Arthur Kopit's *Indians, Buffalo Bill and the Indians*, like *M*A*S*H, Brewster McCloud,* and *Nashville,* is explicitly concerned with performance and with the dramatization of our everyday lives. And like its predecessors, *Buffalo Bill and the Indians* announces its theatricality in its first moment of projection on the screen: while a rising garage door served as the opening curtain in *Nashville,* an American flag is raised up a pole to the accompaniment of morning reveille in *Buffalo Bill.* Emphatic sepia tones evoke the ambiance of old photographs, and graphics cue the unabashed presentational tone of the show within a show we are about to see: **"Robert Altman's Absolutely Unique and Heroic Enterprise of Intellectual Lustre."** From the start, we are being asked not to suspend our disbelief but to hold onto it; we are not to be transported to another corner of the "real" world but to be put in our places as spectators. The pedantic tone of a voice-over confirms these messages, although the words themselves ostensibly refute them: "What you are about to experience," a loud male voice barks, "is not a show for entertainment, it is a review of the down-to-earth events that made the American frontier." The disembodied voice goes on to remind an invisible audience, an audience that is recognized, ironically, by the address of the announcer, that the "foundation" of our knowledge of the future is our knowledge of the past and that this American foundation was not built by heroes but by "anonymous settlers."

The visual images of a shack roofed with sod, of white settlers suddenly attacked by "savage" Indians, are initially framed so as to obscure evidence that this is a staged event, thus to imply that the scenes before us are genuine, photographic documents of the episodes of American history described by the narrative voice. Since few spectators in 1976 or after are so naive as to accept what we are shown as "real" documentary footage, the projected images mock the announcer's "Welcome" to "real events enacted by men and women of the American frontier, to whose courage and strength and, above all, faith our history is dedicated." The contradictions of oral rhetorical claims and visual gestures, such as a deliberately disengaging aerial shot, also remind us of how susceptible we have been to other, equally fabricated, representations of our frontier history.

Ironic and contemplative, controlled yet expansive, historical *and* mythological, *Buffalo Bill and the Indians* has a stillness at its center that appears to contradict its very existence as a motion picture. This is, in part, a matter of the self-conscious absence of a traditional plot. Early in the film, Colonel Ingraham, the Journalist, presses Buffalo Bill's Publicist, Major Burke, for a through-line for the story he is writing: ". . . bull's eye, heroic villians, revolutionize, injuns, whites. . . . What's the plot, Major?" and the Major responds, "Why don't you string those pearls together and devise a nice little Buffalo Bill fable—uniquely original? I'll even give you the legend: foes in '75, friends in '86."

The exchange instructs the off-screen observer as well as the Journalist in how to read this story. The producers provide the basic elements for the drama, but it is the responsibility of the observer to construct not a plot but a fable from the given materials. The form of *Buffalo Bill and the Indians* is closer to that of an essay than that of the dime novel that was the original medium for the amplification of the Buffalo Bill persona. The Publicist knows that there is no self-contained narrative of Buffalo Bill; what exists is the idea of the Star, a role filled by Buffalo Bill Cody and perpetually expanded and invigorated by Bill's supporting cast and crew. The Wild West Show is comprised of episodes and demonstrations whose shifting specific content is constrained only by the requisite glorification of Buffalo Bill; as a form of performance, the Wild West Show conjoins conventions from pageants, theatrical melodrama, the rodeo, and the circus to create its own "unique" hybrid spectacle. A story is told here, but it is not a story with a causally and temporally interrelated beginning, middle, and end.

Buffalo Bill (Paul Newman) enters the arena for his Wild West Show in *Buffalo Bill and the Indians, or Sitting Bull's History Lesson*. (*The Museum of Modern Art/Film Stills Archive, New York City*)

The movie's presentation of events parallels the episodic, multiple performance structure of the Wild West Show. Much as the Wild West Show culminates in the appearance of Buffalo Bill himself, Altman's film generates its energy from two focal appearances—that, first, of Sitting Bull and subsequently that of the President of the United States, Grover Cleveland. Neither of these appearances is exploited through conventional narrative or dramatic devices. Our first knowledge of Sitting Bull's imminent arrival occurs as the disclosure of a secret for some of the Wild West Show company, but the absence on our parts of any foreknowledge of this event combined with the racial bigotry that verbally frames the revelation undercuts any pleasure in suspense or recognition for the viewer. Similarly, the film cuts quickly from a telegraph operator's announcement that President Cleveland will visit the Wild West Show to a shot of President Cleveland and his party already in the audience for the show's "first-time ever" evening performance. The one possible causal link between these two appearances—Sitting Bull's dream that he will meet the "Great White Father" at the Wild West Show—is undermined by "factual" information concerning the President's forthcoming marriage and his struggles with a Republican Congress. And Ned Buntline's reflections on the differing functions of dreams for Indians and for white people further weaken the threat of prophecy in Sitting Bull's dream by distracting us with their ring of half-truths: "Injuns," Ned claims, "gear their lives to dreams and no matter how far-fetched, they'll wait until they die for it to come true." But, he wryly continues, "The Wild West Show is us dreaming out loud, and it's cheaper the Injun way."

There is, however, a common element in the appearances of Sitting Bull and President Cleveland. In contemporary political terms, they are both "photo opportunities." This is literally and figuratively represented by the film's brief but epiphanic emphasis on photography situated precisely between the arrival of Sitting Bull and the news of the President's visit. The topic of photography is raised by Halsey, Sitting Bull's Interpreter, in the first negotiations between Buffalo Bill and Sitting Bull concerning their future business relationship. After presenting Sitting Bull's request for a salary advance, Halsey continues, "Also, he will own his own photographs." Unquestionably more distressed by this than by the previous financial demand, Buffalo Bill explodes, "Hell he will! I've got all photographic rights and historics." Calmly unrelenting, Halsey explains, "Sitting Bull says a man should never let go of his face, therefore he will own his photographs." Bill's only retort is "My ass!"

Westerners have heard from tourists and anthropologists that some "primitive" peoples fear photography because they believe that a photograph of a human being captures the soul. But it is not the loss of soul but of a face (and, perhaps, of face) that Sitting Bull here attempts to prevent. How is a face like a photograph? Both, we might say, are images. Each presents the person to others. If we let go of or sell our image, we lose control of how others see us.

Bill's outraged response does not refute Sitting Bull's understanding of the meaning of a photograph. By conjoining his rights to photographs with his rights to "historics," Bill confirms that he, too, respects the power of photography to represent a person to others and that he comprehends the force of such representations in transporting and securing images over time and space. The dispute is not over the nature of photography but over who will own and therefore control its products.

At least in our presence, this dispute is not verbally resolved. It is therefore not surprising when, not long after this discussion, the issue reemerges in the context of the actual taking of a photograph of the entire Wild West Show company, now including Sitting Bull, Halsey, and several of their Indian tribespeople. Introduced by a series of comments about stardom that conclude with Buffalo Bill's acknowledgment that "He's [Sitting Bull] got to look good in front of his people," the screen is suddenly filled from right to left with a tableau of the entire company, with only Bill himself notably absent. The Publicist's directions, "Try to find places we've picked out for you," and a brief shot of a nineteenth-century camera on a tripod establish our view as coincident with that of the camera and establish the situation of the episode: a company portrait is about to be shot, and, for the first time, it will include the new performers, Sitting Bull and his tribe members.

In an apparent attempt to inspire the company's attention and presentation of their "best" faces, the Publicist reminds the objects of the photograph that "one hundred years from now this picture will still be in existence. This is the way people will remember you." Neither Buffalo Bill nor Sitting Bull need to be reminded of the photograph's power to shape history, and it is because of their shared belief in that power that trouble now occurs. Bill, playing the role of the Star to the last moment, finally joins the rest, but before the photo can actually be taken, he calls a halt to the process. "Hold it," Bill orders his spokesman, Nate. "I don't want Sitting Bull standing next to Annie Oakley—uh—fans won't like it."

It is, of course, Bill who does not like the representation of connection between Annie Oakley and Sitting Bull. Earlier remarks by Buffalo Bill that articulate both his racism and his obsession with the

Annie Oakley's manager and living target, Frank Butler (John Considine); Annie Oakley (Geraldine Chaplin); Buffalo Bill's nephew, Ed Goodman (Harvey Keitel); and Wild West Show producer and public relations man, Nate Salsbury (Joel Grey), pose for the company photograph in *Buffalo Bill and the Indians, or Sitting Bull's History Lesson*. (*The Museum of Modern Art/Film Stills Archive, New York, City,*)

hierarchies of stardom provide us with at least two sources of explanation for this command and for the attempt he now makes, indirectly through Nate, to rearrange the group for the photograph. In an embarrassingly transparent ploy, Nate suggests to his counterpart, Halsey, that "in view of the sun factor it would be better if you and Sitting Bull moved over here." Halsey's unhesitant reply—that Sitting Bull will move for twenty-five U.S. dollars—establishes the rules of the game; if Halsey and Sitting Bull acquiesce to one element of American values, they will at least do so in the American way. Cognizant that such an agreement would mean defeat, Bill delights in a more devious plan. He will allow Sitting Bull and Halsey to stay where they are, near Annie Oakley, and after the fact will reconstruct the photograph. "We're going to put Halsey's face and hat on Buck Taylor," he tells Nate, "and Sitting Bull's on Johnny Baker and vice versa. That way those two Injuns will be over there with the other Injuns. Just don't show them the photograph."

Neither fiction nor history, *Buffalo Bill and the Indians* is an examination of the practice and power of performance and the concomitant practice of politics in American culture. To confront the stillness at the center of this investigation is to comprehend the will to control change that structures desire both for Buffalo Bill (the performer-as-character,[8]) and for politics as a theatricalized institution and practice. Buffalo Bill has no reluctance to manufacture situations or events; for him, the "truth" of history is a matter of relative power and control. There is a sobering echo here of the beginning of Milan Kundera's *The Book of Laughter and Forgetting*:

> In February 1948, Communist leader Klement Gottwald stepped out on the balcony of a Baroque palace in Prague to address the hundreds of thousands of his fellow citizens packed into Old Town Square. It was a crucial moment in Czech history—a fateful moment that occurs once or twice in a millennium.
>
> Gottwald was flanked by his comrades, with Clementis standing next to him. There were snow flurries, it was cold, and Gottwald was bareheaded. The solicitous Clementis took off his own fur cap and set it on Gottwald's head.
>
> The Party propaganda section put out hundreds of thousands of copies of a photograph of that balcony with Gottwald, a fur cap on his head and comrades at his side, speaking to the nation. On that balcony the history of Communist Czechoslovakia was born. Every child knew the photograph from posters, school books, and museums.
>
> Four years later Clementis was charged with treason and hanged. The propaganda section immediately airbrushed him out of history and, obviously, out of all the photographs as well. Ever since, Gottwald has stood on that balcony alone. Where Clementis once stood, there is only bare palace wall. All that remains of Clementis is the cap on Gottwald's head.[9]

Buffalo Bill and the Indians is, of course, not set in Prague but on the frontier of the American West. That is exactly why the episode focused on the company photograph is important. We may pay little heed to dialogue that attests to the inflation of the heroic image of Buffalo Bill, and we may knowingly accept the distortion of past events in their re-creations in the Wild West Show; bluster and melodrama are traditional forms of representation in American culture. But for most of us, the photograph is situated not in the realm of storytelling and half-truths but in the terrain of history and "objective" truth. We take photographs to be records of real events; the camera, we tell ourselves, does not lie or can only be made to lie in a totalitarian country where there is no authentic history. None moved to impeach President Reagan when several sources published accounts of Reagan's lies about his World War II experience,[10] nor was there ever notable outrage when the President's ex-spokesperson, Larry Speakes, publicly confessed in the spring of 1988 that he had invented remarks for President Reagan at the Iceland summit conference with General Secretary Gorbachev in order to augment the President's public image. Americans did, however, move toward impeachment of a President in 1974 when it appeared that he was responsible for the distortion of a record of past events—the Watergate tapes—and it is highly likely we would do the same were we to discover a President or his staff had retouched a politically relevant photograph. Profoundly skeptical about each other's speaking voices, we trust, instead, only mechanical forms of documentation and representation.

By denigrating the "myth" of photography as a special repository of historical truth, *Buffalo Bill and the Indians* reaccentuates its own spoken dialogue. Buffalo Bill's claims that "anything historical is his" and his cohort's claim that "everything" historical belongs to Bill take on more concrete and more threatening meaning. The photograph that is finally taken—of Halsey and Sitting Bull, the only ones who remain posed for the picture after the announcement of the impending visit of President Cleveland—is no more or less an accurate or complete version of this world and its moment than was the original tableau we saw on film or than Buffalo Bill's projected reconstruction of this tableau; only in the interaction among these images do we approach something like "a real" history of the moment. We know also, however, that power and control over the media make a difference in the range of meanings possible for those who have limited access to information. As here and as the one who inhabits the iconically central role, Buffalo Bill has extraordinary control over how others see the world. Prophetically, Altman's (and Newman's) Buffalo Bill and those who speak for him or ventriloquize his message exert this control primarily through terse, self-contained verbal statements. A sampling of these comments reveals their inclusiveness and their autocratic tone:

[said of Sitting Bull] if he weren't interested in the show business, he wouldn't be a chief.

By enlargening our show, we may have disimproved it.

Remember, son, that the last thing a man wants to do is the last thing he does.

... That's 'cause times are bad, gettin' worse, that's when show business flourishes, when show business flourishes.

I want to Codify the world.

We've just signed the most futurable act in our history.

Us whites are smart enough to know you always turn down your first offer.

I hope you realize that we're the only producers who have the courage to show the red and white without taking sides.

Most people will tell you that it's [the Wild West Show] the father of the new show business.

The difference between a President and a Chief is that a President always knows enough to retaliate before it's his turn.

You know, it's a man like that made the country what it is today.

Too bad the Injuns don't learn from the colored.

You ain't changed, Bill.—I ain't supposed to. That's why people pay to see me.'

Halsey don't mean a word he says, which is why he sounds so real.

The difference between an Injun and a white man is that an Injun is red, and an Injun is red for a very good reason, so you can tell us apart.

Many of these lines have a proverbial quality, and as Kenneth Burke has argued of proverbs, we can read these sentences as summaries of strategies for dealing with certain types of situations. Even the lines that do not have the puzzle-like didactic quality of a proverb have that particularly American epigrammatic quality (associated in part with what has been called American "plain style") that characterizes much of late nineteenth- and early twentieth-century American poetry; the poetry of Emily Dickinson, Vachel Lindsay, Robert Frost, and even, to a significant degree, that of T. S. Eliot is frequently marked by epigrammatic lines.[11] In contrast to stichomythia, the classical form of dialogue comprised of single, alternating lines, epigrammatic discourse is monologic and self-enclosed; although the speaking voice is always addressing an other, when it performs epigrammatically, it distances itself from others and simultaneously discourages dialogue while it provokes response.

Epigrammatic speech thus shares much with still photography; each line or photograph is sufficient unto itself and each such line or photograph freezes a moment and a perception forever. Neither a photograph nor an epigrammatic line, however, tells a story in itself, although any set of photographs or epigrammatic lines may allow and often seduces the interpreter to create a narrative by linking the separate shots or statements. The central sequence in Antonioni's *Blow-Up*, in which the photographer creates a narrative of a murder by lining up a series of still photographs in a particular order, demonstrates well the limits and possibilities. "Remember, son, the last thing a man wants to do is the last thing he does" could be spoken in diverse contexts and mean something different in each one; linked with other lines cited above, a context can be imagined and delineated.

Photographs and epigrams both tend to mitigate against a historical understanding of the world while each also seems to still time, to capture and arrest movement. Both this style of speaking and of visually representing the world are thus power-laden practices; controlling photographs like speaking in closed statements is, as Sitting Bull so well understands, a strong means of holding onto one's face or image, of keeping one's own power independent of others. A central interest of *Buffalo Bill and the Indians* lies in the acknowledgment of this mode of asserting power and, concomitantly, in the dispersion of this power so that it is no longer vulnerable to tyrannical usage.

This dispersion of the usually singular authority of the photograph or epigrammatic line is accomplished in *Buffalo Bill and the Indians* in part through continuation of the distribution of focus that was so firmly established in *Nashville* (an approach I have earlier called the promiscuous camera), but Altman takes on a new challenge here of working against a definition of setting and circumstance that would conventionally assume narrow and primary focus on the one character, Buffalo Bill. Resistance to Buffalo Bill's domination of the film, as object or indirect subject is accomplished by repeatedly demonstrating the construction of the character Buffalo Bill and by showing the several authors of this creation in the process of presenting their often divergent tales of origins and subsequent feats. We see and hear pieces of dime-novel writer Ned Buntline's story of his fabrication of Buffalo Bill as Buntline sits, seemingly forever, at the bar on the Wild West Show grounds; we half hear another version of the origin of Buffalo Bill's fame from the Old Soldier whose voice narrates the opening shots and whom we later glimpse continuing his narrative despite the absence of an attentive audience; Nate Salsbury, the Producer of the Wild West Show, repeatedly presents Bill and his interests to others, including the movie viewers, as he believes Bill wishes to be presented; the Publicist and the Reporter present their versions; Paul Newman, as Buffalo Bill, presents his incarnation of the character, a representation that is multiply mediated by viewers' recognition of Paul Newman as a movie star and by the specific attributes Newman carries from previous movie roles. Paul Newman not only brings the status of stardom to the role of Buffalo Bill, but he also carries with him shadows of Brick from *Cat on a Hot Tin Roof,* of Hud and the Hustler, of Cool Hand Luke, and of Butch Cassidy, all characters for whom heroism and personal dignity are achieved or lost primarily through their sexual potency as men, and all men who are committed to sustaining the traditions of American male community as a sphere not only separate from but threatened by women and domesticity.[12]

In addition to these emphatically separate and diverse voices of characters, each of which constructs its own Buffalo Bill, the resources of theatrical and filmic drama become active elements in the destabilization of the image of Buffalo Bill. Painted portraits of Bill offer a flattened, posed point of view; visual and verbal revelations of the costumes or disguises Newman wears as Buffalo Bill (which include a long-haired wig and a buckskin jacket designed for public appearances as opposed to the "real" jacket Bill wants when he goes out to retrieve Sitting Bull) contrast with Bill's own, ever-changing presentations of himself as he performs in the Wild West Show.

While *Nashville* drew our attention to the democratic, polyphonous, composition of American culture, to the many and diverse human beings who, as subjects, make up American culture, *Buffalo Bill and the Indians* displays the other side of the coin. If, as *Nashville* establishes, American society is manifestly and dramatically heteroglot, is, indeed, proudly and perhaps distinctively a dynamic matrix of voices and values, then American cultural products, *Buffalo Bill and the Indians* suggests, including American history, are not one thing or another; they do not present a unitary image to the interpreter but, rather, are plastic permeable texts in which competing and complementary forces strive to control the construction of meaning. We see this multiplicity of the cultural text, even when the object derives from "high" culture, in the display of the diverse reactions among the characters to the performance of operatic song: President Cleveland grimaces, Annie Oakley shows delight, Buffalo Bill is erotically aroused. The movie refuses to explain the meaning of operatic music to Buffalo Bill or anyone in the film; it also refuses, however, to dismiss opera as an authentic form of culture and communication simply because it appears out of place in the context of Buffalo Bill's frontier manners and the popular cultural mode of the Wild West Show.

Confronted with the import of this polyphony for his own sense of self, Buffalo Bill, at the end of the movie, is a character in terror of his dependence on others to ensure his presence in the world. By definition the performer is dependent on the audience for his existence; this is true both in an ontological and a material sense. Buffalo Bill never acknowledges the mutuality of this relationship; what changes over the course of the movie is his confidence in his ability to mount the right strategy to capture the audience of the moment. This confidence is shaken each time Buffalo Bill fails to persuade Sitting Bull and Halsey of his authority as star and as leader of the Wild West Show company; we also witness Sitting Bull's direct assault on the stability of Bill's image when Sitting Bull takes a turn with Bill's pistol and discovers that the weapon employs a scatter-shot mechanism that assures that Buffalo Bill—or anyone using the gun—will hit his target, even with minimal skill.

The most damaging blow to Bill's confidence in his knowledge of the audience is indirectly applied, however, and occurs during Sitting Bull's first performance in the Wild West Show. Obstinately following his own vision of his role in the show, Sitting Bull rides into the arena with quiet dignity and does no more or less than circle the ring repeatedly on his horse. At first, the audience reacts with hostile boos and hisses, an appropriate response given that all they have to go on is the stories they have previously heard—both inside and outside the Wild West Show—of Sitting Bull's savage cruelty to white men, women, and children. The camera, which is now primarily focused, from a distance, on Sitting Bull, captures Buffalo Bill gleefully witnessing this scene of humiliation from behind a fence post. But as the camera returns to Sitting Bull, and we watch him maintain his dignity and remain in the arena, refusing to show signs of humiliation or defeat, we begin to hear a change in the audience's response from angry cries and jeers to respectful applause and cheers. We do not need to see Bill again to know that his self-satisfied grin is gone. If, as Buffalo Bill himself claims, "truth is whatever gets the most applause," than Sitting Bull's interpretation of his history has weakened Bill's exclusive claim on truth.

The destabilization of Buffalo Bill's relationship to the audience is reconfirmed during the special performance of the Wild West Show for President Grover Cleveland and his assemblage. Bill's own appearance and welcoming speech appear to satisfy the audience's expectations of frontier nobility, but the magic of the spectacle is undermined a moment later when Annie Oakley misses her target in her shooting act and hits her husband in the shoulder instead. The

Buffalo Bill (Paul Newman) negotiates with Sitting Bull's interpreter, William Halsey (Will Sampson), while Sitting Bull (Fran Kaquitts) focuses his attention elsewhere in *Buffalo Bill and the Indians, or Sitting Bull's History Lesson.* (*The Museum of Modern Art/Film Stills Archive, New York City*)

camera immediately cuts from the performers to the President, catching Grover Cleveland asking those around him, "Is this part of the act?" The answer is unimportant. What matters here is that the necessary separation of the "real" world of the audience from the created world of theater is troublingly blurred once the audience is unsure of what is or is not "part of the act."

That this is at once a political and an aesthetic problem becomes clear in the next Wild West Show act, the presentation of Sitting Bull. The initial surprise in Sitting Bull's performance is that, for the first time, we and the Wild West Show company hear the Chief speak in his own voice rather than through Halsey, his Interpreter. President Cleveland reassures his companions, however, that Sitting Bull's speech has little political import; grinning, Cleveland proclaims, "I don't understand a word of it." Sitting Bull next makes a gesture that the President does understand. Sitting Bull raises his gun, aims at the President (and at us as audience?), and just as the moment seems too long to be playful, raises his gun and shoots upwards into the air, a motion that simultaneously releases and augments tension, since we now know that the gun was, in fact, loaded. The earlier question recurs for the audience (certainly off-screen and perhaps on-screen): is this, too, part of the act? When we have no reliable grounds for differentiating between theater and the world of our daily lives, we can no longer know when and how to act.

To have genuinely assaulted Sitting Bull when he aimed at the President would have seemed naive and foolish if Sitting Bull were only pretending; not to interfere could be worse than foolish, however, if the Chief authentically intended to harm the President. Our own recent American history and the representation of that history in Altman's Nashville teach us that such moments of real threat can and do occur. Our history has also taught us, however, to assume that most of what we see and hear in public, presented for a public, is a show. How and when we should then take responsibility for others, when others are in our worlds and when they are not, are among our most serious confusions.

It is just such confusions that increasingly trouble Buffalo Bill in Altman's film. Haunted by threats to the continuity of his public and private representations of self, Buffalo Bill's dreams become nightmares when he hears of the death of Sitting Bull. Since Sitting Bull's vision of an authentic conversation with the "Great White Father" was destroyed by Grover Cleveland's unwillingness to hear Sitting Bull's requests, the killing of Sitting Bull by white American soldiers is anticlimactic and predictable. Historically, Sitting Bull was impotent in the face of dominant, racist American policies toward Indians. Theatrically, however, Sitting Bull remains a potent force, as we see in this movie and as Buffalo Bill sees when he arises one night to a presence in his house.

Buffalo Bill's discovery of Sitting Bull in his house is carefully framed and cut so as to appear magical but not dismissible as "only" a dream. The sequence, which occurs near the end of the movie, begins with a shot around a corner through an open doorway of Bill in his bed, apparently aroused by the sense of someone in the house. The camera pulls back to a full shot of the well-lit main room of Bill's house as Buffalo Bill stumbles into the room and there discovers Sitting Bull seated at the end of the table. There is no hazy hue or distortion of space to suggest to us or to Bill that this is a dream: to the movie viewer, objects in this room, Buffalo Bill, and Sitting Bull have equal status and reality. That this scene is a fabricated illusion, in exactly the way that movies are illusions, is articulated a moment later, however, when in one shot Sitting Bull appears to us to be screen right, with Buffalo Bill screen left, and in the next shot the position of the two characters are reversed. The repeated insertion and elimination of the image of Sitting Bull from subsequent shots in this episode, shots that occur while Buffalo Bill is addressing a series of remarks to Sitting Bull, contribute further to viewers' reading of the scene as self-consciously filmic and perhaps as dream-like; whether or not we read the fantastic appearances and accompanying silences of Buffalo Bill in this scene as representations of Buffalo Bill's unconscious mind, we are at least reminded that someone—Bill, Robert Altman, an editor—is denaturalizing the moment and is making Sitting Bull's appearances and disappearances occur before us.

For Buffalo Bill, whose point of view structures this episode, the challenge of Sitting Bull's presence—and disappearances—is to control their meaning, and for Bill, this means reassertion of his understandings of reality and change. "You see," Bill tells Sitting Bull, "in a hundred years, I'm still going to be Buffalo Bill, star, and you're still going to be the Injun." Watching and listening, we know this to be the truth, but not the whole truth. When, in the next and final sequence of the film, we see Buffalo Bill, fully costumed, wigged, and "made-up," enact the defeat of Sitting Bull, now performed by Halsey, the Interpreter, Newman's Buffalo Bill indeed glows like the star he is, and Halsey as Sitting Bull is just the Injun. But a close-up of Buffalo Bill near the end of the movie has shown us his white hair and the wrinkles and pallor of old age, and even without these, the context of our viewing in the last quarter of the twentieth century has already prohibited our unquestioning consumption of Buffalo Bill as Star and Sitting Bull as the stereotypical Indian.

We are on less certain ground with Buffalo Bill's final musings and claims about image making and show business. Looking up at a portrait of himself riding a white horse, an image that has been repeatedly projected throughout the movie, Bill asks Sitting Bull—and us—"Ain't he riding his horse right? Well, if he ain't, how come all of you took him for a king?" Bill had provided one answer to his own question a moment earlier when he told Sitting Bull that he, his friends, his women, and his fans are all curious about what they see as Sitting Bull's self-defeating performance strategy. "I give them what they expect," Bill testifies, "You can't live up to what you expect and that makes you more make-believe than me, 'cause you don't even know you're bluffin.' " If Bill's self-depiction evokes the contemporary network television executive and his description of Sitting Bull recalls Willy Loman's failure to instantiate the image he has created of and for himself of the supersalesman, then perhaps we are in the realm of some fundamental understandings of American culture. As a people that belonged to the land before the land was ours, as a society that self-consciously manufactured itself in history in the context of other cultures whose origins were prehistoric, for us to differentiate between spurious and authentic culture[13] may be neither possible nor desirable. In that case, we Americans are unique among Westerners in separating our heroes from our tragic figures.[14]

*   *   *   *

The form of ritual and the confusion of everyday life conjoin as the wedding party arrives for the wedding reception at the groom's family estate in *A Wedding*. (*The Museum of Modern Art/Film Stills Archive, New York City*)

A Wedding (1978) continues this investigation of the spurious and the authentic in American culture. (Between *Buffalo Bill* and *A Wedding*, Altman directed *3 Women*, which I have discussed in the previous chapter.) Altman has frequently remarked that he made *A Wedding* because he saw the performance of weddings as one of the two remaining rituals of American culture; funerals being the obvious other. In the genealogy of drama, ritual holds a key position; in its necessary repetitiveness and its absence of an audience it is distinctly other than theater, yet in its self-containment and separation from history as well as its dependence on dance, music, recitation, and dialogue it often appears indistinguishable from theater. A film of a ritual is not in itself a ritual, however; nor is it theater. *A*

Wedding thus exists as yet another of Altman's increasingly subtle investigations of performance in its particular role as a means of representing social relations in America.

Recalling *Nashville* even more than it does *Buffalo Bill*, *A Wedding* embraces and pays equal attention to a cast, not of thousands, but of forty-eight people (twice the number of characters in *Nashville*). Defying the normal conventions of both traditional comedy and traditional tragedy, *A Wedding* begins with both a death and a marriage and ends with death. But like *Nashville* if *A Wedding* is, finally, a tragedy, it is one that complicates both the classical notion of the protagonist's flawed character and the modern notion of the evil in particular forms of social structure.

I turn to the terms of conventional theater because *A Wedding* is conspicuously theatrical from its opening shots: a zoom toward and away from the alter of the Episcopal church in which the wedding ceremony is about to occur. Accompanied by heraldic fanfare, we see the mother of the groom and the mother of the bride escorted down the aisle, the latter by the same actor who, as the Coca-Cola truck driver, is the last man seen in *3 Women*. For Altman buffs, this film announces itself as bringing together representatives from Altman's versatile movie-making family. The reverse zoom away from the altar and church instruct us, as do the several reverse zooms in *Nashville*, to watch this film from a thoughtful distance or to approach it in a Brechtian manner of deliberate alienation. As we look at it from a bit of distance, the church appears strikingly empty for this moment in the ceremony; we know the rule that all other guests are seated before the mothers of the wedding couple. This emptiness calls attention to the church as stage for this event, an image extended by the unrolling of the white carpet down the aisle, a gesture that is at once central to the traditional gestures of the wedding ceremony and that stands for the raising of the theater curtain in much the way that the garage door opening functions in *Nashville* and the flag raising functions in *Buffalo Bill*.

Yet what makes this movie move dramatically is not its theatricality alone but its hybridization of conventions drawn from ritual, theater, and film. As Altman obviously knows and exploits, our lives contain so little that is ceremonial that in itself, a conventional, high-church wedding momentarily can transport us from the temporal leadenness of our daily lives to the mythological time and space of "once upon a time." Altman also, however, emphasizes how tenuous and constrained such moments are; the wedding ceremony itself is interrupted for the spectator by cuts to the midwestern mansion where the reception will occur. There we find Nettie Sloan, the groom's grandmother on his mother's side and the ancient matriarch of the family (and, as played by Lillian Gish, the matriarch of drama), and Rita Billingsley, the wedding coordinator (Geraldine Chaplin). When Altman cuts back to the wedding ceremony, it is almost over, and just after we glimpse the recessional, we are returned to Nettie's room where the family doctor and the wedding coordinator pronounce Nettie to be dead. Both marriage and death are but brief preludes in time and space to this movie and to the reception that follows at the midwestern estate of the groom's family. (The estate appears to be an old Sloan family mansion of which Luigi Corelli became the titular head when he married Regina Sloan. But the Sloans still dominate the space.)

During the wedding ceremony, people simply and purely inhabit roles; once relocated to the social space of the reception, each member of the wedding party and their related families must find the particular spaces for their particular characters. And it is only because of film's unique mobility and defiance of the constraints of chronological time that we are able to witness the revelation of forty-eight characters and the interactions of forty-eight men and women in a little over two hours of our "real" time.

As was true in M*A*S*H, Nashville, and Buffalo Bill, A Wedding has stories but no overarching plot. At the beginning of the film, Muffin Brenner, a wealthy young woman, still wearing braces, marries Dino Corelli, a wealthy, handsome young man; at the end of the film, the most erotically appealing man and woman, one a friend of the bride, the other a friend of the groom, die together in an automobile accident. Particular qualities of contemporary American culture, not an ordered series of actions, connect this wedding and these deaths. The wedding of Muffin Brenner and Dino Corelli brings together three types of the American upper class, each of which varies slightly but significantly from its stereotypical version.

Names like Muffin and Buffy are usually associated with female WASPs of families with "old" New England and midwestern money, but while the Brenners are Protestant and rich, they are nouveau riche and southern. Especially in the context of an American movie, Dino Corelli's name (a family name that was, in fact, that of Altman's second wife) and obvious wealth evokes instant associations with the "Mafia"; Dino is, in fact, the son of a marriage between an authentically old, WASP family, the Sloans, and an Italian family of shady background. The Sloans, Corellis, and Brenners are all upper-class Americans (if this category is defined simply by money and U.S. citizenship). It is no accident, however, that the reception occurs at the Corelli's midwestern estate and that the Sloans, who are associated with the Corellis by marriage, dominate the movie and attempt to dominate the wedding and reception. The custom that the bride's family plans and holds the wedding reception is less powerful than the class authority rendered to and assumed by the Sloans, because theirs is old, WASP money. Daddy Brenner's relatively recently acquired wealth is understood by everyone in the film to be inferior in status to the wealth of the Sloans even though the Brenners actually have greater financial assets. Daddy Correli's uncertain Italian roots made him equally subservient to the Sloans.

The image of America as the great melting pot is both confirmed and refuted in the marriage of Dino and Muffin. Dino is already a meld of Old World and New; on his father's side, he represents the first generation of Corellis to be born in the United States, while on his mother's side, he can probably trace ancestors who arrived in America in the seventeenth century. European, midwestern American, and southern American cultures are thus conjoined in this marriage, as presumably are Catholic and Protestant traditions. The secret pact between grandmother Nettie and Luigi Corelli, Dino's father, by which Luigi was allowed to marry Nettie's daughter Regina (Nina van Pallandt) on the condition that none of Luigi's family ever set foot in the Sloan (now Corelli) house, suggests the class consciousness that underlies the American melting pot but also points to the many covenants made possible in a country where past histories and cultural differences can be obliterated with relative ease and within the national code of ethics.

Indeed, between the opening parallel sequences of *A Wedding* and its last moments of the revelation of the deaths of two participants in the wedding, Altman's interest is focused not on the universal characteristics of weddings as a ritual but on the qualities of American culture as revealed in this constrained circumstance. One of the qualities is the division, perhaps especially on occasions such as weddings, between men and women. From the time the families return from the church to near the end of the movie, the editing repeatedly contrasts the worlds of women and the worlds of men in this society. The men meet in Luigi Corelli's basement bar; in the clichéd atmosphere of booze and cigars, they perform their buddy roles with stereotypically little verbal exchange.

The upstairs bedroom and powder room to which many of the women retreat after returning from the church ceremony stereotypically but nonetheless accurately defines a separate women's space. The women, of all ages, encounter each other in various combinations to gossip, criticize, and examine their own appearances. The film's images of women's mutual betrayals and jealousies are often caricatures, and the ritual nature of the occasion encourages cliché-ridden exchanges and melodramatic revelations. If we pay close attention, however, many of these moments provide small but distinct surprises. The attempt of the bride's mother to share confidences about mothering with the sisters of the groom's mother is discomfortingly and predictably strained; the moment is revealing, however, because Carol Burnett tries to mediate this conversation through references to movies, reminding me, at least, of my intuition that in America, movies instigate gossip and are thus a key route to knowledge of others. And if I am embarrassed by such scenes, much as I am by numerous similar vignettes in *3 Women,* it is not because they are reductive or outrageous but because they are too familiar and precise. (My most vivid memory of a recent funeral in my family is of the forty-five minutes I spent in the ladies' room of the restaurant where the post-funeral luncheon wake was held.) Race joins gender and class in *A Wedding* as yet another source of social division. As in so many of Altman's films, the complexities of white racism toward back Americans is noted early in *A Wedding* and becomes a recurrent visual and verbal motif. In one of our first and few glimpses of Nettie, the family matriarch, we see her instruct Randolph, a handsome black family servant: "Be on your best behavior—no stuff between you and my daughter in front of the guests." Subsequent visual and oral hints confirm that Randolph has had a long affair with Clarice Sloan, an affair that is never publicly acknowledged but is known to everyone. The hypocrisy in this situation is highlighted by the image of Nettie holding Randolph's hand as she commands him to "keep his place" during the reception.

The presence of Nettie's unshakably left-wing sister Beatrice, also calls attention to the political multiplicity and biases of American culture. The same family that produced aristocratic Nettie brought forth a Beatrice who is so accurately costumed and portrayed that she is a fulfillment of the type of the radical old-lady American rather than a stereotype. Beatrice's wedding present of a nude portrait of the bride painted by a socialist artist embarrasses both families but has a kind of historical accuracy in reminding us of the conjoining of aesthetic, sexual, and political battles in the struggles of an earlier generation of liberated women. Neither the drug addiction of one of her nieces nor the pregnancy of her grand niece the bride's sister, who has been impregnated by the groom, suggests that American women's conditions have improved considerably or become more liberated in constructive ways since Beatrice's youth.

Geraldine Chaplin's role as the professional wedding coordinator who eventually reveals her sexual preference for women further complicates this movie's depiction of gendered relationships. While incarnating the well-established dramatic function of the *raisonneur* or commentator on the action, a position that Chaplin herself played previously in *Nashville* and which Altman, as I earlier noted, often includes in his movies, Chaplin as wedding coordinator also calls attention to the ignorance and anxiety of contemporary Americans in respect to the rituals and performances of sexuality. Chaplin is needed to construct and instruct the family on the cultural rules of weddings. The wedding is therefore not, in this world, a ritual whose conventions are naturally understood by all involved but is a reconstructed ceremony that requires a voice of authority to ensure its propriety. Without such experts, Americans, who recognize the relative plasticity and fragility of their cultural forms, would appear to be lost. What happens then to our confidence in such authorities when they reveal (as Chaplin does when she fervently kisses the bride) their own unconventional sexuality? We know from the non-fictional cases of presidential candidate Gary Hart and John Tower, the rejected candidate for Secretary of Defense in 1989, that in the eighties, in public arenas, such revelations call into question the integrity and thus the authority of any particular expert. In this instance, where the overbearing officiousness of the character has already established her distance from the audience, we can read the revelation of her sexual preference for women as either the film's (and therefore Altman's) gesture of hostility toward lesbians or simply as one of a long list of ironic gestures with which Altman continues to detail his imaging of the contradictions in the landscape of American culture.

A far better articulation of Altman's often bitterly ironic imaging of American culture occurs near the end of the film, as many of the family and guests are departing. For the first time since the opening church sequence, the camera cuts away from the Sloan-Corelli estate to a nontheatrical space, a "real" highway where we see a shot of an ambulance and then a shot of an oil truck and the bride and groom's white Mercedes, jackknifed and burning. The Brenners, the bride's parents, are on the highway, too, and when they see this sight, they return, in genuine hysteria, to the Sloan-Corelli's house. Hugh Brenner, the bride's brother, announces the deaths of the bride and groom, and the stoned and drunken scene of the waning wedding celebration instantly transforms into a verbal battleground of accusations and attributions of blame. In the midst of this cacophony, Muffin and Dino, the bride and groom, appear on the stairway, obviously unharmed. The relief among all present is palpable. It is also profoundly disturbing because the escape from horror and grief is sustained even when, immediately, Dino notes that the occupants of the car must have been his friend Briggs and his ex-girlfriend Tracy, reminding those in the film and outside it that although the bride and groom are safe, two young people have just died.

More than at any moment since the first few segments of the film, Altman is now in strategic control of the relationship between the world screened and the movie audience. The visual and oral absence of grief for the two who have died and the lack of concern among the wedding guests for the families of the dead is both appalling and shaming. It might remind us of the young people killed in automobile accidents every day in America and, more important, bring home that in most instances we remain as distant from those deaths as we are distant from the movie deaths of Briggs and Tracy. As long as they are not "our kids," we can ignore it (whatever the "It" is). Our sense of care and responsibility is not social or communitarian but personal and private.

The only character in A Wedding who takes a contrary position, a position of rage at these deaths and responsibility to the families of the dead, is Luigi Corelli, the groom's father, whose suffering is captured as he bangs his fist on the stairway railing. It is he who insists that someone close to Briggs and Tracy call their respective families. In sharp contrast to Luigi's responsible and caring behavior, his wife declares that "Briggs had no right to take that car," and Tulip Brenner takes this event as a sign that her brief but passionate liaison with another wedding guest must be terminated. As is so often the case in Altman's movies, it is not the man or women who stands up for personal rights but the one who takes on responsibility for others whom Altman establishes, often in a surprising moment, as the genuinely virtuous American. Luigi Corelli departs from this movie, as from his family and home, with a mantel of human dignity that distinguishes him from all forty-seven of the other characters. Paying his respects to the dead Nettie, he takes his leave with the assurance to Nettie and the audience that he has kept his promises, that his family is secure, and that there is nothing more he need do in the world we have witnessed as the estate. It is not coincidence that, as he departs, we hear on the sound track Leonard Cohen's song "Like a Bird on a Wire" or that the film really ends as Luigi drives off to the Cohen line, "I have tried, in my way, to be free." Like Wade's freedom in Nashville, Annie Oakley's in Buffalo Bill and the Indians, and

Millie's in *3 Women*, Luigi's freedom is not a simple matter of detachment from others but a liberty gained through the acknowledgment of responsibility *to* others.

Altman, too, tries, in his way, to be free. The failed moments in *A Wedding*, as in many of his films, are those not of radical invention or incoherence, despite his unconventional narrative style, but of the evidence of trying too hard, of straining to be satiric or ironic or inclusive or profound. The inclusion of a video crew employed to record the wedding and reception does not, for example, add any new insights to Altman's previously established acknowledgments of the intrusion of all kinds of media in our daily lives. And the unannotated catalogue of contemporary human foibles and resistances to dominant practices apparent in *A Wedding*—from drug addition, to adultery, racism, class elitism, homosexuality, and voyeurism—weakens this movie's ability to perturb viewers' understandings of American society. Because so much is thrown into the suitcase of post-modern American cultural practices, and because the separate pieces of the cultural baggage that is Altman's America are less inventively delineated in *A Wedding* than in *Nashville* or *Buffalo Bill and the Indians* or *Come Back the the 5 and Dime, Jimmy Dean, Jimmy Dean*, the audience for *A Wedding* need not be caught in the trap of cultural recognition that Altman persistently sets. We can know that this movie calls our attention to the proximities of racisms and interracial relationships, of sentimental romance to homosexuality, but nothing that happens until the end of the film requires that we rethink our understanding of the meaning of America.

*   *   *   *

Different limits are apparent in the two movies Altman made immediately after *A Wedding*, *Quintet* and *A Perfect Couple*. Both these films were released in 1979; along with *Buffalo Bill and the Indians*, *3 Women*, *A Wedding*, *Health* (1980), and *Popeye* (1980), *Quintet* and *A Perfect Couple* were increasingly the products of Altman's own company, Lion's Gate Films. Established initially in 1970 as a group of offices, by the mid-seventies Lion's Gate had its own studio, which was particularly strong in audio facilities. One of the well-known characteristics of Lion's Gate was its ability to produce interesting low-budget films; unfortunately, in contrast to Lion's Gate's other productions, *Quintet* and *A Perfect Couple* feel like low-budget films that were not just made on relatively little money but that were also imaginatively and thematically constrained. Neither was a success at the box office or with film reviewers, and this was the case not because they were too experimental in the terms Altman had previously established but because they were not compelling movies. These two films, while resembling some earlier Altman works like *Images* in their relatively narrow focus and domains, have the most blurred signatures of any of Altman's productions.

Quintet, Altman's first attempt at science fiction, shares with other Altman films a theatrical approach to space, but whereas the assertively framed locations of *Nashville* or *Buffalo Bill* or *A Wedding* are settings for the dramas that occur within the site they define, the set in *Quintet* is the most important single signifier in the movie. This set represents a futuristic city of glass and metal, drastic angles and glaring colors, a twenty-first -century vision of purgatory. The film begins outside this post-modernist city; on a field of white, accompanied by windy sounds reminiscent of the beginning of *McCabe and Mrs. Miller,* two dots of gray appear and gradually emerge as a man and woman, cloaked like conventional Arabs of the Middle Eastern desert. The man, Essex (Paul Newman), once lived in the city they are approaching and is returning, in part, to find his brother. The woman, Vivia (Bridgette Fossey), is young, inquisitive, and pregnant. Just before their arrival in the city, Vivia sights a bird flying north and remarks that she did not know that there were any such birds left. Blatantly, too much so I think, the bird and Vivia's pregnancy suggest the possibility of life outside of the chilling cold of the snow-covered plain and the equally chilling atmosphere of the murder-structured city we, Essex, and Viva are about to enter.

The characters who inhabit the city, in contrast to Essex and Vivia, are like Italian Renaissance commedia dell'arte players; their Renaissance costumes and stylized speech and movement suggest stock characters, and their playing of the game Quintet, a game of life and death, is their profession. Like the commedia players and not unlike most of the characters in Altman's films, the figures who appear in *Quintet* win or lose, hold our attention or fail to do so, by virtue of the skill of their improvisations within the limits of the stock or "type" characters. In large part because of the masked quality of these characters, *Quintet* invokes both the terrors and inversions of Carnival in Venice.

Between the arrival in the city of Essex and Vivia and Essex's departure at the very end of the film, only two events occur. Shortly after the arrival of Essex and Vivia, Essex's brother and Vivia are killed by a bomb explosion in the brother's apartment; from that point on, Essex becomes a participant in the game of Quintet, a game for which the rules are never clear but that obviously, from what we see, involves murder and a hit list of opponents. The "game of life" to which the opening song in *M*A*S*H* referred has, paradoxically, become the game of death in this futuristic world. None in the city has reproduced in so long that Vivia's pregnancy is a wonder and a threat to the city's inhabitants. But Essex poses no genuine threat to his opponents or to us; when he departs at the end of *Quintet,* following the gull heading north, we are, I infer, meant to take courage to escape our own technological worlds, to have faith that "decent" people can survive cynicism and violence. But I understand this world no more or less than I did at the beginning of the film. Removed from the roots of American culture, *Quintet* takes place in a no-man's land that detaches itself from history and authentic modern culture. It is far from the land where Altman's work works.

Among the oddities of *Quintet* in the context of Altman's other movies is its relative silence. Following the embarrassingly predictable dialogue between Vivia and Essex as they approach the city, there is neither a single line of dialogue nor a moment that captures multiple voices that is worth remembering. Even the silence is detached from meaning.

*   *   *   *

Altman's next film, *A Perfect Couple,* is, in contrast to *Quintet,* a noisy film, but it, too, never achieves the depth of focus in sound characteristic of Altman's films, and it presents no lasting images. As in *A Wedding* and *Quintet,* the key questions in a *A Perfect Couple* are: "What is this game?" and "What are the rules to this game?" The game here is courtship. The key players are Alex Theodopoulos (Paul Dooley) and Sheila Shea (Marta Heflin). They meet through a computer video dating service whose accuracy in creating "perfect couples" is both satirized and confirmed by the episodes that comprise Alex and Sheila's courtship.

The essential sources of conflict in *A Perfect Couple* are situated in the very different cultural and, more specifically, family contexts of Alex and Sheila. Alex comes from and, in his forties, remains dominated by, an aristocratic, traditional Greek family. Sheila's "family" is the rock-and-roll group with whom she performs. Alex's father is a tyrant who rules his family with an ominously authoritative voice; the band leader of the group to which Sheila is attached repeatedly appears to be tyrannical and cruel to his fellow musicians. Music is central to both their lives. Alex's younger sister, Eleausa (Belito Moreno), is a cellist with the Los Angeles Philharmonic orchestra; Sheila sings rock and roll.

The computer brings these two people together because each wants a "meaningful experience." But the computer's categories for matchmaking apparently exclude indications of cultural preferences and class biases. The computer's vision, to the degree that one can talk about a computer's "vision," is of an idealized, democratized American society in which desires transcend specific cultural rules and restraints, at least in the attachments of women to men and men to women.

In order for the computer's predictions to be accurate, Alex and Sheila must either perfectly fulfill a "type" of character with no more or less definition than the type requires, or each must be an exceptional version of the types they appear to fulfill. Each of the two worlds of *A Perfect Couple*—that of the old, aristocratic Greek family and that of the hippie rock group—is stereotyped, but neither Alex nor Sheila is a stereotype. Alex is not, in part, because he is unlike other roles Paul Dooley has played and will subsequently play, as the mushy husband in *A Wedding* or the buffoon politician in *Health*. Alex also defies the stereotype of the upper-class nebbish when, after failing to defend Sheila from his father's condemnation of her as a whore (this occurs when Papa invades Alex's bedroom and finds Sheila there with Alex), he seeks her out and starkly apologizes.

Sheila defies stereotypical images of the female rock-and-roll star immediately by her application for a mate to the computer service and, later, in her obvious dissatisfaction with the superficial bonds of attachment in the rock group. Marta Heflin's gangly, stringy-haired, anorexic Sheila also does not look like a rock-and-roll singer (in contrast, for example, to Mary in *Nashville*).

The problem with Sheila and Alex is that they do not *do* enough to interest us in their separate lives or their lives together as a couple. Precisely because they come from such different cultural contexts, because (in the sixties terms that shadow this movie) Alex comes from a biologically related, cultured family and Sheila from an invented, countercultural family, the possibility of their union re-creates the uniquely American mythology of marriage as the key institution for the assimilation of immigrants and the production of an authentically American culture. But for their differences and their union to make a difference to us we must feel pleasure in their company—their pleasure and ours. We have precedents in such American movies as *It Happened One Night* or *Do the Right Thing* for celebration of difference—of gender, of class, and of ethnicity—so we know what it looks like, and this is not it.

The troubling irony in *A Perfect Couple* is that for the first time, Altman positions a romantic relationship between a man and a woman in the foreground of his examination of American culture, and given everything he has shown us previously of relations between American men and women, the poverty of this relationship only confirms his previous demonstrations of skepticism about modern gendered relations. Although I tend to think of Altman's films as absent of romantic male-female relationships, this is not precisely the case, as Robert Self has argued in his ruminations on "perfect couples" in Altman's work.[15] The construction and deconstruction of male-female couples contribute significantly as plot elements and signs of social malaise in all of Robert Altman's films. But only in one earlier film, *McCabe and Mrs. Miller,* is the attraction between a man and a woman a source of pleasure and desire for the spectator, and even in *McCabe and Mrs. Miller,* this triangulated attraction of characters and spectator is subordinate to our and their design for knowledge and survival. Altman's consistent vision of relations between men and women is of encounters that are fragile, fragmented, and self-oriented, of detachments rather than attachments.[16]

The reunion of Sheila and Alex, allegorized in the final joint performance of the Los Angeles Philharmonic orchestra and Sheila's rock group, Keepin' Them Off the Streets, must either then be read as a transcendence of the gendered flaws and social constraints that dominate Altman's America or as incoherent with much of this film and most of Altman's other work. What we see of this reunion within its own frames is perfectly clear in its meaning. Sheila and Alex are reunited in the theater/concert hall and go to the center box, where they drink champagne out of silver goblets; Alex feeds Sheila olives, nourishing her with elments of his culture; Sheila offers marijuana, and Alex readily accepts. In context, however, a context with which Altman provides us, the meaning of this match is more ambiguous. Intercut between shots of Alex and Sheila are shots of the iconic other "perfect couple" whom we have seen throughout the film (much like the tricycle man in *Nashville*) how they are not talking to each other, they have moved out of the center box, and most threateningly, we watch the woman of this couple burn the man with a cigarette held in a long cigarette holder. Has one ostensibly perfect couple only been replaced by another, equally ill-fated couple? Or is the replacement, like Hal Phillip Walker's Replacement party in *Nashville*, a substitute that only superficially signals change?

Because similar questions, in a louder and more ringing voice, are provoked by *Nashville*, it is possible to see *A Perfect Couple* as simply a miniature of Altman's larger canvases, of films like *M*A*S*H; Nashville; Buffalo Bill;* and *Health*, the film that follows *A Perfect Couple*. What I am missing in such a reading of *A Perfect Couple* is the theatricality and the self-reflexivity of performance that should be innate or at least natural to this movie, given its juxtaposition of Greek-American family culture and rock-and-roll performance culture. Even when, at the end of *A Perfect Couple*, Alex and Sheila are in a theater, their presence to us is the deflated presence of video, almost as if to say that to be a spectator is no longer to be witness to a spectacle.

*   *   *   *

Before Altman presses this possibility further, as he will come to do in most of his films of the eighties, he does return twice more to the broad canvases and carnival spirit of *Brewster McCloud, M*A*S*H, Nashville,* and *Buffalo Bill. Health,* released in 1980, is the first of these last two spectacles (*Popeye* is the other). Once again, in *Health* the setting tells the story. The entire film occurs within the physical and narrative boundaries of a health-food convention occurring in St. Petersburg, Florida. While the blatantly dominant colors of *Nashville* were red, white, and blue, here the striking colors, are, appropriately, orange and green. (The comic qualities of these colors and their referents are blatantly displayed in a character walking around the convention costumed as an orange.) What plot exists concerns the competition for the presidency of the national health-food association; the two leading candidates are women—Esther Brill (Lauren Bacall), an eighty-three-year-old fanatic, and Isabella Garnell (Glenda Jackson), a domineering, ivory-tower intellectual. There is a third "independent" candidate—Harold Gainey (Paul Dooley)—but he is, to his fury, never taken seriously by anyone but himself.

Like the football game at the end of *M*A*S*H* that is literally about the function of football in American culture and simultaneously an extended metaphor for war, *Health* is at once a satire on the contemporary American obsession with health and an allegorical commentary on national politics in the United States, especially as it was played out in the presidential campaign of 1980. From the start, the world of *Health* is that of a carnival. Everything seems to be happening at once, while paradoxically there is little plot movement; roles and rules are turned topsy-turvy; behavior that is hidden or disguised in ordinary life is exaggerated and displayed; every moment is perceived from multiple points of view, and absurdity reigns.

Health's first sounds and images tell us that this is a film about American presidential politics in which the power structures of the national election campaign are re-presented intact while the specific social characteristics are reversed or distorted, as the opening reverse zoom and the domination of the election by women suggest. The initial setting is a show within a show. Dick Cavett, playing

Eighty-three-year old Esther Brill (Lauren Bacall) takes a sudden nap while appearing on the Dick Cavett Show with the U.S. President's representative, Gloria Burbank, (Carol Burnett), and her opponent for the presidency of the National Health Organization, Isabella Garnell (Glenda Jackson), in *Health*. (*The Museum of Modern Art/Film Stills Archive, New York City*)

himself, is about to tape a program in which the two leading candidates, Esther Brill and Isabella Garnell; and Gloria Burbank (Carol Burnett), the White House's health advisor, are appearing as guests. This immediate image of the Cavett show is an efficient device for character revelation and for altering the audience to the movie's reliance on allusions and metaphoric gestures. Most obviously, in the health-industry election campaign, the leading candidates are women, and a man is the independent candidate who is never taken seriously or even paid public attention. The male candidate is absent from the Cavett show.

Eighty-three-year-old Esther Brill deliberately reveals that the secret of her youthful appearance and longevity is sexual chastity; like the memorable general in Stanley Kubrick's *Dr. Strangelove,* Brill believes that we literally lose ourselves in sex. The sudden, on air, stand-up nap that she takes is equally revealing, but not an act of Brill's choice. The suddenness of Brill's nap lapse is funny; her unconscious state also refers unquestionably, and seriously, to the nap-taking inclinations of then presidential candidate Ronald Reagan, in whom the disparity between appearance and age is analogously evident. That Brill is played by Lauren Bacall, a well-known Hollywood star of approximately the same vintage as Ronald Reagan, also contributes to the spectators' association of Brill with Reagan.

A similar but more complex analogue is established by the characterization of the other major candidate, Isabella Garnell. Isabella only speaks in paragraphs and assumes the transcendence of her mind over her body. Her narcissism and need to control are aptly illustrated during the opening Cavett show sequence when she unselfconsciously takes out her own tape recorder and microphone to record some lines for future use. Throughout the film, she is associated with Adlai Stevenson, most notably when, later in her own room, we glimpse a hole in the bottom of her shoe that recalls a similar hole in one of Stevenson's shoes. The film's identification of her with Stevenson, however, is less direct and more ambiguous than is Brill's with Reagan. Cavett quotes Stevenson in the opening episode as stating that "health, next to character, is a man's best asset"; having thus brought Stevenson's voice on screen, we are prepared to recall Stevenson when we hear Isabella's careful, intellectualized talk. It is not clear, however, how this association is meant to affect us as viewers/voters. Glenda Jackson's performance of Isabella is parodic and critical; in contrast to my memories of Stevenson, which are characterized by admiration, respect, and even warmth, I am repulsed by my sense of Isabella's manipulativeness and ideological tyrannization of others. Either the match between Isabella and Stevenson is meant to link them weakly or, potentially of more interest, Altman is attempting to re-create the negative experience of the majority of Americans in relation to Stevenson for the minority who saw him positively. Under the latter conditions, we who admired Stevenson would see him as did others who denigrated him—as a detached, frigid, academic, liberal un-American statesman.

Stevenson, of course, was not running against Ronald Reagan in 1980; Jimmy Carter was. Nor does Esther Brill's behavior or appearance in any way suggest Stevenson's actual opponent, Dwight Eisenhower. *Health* cannot, therefore, be read as a straightforward political allegory, even though Gloria Burbank, the White House representative at the health convention, at one point proclaims that "It's Ike and Adlai all over again." Haven Hamilton is right when he cries out at the end of *Nashville*, "This isn't Dallas, it's Nashville." But for the audience, both in Nashville and in the movie theater, Hamilton's denial is self-defeating; his denial in fact confirms the validity of associating Dallas and Nashville. Similarly, the diversity and historicity of the associations of the candidates and election phenomena of *Health* with the U.S. presidential election campaigns of both 1956 and 1980 make *Health* more rather than less interesting as political satire. There is a political memory present in this movie that illuminates more than just one election campaign.

The link between the health-food enterprise and national politics is personified in the character of Gloria Burbank, who is explicitly attending the convention to make certain that the U.S. President's "support for health" is publicized by the media. Although she does not stand for or allude to any particular political figure in the way that Esther Brill and Isabella Garnell do, like these other women, she, too, ventriloquates and must be heard much of the time as two voices speaking at once or as a hybrid voice.[17] Each of these women is also, notably and blatantly, speaking for a man; the fact that women are in these particular roles is such an obvious reversal of the norm that it unquestionably names gender and power relations as a central theme of the film without the *auteur* having to do anything further with these characters or with plot. When Gloria eventually discards her official, nonpartisan voice and passionately embraces the candidacy of Isabella Garnell, she explains her comically confused motivation both in terms of her identification of Isabella with Adlai Stevenson and in terms of her wistful assertion that 'Someday a woman will be president.'"

Dick Cavett's role "as Himself" (as emphasized by the opening credits), the talk-show host, is at once reassuring in its familiarity and disconcerting in its injection of the "real" world into an otherwise fictitious world. Cavett's presence in the film as himself recalls the brief appearances of Julie Christie and Elliot Gould "as themselves" in *Nashville* and foreshadows the mixture of "real" people and actors in *Tanner '88*. Precisely because the other actors and actresses in *Nashville* are all playing invented characters, Christie's and Gould's less mediated roles not only catch our attention but mark our memory of the movie. Such mixtures of real and fictional people unfix our positions as spectators because they call attention to the movie as a fabricated product and because by defying the classical Hollywood conventions of separation of documentary from fictional cultural forms they prevent us from losing ourselves in the movie. Starting in the sixties, many mainstream American movies did borrow from documentary style by shooting on location as opposed to in a studio, by encouraging improvisation, by employing more explicit montage techniques in editing, by the use of hand-held cameras, and more natural lighting, but for the most part, they did not include actual men and women and fictitious characters in the same movie.

In one sense, this device, which becomes key to several of Altman's productions in the eighties, is contiguous with his use of music and his zooms; all of these gestures "denaturalize" the world on the screen, and in what can well be called a Brechtian approach to drama, these gestures distance the spectator from the world viewed and are intended to perplex.[18] European film directors have used comparable Brechtian alienation effects since the sixties, and a few American directors—Woody Allen comes immediately to mind— have been concerned with disorienting viewers' relation to film, but Altman's persistence in exploring this terrain is unusual in the domain of American movies.[19]

For Altman, the blurring or removal of the line between reality and fiction is not just one of many devices used generally to reinflect what we see and hear on screen. In the eighties, in a country with a movie star as President, a country that makes no attempt to disguise the dramatization of both politics and ordinary life, the role of moving, talking pictures is a specific and serious matter. The point is not simply that we be distanced sufficiently from the world on the screen to regard it thoughtfully but that we specifically think about what it means to be unable to tell the difference between a political persona created to attract our votes and a dramatic persona created to attract our money.

Who or what, then, is Dick Cavett as we see him doing his show at the beginning of *Health?* He is a well-known talk-show host, playing his role of interviewer much as he played it on television. But as well as we know that his "guests" only exist within the frame of this movie, we know that outside this frame Dick Cavett remains Dick Cavett, while Esther Brill vanishes and Lauren Bacall appears. On his talk show, Cavett seems to be in control of the frame and its content; in *Health,* Altman controls the frame, and within that context, reverse zooms and distance shots as well as an overwhelming arched HEALTH sign visually diminish Cavett. Further attention is called to Cavett's relatively small body when a chorus of four young women greets him with a song and a bridge comprised of their arms, as in the familiar "London bridge is falling down" game; the chorus has underestimated his height and must ask them to raise their arms. These various gestures make it clear that the movie's interests dominate Cavett's own or those of "his" show. Cavett appears to instantiate the conclusion asserted to Isabella Garnell by the health association's apparent behind-the-scenes power, an old man who identifies himself as Colonel Cody: "You are for real. That means you are no threat to anyone." We can read "for real" here as meaning both sincere and undisguised. Both meanings are true of Isabella (within the world of the film, although not, obviously, if we take into account that she is a role played by an actress, Glenda Jackson), and Cody's interpretation of the causal relationship between her integrity and politics is given credence by the final election results—Esther Brill is victorious.

In *Health,* not to be "for real" means to appear to others behind a mask consciously worn to manipulate others in particular ways. Although Esther Brill partially fits this description, it is the men in *Health* who most blatantly take on disguises in order to fulfill individual desires. Cody, whom we finally learn is not a wealthy and powerful tycoon but the dependent younger brother of Esther Brill, is nonetheless, threatening to Gloria Burbank and to us because he behaves as if he does have power and because his fury is particularly directed at women in politics. "You work for me, woman, you work for me," Cody tells Gloria, "You people have got no control and you are just a damn female. That's spelled *f e e*—for your information, that is a whore."

An equally blatant disguise is taken on by Bobby Hammer (Henry Gibson), a notorious political manueverer whose interests can clearly be bought. In order to undermine Isabella Garnell, he dresses up as a woman and subsequently accuses Isabella of "really being a man" who has had a sex-change operation. Hammer says he knows this because he had a similar operation at the same time. This is all made ridiculous by the obviousness of Hammer's presentation of himself as a woman. What it means to be seen as a woman or man is not, however, a trivial issue for Altman, as we have already seen. When a transformation of gender is meant seriously by the subject, as with Helen, the transvestite in *California Split,* or Joanne in *Come Back to the 5 and Dime, Jimmy Dean, Jimmy Dean,* Altman's films treat the transformed character with dignity and respect. But when gender is deliberately misrepresented to manipulate others, as with Hammer, Altman releases the camera's potential for cruelty and mockery.

That potential is most strikingly fulfilled in the last episode, a brief epilogue to *Health.* As if taking its cue from Isabella's style, the movie itself is comprised of a series of filmic paragraphs, several of which are memorable as discrete entities but only a few of which are meaningfully linked to what immediately precedes or follows them. Mostly what we remember are moments that are funny, either because they are sight gags or comical remarks. Gloria Burbank is so frightened of being on Cavett's television show that when Cavett "reassuringly" puts his hand on her bare thigh, she crosses her other leg over his hand, simultaneously naming and deflating the sexism in his gesture; the double entendre in Esther Brill's campaign slogan, "Feel yourself," is amusing both because of Esther's claims for sexual abstinence and because of its satiric reference to a whole number of comparable pitches from New Age advocates.

The conclusion of *Health* is not at all funny, however, and is particularly striking because it uses devices already well established in the film to effect its lasting chill. The final sequence begins with Gloria Burbank slapping down her ex-husband Harry's fondling hand because, as she tells him in no uncertain terms, he has knowingly, the night before, exploited his knowledge of her erotic reaction to fear and hidden his knowledge that her fear was unfounded. The camera then moves through a crowd, creating the same kind of mobile montage of faces and voices and themes screened in the last segment of *Nashville*. Finally, the camera lands where it began to shoot, near the entrance to the hotel and the site of the Cavett show. With the Cavett show set as a backdrop, a black woman, identified earlier as the public relations director for the hotel, firmly informs Esther Brill and her brother, Lester (alias Cody), that they must leave to make way for the next convention, a meeting of hypnotists; there are some circumstances, at least, in American culture, when a black woman is empowered, even if they are, for the moment, relatively trivial. It is over the end of this scene that we begin to hear the voices of the Steinettes, the hotel chorus, singing a song that is unmistakably identifiable with German cabaret music of the late twenties and the thirties. When the camera finds the Steinettes, poised on the entryway stairs, they confirm the cultural association. The four women are dressed in men's tails and top hats and their movement and accents are those that we now associate with fascist Germany. As this chorus sings their last line—"We welcome you and want you to join us—in sleep"—one member raises her arm in a gesture that imitates Esther Brill's "nap" gesture but also associates that gesture with salutes to Hitler. The other three chorus members drop their heads as if in sudden sleep on command. And for those who remain to watch the credits, the final, ironically placed music is the "Star-Spangled Banner."

Health is a funny and sometimes silly film, but it is also a film with an unmistakable political agenda and a scathing critique of American culture as we arrived in the eighties. That it followed two Altman films that were failures at the box office—*Quintet* and *A Perfect Couple*—did not set it up well as a product for big box-office returns in mainstream America. It is therefore not surprising that Twentieth Century-Fox, which was to distribute *Health* in 1980, refused to do so, despite the prizes the film won at the Venice and Montreal film festivals and the subsequent successful, if brief, run in Los Angeles.

In *Health,* more openly than in any of his previous movies, Altman asserted the relevance of his ongoing critique of American culture to specific American political events. Despite his persistent public disclaimers of political intentions, there is little question while watching and listening to *Health* that this is a political as well as cultural vision at work. Beyond the understanding that this is a critical vision, however, there are uncertainties and complexities as to where Altman stands in relation to American history and the future of American society. His next film, *Popeye,* although in part intended to be a commercial success and therefore compensate for the losses incurred by his previous three films, clarifies that stance in both predictable and surprising ways.[20]

* * * *

For those who approach Altman's work as a series of genre critiques, *Popeye* is unquestionably Altman's musical. Altman had lingered in this terrain many times before—in *Nashville* most explicitly, but also in more constrained ways in *McCabe and Mrs. Miller, California Split, A Perfect Couple,* and *Health. Popeye,* however, not only extends Altman's previous uses of music but models its integration of music and dance, talk and event, on the classical Hollywood musicals that, along with Westerns, are among the relatively few cultural forms fully made in the U.S.A.

Consonant with the traditional Hollywood musicals of the thirties, forties, and fifties, *Popeye,* enthusiastically embraces its folkloric setting and characters, drawing and giving its pleasure by exaggerating the ordinariness of ordinary people and their lives. From the dozens of vignettes told in comic strips by E. C. Segar, the cartoon creator of Popeye, Altman, writer Jules Feiffer, composer Harry Nilsson, and the movie cast have distilled what Altman himself called "a morality play."[21] With the notable exception of Olive Oyl (Shelley Duvall), characters are unambiguously good or evil; a series of episodes enact the struggle between good and evil, and

Popeye (Robin Williams) enters the theatrical world and fabricated town of Sweethaven in search of his father in *Popeye*. (*The Museum of Modern Art/Film Stills Archive, New York City*)

good, of course, wins in the end. The plot line that presses the movie forward is deceptive in its apparent simplicity; a son seeks his father, a son becomes a father, and a good man competes with a bad man for the same woman. Each of these story lines is linked to the other two by a common protagonist, Popeye (Robin Williams), and each story has a familiar mythical base in a man's search for knowledge of his own identity.

While the film's narrative structure is built around these interlinked stories of Popeye's individual struggles, Sweethaven, the town that contains all of the film's action, is the center of the film's interest. Sweethaven is a place and a community, and both aspects of it were built, on Malta, specifically for the movie. Isolated for a considerable time in their own little village, the crew and cast, many of whom had worked with Altman and each other before, apparently became an authentic community on and off camera. Of the several accounts of this production, Jules Feiffer's description of Robert Altman is particularly revealing, especially since several other sources have recorded tensions between Feiffer and Altman over the script for Popeye:

> What struck me during the first couple of weeks of shooting was that I couldn't figure out where his authority came from, because he's not charismatic in any sense of the word. He doesn't order people around. He's very relaxed and reflective on the set, or sometimes tense and concentrated. But whatever his mood, there's nothing bossy about it. He doesn't dominate anybody.[22]

To describe Sweethaven as a community, on or off camera, may be misleading in a post-sixties context. I do not mean to conjure a vision of countercultural flower adults, all happily and uncompetitively working together for the common good. Sweethaven is not a utopia; to the contrary, as Altman himself describes it, it is "a microcosm of an oppressed society."[23] I do mean to suggest, and that is why I related Feiffer's comments, that Sweethaven appears on the screen as at least an extension of Altman's previous attempts to incorporate many points of view in the movie itself and to establish the ambiance of a company, of a collaborative endeavor whose success depends (in contrast to that of the inhabitants of the fictional town) not on one voice that is dominant because of its particular role or resources or power but on the cooperation and mutual sense of responsibility of all involved.

Sweethaven is also a notably theatrical space, self-contained and distinct from any world accessible to the spectator. The angles of the roofs of its houses are too acute, the clothing of its inhabitants too bizarre, and the inclination toward song and dance too present for this to be a "real" place. Popeye enters Sweethaven, with us, like the first actor making his entrance on stage, and we know from that entrance that Sweethaven is not a town we can enter, even though we instantly recognize its similarity to our towns. Altman has created nearly comparable settings before—the base in *M*A*S*H* and the Wild West Show in *Buffalo Bill* are vivid examples—but here, for the first time, the theatrical uniqueness of the space is a given, and the possibilities within it for magic to occur are inherent to its definition.

More than in any movie since *Nashville*, in *Popeye* Altman and his co-workers exploit every element of theater and film. Although character portrayals are deliberattely flattened to suggest the characters' roots in comic strips, no single moment or character is entirely flat because odd camera angles; overlapping sounds and voices; blantantly stylized costumes, movements, and gestures; music, dance, and verbal wit come into play often and unexpectedly. Of all these elements, it is the distinctive physical movements of the characters—and not the movement of the camera—that identifies *Popeye* with movie musicals. We can learn from *Popeye* that to call this kind of film (or live show) a musical is a misnomer. It is dance more than singing that gives movie musicals their distinctive aura, as we immediately know if we look back at any number of movies in which Fred Astaire or Gene Kelly starred. Although Altman deliberately obscures or transforms conventional dance steps in *Popeye,* it is the particular movements of Robin Williams and Shelley Duvall that most vividly reveal their characters and separate them from ordinary beings. Robin Williams's somersaulting falls and spins in his first fight with Bluto and his "fancy dancin' " in his boxing match with Oxblood Oxheart, and Shelley Duvall's dance in her size-14 shoes to "He Needs Me" recall the transcendentally graceful klutziness of Charlie Chaplin. Duvall's physical makeup and gestures *are* Olive Oyl from the first moment we see her dressing for her (fourth) engagement party and complaining about the ugliness of her hat, but in the moment of her recognition that "he needs me," her tuberous arms and legs, her unsettled head, and doll-like hair all conjoin to float her above the pavement of Sweethaven and any world we are likely to come across.

Once we are in the world of the unearthly, anything can happen, or at least anything that does not disturb the common values and beliefs (the common sense, in Clifford Geertz's usage) of the folk who inhabit this world. In *Popeye,* anything that can happen does happen. Olive Oyl cannot bring herself to marry Bluto, even though, as she proclaims in her first song, he is large. (While classi-

Olive Oyl (Shelley Duvall) dances her ambivalence about everything—especially her engagement to Bluto and her attraction to Popeye—in *Popeye*. (*The Museum of Modern Art/Film Stills Archive, New York City*)

cal movie musicals only depicted sexuality in metaphor, *Popeye* finds a whole number of double entendres to express its simultaneous innocence and erotic knowledge.) Bluto susbsequently destroys much of the Oyls' house, which remains in its demolished state for the rest of the movie. Stopped and distracted by Popeye in her attempt to escape Bluto and Sweethaven, Olive quickly finds herself emotionally entangled with Popeye and attached to a baby in a basket that has been substituted for the traveling basket Olive was carrying.

The baby's arrival is both magical and mundane. Twice before the baby is uncovered, we are shown images of a stork sitting nearby on a railing; on the other hand, there is comically familiar note attached to the basket that declares that the baby's mother was destitute and would not be able to care for the child for at least twenty-five years. None of this is as surprising, however, as Popeye's reaction to the baby, whom he names Swee' Pea. While Olive's first reaction is to disassociate herself from the baby, Popeye instantly claims his attachment to Swee' Pea: "Look at this!" Popeye exclaims, "I came lookin' for me Pap an' now I'm a mother." So much for Oedipal journeys and biologically determined gender roles.

Two conventional patterns are reversed here and for much of the remainder of the movie. Traditional narrative and social customs would have courtship and marriage precede the arrival of a baby, but in *Popeye,* it is the baby who signifies and mediates an attachment between Popeye and Olive Oyl. In a sequence at a boxing match not long after the discovery of the baby, Popeye and Olive dispute the similarities between Swee' Pea's features and each of theirs, then slide into talk about their dreams for the baby's future. In the process of imagining Swee' Pea at school, Swee' Pea punching other kids in the mouth, and Swee' Pea living in a vine-covered cottage, they recognize their own attraction for each other, and Swee' Pea giggles as they sing the requisite romantic duet "Stay with Me."

Traditional expectations of gender roles would dictate that Olive Oyl feel an instant "maternal" affection and responsibility for the baby, but in this movie, it is Popeye who feelingly and knowingly becomes the primary caregiver to the infant. It is Popeye who objects to the exploitation for financial gain of Swee' Pea's apparent ability to predict the future, including who will win in the toy horse races that are subject to heavy wagers in Sweethaven. Olive argues that Swee' Pea can simply help make their lives easier, but Popeye, concerned about Swee' Pea's moral sensibility, counters that "wrong is wrong even when it helps you." This dispute sets up Popeye's key revelation song, "What Am I? I Yam What I Yam," the lyrics of which establish his integrity and his immobility in the face of his countercultural position in Sweethaven.

Popeye's suffering begins just one step beyond this assertion of self, a step in which Popeye allows himself to be carried about town as a hero for putting the ever-present tax man in his place—down a chute and into a lake. While Popeye and most of the townspeople of Sweethaven are celebrating their victory over the tax man, Swee' Pea is kidnapped. Popeye blames himself for this woeful turn of events: "Olive was right," he mumbles to himself. "Even an orphan needs a mother and a father and if I was going to be his mother I should have at least let her be his father. I wasn't man enough to be his mother."

No attempt to interpret these lines would do them justice. Suffice it to recall that in the end Altman again paradoxically reverses and confirms the old stories. This Popeye, unlike the cartoon character, hates spinach, but forced to eat it as a punishment by his evil competitor Bluto, Popeye gains superstrength by which he is able to save both Olive and Swee' Pea from a dreadful monster. In addition, in confronting the forces of evil in Sweethaven, Popeye discovers that the invisible power and authority behind the town, the Commodore, is none other than his own Pap, who, upon being reunited with his son, instantly transforms from bitter, absent tycoon into loving father and generous citizen. All's well that ends well, even if getting there requires significant subversions of common practices and beliefs.

For Altman and his company, *Popeye* did land well, but not well enough. A commercial success in theaters and subsequently on video casette, *Popeye* freed Altman from financial constraints and might have given him greater authority in the filmmaking world had the film not been damned by most of the critics. Even reviewers like Vincent Canby and Pauline Kael, writers who had admired much of Altman's previous work, criticized *Popeye* for its detachment from its characters and its audience, created in part by what these critics viewed as the film's intellectual restraint and self-conscious stylization.[24]

My guess is that *Popeye* disappointed most critics because it never is what Michael Wood aptly calls "the vehicle of an all-purpose joy," and it is that joy that we are missiing when *Popeye* is over. Its model, although it certainly never equals it, is Brecht's *Threepenny Opera* not *Flying Down to Rio* or *Top Hat*. One source of that peculiar, all-purpose joy in musicals is surely the knowledge that it is within the range of human possibility to move like a Chaplin or an Astaire but that, at the same time, these stars are extraordinary performers, and we are blessed to be their audience. Robin Williams and Duvall fit their roles wonderfully, but neither embodies a spectacular or transcendent style. Their style is more like Chaplin's than it is like that of Astaire and Rogers, but while we would be happy to see Chaplin or Astaire perform the same numbers again, we are satisfied with one rendition of each number performed by Williams or Duvall. When Popeye transcends what we normally expect of the human body, as in his encounters with Bluto, Oxheart, or the giant octopus at the end of the movie, the impression conveyed is of a joint effort of actor and movie technology, not of an effortless, solely human grace. Nor is the dance or singing of Williams and Duvall a metaphor for a special eroticism, as it is with Astaire and Rogers.

That Williams and Duvall are not Astaire and Rogers may be a failure of wish fulfillment but is not in itself a cinematic flaw. Their limits may arguably be strengths in this case, since both Feiffer and the body of Altman's work attest that Altman was, all along, more interested in the peripheral characters of Sweethaven than in his two "stars." The more vexing issue is what it means to make a musical situated in the world of Sweethaven as conceived by this group of moviemakers. Here again, Michael Wood's reflections on two types of movie musicals are helpful:

> To put it crudely, one kind of musical blatantly puts music where there is none, providing an arrant compensation for a dreary lack of music in our daily doings. The other kind hints that music is everywhere, scattered all about us if we will only look and listen. Astaire and Kelly are agents of hidden truths rather than pure fantasies, they are our own voices and our own feet, dancing and singing through those times when we really feel that way about our lives.[25]

Sweethaven is not a town obviously "filled with pretexts for song and invitations to the dance."[26] It is the setting for a world that may have a memory of music, but that, until Popeye's arrival, has been a dour place where the tax collector charges fees for every imaginable source of pleasure and where music is just too costly. Popeye enters Sweethaven singing, and at times he does succeed in making music natural for others, including the audience. But *Popeye* also eludes both Wood's categories because it is, decidedly, a post-sixties musical. Its music is neither absent nor present in Sweethaven but is rather an oppositional activity, a commentary on society and invitation to dance and sing despite the tax collector's fees. Popeye does not so much bring music with him as he gives the citizens of Sweethaven permission to dance, sing, and confront their oppressors.

Popeye is, then, a hero, but in Robin Williams's incarnation of the character, he falls short of mythic proportions. Looking backwards, he must compete with the sublimity of Astaire; in his own movie time, Popeye's superhuman strength forces comparisons with more radiant movie superheroes: Superman himself, Batman, Luke Skywalker, and Indiana Jones. It is typically Altman to create a countercultural superhero, a man who subverts both the genre that instatiates him and the society that recognizes him. And in several ways this collaborative creation succeeds. But when it counts most, in his final battles with Bluto and with the giant octopus, Popeye the character and Popeye the movie both suffer from our overexposure to sexier superheroes and sexier special effects. The film simply fails in its last twenty minutes to offer an imaginative alternative to either the final burst of music we expect from musicals or the last magical act we anticipate in fantasy movies.

In the end, *Popeye*'s problems are political as well as aesthetic. Most of Altman's films suggest you can change what and who you are, but to do so requires either an epiphany or the cooperation of others. Joanne, in *Come Back to the 5 and Dime, Jimmy Dean, Jimmy Dean,* for example, cannot simply declaire, "I (y)am what I (y)am." Yet this is Popeye's theme song, and it is difficult to read it as doing anything other than affirming a staunch and static individualism. Even as a claim against the conformity and impotence of the oppressed people of Sweethaven, Popeye's heroically portrayed individuality is disturbing because it refutes the collective activity that characterizes the film's production process as well as the meaning of most if not all of Altman's previous movies. There is not much thematic distance between 'I yam what I yam" and "It Don't Worry Me" from *Nashville*, but there is a perplexing absence in *Popeye* of a place from which to ponder the merits of such self-satisfaction and detachment from others.

*   *   *   *

In this and other ways, *Popeye* is, retrospectively viewed, a bridge between Altman's work of the seventies and his work of the eighties. After *Popeye* and an aborted attempt to direct a film that was to be called *Lone Star*, Altman sold Lion's Gate Films and announced that he was turning away from commercial filmmaking. What he turned to—directing scripts conceived for live theater—was not as out of character as some critics proclaimed. Altman's preference for discrete, self-enclosed settings, his repeated use of the same actors and actresses as well as his efforts to create companies of actors and crew for each of his films, his encouragement of improvisation and his attention to dialogue, music, and noise are all familiar aspects of contemporary live theater, while they are unusual elements of commercial filmmaking. I have talked at various points in this book about Altman's attraction to spectacle, carnival, and theatricality; this attraction is apparent not only in the style of representation that characterizes Altman's films but also in the cultural situations they explore; the pop and country-music scene in *Nashville*, the circus in *Brewster McCloud*, the Wild West Show in *Buffalo Bill and the Indians*, popular and classical music performance in *A Perfect Couple*, and ritual in *A Wedding*. If, in Altman's movies of the seventies, Americans' propensity for theatricality was often an object of reflection, in the eighties, when theater took over the White House, it had to become the medium and the message had to become more subtle.

Altman himself has stated publicly several times that he sees little difference between directing for film, live theater or television.[27] Pressed on this issue, he has more than once suggested that the key difference he perceives among these dramatic media is in their relationships to the spectator's point of view. In theater, each audience member sees the show from a distinct "point" of view, one not only chooses what to look at and listen to at every moment but is also fixed in a seat that allows a singular point of view. In most film and television, all specators share the same point of view (at least in a technical and non-historical sense), and that point of view is one established by the camera. Movies and video are thus more egalitarian but, paradoxically, also potentially more manipulative and tyrannical than theater.

I trust Altman's comments on these similarities and this key distinction primarily because I find ample evidence of both in his film and video work of the eighties. Beginning with *Come Back to the 5 and Dime, Jimmy Dean, Jimmy Dean* (written by Ed Graczyk, 1982), Altman has directed eight scripts initially intended for live theater: *Precious Blood* and *Rattlesnake in a Cooler* (written by Frank South, 1981–82), *Streamers* (written by David Rabe, 1983), *Secret Honor* (written by Donald Freed and Arnold M. Stone, 1984), *Fool for Love* (written by Sam Shepard, 1985), *Beyond Therapy* (written by Christopher Durang, 1987), and *The Caine Mutiny* (written by Herman Wouk, 1988). He has directed all of these works for video or film but has also directed several of them— *Come Back to the 5 and Dime, Jimmy Dean, Jimmy Dean; Precious Blood; Rattlesnake in a Cooler;* and *Secret Honor*—for live theater. Produced on tape or film, each of these works required a relatively small budget. In nonmaterial terms (but obviously relevant to the lesser costs of these films), these works are also tighter and more narrowly focused than are Altman's most characteristic works of the seventies; that is, *M*A*S*H, Nashville, 3 Women, Buffalo Bill and the Indians, A Wedding, Health,* and *Popeye.* (*Health* and *Popeye* were released in 1980 but made in the late seventies.) The films of the eighties fit in the corpus of Altman's work as explorations of the crevices of American culture. They differ from Altman's films of the seventies in their complex dialectic with the scripts on which they are based.

Prior to directing these dramas written for the stage, Altman's scripts tended to be outlines that would be filled in by the director and cast during production. Altman's "text" in these instances was as much the particular area of culture cornered by the story and his actors' interpretations of that terrain as it was a written script. Once he turned to filmic representations of scripts conceived by their authors not as outlines or screen treatments but as complete works of drama, his relationship to the written work changed considerably. In Altman's dramatic productions of the eighties, the words come from the playwrights; everything else comes from him and his actors and crew. And the words are never, in these productions, unimportant.

For the *auteurist* critics of the fifties and since, the major film directors were those who controlled not only the shooting style and editing of their works but also finally shaped the story. Altman's movies of the seventies clearly fit these criteria. His dramatic work of the eighties is more problematic in these *auteurist* terms because of his more explicit engagement with powerful scripts that he has not written himself. Yet Altman is equally effective when he acts as a reader of a script that is already an interpretation of American culture.

Come Back to the 5 and Dime, Jimmy Dean, Jimmy Dean is a first and lasting indication of Altman's empowerment by a playwright's script. Since, from the start, the authorial point of view is shared with the playwright in *Come Back to the 5 and Dime, Jimmy Dean, Jimmy Dean*, Altman can disperse the camera's point of view with ease and can experiment with film's unique possibilities for conveyance of points of view from diverse temporal contexts. Here and again in his next filmic drama *Streamers*, Altman places the camera in the middle of the single, enclosed space (the 5 and Dime in *Come Back to the 5 and Dime, Jimmy Dean, Jimmy Dean*, an army barracks in *Streamers*) and wanders about in that space in a manner consistent with but more subtle than the promiscuous camera work in his films of the seventies. A difference between these works and Altman's previous movies is to be found in the subordination of his own conventions to the meanings he finds in the scripts. In contrast to the relationship between Arthur Kopit's *Indians* and Altman's *Buffalo Bill and the Indians*, there is never a question in *Streamers* or *Come Back to the 5 and Dime, Jimmy Dean, Jimmy Dean* of the function of the script. What we are offered in these instances, as well as in *Fool for Love* and *Secret Honor,* is a brilliant reading of these scripts made "thick" by Altman's ability to harness the techniques and energies of actors in any medium and of film. Of these later works, *Streamers, Beyond Therapy,* and *O.C. and Stiggs* are the most predictable productions; all three reiterate Altman's concerns with the injustices of American society in terms that are made accessible primarily by Altman's attentiveness to the actors. Bigotry, especially in its emergence as cruelty toward gay men, is the object of critical scorn and deconstruction in all three of these films, and racial prejudice comes in a close second as an appropriate and distinctly American target of disgust. What Altman does by bringing these works to the movie screen and, more effectively, to cable television is to amplify and record the meanings produced by the playwrights who wrote the scripts for these productions. These movies reconfirm elements of Altman's work that I have discussed earlier in this book. These is nothing I can say about them that would add to my reading of "Altman's films" and American culture.

Fool for Love suggests a more complicated relationship between playwright, director, and actors. In the first place, the match between Shepard and Altman seems perfect; of all contemporary American playwrights, it is Shepard who has demonstrated the most tenacious, affectionate and perverse concern with American culture. The characters Shepard has created could walk into any Altman film of the seventies with ease; they are the not-quite-lost but disoriented men and women of a mobile society seeking to be fixed and looking for a fix; like Altman's own characters, Shepard's are people who surprise. Both ordinary and surreal, Shepard's characters belong in the movies, and once one knows *Fool for Love,* it seems inevitable that these characters would find their ways into an Altman movie.

Fool for Love, the movie, is Altman's first full encounter with a story of passionate attachment between a woman and a man. The closest Altman had come previously was in *McCabe and Mrs. Miller;* in the end, *A Perfect Couple* is not a representation of love kindled by sexual attraction but by need and loneliness, and the affection between Popeye and Olive Oyl is lyrical rather than passionate. Shepard's script well meets Altman's tensions between groundings in very authentic, specific American contexts and dramatic structures that subvert the realism so easily attached to those contexts. Altman is thus freed in *Fool for Love* to re-explore the possibilities of sound and image. *Fool for Love* is explicitly a dialogue between speech and sound, words and image; this had been true of moments, at least, in many Altman films, but here, where the words are so strong and carefully arranged, there is no space for the self-consciously experimental combinations or mere cleverness that sometimes undermine even Altman's most illuminating scenes.

Fool for Love begins with the assertion of Altman's signature, in landscape, near silence, and soft ambient sound. Shepard's stage directions call for an interior, "stark, low-rent motel room on the edge of the Mojave Desert." Altman starts with the largest context of that setting, the desert, with sun spotting the air and mountains in the background. From these he closes in slowly to what is more accurately called a small collection of buildings set in a circle than a town; on one side we see pieces of old cars and trucks junked in their graveyard. Now and throughout the film, there is more neon here than on 42nd Street and Broadway.

The world on screen is so quiet at this point that the sound of a squeaking door is threatening. Softly, a harmonica begins to play someplace nearby as the credits roll. Various noises follow: of a rundown old truck approaching, of water in the sink as a woman washes dishes, and soon of country music. As the camera cuts to a car radio, the country-song's lyrics narrate the thoughts of the woman at the sink: "I can hear the sound of your headlights on the ground looking for me. . . . c'mon, baby, let's ride." This is Altman territory, a frontier not far from Presbyterian Church, the mining town of *McCabe and Mrs. Miller,* and not so far either from the desert of *3 Women* or Mattie's Grapes Motor Home, the setting for the penultimate scene in *Thieves Like Us*.

Into the stillness of this desert oasis, in a rundown truck with a horse trailer, rides Eddie, a late-thirties, over-the-hill cowboy, who once made his living playing rodeos. He has traveled 2,480 miles to find May, his sometimes lover. May is now what she calls "a regular citizen." She has a job "cookin'," presumably at the small café

Angry at his half-sister May's (Kim Bassinger) rejection of his erotic overtures, Eddie (Sam Shepard) regresses to his rodeo cowboy role in the neon-
lit courtyard of *Fool for Love*. (*The Museum of Modern Art/Film Stills
Archive, New York City*)

located in one of the half a dozen buildings on the site. The café and
motel are apparently (but never clearly) owned and run by "an old
man" whom we see playing his harmonica, rocking and watching
for a long time before he utters a word.

Both Shepard's play and the film evolve from a gradual revelation to the audience of the complicated genealogical and emotional relationships between May, Eddie, and the old man. Martin, the one other character in the play, is narratively present as May's date for the evening; structurally, he functions to catalyze the expressions of feeling between May and Eddie. He also serves as a chorus or surrogate audience for the diverse stories of their common history, told, in the last third of the drama, by Eddie, May, and the old man.

Key to the relationships among these characters is their difficulty articulating their attachments to each other. This is perfectly reasonable, once we know that Eddie and May are half brother and half sister, that the old man lived a bigamous life that remained secret until Eddie and May were teenagers; and that, soon after Eddie, May, the old man, and his two wives all became cognizant of this complex family structure, Eddie and May fell blindly in love, and May's mother shot her own brains out.

It is in the hollows of Shepard's characters' verbal canyons that Altman's contributions echo. From the moments before Eddie's arrival until the oasis setting goes up in flames at the end of the movie, there is a rhythmic pattern in the relationship between Eddie and May that repeatedly moves from quiet to noise, from watching to engaging, from affection to fury, and distance to intimacy. At each major change, there is a sudden surprise, an instantaneous, seemingly unmotivated change of ground, intensity, and feeling. Altman redramatizes these surprises by filling the space between each of the characters with the sounds and images of the desolate, unrooted world that May, Eddie, and the old man inhabit. Eddie dreams of a farm in Wyoming with chickens and vegetables; May's experience transforms this dream into a scene she recalls as "sittin' in a tin trailer for weeks on end with the wind rippin' through it. Waitin' around for the butane to arrive. Hiking down to the laundry in the rain."[28]

What we see through Altman's camera and hear on the film track is a lot closer to May's vision than it is to Eddie's. The sounds of Eddie's truck clank in the desert stillness as he arrives and departs and arrives again. Another couple, with a child, arrive at the motel, and we, explicitly put in our voyeuristic places, only hear signal sounds: a car door opening and closing, footsteps, and a child sobbing. In the movie we also see the man of this other couple depart for a while, then return, and during his absence, the little girl plays in the paltry motel playground where she is eventually joined by May. Later, while the old man tells a story about May's childhood, we see the man, woman and little girl depart together in their car. As the old man's story continues in voice-over, the unidentified man gets out of the car with the little girl and carries her in the barely penetrable darkness to a field where they suddenly appear surrounded by strange, slow-moving shapes that turn out to be cattle. In Shepard's stage script, we only hear this story as told, verbally, by the old man. In the Altman/Shepard movie, images and sounds—of the girl's sobs, the car door opening and closing, and finally of a moaning "moo"—parallel the old man's oral narration. The movie makes no attempt to clarify whether the unidentified man, woman, and child are "real" people who recall May and her mother for the old man or if all this projected for us in the old man's fantasy.

Altman takes his cue for these scenes from an exchange between Eddie and the old man. The old man points to a blank wall and tells Eddie to take a good look at the picture on the wall. The old man then tells Eddie that the "picture" is of Barbara Mandrell, to whom he was once married. Eddie assents to the existence of a picture but denies that he believes the old man was married to Barbara Mandrell. "Well, see, now that's the difference right there," the old man retorts. "That's realism. I am actually married to Barbara Mandrell in my mind. Can you understand that?"

The external images and sounds of the playground, car, and field are Altman's picture on the wall, his contribution to a conversation in which Shepard's scripted dialogue as well as his performance of Eddie are equally vital. Even if we have not read the play or seen it live in the theater, we know these moving images and sounds are Altman's work because it is the kind of work only film can do. Only a camera can move this fluidly from interior to exterior, up a road to a desert side-stop, and back to the playground and outside windows that disclose the interior lives of the characters. Only in the movies is point of view so naturally, oddly, acceptably mobile and as real when it presents what is in a mind as what is outside a mind in a world. This is, of course, Altman's natural mode, but it corresponds eerily to Shepard's dramatic form. Our interest in *Fool for Love* is maintained primarily by offerings to the audience of narrative that for a long while arrive only in bits of elusive and allusive pieces. Then at the end, when Eddie, May, the old man, and Martin come together in the coffee shop and Eddie, May, and the old man finally get their chances to really tell their tales, what we get are three congruent but conflicting stories. Altman's strategy is to avoid offerings of neat clues that might solve the mystery of these relationships. Instead, he thickens and enriches our evidence of the contexts. We thus not only see and hear the affinity between the lonely little girl and May, but we also see and hear, from a distance, a Mercedes that twice drives past the motel, and we see the car's striking female passenger, who is, perhaps, one of Eddie's other women, "The Countess." (Again, in the stage script, the audience never sees The Countess, although we do hear gunshots and the squeal of tires, and May reports that the car is a Mercedes.) If The Countess is only "real" in May's mind, a figment of her jealousy, something else is shooting a gun outside, and Eddie is at least in part in collusion with May's fantasies. Altman's use of darkness and light to make the images of these "fantasy' moments surreal works well to maintain their ambiguity.

This is not the working-class world of northeastern factories or indebted midwestern farmers. This is the place where people from the Northeast and Midwest end up when they cannot find the promised work in Texas for which they left their hometowns. It is the downtrodden world of the Southwest, a place of wanderers, migrants and poor homesteaders, people looking for a place to rest their feet and their memories. Wim Wenders's *Paris, Texas*, which shares with *Fool for Love* a screenwriter (Sam Shepard) and a lead actor (Harry Dean Stanton), is not far away. Like Wenders, Altman does what Shepard's script suggests but cannot fulfill on stage; the film director realizes this struggle between a man and a woman in a particular social and material place. Each detail of the motel room in *Fool for Love* is named; several details are changed in the movie, but it is as careful as the play in the props and colors it selects to establish this world. The thin mattress, nondescript bed sheets, motel towels, and scattered dirty clothes whimper the non-news that this is not the promised land.

This is the world of country music, as Altman and Shepard both understand. Since the sixties and *Easy Rider*, movies have recognized the narrative possibilities of popular songs, and Altman has been a significant exploiter of varieties of popular music. Sometimes, as in *Thieves Like Us*, Altman uses songs to evoke a particular historical period and place; *Nashville* and *Popeye* use songs as soliloquies to reveal characters' inner speech. Songs in *Fool for Love*, however, function as an additional narrative voice, as did Leonard Cohen's songs in *McCabe and Mrs. Miller*. Unlike the deliberate anonymity of many movie narrators, however, the country songs that augment the narrative of *Fool for Love* are sung by particular voices that are at home in this place and with these inhabitants.

The songs in *Fool for Love*, like the visual images of the little girl and The Countess, complicate the stories of May and Eddie and the old man, but they do not explain the ambiguities in their stories. These songs intensify the pain of love lost and reclaimed that animates the film, but they accomplish this, too, without deciphering the relationship between Eddie and May. As one of several narrative voices in the film, the country songs also remind us of our distance from the characters.

Such reminders of our spectating are frequent throughout Altman's work but are particularly abundant and appropriate in *Fool for Love*. Like the alternation of calm and fury in the relationship between Eddie and May, we are brought close enough to their passion to feel its heat and then suddenly cast away. In addition to the music, much of this process of admission and rejection of the viewer is accomplished through the recurrent motif of windows and mirrors. Mirrors and windows are metaphors for viewing and for self-reflection in most of Altman's films, beginning with *That Cold Day in the Park*. Sometimes, as in the window/mirror reflection of Roger Wade's suicide in *The Long Goodbye* and the mirror behind the soda fountain that repeatedly becomes a window to the past in

Come Back to the 5 and Dime, Jimmy Dean, Jimmy Dean, the mirror/window's simultaneous transparencies and reflections are a perfect form of mediation for the action. At other times, as in *Images* or *3 Women,* mirroring, glass, and transparency seem only to restate meanings that are already evident.

There is no sense of strain for a motif or a metaphor in *Fool for Love.* The motel setting and the narcissistic love of Eddie and May naturalize recognitions through windows and mirror reflections. May first sights Eddie's truck through her motel-room window; his arrival is threatening but stiill at a manageable distance. Eddie locates May's room by peering through her windows; she has hidden in the bathroom, but the windows allow him to perceive her things and thus give him access to her. Twice after recognizing Eddie's truck, May looks in her bathroom mirror, smoothing her hair and her face. We learn from these glimpses that May cares about how the person in the truck sees her, and the mirror, the "glass of time,"[29] tells her of aging and of her separateness from others.

Mirrors are, throughout literature, painting, and film, associated with women. Windows are, in gendered terms, bidirectional. Women look through windows from the inside, from interiors, and stare outwards at a world they often cannot or will not enter. Men look through windows from the outside in, as voyeurs of objects, persons, and situations that they wish to know but from which they wish to remain unknown. May's and Eddie's relations to windows are consistent with these patterns. Eddie looks through the window into May's room, he looks through his truck window, and through the window of the café at The Countess. May and the young girl each look from inside out. While point of view shifts between May and Eddie throughout *Fool for Love,* in the end, there is a screen between us and Eddie and us and May, as they both disappear down the road, and there is a more protective screen between us and the fire that consumes the motel and leaves the movie with no place to be.

Fool for Love is more demanding and more troubling on a television set or monitor than it is on the large screen of a movie theater. To assault us as voyeurs, as this movie does, is to locate viewers in a place they think is safe and private. On television, the nonchronological storytelling of *Fool for Love* is not much different than the evening news. On a movie screen, we anticipate spatial and temporal mobility but with conventions that assure us of continuity. Although there is a past that shapes the present in *Fool for Love*, Altman/Shepard's work dissolves temporal boundaries and evokes the ambiguous past/present tense of television rather than the historical absence of movies. In Shepard's theater script, the last word, spoken by the old man, is "forever." In the movie *Fool for Love*, May, walking down the road with her suitcase, has the last words, and they are about Eddie: "He's gone." Recalling, almost comically, the cowboy of American Westerns, Eddie has ridden down the road on a horse. He is not, however, riding off into the sunset because he has done what a man's got to do; he is riding out of the remnants of the American Dream. And the flames we see at the end of the movie devour that dream in much the same way that dust and dirt tarnish the setting at the end of *Come Back to the 5 and Dime, Jimmy Dean, Jimmy Dean*. Before those flames, as I watch first Eddie and then May go down the road, I remember a question: "Ah, when to the heart of man / Was it ever less that a treason / To go with the drift of things, / To yield with a grace to reason, / And bow and accept the end / of a love or a season?"[30]

*　*　*　*

The amazing grace that appears for a moment near the end of an Altman film is not to be found in *Fool for Love*. Perhaps Altman had expended his quantity of grace in the picture he made just before *Fool for Love*, a movie called *Secret Honor* (1984). I have postponed my reflections on *Secret Honor* in large part because, as a film that is barely known but heralded as unique in Altman's work when known, it was important to talk first of the "other" Altman movies. Yet another transformation of a stage production into film, *Secret Honor* defies not only Hollywood practices and American political rules but initially appears to counter Altman's own moviemaking conventions. A movie with only one actor, *Secret Honor* presents ninety minutes of Philip Baker Hall's performance of Richard Nixon recording (on video and audio tape) his defense for an imagined judge and jury of his life, his presidency, and his culture.

Altman went far from Hollywood, to the University of Michigan, to direct *Secret Honor,* first as a live stage production and subsequently as "a teaching exercise" on 16-mm film. The original script was written by Donald Freed and Arnold M. Stone; Freed had written several other theatrical scripts primarily concerned with politics and conspiracies; his writing always teetered on the edge of self-indulgent eccentricity while remaining interesting despite itself. The setting for the screenplay is one large, wood-paneled room, divided by an archway into a library and study. The room floats in some nonspecified, probably urban location; what we see of the outside surroundings comes from watching Nixon on a security monitor as he enters on a ground floor, passes through a lobby and hallway, goes up a half-flight of stairs, and turns his key in his own door. Subsequent speeches locate the movie temporally in a period after Nixon's resignation, but not too long afterwards, since he appears to be young and vigorous and without distance from his past in public office.

The setting has much to say to the viewer. The wood-paneled walls, leather-upholstered chairs, and solid, well-polished desks suggest a luxuriously spacious den that is both home and office. It is unambivalently a man's space. Large formal portraits define the walls; all but one of these portraits, we eventually see, are of well-known public figures—Kissinger, Eisenhower, Lincoln, Washington, and Wilson. This is not, then, just the retreat of a wealthy man; this man sees himself surrounded by a very specific elite. A grand piano and a full liquor decanter make the room more particularly Nixon's: the man Nixon was a competent pianist and a drinker, despite his Quaker background. A grandfather clock in one corner of the room is at once consistent with the furnishings and a specific reminder of the temporal, historical situation of Richard Nixon.

The one incongruent element of the setting is the bank of four video monitors and a stationary video camera situated near the front door on a long sideboard. Along with a large microphone and audio tape deck that we seen about ten minutes into the movie, these video monitors and camera are inappropriate to the warm, woody ambiance of the room but a natural extension and reminder of our recollections of Richard Nixon.

We enter this room before Nixon. Indeed, the camera tracks the room during the opening credits as if to make us familiar with its shape and contents. Nixon's entrance is a relief after several seconds of watching his approach on video monitors with weak, black and white resolution. In characteristic Altman fashion, it is a while before we actually hear Nixon's voice—or any human voice. The man enters, immediately pours himself a drink, and sits in front of a fireplace. The camera cuts to the video monitors, as it will do periodically throughout the movie, showing Nixon on the screen and a portrait of Eisenhower. We are then returned to Nixon (now one step less mediated) getting a bottle of Chivas Regal and pouring himself another drink.

A depth-of-focus shot from the "office" part of the room through the archway shows Nixon changing his suit jacket for a maroon-velvet smoking jacket. After re-dressing himself for his private world, he removes a gun from a wood box he was carrying on entering, places the gun on a pedestal at the front center of his desk, and puts the box in its place in a hidden set of desk file drawers.

Each of Nixon's moves to this point conveys a sense of ritual. Everything we have witnessed thus far seems a prelude, but we do not know to what. When Nixon removes the gun from its box, there is an immediate possibility that what we have seen is a prelude to suicide. That, however, proves not to be the case.

With the gun, carefully placed, Nixon picks up a microphone and then, in a wonderfully funny scene, tests the tape deck in front of him. His first words, "testing, one, two, three, four," are disconcerting after the long opening silence. They are also, of course, because of their association with the Watergate tapes, the most potent sign available to situate Richard Nixon in history. Nixon's discovery, a moment after beginning testing, that he does not have a cassette in the recorder, ironically reaccentuates the incompetences that led to his resignation.

For the next seventy-five minutes, the Nixon character records his story and his reflections on that story. In bits and spurts, in nonchronological order, he tells of how he came to run for Congress in reponse to an advertisement, of the early deaths of two of his brothers from tuberculosis, and of the conspiratorial Committee of 100 who have met since the forties in Bohemian Grove and who supported and controlled him in order to make and control money and power. What truth we think we know of the rise and fall of his presidency is far from the truth, he warns. In "fact" he argues, Watergate was not about a cover-up but was a cover-up itself, a distraction from his much more significant crime as the continuing object of manipulation by the Committee of 100. He did not know, he confesses, that he was "signing a pact with the devil." He should be respected by the American people, he claims, because he chose "secret honor" and public shame in order to preserve the "system" of American democracy.

What we hear and see is a mixture of several forms of discourse. In the beginning especially, Nixon's tone is that of a subject recording his autobiography for posterity and, more immediately, for his long-time aide, Roberto, who apparently, from Nixon's comments into the mike, transcribes and categorizes the audio tapes Nixon makes. Fairly quickly and intermittently, Nixon changes voices and audience and explicitly addresses a judge or jury as his own defending lawyer. At other moments, his speech resembles that of a patient in psychoanalysis. As the taping continues, Nixon's voice increasingly dissolves into sounds, words, pleas and cries that suggest an inner voice exploding and no longer comprising any identifiable form of discourse.

All that appears to remain is the monologue. "What is there to keep me here?" Clov asks in Samuel Beckett's *Endgame*. "The dialogue," Hamm retorts. Superficially, the world of *Secret Honor* is further reduced; not dialogue but monologue is all that apparently keeps us watching. But this is not really what we hear and see. Or, more precisely, it is not because of the verbal sources but because of the presentation of sounds and images that we know that *Secret Honor* is only disguised as a monologue. We only hear one actor and one character speak, but he speaks in many voices. Sometimes he speaks as President of the United States, sometimes he speaks as a lawyer, sometimes he speaks as an ordinary American struggling to make his way up the ladder and achieve the American Dream. His voice changes primarily in relation to whom he is speaking. Many of those to whom he speaks appear in the portraits on his walls and are found and displayed by the camera; thus when Nixon mentions American foreign policy and, with fury, names "Henry Asshole Kissinger," we see the portrait of Kissinger on the wall, staring benignly back at us. Similarly, in the second half of his tirade, when Nixon begins to fall apart and addresses his mother, it is her unyielding portrait that we see as he rants and pleads. Nixon also approaches the large microphone with increasingly intense fervor, and, as a result, the microphone becomes a presence, a party to a dialogue that emerges from Nixon's monologue. It is a kind of parody of Plato's *Apology*, with Nixon playing the role of Socrates to an inarticulate crowd/jury.

The dissolution of Nixon's speech into inarticulate babble is captured perfectly in a visual metaphor of an increasingly rapid tracking shot of the video monitors. As the film and Nixon's ramblings progress, there are increasingly frequent cuts to the video monitors; these mediated images serve both to relieve the audience of embarrassment as Nixon becomes more maudlin and vulnerable and to remind us that this image of Nixon is multiply mediated and constructed—by television, Nixon himself, those who controlled Nixon the President, and, in the case of this movie, director Robert Altman, Philip Baker Hall, the actor, Freed and Stone, the screenwriters, and Pierre Mignot, the cinematographer. In the last moment of the movie we see nothing other than the rapid tracking shots of the monitors, and the image dissolves into visual noise as, ironically, we hear a crowd of voices calling for "four more years."

I claimed as I introduced *Secret Honor* that it would at first appear to be at odds with Altman's previous work. I want now to return to that point. A talky movie with one actor playing one character confined to an enclosed interior hardly seems like typical Altman fare, despite some of the preceding adaptations of theatre to stage. *Come Back to the 5 and Dime, Jimmy Dean, Jimmy Dean* and *Streamers*, while performed on one unitary set, at least divide the camera's attention among half a dozen characters and points of view. Such persistent Altman concerns as gender and race were also key issues in these dramas, in contrast to *Secret Honor*. Perhaps even more disorienting, *Secret Honor* is explicitly about an actual historical figure and "real" events in American history, and while the film evokes some surprising empathy for Nixon (empathy that I have found to be problematic for several of my liberal and progressive friends), it is surely an unhesitant assault on the American political system that the Nixon character unequivocally says he represents. Where, in this representation, is the Altman of allegory and allusion?

Right there in front of us, I want to maintain, as present as Altman was in *Buffalo Bill and the Indians* or *Nashville.* The portraits on Nixon's walls are alter egos for Nixon in much the way that Bill's portraits of himself are his alter egos. Nixon, like Buffalo Bill but also like John Triplette the candidate's front man in *Nashville,* is busy constructing an image of a political and cultural leader. The more important continuity has to do with Nixon's representation and relationship to us. To say that he, too, is a human being, is a sentimental cliché. To convince us that this is true and meaningful is another story, and that is the story Altman tells. No more or less than Haven Hamilton in *Nashville,* Nixon, if he is human and not only a media creation, is unpredictable, and no matter what he does, it is possible to care about him. We who felt our rage at the Vietnam war satisfied by Nixon's resignation may not enjoy such empathy, but that Altman makes it possible is to make us thoughtful. Ours is not to judge Nixon as a soul but as a fellow citizen. Altman's own comments on the portrayal of Nixon in *Secret Honor* confirm this response:

> The interesting thing I've found about *Secret Honor* is that the people who were big Nixon supporters don't hate the film at all. . . . And the people who've hated Nixon have said I'm not sure I like that piece, it makes him almost human. I don't think it's in any sense pro-Nixon, but I think it's good to shake people out of that real hard polarization where he is just some kind of cardboard figure.[31]

"I'm not the American nightmare, I am not President of some forgotten planet, I'm the American dream," the Nixon character says, claiming that the American system works because he *is* the system. After accompanying himself at the piano to a rousing chorus of "The Reds, the Reds, the Reds, the Reds," Nixon chants that he believes in America and in real estate. And perhaps because he is so vividly struggling with a sense of his own sin, I am reminded of Hawthorne's Clifford Pyncheon warning, "What we call real estate—the solid ground to build a house on—is the broad foundation on which nearly all the guilt of the world rests."[32]

Nixon's testimony supports Clifford Pyncheon and not his own claim. Yes, he tells us, his father only went to school through sixth grade and his Quaker upbringing was humble, like that of his hero, Abraham Lincoln but his own narration argues that he did not become President because of hard work and virtue (the ideal means of the American Dream) but because he allowed himself to become the pawn of a group of powerful rich men who wanted to get richer. And, finally, he reminds us, we, the people, elected him knowingly, with all of his baggage of dirty tricks. "Fuck 'em," he shouts as the rapid tracking movement of the camera dissolves the last image on the monitors into chaos. " 'Em" is us. And "Four more years" and "Fuck 'em" interanimate each other, blur and become one blurred cry.

At the beginning of *Secret Honor*, just before we are shown the setting, a message appears on the screen in white letters on a black background. The form of this message is a disclaimer. Ostensibly the filmmakers are protecting themselves from possible libel suits. But the words say more than they need to say:

> This work is a fictional meditation concerning the character of and events in the history of Richard M. Nixon, who is impersonated in this film. The dramatist's imagination has created some fictional events in an effort to illuminate the character of President Nixon. This film is not a work of history or a historical re-creation.
>
> It is a work of fiction using as a fictional character a real person, President Richard M. Nixon, in an attempt to understand.

Hawthorne again comes to mind. Not unlike some of his contemporaries, Hawthorne framed *The Scarlet Letter* in what purported to be a historical account of the discovery of a document that related the story of Hester Prynne. To pretend that the fiction was history was to give the story more credence, even if author and reader understood this to be a rhetorical device. Truth then, appeared to dwell in history, while in the eighties, we must turn to fiction to understand.

*   *   *   *

Ironically as much a claim as a disclaimer, the preface to *Secret Honor* could well stand as directions to all of Altman's films. But it is in *Secret Honor* and *Tanner '88,* the 1988 television series based on an imaginary candidate for the Democratic presidential nomination, a man named Jack Tanner (Michael Murphy), that the function of Altman's work becomes explicitly political, not just in the sense of a concern with power but in terms of overtly beholding contemporary events, practices, and persons in the arena of American politics. I want to close this book with some reflections on the *Tanner* series because it is in this series that I see the future.

The *Tanner* series is a set of ten television programs, the first of which was one hour in length, the rest a half an hour each. Written by cartoonist Garry Trudeau and directed by Altman, the series was produced by HBO and aired by HBO in approximately two-week intervals between early February and July. The airing of the first episode was timed to occur shortly before the New Hampshire primary, and the last episode was aired shortly after the Democratic convention.

"Tanner: The Dark Horse," the first program in the series, immediately establishes the tension between the character Jack Tanner and the fabrication of the candidate Jack Tanner. All of our first glimpses of Tanner are mediated. The program begins at the Tanner campaign headquarters in New Hampshire, where, in a familiarly Altmanesque fashion, the camera repeatedly scans and tracks the room, roaming amidst flyers, buttons, posters, television monitors, and a gaggle of campaign workers, directed by Mrs. T. J. Cavanaugh, who is instantly identifiable as the campaign manager by her authoritative tone, quick wit, and intelligence. Jack Tanner is immediately but indirectly present on one of the television monitors inside the campaign headquarters; he is the guest to be interviewed on local news. Through this efficient device, we find out that Tanner was an Air Force brat, who grew up in half a dozen American towns as diverse as East Lansing, Michigan; Warm Springs, Georgia; and Riverside, California. He *is* the American Dream, from his birth in Pearl Harbor on. As played by Michael Murphy, one of the long-term members of Altman's company and Triplette, the candidate's front man in *Nashville,* Tanner is boyishly charming, confident but not arrogant, and refreshingly and seductively candid. He may well remind viewers of John F. Kennedy. Once a popular congressman, Tanner dropped out of politics for several years to take care of his daughter who was seriously ill but has now recovered. Tanner also has a Ph.D. What more could a good, liberal Democratic voter want in a presidential candidate?

Our next introduction to Jack Tanner is even more blatantly mediated. Deke, a perfectly captured caricature of an ambitious, independent video producer, presents his Tanner bio tape to the rest of the campaign staff. What we and they see is both funny and appalling. The first shots of Tanner shoveling snow in front of his substantial, two-story white frame house are wonderfully predictable; we know what we are meant to read here: Jack Tanner is a man of some but not too much substance, he is a stable family man who exudes good health and physical vigor, and he does such tasks as shoveling snow just like the rest of us. From this reassuring context, we follow Tanner up to but not through his front door as he rushes in to take a phone call. Through the front window, in an obviously staged scene, we see and hear Tanner receiving a call from an unknown supporter. There is no ambiguity in the message.

Except of course, there is, because we are watching this on our television sets but from the point of view of the campaign staff, all of whom presume that the consideration is how persuasive the propaganda, not its basis in some kind of historical reality. The Tanner bio tape gets worse as it goes on in its undisguised and often unsuccessful attempts to gain the favor of the viewer/voter. It is, nonetheless, shown to a focus group of New Hampshire citizens whose function is to prejudge the overall impact and the specific flaws and achievements of the tape. A low-key academic expert laboriously informs the focus-group participants of their task and how they are to push which buttons at what time to demonstrate their responses to the tape. Not surprisingly, the expert's analysis shows that the focus group does not like the tape and responds especially negatively to its most obvious manipulations. In addition, since we have witnessed the conditions and process of the focus group, which included evidence of the participants' annoyance at the freezing temperatures in the room and the chaos of coffee, pizza and blankets brought in to compensate for the cold, we are unclear as to the validity of the findings based on the focus group.

After the focus group, the program cuts to Jack Tanner on the campaign trail with his daughter, Alex. Along the way, Tanner encounters several of the other candidates, including Republicans Pat Robertson and Bob Dole and Democratic not-quite-candidate Gary Hart. In each of these instances, the candidates are represented by themselves, and they play their parts in relation to Tanner with unhesitant aplomb. We might think of the appearances of Robertson, Dole, and Hart as elements of the setting that signify the illusion of a real world aimed for in location settings as compared to studio re-creations. More than one film critic, most notably André Bazin, has argued that in film, objects and persons take on the same status. But few people would attempt to argue that all objects and all persons have exactly the same force in film. The most famous evidence of this, the forks and rolls that Chaplin transforms to legs and shoes in *The Gold Rush*, have an obviously different place in our memories than do dozens of other objects in Chaplin's films or in any film; equally obviously, the performances of Monroe in *Some Like It Hot* or Chaplin in *City Lights* are of a different potency than that of say, William Hurt as the anchorman in *Broadcast News*. Robertson, Dole, and Hart have an inordinately powerful presence on screen, not because of any particular attributes of their performances but because the context is that of a world both discovered *and* imagined.

Comprehension of this peculiar context requires turning to candidate Tanner at the end of the first program. Exhausted at the end of a typical campaign day of late airplanes and rushed meetings with New Hampshire's citizens, Tanner arrives at his own headquarters frustrated but nonetheless able to reinvigorate his staff with a spontaneous, impassioned pep talk about America's real needs for change. His speech is surprising and well performed as an outburst of authentic caring and provocative political thinking; we thus need the reminders that Tanner is not "for real" provided by cut-away shots that discover Deke, the video man, surreptitiously videotaping Tanner's whole impetuous speech. And, finally, just in case we are still tempted to separate Deke's vision of everything in the world as a potentially good video product from Jack Tanner's campaign, T. J. Cavanaugh, the campaign manager asks Deke the moment Tanner is gone, "Did you get it?" The "it" is the speech; "getting it" refers to recording the moment on video. There is no space for the campaign workers to be moved or inspired here; even in virtuous Jack Tanner's campaign, all that matters is the product and its success.

The virtues of the combination of Garry Trudeau and Robert Altman are clear in this opening program in the series. The script is tight and droll; the characters are painfully accurate fulfillments of the types of people who staff a political campaign. Even if we did not know the political campaign scene before, watching this program we recognize the roles and are convinced by the precision in the performances. Whereas in *Fool for Love* I can to some extent locate and separate Altman's contributions from Shepard's, in *Tanner '88* I find a seamless world so precisely conceived that the collaboration is invisible as a process but rich in its results.

Altman's audio/vision throughout the *Tanner '88* series is as complicated and dense as it was in *Nashville*. He repeatedly cuts to signs, objects, monitors, or to shots of characters mirrored on table surfaces and windows. Often the angles of shots are so bizarre as to be funny. The threat of the program, however, is that we need all of these cinematic alienation effects to remind us of the fictional quality of Jack Tanner. Trudeau and Altman are educating us in our election process, but there is so much similarity between their fiction and the constructions of the other candidates that we have to work to make distinctions. That, of course, is just the point.

Self-reflexively, the second program in the *Tanner* series, subtitled "Tanner for Real," begins in a bar where a Tanner ad is being screened on television. The ad is comprised primarily of a cut from the spontaneous speech Tanner gave his staff at the end of the first episode. The response of one man in the bar is: "What the fuck was that?" T. J., who is also in the bar, wryly notes that the reason the Tanner people are doing better in the polls must be the "what the fuck is that approach."

Together, the ten episodes in the series touch on every issue that was actually raised or implied in the 1988 campaign. The problem of drugs is a recurrent theme in the series, as is race, sex, the environment, nuclear proliferation, and the relations between the media and the election campaigns. But if the issues are predictable, the Altman-Trudeau approach to them is not, and each program in the series takes risks and holds surprises in its specific representations of the topics and methods of American campaigning. In the second and third episodes, we are given hints that Jack Tanner has an erotic relationship with an elegant woman who is eventually identified as Joanna Buckley. We know by now that Tanner is divorced from his daughter Alex's mother; we soon find out that Joanna is the deputy campaign manager of Michael Dukakis. Like most of the motifs in *Tanner '88*, this one is linked to others. The reporter who first observes the relationship between Jack Tanner and Joanna respects their privacy and finds a moment to let Joanna know that he knows but considers it none of his business unless she wants to talk publicly about the relationship. Other reporters on the Tanner bus, however, are avidly looking for dirt and drama, and when they get a whiff of the Joanna–Jack Tanner relationship, they blare it out over television and in newsprint. (Ironically one of the reporters who makes this information public is soon aftrwards fired by NBC, thus suggesting that getting this kind of scoop is not a guarantee of anything.)

The relationship between Tanner and Joanna, while obviously echoing Gary Hart's dalliances with Donna Rice, is deliberately underemphasized in the first several programs. Although we, like the reporters, catch brief glimpses of this relationship early on in the campaign, rather than the immediate exploitation of the romance I anticipate once a clue is presented, the relationship is kept out of our view successfully for a time period parallel to that during which most of the press are also ignorant. Once the news of the relationship is public, the responses of the key characters also go counter to expectations. Jack simply suggests that they get married, since attempts to conceal the relationship have failed; Joanna coolly suggests that she would at least like the opportunity to resign from her job with the Dukakis campaign before announcing her marriage to Jack. There are even surprises once the wedding plans are in process. At the last minute, following a series of minor disasters that include Jack's father's wedding-dinner attack on Joanna's virtue, Jack suggests that they postpone the wedding until November, after the election, and Joanna happily agrees. Jack appears to understand that his daughter, Alex, has become problematically obsessed with the wedding and that to marry in the middle of the campaign to deflate the scandal surrounding his and Joanna's relationship is hypocritical.

The coda, in the last episode of Tanner '88, to the relationship of Jack and Joanna is poignant and mind-boggling. This episode, called "The Reality Check," finds Tanner and his staff in Atlanta at the end of the Democratic convention, after the Dukakis victory. One of the key vignettes is a meeting between Joanna and Kitty Dukakis. On Kitty's suggestion, the two women meet for coffee to confront the strained relations between them since the revelation that Joanna was Jack's lover. Kitty admits that she and Mike were at first hurt and felt betrayed, but subsequently, she says, both came to understand Joanna's duplicity on the grounds that love matters more than politics. Only somewhat ironically, Kitty then proceeds to ask if Tanner will support Dukakis for President, and when Joanna hedges, Kitty urges her to encourage her lover to do so. The oddest and yet most convincing gesture of this encounter is Kitty's presentation to Joanna of a "Mikey" doll that squeaks. It is an absurd object but an offering that captures the right quality of intimacy, humor, and distance between the two women.

For those who have followed the series, the introduction of a "real" person in the last episode is not news; by this point in the series, we have witnessed the appearance of dozens of "real" people as themselves, including a long, advisory conversation between Bruce Babbit and Tanner as the two stroll along the Potomac River in Washington, D.C. Kitty Dukakis's appearance as herself is nonetheless disconcerting, perhaps because the role she plays with Joanna requires that she present herself as a particular person and friend, not just as the candidate's wife, in a situation that she, we, and the actress playing Joanna know to be fictional.

Although the *Tanner* series is not *Health,* and the major candidates here, as they are in the real world, are men, the series also subtly portrays the importance and complexity of women in these scenes of mainstream American politics. T. J. Cavanaugh's range of behaviors and moods over the ten episodes is remarkable, since the actress manages to always present a coherent, substantial character. It matters, too, in terms of gender stereotypes, that T. J. is rational, smart, pragmatic, and tough, while never appearing to be a castrating or asexual woman. Her life is humorously accented by persistent, apparently amorous, calls from Joe Kennedy, Jr.; her commitment to Tanner is only superseded by her commitment to progressive goals and to winning. Her most appealing and interesting relationship is with Andrea, a young, naive campaign worker who matures considerably during the months covered by the series. A scene in a steam room in the last episode of the series shows T. J. and Andrea equally weary and depressed and more connected by their fatigue and sense of themselves as women than they are separated by age and sophistication or lack thereof.

Of the dozens of similarly apt scenes in the five and a half hours of the *Tanner '88* series, the most daring ten minutes remains for me almost beyond interpretation. That ten minutes occurs in the seventh program, subtitled "The Girlfriend Factor." Ironically, the program pays little attention to the "girlfriend factor"; the title in retrospect is a red herring. Instead of sex and scandal, we get three separate images of politics in the state of Michigan. The first of these images finds Tanner in a state park knowledgeably arguing for environmental controls. The second vignette finds Tanner in a Detroit robot-manufacturing factory, where one of the robots confronts him on his radical drug policy proposals. Finally, Tanner arrives at a small park in a poor black area of Detroit, where a community group called SOSAD is meeting and waiting to talk with him. SOSAD, which originated in Detroit in the late eighties, exists in real time in the real world. The acronym stands for Save Our Sons and Daughters. The group came together out of the grief and anger of black parents who had in 1987 alone, lost seventy-seven children to gang warfare.

At the end of the promotional video screened early in the first program of the *Tanner* series, Jack Tanner claims his ability to listen as one of his key attributes. His meeting with SOSAD is the test of that claim for the character Tanner and also for Altman and Trudeau. Even before Tanner arrives, we are asked to listen—to a young black man wearing a cap and an orange jacket, who recites a rap poem he has written about the children who have died in recent years in Detroit's drug wars. Midway through the recitation, we see Tanner standing, unobtrusively listening, at the back of the crowd. The camera soon cuts to a circle of people from the community, sitting and talking with Tanner, still in the playground setting.

During the next ten minutes, we hear and see little from Jack Tanner and a lot from the people of this community. Tanner tells the group that he is there to find out what's going on, and at one point, he explicitly instructs the small crowd to "take advantage of our presence and these cameras and tell these people what's goin' on." A barrage of questions and comments from the men and women of the neighborhood follows. Strikingly, their views are diverse. What we hear and see is not a monologic "black" discourse but authentically dialogic speech. Several people oppose Tanner's proposal to legalize drugs. Another explains that the people who live in these projects need genuine employment alternatives; as long as they can make much more money dealing drugs than doing other kinds of legitimate work, they will keep dealing drugs. A man in a suit argues that the United States should use the army in the war on drugs if it is really serious about this issue. Another argues that blacks should work in their own communities on limiting the demand side of the drug problem while white politicians like Tanner should work on the supply side. A minister very articulately suggests that the Iran-Contra scandal was actually a cover-up for the more lethal Contra-cocaine scandal that has only been hinted at in the media. He echoes one of the messages of *Secret Honor*—the deceit and corruptions we know about are only the tip of the iceberg of evil in the American political elite. Tanner's goal, the minister argues, should be to get rid of "the administration cocaine push-ers." Eventually one black woman interrupts and urges that the conversation get back to the kids. "Change has to do with us," she argues. "Mothers and fathers." A man injects a less positive note, "None can help us and we cannot help ourselves." Then another woman retorts that SOSAD is the first visible movement in twenty years, and in a voice devoid of sentiment, she refers to her loss of a sixteen-year-old son.

The rap song whose theme is "changes," a chant we have heard since the beginning of this program, picks up again as the talk session ends and Tanner and his group exit. As he leaves, Tanner suddenly sights the body of a young black boy half-hidden by a bush. Distressed and disoriented by this "real" evidence of what everyone has been talking about, Tanner has nothing to say at the moment. We just watch someone approach the boy, and we watch the dismay on Jack Tanner's face. At the moment, the actual sight-ing of the child's body seems superfluous, an image as unnecessary as the dream sequence in *3 Women*. If we have listened to the voices of the men and women in this neighborhood, we do not need a visual, onstage demonstration of the destruction of life. When, how-ever, in the very next episode Jack Tanner begins a speech with reference to this moment, I am not sorry it was included:

> I came here today because I thought I knew everything there was to know about life in the inner cities of America. But I found out a few days ago that I don't know anything at all. I came out of a meeting and crossed a vacant lot and came across an eight-year-old boy who had been shot three times and left to die.

Following this speech, Tanner leads his audience, a large group of teenagers, out into the streets to protest urban conditions. We later find out that they are stopped by police who argue that the group needs a permit for a demonstration. This is a part of urban life in America that we do know about. Some, but hardly all, Americans want changes, and the voices of those who do are often silenced by those who do not.

"TV can cover a war, TV can cover a birth, TV can cover a

highway accident," television commentator Linda Ellerbee tells Jack Tanner after a (fictitous) televised debate starring Dukakis, Jackson, and Tanner. "But what TV can't cover very well is change." If TV, for anyone close to the medium, means television news, as I infer it does for Ellerbee by her use of the verb, "cover," then she is probably correct. I am not certain that it is inherent to the medium and the genre, but even outside of the United States, in Moscow, say, or in Beijing, television news, constructed increasingly out of sound "bites" and symbolic, decontextualized images, presents conclusions, products, and effects; at best, it covers the results of changes not the processes that constitute the activity of change.

If Ellerbee is correct, then television is not the dramatic medium that I and others have taken it to be. Drama, after all, does "cover" change, even if, in the theater, that has most often meant revelation rather than alteration. And film, our most obvious modern dramatic form, always contains the option of going a step beyond recognition. It can show the world, including the people in it, in the process of transformation. Film can also, as Altman's work demonstrates, change viewers so that they see the world a bit differently. We may even hear pronouncements like Ellerbee's with a questioning ear because we see her not "straight on" but in angles through mirrors in Tanner's dressing room, shots chosen to denaturalize the speaking voices and transform our ways of seeing and hearing.

But this supposes and proposes that, within the frame of Ellerbee's implied definitions, the *Tanner '88* series is a film, not television, or that the *Tanner '88* series is a hybrid of the two media. I incline toward the notion of hybridization, not to avoid the question of the distinctions between television and film but to acknowledge current technical and cultural changes that are making those distinctions less relevant to the ways we live our daily lives. Television's unique ingredients have always been its instantaneousness (as in "live" from Beijing) and its coverage of the actual world. Film compresses and manipulates time and space; television transcends space and exists only in the present tense. The *Tanner '88* series appears to (and often does) monitor current events. It also presents itself to us as a series, a sequence of representations, not unlike serialized novels or any of dozens of ongoing television programs that maintain our attention because of the continuity and familiarity of spaces, events, and characters and because of the expectation (even if false) that someplace along the line things will change.

Tanner '88 fulfills that promise in several ways. Some characters in the program do change, most notably the young woman named Andrea, whose initial awkwardness and lack of tact are difficult to watch. At the end of the series, visually and aurally transformed from an awkward, bumbling kid inspired by *The Prophet* to a self-confident, attractive woman, we see her responding to a reporter's inquisitive stare. "You're wondering how I've changed, right? I'll tell you. I'm not a nice person anymore." Jack Tanner has also changed, if we accept his own confession, from a man who thought he knew everything about urban America to one who knows, after Detroit, that he does not even know the questions to ask.

But, then, people asking the pertinent question was always what Jack Tanner thought "the American experiment" was all about, or so he said in that intendedly private speech at the end of the first episode. "Our noisy dissent," he argued, "didn't weaken us. Why? Because throughout our history we've been willing to reinvent ourselves for the common good."

"Reinventing ourselves" is as good a phrase as any to describe what Robert Altman's work has been all about. This reinvention must begin, Altman's films urge, with a reevaluation and re-presentation of gender in American culture. In Altman's movies, and in American society, *women* have begun the transformations that are necessary to re-create an authentic and decent life for each and every citizen. From Hot Lips Houlihan in *M*A*S*H* to Andrea in *Tanner '88,* it is the women in Altman's films who demonstrate to us the possibilities and directions of change. The directions to which they point are not, as is often the case in contemporary feminism, those of autonomy and individual subjectivity but are those of interdependence and the social construction of gender. Who we are, in terms of gender, politics, and theater, is not a matter of choices made alone but of the consciousness of self we build with and in relation to others.

More often than not, the men in these films remain rigid; they cling to hollow, confused images of manhood and fraternity and assert their power to freeze images of themselves as invulnerable heroes who make and control our history—to memorialize themselves as photographs. The few men in Altman's films who attempt to change themselves in the interests of a different figure, men like Joe in *Jimmy Dean* and Jack Tanner in *Tanner '88,* are men who find either virtue or necessity or both in the feminization of American culture. Like the women in Altman's films, these men are vulnerable and marginal in the social worlds they inhabit, even while they dominate the movie screen. The challenge to the audiences of Altman's films is to imagine and create a society in which power is as manifold and dialogic and difference is as celebrated as it is in his films. Altman's films suggest that it is from women, and from accurate and authentic representations of women, that we can learn how to be responsible citizens, but if the society is to reinvigorate itself, men will have to do most of the changing.

To accomplish the reinvention to which Altman directs us, *for the common good,* in America, at the end of the twentieth century, may well require, as the *Tanner '88* series and *Secret Honor* suggest, that we rethink the lines between the imaginary and the actual, that we use transmissions of the real world, say on television, to understand the world of the imagination, and that, harder still, we use the works of the dramatic imagination, call them film and theater, to experiment with change.[33] After all, not all reinventions serve the common good. For eight years we watched a President of the United States reinvent himself and his past, pretending, as Garry Wills succinctly puts it, that "there was no pretense."[34] But many Americans pretended along with Reagan that there was no pretense, or, at the least, that the persona Reagan invented for himself did serve the common good. We knew he had been an actor professionally, but by 1980, most Americans ignored or applauded that preparation for public life.

The pertinent question then, is how we distinguish Jack Tanner from Ronald Reagan. We might also ask how and why we distinguish between the mythical Buffalo Bill, Altman/Newman's Buffalo Bill and the "real" historical figure or how we distinguish between Nixon of *Secret Honor* and the "real" Nixon. This requires that we offer criteria for determining who the real Nixon or the real Buffalo

Bill is. HBO conducted a straw vote just before the California primary in which approximately 41,000 votes were cast between four presidential candidates. The results of this unofficial vote were: Tanner, 38 percent; Bush, 22 percent; Jackson, 21 percent, and Dukakis, 19 percent. One way to look at these results, Linda Ellerbee suggests in a preprogram report, is "that a make-believe candidate won a make-believe election." Another way to look at these results is that they are evidence that people who watch HBO voted for Tanner as a protest against the mediocrity of the "real" candidates. The HBO viewers might also have been so ignorant of the "real" political scene that they took Tanner to be a "real" candidate. Or perhaps, for many Americans, there are no meaningful or available criteria for distinguishing between Michael Murphy playing Jack Tanner and George Bush playing George Bush.

Provoking these questions is the stuff of which Robert Altman's work has been made. There are, Altman's movies remind us, diverse examples of possibility for a dramatized society in the world of mechanical reproduction. On and off, the history of drama has been a history of public discourse, of representations that provoke and comprise common talk about the contested terrains and values in our daily, shared lives. Robert Altman's movies, and his recent programs for television, speak to and from that history. If sometimes, in the process, Altman makes masterpieces, that is laudable but beyond the point. His movies set a frame within which we can think about what it means to be a woman, a man, an American in our present time, and we can trust that his production will change as we change. Altman's moving pictures do move, and the voices that subvert and accompany these pictures do encourage us to reinvent ourselves—for the common good. Altman's work began in the context of a cacophonous American cultural revolution. It continues, as we enter the nineties, in a society that has viewed change itself as a threat. But our children are waiting, with increasing impatience. And so, perhaps, are his.

FILM CHRONOLOGY

Come Back to the 5 and Dime, Jimmy Dean, Jimmy Dean	1982
Streamers	1983
Secret Honor	1984
Fool for Love	1986
Beyond Therapy	1987
O.C. & Stiggs	1987
Vincent and Theo	1990

For Cable Television*

Precious Blood and *Rattlesnake in a Cooler*	1983
The Laundromat	1985
The Dumb Waiter and *The Room*	1987
Tanner '88 (ten episodes)	1988
The Caine Mutiny	1988

*Note: A complete listing of Altman's work for network television (1955–1968) can be found in Virginia Wright Wexman and Gretchen Bisplinghoff, *Robert Altman: A Guide to References and Sources*, (Boston, 1984). Wexman's book is the best source for production details and references to Altman's work through 1982. For production information since 1982, see Patrick McGilligan *Robert Altman: Jumping Off the Cliff* (New York, 1989), "Notes and Credits."

NOTES

Chapter 1. The Altman Signature: A World in Motion

1. The precise number of Robert Altman's films can be counted in several ways. The number twenty-three here refers to full-length features made for theatrical release between 1968 and 1989. In addition, Altman directed three films—*The Delinquents* (1957), *The James Dean Story* (1957), and *Nightmare in Chicago* (1964)—prior to 1968 and at least fifty television episodes during this earlier period. Finally, in the eighties, Altman produced and directed several dramas for live theater and cable television and directed the *Tanner '88* series comprised of ten programs for HBO; the latter are currently being re-edited into a two-hour version for video tape sale and rental. While this book was in production, Altman released another full-length feature film, *Vincent and Theo*.

2. Michael Holquist, "The Politics of Representation," in *Allegory and Representation,* edited by Stephen J. Greenblatt (Baltimore, 1981), 163–183. Also published in *On Metaphor* (Chicago, 1988).

3. See note 1 for explanation of the counting of Altman's films. See also the Film Chronology at the end of this book.

4. I owe much of the motivation and substance of my discussion of *auteur* theory and its particular application to the work of Robert Altman to the extraordinarily generous and insightful readings of various versions of the manuscript for this chapter by John Cameron, himself an unheralded, self-disguised film critic.

5. Articulations of *la politique des auteurs* began in the pages of

Cahiers du Cinéma in 1953 with somewhat elliptical comments by Fran-çois Truffaut. In 1957, André Bazin provoked a more analytic discussion of *auteur* theory in an article published in April 1957 in *Cahiers du Cinéma* in which he aptly remarked the flaws and holes in the "theory" as established at that time. It was not until 1962, however, that American critic Andrew Sarris actually published what has come to be seen as the most definitive, if also narrowest and most extreme, statement of *auteur* theory in his "Notes on the Auteur Theory in 1962," in *Film Culture* (Winter 1962–63).

6. Pauline Kael, "Circles and Squares," in *I Lost it at the Movies* (New York, 1963), 292–319. First published in *Film Quarterly*.

7. Ian Cameron, "Films, Directors and Critics" in *Movie* (Sept. 1962), cited in Andrew Sarris, "A Theory of Film History" in *Movies and Methods*, edited by Bill Nichols (Berkeley, 1976), 248.

8. See Robert Self, "Robert Altman and the Theory of Authorship" in *Cinema Journal* 25, no. 1 (Fall 1985): 3–11. Self situates the idea of Altman as *auteur* in contemporary debates concerning the permeability and fluidity of a text and the multivoicedness of what Michel Foucault calls the "author-function." I am essentially in agreement with Self's depictions of the ideas of author, text, and interpretation as metonymic devices for momentarily stabilizing meanings, and with his emphasis on the heterogeneity of conventions and ideas in Altman's films. But, as I go on to suggest, I locate my understanding of Altman as *auteur* in the interanimation of Altman's discourse as a particular set of readings of American culture, the role of a director as defined by Altman, and the concept of dialogism as presented in the work of M.M. Bakhtin.

9. Thanks to Tracy Strong for this poem by Peter Mullen.

10. Robert Self, "Robert Altman and the Theory of Authorship."

11. Michel Foucault, "What is an Author?" in *Language, Counter-Memory, Practice*, edited by Donald F. Bourchard (Ithaca, 1980), 123.

12. M.M. Bakhtin, *The Dialogic Imagination* (Austin, 1981). Bakhtin's ideas are key to my interpretations of Altman. For a detailed discussion of some of Bakhtin's concepts, see my "Drama and the Dialogic Imagination," in *Modern Drama* (Spring 1991). As I elaborate in this article, there is an obvious confluence of Bakhtin's idea of dialogism with several elements of feminist theorizing. What Elaine Marks and Isabell de Courtivron in *New French Feminisms* (New York, 1981), 36, describe as "attempts to find a discourse that is not governed by a prime signifier—a discourse compatible with rigorous atheism, a discourse that is not God centered— . . . attempts at decentering the reigning phallus from its dominant position in the symbolic order" are strikingly compatible with Bakhtin's celebration of dialogism and heteroglossia in language. Carol Gilligan, Jean Elshtain, and Evelyn Fox Keller also point to forms of discourse that resist governance by a "prime signifier" and that are dynamic and in-

teractive. See also Kaja Silverman's discussion of authorship from a feminist and psychoanalytic perspective in the chapter entitled "The Female Authorial Voice" in her *The Acoustic Mirror* (Bloomington, 1988), 187–234.

13. See Michel Foucault, especially *Language, Counter-Memory, Practice*, 113–38.

14. John Cameron's unpublished notes for film classes. These are the best comments I know of on Altman's films as post-classical movies.

15. Stanley Cavell, *Pursuits of Happiness* (Cambridge, 1981), 28.

16. Robert Kolker, *A Cinema of Loneliness* (New York, 1980), 338.

17. Ibid.

18. Judith Kass, *Robert Altman: American Innovator* (New York, 1978), 21.

19. Pauline Kael, *Reeling* (Boston, 1976), 451.

20. Robert Kolker, "Radical Surfaces," appears as the chapter title for Kolker's piece on Altman in *A Cinema of Loneliness*.

21. Stanley Cavell, *The World Viewed* (New York, 1971), 33.

22. Pauline Kael, "The Man from Dream City," the *New Yorker* (July 14, 1975).

23. Stanley Cavell, *The World Viewed*, 35.

24. At issue here are the spectators' persistent desires to remake the films they see. Perhaps because of film's transience and its superficial similarities to dreams, we "what if" the movies we see almost instantly after viewing them. The mistake here is that we behave as if any movie were our own dream, not the dream of another or others. Oddly, we tend to treat our own dreams as if they were fabricated by another and the movies we see as if they were ours to shape. For a related discussion, see the first section of Cavell's *The World Viewed*.

25. I originally used the term "syntagma," borrowed from the film semiotics of Christian Metz, to name these units of film that are comprised of shots whose relation to each other has an identifiable pattern such as parallelism or chronology. Since this term, as Metz himself acknowledges, is very close in its meaning to what we ordinarily call a "sequence" in film, and is only better because it avoids the semantic problem of speaking of an achronological sequence, I have revised my usage such that I now use "syntagma" primarily where chronology is an issue and otherwise use the more common terms of "sequence," "scene" and "shot" to describe basic film units of differing size.

26. Christian Metz, *Film Language* (New York, 1974), 124–30.

27. Bela Belazs, "The Close-Up" in *Film Theory and Criticism,* edited by Gerald Mast and Marshall Cohen, 2nd ed. (New York, 1979), 288.

28. Ibid., 289.

29. Ibid., 291.

30. Roland Barthes, "The Face of Garbo," in *Film Theory and Criticism*, 720–21.

31. Kolker, *A Cinema of Loneliness*, 276–77.

32. Ibid., 276.

33. Ibid., 298. To be fair here, Kolker does suggest something like this possibility of community in his discussions of *3 Women* and *Thieves Like Us*.

34. Robin Wood, ". . . A New Look at Renoir," *Film Comment* (Feb. 1978).

35. Pauline Kael, *Reeling*, 451.

36. See Kaja Silverman, *The Acoustic Mirror* (Bloomington, 1988).

37. Alex Eisenstein has remarked a similar activity in the films of Stanley Kubrick in his "Letter to the Editor," *Journal of Popular Film* (1980). It is worthwhile to note that while Kubrick and Altman seem superficially to be engaged in very different enterprises, they share both an eclectic film style that absorbs and exalts in film history and an unabashed confrontation with contemporary political life. Kolker's inclusion of Kubrick and Altman in *A Cinema of Loneliness* is a good example of the merits of juxtaposing these two filmakers.

38. Judith Kass, *Robert Altman*, 19.

39. Ibid.

40. Michael Goldman, *The Actor's Freedom* (New York, 1977). Goldman introduces the notion of the actor-as-character early in his book and pursues it throughout. While I have hesitations about this concept in terms of much live theater, as elaborated in my "Theater Games, Language Games and Endgame," *Theater Journal* (May 1979), I find the term apt for Altman's filmic treatment of persons.

41. Robert Kolker, *A Cinema of Loneliness*, 294–95.

42. Ibid., 277.

43. Stanley Cavell, *The World Viewed*, 48.

2. Power and Morality: The Fraternal Films

1. See Stanley Cavell, *The World Viewed* (New York, 1971), ix–xv, 3–15; and Pauline Kael, "Trash, Art and the Movies" in *Going Steady* (New York, 1968), 103–58.

2. See Molly Haskell, *From Reverence to Rape* (New York, 1973), 323–36.

3. Ibid.

4. Wilson Carey McWilliams, *The Idea of Fraternity in America* (Berkeley, 1973), 506.

5. Ibid.

6. Interview with David Denby, *Atlantic Monthly* (Mar. 1971).

7. I am thinking here of Joan Scott's definition of gender as "a process of constituting social relationships based on perceived differences between the sexes" and as "a primary way of conceptualizing relationships based on perceived differences between the sexes" and as "a primary way of conceptualizing relationships of power." See Joan Scott, "Women's History and the Rewriting of History" in *The Impact of Feminist Research in the Academy*, edited by Christie Farnham (Bloomington, 1987), 334–50. Feminism can refer to the evolving body of feminist theory and criticism but is more usually taken to index the women's movement and related political and social activities in society.

8. Michael Altman, lyrics; Johnny Mandel, music.

9. Judith Kass argues that the gambling metaphor repeatedly informs Altman's work; her summary of Altman's life and work emphasizes his gambling habit, modeled, she suggests, on his father's identity as "an inveterate gambler." Patrick McGilligan's *Robert Altman: Jumping Off the Cliff* (New York, 1989) also makes much of the Altman family gambling habit as resource and metaphor in Altman's life and work. I might note here that McGilligan's book, primarily a biography of Robert Altman, was published after I had completed the final manuscript for this book and thus was not available as a primary resource during my research and writing. What commonalities exist, therefore, between McGilligan's comments and mine about particular films are wholly coincidental. My reading of McGilligan's book, subsequent to completing my manuscript but prior to publication of my own work, did not lead me to make any revisions in my own claims, although I found, here and there, details that were and are of interest to those concerned with Altman's life and work.

10. M.M. Bakhtin, *The Dialogic Imagination*, 358–61.

11. Hugh Kenner, "Life in the Box," *Twentieth-Century Interpretations of Endgame*, edited by Bell Gale Chevigny (New Jersey, 1969), 57. I have my doubts about Kenner's claims of the cause-effect relationship between the "fatalistic attention" of the film audience and Beckett's dramaturgy, but the temporality of film can be no better described than by "Something is taking its course."

12. A number of uncertainties inform my caution here. I hesitate to assume that, for most first-time viewers, images of military helicopters will call forth a set of feelings particular to the war in Vietnam. I am reasonably confident that my experience of referring to the war in $M*A*S*H$ as the war in Vietnam was similar to that of most Americans who first saw the film at or near the time of its release in 1969; I would also guess that this held true for the seventies' television audience for the $M*A*S*H$ TV series, whether or not the television viewer had ever seen Altman's film. At the same time, I want to resist the claims that no one born after, say, 1965 or no

one outside American culture can "really" understand or appreciate *M*A*S*H*. The arbitrary elitism and assumption of an authoritative, singular, and stable meaning in that position are untenable. The trickier issue is that raised by Jean-Pierre Vernant's historically contextualized interpretations of Greek tragedy. Drama may privilege its original audiences more distinctly than do other cultural forms, and it may even be the case that the very works that seem to have transcended the historical moment of their creation—the "classic" plays and "classic" films that engage human beings decades and centuries after their inception—are more specifically embedded in their original cultural contexts than their forsaken companions that never achieved the status of the "universal." Especially if we allow this to be likely, we will have to pause before Vernant's argument that an "authentic sense' of any particular drama (Vernant's studies are focused on Greek drama, but he explicitly asserts the universal validity of this position) requires knowledge of the historical context in which it was conceived. Applied to *M*A*S*H*, this would mean than an "authentic" experience of the film is available now and will be indefinitely for anyone who knows what the historical moment of 1969 looks like. Epistemologically, this implies that *M*A*S*H* does not necessarily privilege viewers who "lived through" the sixties and the war in Vietnam, but it does privilege those who share a common body of knowledge specific to that particular historical moment. For further discussion of this position see Vernant, "Greek Tragedy" in *The Structuralist Controversy*, edited by Richard Mackey and Eugenio Donoto (Baltimore, 1970).

13. "An Interview with Robert Altman," by Frank Beaver in *Michigan Quarterly Review*, vol. 22 (1983), 47.

14. I will return to this topic and to the similarities and differences between the functions of allusions in theater and in film in the last chapter. It is worth noting here, however, that Vernant makes a convincing case for the necessity and vitality of allusions in the creation and maintenance of Greek theater.

15. André Bazin, "Theatre and Cinema," reprinted in Mast and Cohen, *Film Theory and Criticism*, 392.

16. Although this was not the first of Altman's films to have a discernible relationship to a script written initially for live theater. (*Buffalo Bill and the Indians* is officially "based on" Arthur Kopit's play, *Indians*, and the dramatic script penetrates several segments of the film). *Streamers* was the first of the series of Altman's experiments with films as the medium of refraction for a dramatic script or score. In subsequent explorations of dramatic scripts—*Come Back to the 5 and Dime, Jimmy Dean, Jimmy Dean; Secret Honor; Fool for Love*—Altman finds precise and efficient aesthetic catalysts to transform the closed theatrical space into open filmic space. I will return to this question of the distinction between theatrical and

filmic space but wish, for the moment, simply to mark its centrality to Altman's concerns.

17. In Susan Sontag's words, "The history of cinema is often treated as the history of its emancipation from theatrical models." Susan Sontag, "Film and Theatre," *Styles of Radical Will* (New York, 1966).

18. Robert Warshow's "Movie Chronicle: The Westerner" remains the most elegant statement of the cinematic and moral elements that combined to make the Western what Warshow claimed to be one of the most successful creations of American movies, the other being the gangster film. Robert Warshow, *The Immediate Experience* (New York, 1975) 135–54.

19. Stanley Cavell, *The World Viewed*, 56. Also see Chapter 1 of this book.

20. See Stanley Cavell, "Ending the Waiting Game" in Cavell, *Must We Mean What We Say?* and my "Theater Games, Language Games and Endgame" in *Theater Journal* (May, 1979) for examples and discussion of an ordinary language approach to reawakening language in dramatic texts.

21. The closest analogue to this structure may be that of the "story-tree," a concept employed by folklorists to describe collections of tales in a variety of media that grow from a common trunk, that are often collectively or cooperatively developed, but that take off in a range of directions with neither sequential nor causal connections among them. *M*A*S*H* is not, of course, a "natural" story-tree; it is a cultural production, conceived as a whole that at most represents a story-telling structure somewhat like that found in communities of folk with shared interests or boundaries. And because *M*A*S*H* is a film, intersections of meaning are provoked and do occur among incidents or episodes, not the least because these are edited, linked together in an order that is never coincidental or trivial. See article on *Star Trek* groupies and women's writing in *N.Y. Times Book Review*, Nov. 15, 1986.

22. See Clifford Geertz, *The Interpretation of Cultures*, esp. "Deep Play: Notes on the Balinese Cockfight" (New York, 1973), 413–53.

23. See Molly Haskell, *From Reverence to Rape* (New York, 1973) for what has become the standard treatment of the "types" and, more accurately, the stereotypes of women portrayed in film. Her discussions of the woman as goddess are particularly perspicacious. Less directly and less categorically, Joan Mellen's *Women and Their Sexuality in the New Film* (New York, 1973) remains an important ground for the subsequent discussions of gender and sexuality in the movies that have appeared in the last 15 years in American film criticism, which, often in the eighties, has been dominated by French psychoanalytic and feminist film criticism.

24. Laura Mulvey, "Visual Pleasure and Narrative Film," in *Visual and Other Pleasures* (Bloomington, 1989), 20. First published in 1975 in *Screen*.

25. Ibid., pp. 808–16. See also Kasell and Meehan above, and Bill Nichols, *Ideology and the Image* (Bloomington, 1981), esp. 34–42.

26. For an excellent discussion of "the aesthetics of the zoom," including some particularly helpful comments on Altman's use of zoom shots, see "The Bionic Eye: The Aesthetics of the Zoom," by John Belton and Lyle Tector in *Film Comment*, vol. 16, no. 5 (Sept./Oct. 1980).

27. See Stanley Cavell, *Pursuits of Happiness*, 106–7.

28. Joan Mellen, *Big Bad Wolves: Masculinity in the American Film* (New York, 1977), 312–14. To the best of my knowledge, this remains the only book-length work published to date on masculinity in American film. I have been, in a number of general and specific ways, confirmed and informed by Mellen's work, despite and sometimes because of the many specific points on which I disagree with her interpretations.

29. I have addressed the large and sticky issue of interpretations and ways of seeing in Chapter 1, but this seems a good place to recall both my own remarks and Cavell's discussion of interpretation in *Pursuits of Happiness*, especially the passage in which he points us to Wittgenstein's notion (in *Philosophical Investigations*, Part II) of "seeing an aspect." I note, particularly, Cavell's emphasis on the requirement that "there must be a competing way of seeing the phenomenon in question" (*Pursuits of Happiness*, 36). In an important sense, I am only able to see that aspect of *M*A*S*H* that I take to be a critique of movie misogyny because it is also possible to read this film as demeaning to women.

30. Joan Mellen, *Big Bad Wolves*, 313.

31. Ibid.

32. Sarah Kofman, "Baubo: Theological Perversion and Fetishism" in Michael Allen Gillespie and Tracy B. Strong, eds., *Nietzsche's New Seas* (Chicago, 1988), 195.

33. Kofman, 191.

34. Vincent Canby, *M*A*S*H*, *New York Times*, Feb. 1, 1970.

35. Stanley Cavell, *The World Viewed* (New York, 1971), 48.

36. Raymond Williams, *Problems in Materialism and Culture* (London, 1980), 39.

37. Here, as with the notion of "selective tradition," I draw on the work and terms of Raymond Williams, especially as they are articulated in *Problems in Materialism and Culture*. Williams identifies three types of cultural activities, all of which will be present in any cultural system but in varying forms and force, dependent on other historical and material aspects of the historical moment. These he names residual, dominant, and emergent cultural forms.

38. It may be worth noting the ironic allusion here to the war in Vietnam. For many viewers, the similar sounding name "Mylai" evokes memo-

ries, not of the saving of innocent lives but of Lieutenant Calley and the massacre of Vietnamese civilians in the village named "Mylai."

39. See Norman Kagan's *American Skeptic* (Ann Arbor, 1982) for the most elaborate treatment of this and other Altman films as "genre-commentaries." Almost every review contemporary to the release of *The Long Goodbye* remarked, both negatively and positively, on the relationship of Altman's film to the detective genre. See especially "Knight Without Meaning" in *Sight and Sound*, vol. 43, no. 3 (Summer): 155–59 and John Coleman's "Marlowe and His Society" in *New Statesman* 86 (Nov. 2, 1973): 660–61.

40. Robert Kolker, *A Cinema of Loneliness*, 307.

41. Ibid.

42. Ibid, 308.

43. Robert Kolker calls attention in *A Cinema of Loneliness* (p. 309) to this scene from *The Big Sleep*, which Kolker hypothesizes may motivate what he sees as Altman's thematic emphasis on the impotence of the detective-hero in the face of the vast complex of corrupt forces controlling contemporary society.

44. Raymond Chandler, "The Simple Art of Murder" in *The Second Chandler Omnibus* (London, 1962), 3–15. This and subsequent quotes from Chandler are all cited from this source.

45. While I think we can discern this voice even if we cannot locate its specific origin in Chandler's essays or in Altman and his casts' readings of Chandler's essays, it is probably worth noting that several members of the cast of *The Long Goodbye* as well as Altman himself have told interviewers that Altman assigned Chandler's essays to everyone involved with the film.

46. From Charles Baudelaire, *The Painter of Modern Life* (1859) cited in Cavell, *The World Viewed*, 55.

47. Chandler, *Second Chandler Omnibus*, 15.

48. Cavell, *A World Viewed*, 58.

49. Robert Warshow, "The Gangster as Tragic Hero" in *The Immediate Experience* (New York, 1975), 131.

50. Clifford Geertz, "Common Sense as a Cultural System" in *Further Essays in Interpretive Anthropology* (New York, 1983). There are metaphors within metaphors and allusions to allusions here, as those who know Geertz's essay will immediately recognize. Geertz launches his discussion of common sense from the pedestal of Ludwig Wittgenstein's wonderful passage on the commonalities between "knowing how to move in a culture." I simply, or not so simply, am walking back through the metaphoric series and returning it on its feet.

51. Warshow, "The Ganster as Tragic Hero," 132.

52. Although his interpretation of the meanings of this scene and its

mode of presentation differs from mine, I should note here that Norman Kagan makes a similar observation about the counterconventional approach to the killing of Lennox. See Norman Kagan, *American Skeptic, Robert Altman's Genre-Commentary Films* (Ann Arbor, 1982), 95–97.

53. See Chapter 4 for a detailed discussion of *McCabe and Mrs. Miller* and of this scene in particular.

54. For a detailed and alternative reading of this last sequence, see Kolker, *A Cinema of Loneliness,* 314–17. Kolker attends to many of the same elements of this sequence to confirm Marlowe's passivity and ineffectuality and to be consistent with the despair of *McCabe and Mrs. Miller* and *Nashville,* whereas I take Marlowe to be the last surviving actor in a ritual that Altman takes to be moribund.

55. Virginia Wright Wexman, "Critical Survey" in Virginia Wright Wexman and Gretchen Bisplinghoff, *Robert Altman: A Guide to References and Resources* (Boston, 1984), 17.

56. I should note here that Norman Kagan draws attention to these lines in his *American Skeptic: Robert Altman's Genre-Commentary Films,* 111. I would, and on occasion do, dispute some of Kagan's specific claims, but in general, Kagan's discussion of *Theives Like Us* is illuminating and has led me to curtail my own comments on this film with the sense that often what I might have said would be simply redundant with his remarks.

57. Kolker, *A Cinema of Loneliness,* 41.

58. See Pier Paolo Passolini, "The Cinema of Poetry" in Bill Nichols, ed., *Movies and Methods* (Berkeley, 1976), 551–58.

59. Cavell, *The Pursuits of Happiness,* 83.

Chapter 3. *Nashville:* New Roots for the Nation

1. For this and many other understandings of *Nashville,* I owe much to conversation with Ken Gewertz, Helen Von Schmidt, and Tracy Strong. I also thank Marguerite Waller and John Cameron for their helpful readings of a draft of this piece. A number of students who have patiently participated in my obsession with Altman's films also deserve special thanks; I single out Heidi Reavis for the constant supportive glimmer in her eye.

2. V.F. Perkins, "Participant Observers," *Film as Film* (London, 1972), 134–57.

3. Pauline Kael, *Reeling* (Boston, 1976), 452.

4. Ibid., 451.

5. Christian Metz, *Film Language* (New York, 1974), 145–30.

6. From the song, "200 Years," lyrics by Henry Gibson, music by Richard Baskin.

7. I am reminded at various moments in *Nashville* of the fictional

worlds of William Faulkner. Haven Hamilton may never achieve the authority of the "They endured" at the end of *The Sound and the Fury,* but he and Dilsey have only the distance from Nashville to Memphis between them.

8. I use "camera" here and elsewhere not only as the recording instrument that photographs the world but also as a metaphor for the mechanical intermediary between us and the world projected.

9. Metz, *Film Language,* 126.

10. Ibid.

11. Leonard Quart, "On Altman: Image as Essence," *Marxist Perspectives* I, no. 1 (Spring 1978): 118–25. I cite the entirety of Quart's essay because I am arguing against the basic thrust of his claim that "Altman's profoundly American sensibility focuses on individuals living in a present devoid of a sense of history or any notion of collective social context" (p. 118). That Altman's characters do not have the "ability to stand back and analyze their condition" (Quart, p. 123) does not mean that they do not have a sense of history through their behavior in the present, especially in the songs they sing. Part of that behavior, as I suggest at the end of my essay, is a particular, Dionysian expression of community. Quart also errs in his judgment that "He [Altman] never conveys the notion that institutions are intricate, powerful mechanisms characterized by subtle power relationships, explicit and implicit ideologies, and real functions." The early scene in the recording studio and the fund-raiser at which Sueleen Gay strips seem to me vivid examples that refute such a claim. I concur superficially with Quart's last statement in his essay, "But at those moments when his suggestive metaphors work, they resonate on deep unconscious levels untouched by other more conscious and articulate analysts of America," but find that there are many more such moments than Quart allows. I am uneasy, too, about the connotation of "deep unconscious levels" especially in relation to film and Altman. Altman's films often deny reduction to overt explanations and meanings, but they tend to depict a world in which a Freudian image of the psyche contends with alternative readings of mind and its relation to others or is irrelevant. As I argue in Chapter 4 in my discussion of *3 Women* and in Chapter 5 in my comments on *Secret Honor,* the moments when Altman's films do represent the interior world of characters in psychoanalytic terms are often redundant or carry with them an ambiance of inauthenticity. I also argue in Chapter 4 that when Altman's films do address us from a psychoanalytic perspective, the frame seems more Jungian than Freudian.

12. Here, again, and specifically I must mention my gratitude to Helen Von Schmidt for affirming and exploring with me the importance of red, white, and blue in *Nashville.*

13. Umberto Eco, "On the Contribution of Film to Semiotics," *Quar-*

terly Review of Film Studies (Feb., 1977); reprinted in Gerald Mast and Marshal Cohen, eds., *Film Theory and Criticism*, 2nd ed. (New York, 1979), 232–33.

14. Peter Wollen, *Signs and Meaning in the Cinema* (Bloomington, 1969), 122–23.

15. Metz, *Film Language*, 127.

16. Robin Wood, ". . . On Renoir," *Film Content* (Feb. 1978).

17. Stanley Cavell, *Must We Mean What We Say?* (New York, 1969), 121. The affinities between hallucination and critical "insight" are imprinted in my thinking by Cavell's articulation of such an experience in the essay, "Ending the Waiting Game."

18. Walter Benjamin, "The Work of Art in the Age of Mechanical Reproduction," *Illuminations* (Frankfurt, 1955). English trans. New York, 1968; reprinted in *Mast and Cohen*, 618.

19. My understanding of the distinctions between the relationship of film to audience and of live theater to audience are informed by my readings of Stanley Cavell's *Must We Mean What We Say?* and *The World Viewed* (New York, 1971).

20. Friedrich Nietzsche, "The Birth of Tragedy," *Basic Writings of Nietzsche*, edited by Walter Kaufmann, (New York, 1968), 59.

21. "It Don't Worry Me," lyrics and music by Keith Carradine.

22. Friedrich Nietzsche, "The Birth of Tragedy," 60.

23. The friend to whom I refer and whose notion of being transported I have lifted and twisted in the service of my argument is professor George Kateb, with whom gossip about film is always in itself transcendent.

Chapter 4. The Unconquered: The Feminization of Altman's Films

1. Leonard Cohen, "The Stranger."

2. Or at least the title may function to draw attention away from some aspect of the film that might discourage audiences from attendance. Robert Stone's novel, *Dog Soldiers*, for example, appeared as *Who Will Stop the Rain?* in its movie version. The film title did little to suggest the activity of the narrative but was invented to distract attention from the story's concern with war and Vietnam, subjects that the director and producers felt were not attractive to audiences in the late seventies.

3. Roland Barthes, *Mythologies*, translated by Annette Lavers (New York, 1972), 114.

4. Robert Kolker, *A Cinema of Loneliness*, 28.

5. Ibid., 283–84.

6. Stanley Cavell, *The World Viewed*, 48.

7. Roland Barthes, *Mythologies*, 118.

8. Ibid., 117.

9. Ibid., 143; and see Tracy Strong, *Friedrich Nietzsche and the Politics of Transfiguration* (Berkeley, 1975), especially Chapter 9.

10. Peter Wollen, *Signs and Meaning in the Cinema* (Bloomington, 1972), 122, 124.

11. Kolker, *A Cinema of Loneliness*, 281. Kolker is particularly insightful in his discussion of the use of the telephoto lens.

12. Roland Barthes, *Mythologies*, 119.

13. Sergei Eisenstein, "Collision of Ideas" in Richard Dyer MacCann, ed., *Film, A Montage of Theories* (New York, 1966), 36.

14. Robert Warshow, "Movie Chronicle—The Western" in *The Immediate Experience* (New York, 1970).

15. M.C. Kolbenschlag, "The Female Grotesque: Gargoyles in the Cathedrals of Cinema" in *The Journal of Popular Film*, vol. vi, no. 4 (1978): 328.

16. Kolbenschlag, 334.

17. Kolker, *A Cinema of Loneliness*, 330.

18. What I am suggesting here is consistent with Eisenstein's implied understanding that the crucial point of view established by montage is that of the spectator. This is in contrast to André Bazin's argument that montage asserts the director's point of view and constrains or asserts (monologically, Bakhtin would say) the spectator's point of view.

19. There are, of course, aesthetic curiosities like *Lady of the Lake* that attempt to consistently establish a subjective point of view. To the best of my judgment, however, no film yet made fully succeeds in sustaining a subjective point of view. Hitchcock's films might well be seen as precedent to Altman's in their frequent and effective use of subjective point of view employed to emphasize the experience of one character and to complicate the experience of the spectator; both *Psycho* and *Notorious* are notable examples of effective use of point of view shooting. The films of Bergman, Truffaut, and Godard, are also relevant to further discussion of this issue.

20. Kolker speaks illuminatingly of the use of sharp focus in *Images*, Kolker, *A Cinema of Loneliness*, 331.

21. René Girard, *Violence and the Sacred* (Baltimore, 1977), 58.

22. Ibid., 57.

23. William Shakespeare, *The Comedy of Errors* I, i, lines 30–40.

24. Pier Paolo Pasolini, "The Cinema of Poetry" in Bill Nichols, ed., *Movies and Methods* (Berkeley, 1976), 553.

25. I should note here that I believe Pasolini is mistaken in his argument that free, indirect, subjective point of view is only a matter of style, not linguistics. Free indirect subjectivity constrains the possibilities of editing and thus affects the grammar of film.

26. Kolker, *A Cinema of Loneliness*, 333.

27. Judith Kass, *Robert Altman: American Innovator* (New York, 1978), 224.

28. Vincent Canby, "Laurel and Hardy," in Stuart Byron and Elisabeth Weis, eds., *Movie Comedy* (New York, 1977), 46.

29. Susan Sontag, *Against Interpretation* (New York, 1966), 21.

30. Kolker, *A Cinema of Loneliness, 333*.

31. Stanley Cavell, *Pursuits of Happiness*. See especially Chapter 6, "The Courting of Marriage: Adam's Rib" and see as well Cavell's "More of the World Viewed" in the *Georgia Review,* vol. XXVIII, no. 4 (Winter 1974): 5, particularly 604.

32. Stanley Cavell, *Must We Mean What We Say?* (New York, 1969), particularly 337–53, although to fully appreciate Cavell's arguments about the privilege of being a member of an audience and our ability to know and acknowledge others, one should begin at least with the chapter "A Matter of Meaning It." See also Helene Keyssar, "I Love You, Who Are You? *PMLA* (Mar. 1977), 297–306.

33. C.G. Jung, *Psyche & Symbol* (New York, 1957), especially 6–9.

34. Pauline Kael, *When the Lights Go Down* (New York, 1975), 442.

35. Stanley Cavell, *The World Viewed* (New York, 1971), 108–18, and Walter Benjamin, "The Work of Art in the Age of Mechanical Reproduction" in *Illuminations* (New York, 1969), 217–52.

36. C.G. Jung, *Psyche & Symbol,* 137.

37. Kolker, *A Cinema of Loneliness,* 338.

38. See Kaja Silverman, *The Acoustic Mirror* (Bloomington, 1988), 126–29 for a persuasive, Freudian psychoanalytic discussion of *3 Women,* with particular emphasis on the representation of the maternal. Silverman reads the pile of tires at the end of the film as meaning that "the three women have reduced Edgar's phallic regime to the status of trash or waste." This seems to me as good as any interpretation of the pile of tires, since I, too, find phallic resonances in this image. But, in the end, I take this image to be deliberately open in its signification, perhaps a post-modern alternative to mythically laden phallic images that Willy paints. This is a good place to note, more generally, that, while *3 Women* is the only Altman film to which Silverman pays close attention in her book, her work as a whole makes a rare contribution to our understanding of the "acoustic" dimensions of film and, as such, is particularly relevant to Altman's movies.

39. Bill Nichols, *Ideology and the Image* (Bloomington, 1981), 3.

40. For a discussion of presence, presentness, past and present, and absence in the two media of theater and film, see Stanley Cavell, *Must We Mean What We Say?* (New York, 1969), 1955, and *The World Viewed* (New York 1971), 22–29, 155–60.

41. Nichols, *Ideology and the Image,* 35.

42. J.L. Austin, "Pretending" in *Philosophical Papers* (London, 1970),

253–71, esp. 256. There is difference here, of course. Austin rightly notes that a person who, while acting like a hyena, takes a bite out of someone else's calf can no longer be said to be pretending. But it is not the case that we would then say the person on all fours is really being a hyena. In the instance of Joe and Joanne, we may want to say that Joanne is really being a woman.

43. I am informed here by Tracy B. Strong's discussion of passages from Wittgenstein's *Philsophical Investigations* that concerns these issues of seeing, interpretation, and communities of discourse in Tracy B. Strong, *The Idea of Political Theory* (Notre Dame, 1990), 94–99.

44. Laura Mulvey, *Visual and Other Pleasures* (Bloomington, 1989), 13.

45. Ibid.

46. I borrow this term and have learned its use from my colleague Michael Cole. I think of the word as part of a cluster of terms that includes Paolo Freire's concept of re-admiring and Bakhtin's notions of interanimation and refraction.

Chapter 5. Democratic Vistas: Spectacles, Screens, and Monitors

1. Cited in *Best Plays of the Early American Theatre*, edited with an Introduction and Notes by John Gassner (New York, 1967), xxix.

2. Raymond Williams, "Drama in a Dramatized Society" (Cambridge, England, 1975).

3. See John Cameron, "Notes," 68.

4. As detailed in my earlier discussion of *Nashville*, this Eisensteinian mode of montage (editing) is based on a dialectic notion of the collision of ideas and images. Altman augments the conventional Eisensteinian practice both by fully utilizing audio signs and by establishing and arranging scenes such that they indirectly comment on each other.

5. Tracy B. Strong, *Friedrich Nietzsche and the Politics of Transfiguration* (Berkeley, 1975), 15–16. For a more elaborate discussion of this concept, see also pp. 29–49.

6. Ibid., 16.

7. Frank Beaver, "An Interview with Robert Altman," in *Michigan Quarterly Review*, vol. 22 (1983): 55.

8. Michael Goldman, *An Actor's Freedom* (New York, 1977). Goldman argues for the term, "the actor-as-character" as best capturing the effective nature of dramatic personae in performance. Elsewhere, (see note 39, Chapter 1, and my comments at the end of Chapter 1) I have suggested both the usefulness of this concept and some of the problems it raises. Goldman's "actor-as-character" is, however, certainly in the back of my

mind when I here invent the notion of the "performer-as-character." As my discussion of *Buffalo Bill and the Indians* goes on to suggest, Paul Newman as William Cody (Buffalo Bill) tends to obliterate the "real" person that lingers in the idea of the actor and to leave, in Paul Newman's presence, only the shadow of the actor, as the bonding of performer and character occurs, in *Buffalo Bill*.

9. Milan Kundera, *The Book of Laughter and Forgetting* (New York, 1980), 3.

10. The best account of President Reagan's fabrications of his autobiography occur in Garry Wills's *Reagan's America* (New York, 1988), especially 192–201, 448–60.

11. I owe this understanding of the style of much of American poetry to a course that I took with critic Alfred Kazin at the State University of New York at Stony Brook more than twenty years ago. As I make this acknowledgment, it also occurs to me that I perhaps owe even more to Alfred Kazin, since it was he who chastized me and others for paying insufficient attention to contemporary work.

12. See my book-review essay on Jill Dolan's *The Female Spectator as Critic* in *Theatre Journal* (Fall 1989) for more detailed discussion of this feminine threat.

13. Sapir, "Culture, Genuine and Spurious" in *Selected Writings of Edward Sapir in Language, Culture and Personality,* edited by David Mandelbaum (Berkeley, 1949), 308–31.

14. It is in the context of this reading that I concur with Robert Self's argument that *Buffalo Bill and the Indians,* rather than being the failed intellectual exercise that some have judged it to be, is an achievement whose significance can be appreciated by placing the film in the critical framework of post-modernism and deconstruction. See Robert Self, "Robert Altman and the Theory of Authorship" in *Cinema Journal* 25, no. 1 (Fall 1985): 3–11. But this also may be why viewers are in such discord in their judgments of this movie.

15. Robert Self, "The Perfect Couple: 'Two Halves are Better than One' in the Films of Robert Altman," *Wide Angle,* vol. 30, no. 4 (1983): 31–37.

16. Carol Gilligan, *In a Different Voice* (Cambridge, Mass., 1982).

17. See Michael Holquist, "The Politics of Representation" in *Allegory and Representation,* edited by Stephen J. Greenblatt (Baltimore, 1981), 163–83.

18. Bertolt Brecht's ideas about drama, politics, and aesthetics are most readily accesible in English in the collection *Brecht on Theatre,* translated by John Willett (New York, 1964). Paolo Freire's concept of re-admiring texts and events as discussed in his *Cultural Action For Freedom* (Cambridge, 1970) is notably similar to Brecht's notion of alienation.

19. Virginia Wright Wexman in "The Rhetoric of Cinematic Improvisa-

tion," *Cinema Journal 20*, no. 1 (Fall 1980): 29–41, differentiates between documentary and theatrical realism. What she means by "theatrical realism"—". . . making us aware of the experience of a group of people gathered together to make a film"—is close to what I am here associating with Brecht's alienation effects, but I hesitate to use her term for fear of its confusion with the concept of realism in drama. In Wexman's terms, Altman's approach to the world staged and recorded in *Health* as well as in most of his movies combines the sense of "actual people in actual situations" that characterizes documentary realism with the self-consciousness of the medium by which Wexman defines theatrical realism.

20. When I visited Lion's Gate Studios in the fall of 1980, Altman and his staff had just returned from shooting *Popeye* on Malta. The public relations person with whom I spoke candidly described the company's enthusiasm for *Popeye,* its hope that it would be a commercial success in contrast to *Health, Quintet* and *A Perfect Couple,* and its attempts to create an extended market for *Popeye* through sales of related toys, tokens, and clothing.

21. *American Film,* vol. 6, no. 3 (Dec. 1980): 31–36, 73–74.

22. "The Stormy Saga of Popeye," in *American Film,* vol. 6, no. 3 (Dec. 1980): 73.

23. Ibid., 74.

24. Vincent Canby, *New York Times,* (Dec. 12, 1980; Pauline Kael, the *New Yorker* (Jan. 5, 1981). These and other negative reviews are also cited in Gerard Plecki, *Robert Altman* (Boston, 1985), 124.

25. Michael Wood, *America in the Movies* (New York, 1975), 147–48.

26. Ibid., 147.

27. I heard Altman make remarks along these lines at a preview of *Streamers* at UCLA in 1983. In an interview with Sylvie Drake (*Los Angeles Times,* May 28, 1981) when he was in rehearsals for the Frank South plays at the Los Angeles Actors' Theater (LAAT), Altman argued that "It's all basically the same, you know. You're dealing with text, content, style, actors and an audience."

28. Sam Shepard, *Fool For Love* (San Francisco, 1983).

29. Jenijoy La Belle, *Herself Beheld* (Ithaca, 1988), 76–99. I have puzzled for several years about how to address Altman's persistent use of mirrors and windows. The reminder that we, the audience, are voyeurs and outside the world of the film seems important, but I have always felt that something was missing in my understanding. LaBelle's intriguing book, while primarily a literary survey, gives a partial answer in terms of Lacan's mirror stage and the discovery of self and others and women's relation to the mirror on the temporal inquisitor.

30. Robert Frost, "Reluctance" in *The Poems of Robert Frost* (New York, 1946), 31.

31. Robert Altman, "In a Lonely Place," *Monthly Film Bulletin*, vol. 52, no. 612 (Jan. 1985): 5.

32. Nathaniel Hawthorne, *The House of the Seven Gables* (New York, 1961), 229.

33. Here, as elsewhere, I am indebted to several of Stanley Cavell's sentences, especially those from *Themes Out of School* (Chicago, 1983), 177–83.

34. Garry Wills, *Reagan's America* (New York, 1988), 191. Wills provides numerous examples of Reagan's invention of himself: Reagan claimed, for example, more than once to have filmed Nazi concentration camps, when he was never out of the United States; similarly, he claimed to have visited Nicaragua when he never did. The stories are endless. Michael Rogin's *Ronald Reagan, the Movie* (Berkeley, 1987), provides an excellent, detailed account of the relationship between Reagan's Hollywood roles and the self he and others created for his political life. Many of my reflections on Altman's reflections of the making up of American history by drama, and film in particular, have evocative parallels with Rogin's analyses of the ongoing relations between American politics and American movies.

INDEX

A Perfect Couple, 17; analyzed, 293–
96; and games and rules, 294; and
family 294; and myth of marriage,
295; lack of self-reflexivity, 296
A Wedding, 16, 25, 32; family in, 42;
analyzed, 284–91; and ritual, 284f.;
and theater, 285; social class
relations in, 285f.; embarrassment,
287; race, class, and gender in, 287;
and irony, 289
Adam's Rib, 77f., 212
Allen, Woody, 13, 301
allusions in Altman's films: as
intertextual or referrential, 58f.; as
democratic or elitist, 59
Altman, Robert: and the American
Dream, 4, 62; and American history,
5–6; as *auteur*, 10–13, 52; and
modernism (self-referentiality), 13–
14; and genre, 14; and democracy,
15, 32; and making sense, 16f.;
experience of watching a film by,
16ff.; compared to Bergman and
Renoir, 20; and the metaphysical, 21;
social not psychological 21; and
knowledge of his characters' part
histories, 29–30; and elements of the

American character, 31; and
revelation, 34; and Puritanism, 35;
and promiscuous camera, 35f.; way
of seeing as aural, 36; and
complexity of filmic space, 37; and
production company, 38ff.; not a
romantic, 44; and community 44;
early television work, 52; and
gambling, 56f.; skill in making
common sense, 98; and semiotics,
146f.; and voyeurism, 162; and
freedom, 172; and respect for
women, 199; as male director, 206;
absence of the erotic, 210; and
muteness, 226; as female point of
view but not identity, 258; and irony,
289; skepticism about gendered
roles, 295; as director of live theater,
314f.; and the transformation of
women, 342; and the rigidity of men,
342f. *See also specific films*
America(n), 30ff.; irony of 1960s'
politics in, 51; mobility in, 62f.;
heroes for, 98; political parties in,
167; and freedom, 172f.; iconic use
of the flag, 243; as a dramatized
society, 262; performance and